World War I
Media, Entertainments
& Popular Culture

World War I
Media, Entertainments
& Popular Culture

Edited by
Chris Hart

Midrash Publications

ISBN (pbk) 978-1-905984-21-3
© Chris Hart 2018

Apart from any fair dealing for the purposes of research or private study, or criticism or review, as permitted under the Copyright, Designs and Patents Act, 1988, this publication may be reproduced, stored or transmitted in any form, or by any means, only with the prior permission in writing of the publishers, or in the case of reprographic reproduction, in accordance with the terms of licences issued by the Copyright Licensing Agency. Inquiries concerning reproduction outside those terms should be sent to the editor.

Editorial arrangements and Introduction ©2018 *Chris Hart*

Chapter 1 ©2018 Michael Paris
Chapter 2 ©2018 Christopher Hart
Chapter 3 ©2018 Guy Hodgson
Chapter 4 ©2018 Maria Rikitianskaia
Chapter 5 ©2018 Andrijana Rabrenović
Chapter 6 ©2018 Eneko Bidegain
Chapter 7 ©2018 John Dilley and David Penman
Chapter 8 ©2018 David Goldie
Chapter 9 ©2018 Jesús Jiménez-Varea and Antonio Pineda
Chapter 10 ©2018 Tom D. C. Roberts
Chapter 11 ©2018 Dietrich Helms
Chapter 12 ©2018 Rosie White
Chapter 13 ©2018 Lucy Claire Church
Chapter 14 ©2018 Sonja Andrew

British Library Cataloguing in Publication data
A catalogue record for this book is available from the British Library

Editor: Chris Hart
Copyediting: By *Beverley*
Proofreading: By *Beverley*
Cover design: Chris Hart

Typeset by Midrash Typesetting
Typeface, Baskerville
Printed and bound in Great Britain by
Lulu Press Limited

World War I
Media, Entertainments & Popular Culture
Edited by Chris Hart

Contents page

List of figures
Acknowledgements

	Chronology of events during World War I referred to in this Book	1
	Introduction Christopher Hart	9
Chapter 1	**What Shall We Tell the Children? The Great War, Propaganda, and British Children** Michael Paris	45
Chapter 2	**Remember Scarborough. Re-Active Propaganda as Natural ethics** Christopher Hart	69
Chapter 3	**Causing Unnecessary Anxiety? British Newspapers and the Battle of Jutland** Guy Hodgson	101
Chapter 4	**Listening to 'Concert of Europe': Pioneering Radio Amateurs During World War I** Maria Rikitianskaia	123
Chapter 5	**The Role of Political Posters in Montenegro and Serbia during World War I** Andrijana Rabrenović	145

Chapter 6	**Basque Writers' Reportages in** *Eskualduna*, **during World War I** Eneko Bidegain	167
Chapter 7	**How Local Newspapers Scooped the National Press to Tell the Truth about the First World War** John Dilley and David Penman	195
Chapter 8	**Romance by Other Means: Scottish Popular Newspapers and the First World War** David Goldie	231
Chapter 9	**"And Yet They Tell Us Not to Hate the Hun" Atrocity Propaganda, and War Patriotism in Winsor McCay's** *The Sinking of the 'Lusitania'* Jesús Jiménez-Varea and Antonio Pineda	259
Chapter 10	**The Murdochs and Gallipoli: Entertainments in Service of Myth** Tom D. C. Roberts	287
Chapter 11	**All Quiet on the Musical Front? German Music Production as a Source for a History of Attitudes of the First World War** Dietrich Helms	327
Chapter 12	**Englishness and the 'Other'. Mata Hari and Edith Cavell On Celluloid** Rosie White	349

Chapter 13	**Defining Musical 'Germanness'. The Reciprocal Influences of Music and National Identity Formation** Lucy Claire Church	367
Chapter 14	**Dichotomies of Representation and Interpretation. A Pacifist's Story** Sonja Andrew	399

List of figures

Figure 1   Poster advertising *The Martyrdom of Nurse Cavell*, January 1916

Figure 1.1   *Scouting for Boys*, 1908 and 1815
Figure 1.2   Best selling in 1915, *A Hero of Liege*
Figure 1.3   G.A. Henty's 1902, *To the Herat and Cabul*
Figure 1.4   O'Neill's book for boys and girls explaining the war
Figure 1.5   Popular periodical for children on the war
Figure 2.1   'Remember Scarborough' published in early 1915
Figure 2.2   Photographs and names of children killed
Figure 2.3   Scarborough pre-war
Figure 2.4   *Lustige Blatter* in January 1915. Artist W. A. Wellner
Figure 2.5   German newspaper report of attacks
Figure 2.6   'Enlist Now' published early 1915
Figure 2.7   'Men of Britain', published early 1915
Figure 3.1   Six of the main battle-ships lost listed in June 3 *The Daily Mirror*
Figure 4.1   Wireless World responds to the war
Figure 4.2   Horace Hurm's 'Ondophone'
Figure 5.1   Nikola I Petrović-Njegoš was the ruler of Montenegro from 1860 to 1918
Figure 5.2   Order No. 8676 from 1914, of the Supreme Commander of His Royal Majesty the Crown Prince Alexander, to his Serbian Army for 15 December
Figure 5.3   German cartoon mocking the Allied countries as a rag-tag of bandits
Figure 5.4   The defeat of Austria was an opportunity to mock them
Figure 5.5   Mobilisierungs-Kundmachung, 1914
Figure 6.1   Front page of the *Eskualduna* 7 August 1914
Figure 6.2   Monument des Basques (1928)
Figure 7.1   Front page of the *Market Harborough Advertiser*
Figure 7.2   Front page of the *Ashbourne Telegraph*
Figure 7.3   Ernest Dunlop Swinton 'Eyewitness'
Figure 7.4   1457 Pte. Frederick Bull killed 9 April 1915, aged 26
Figure 7.5   2549 Pte. F.G. Luck Killed 29 October 1915, aged 19
Figure 8.1   *Sunday Pictorial*, 14 March 1915
Figure 9.1   Winsor McCay 1906
Figure 9.2   Women and children as victims of atrocities
Figure 9.3   Divine vengeance against the forces of evil?
Figure 9.4   The Lusitania and the Statue of Liberty
Figure 10.1 Poster for 'Gallipoli'
Figure 10.2 Photograph of Keith on the peninsula

Figure 10.3 'Splendid Men' photograph (Australian War Memorial)
Figure 10.4 'Men love the beaches' article
Figure 10.5 British officers drinking tea
Figure 10.6 Cut from British officers drinking tea to men charging
Figure 11.1 Lyrics of 'Argonnerwald Lied'
Figure 11.2 Cover page of 'An Zeppelin'
Figure 11.3 Number of entries touching the topic of grave (absolute numbers)
Figure 11.4 Number of entries touching the topic of death (total and related to war)
Figure 11.5 Number of entries touching the topic of mourning (absolute numbers)
Figure 11.4 Total of entries on death, mourning (war related) and grave (war related)
Figure 11.5 Relative and absolute numbers of entries on mourning, death and graves
Figure 11.6 Entries with the keyword Frieden (peace)
Figure 11.7 Entries with the keyword 'Sieg' (victory)
Figure 12.1 Margaretha Zelle MacLeod, as Mata Hari. n.d
Figure 12.2 Poster for 1938, *Nurse Edith Cavell*
Figure 13.1 *Jean-Christophe*, a novel in 10 volumes
Figure 13.2 Cover of *Des Knaben Wunderhorn; Alte deursche Lieder* – folk songs
Figure 13.3 Wagner's *Judism in Music* (org. Published in 1850)
Figure 14.1 Extract from the diary of Myrtle Andrew 2004
Figure 14.2 Extract from the diary of Myrtle Andrew 2004
Figure 14.3 Extract from the diary of Myrtle Andrew 2004
Figure 14.4 Images from the cell block at Richmond Castle, and Richmond Castle ruins, North Yorkshire.
Figure 14.5 Drawings on the cell walls in the prison block at Richmond Castle, North Yorkshire.
Figure 14.6 Panel one from the triptych 'The Ties That Bind'.
Figure 14.7 Stamp detail from the triptych 'The Ties That Bind'.
Figure 14.8 Centre panel detail from the triptych 'The Ties That Bind'.
Figure 14.9 Family photograph of Myrtle and Jack Andrew
Figure 14.10 The second triptych 'The Ties That Bind' displayed at the Bankfield Museum, Halifax, West Yorkshire.
Figure 14.11 'The Ties That Bind ' panel one detail
Figure 14.12 'The Ties That Bind' centre panel detail of Harriet Bell, John Edgar Bell's wife

Chronology of Events during World War I referred to in this Book

1914

June 28th 1914
   Archduke Franz Ferdinand of Austria is assassinated in Sarajevo, Serbia. His death is the event that leads European countries into war with each other. The reason for the assassination was to get Austria-Hungary to release South Slav provinces under their control. The government of Austria-Hungary blamed the Serbian government for the assassination of Franz Ferdinand and his wife and subsequently, on the 28 July, declared war on the Kingdom of Serbia.
   Austria-Hungary was part of the *Triple Alliance* with Germany and Italy and, therefore, had the support of Germany.
   Russia was allied with the Kingdom of Serbia, and, through their alliance with France, called on the French to mobilise with them against Austria-Hungary.
   Under the Secret Treaty of 1892, Russia and France were obliged to mobilise their armies if any of the Triple Alliance mobilised. Austro-Hungary and German reacted to the Russian call to France by mobilising their armed forces.
   Soon all the Great Powers had chosen sides. Russia and France were part of the *Triple Entente* (of 1907) with Britain.

August 3rd 1914
   Germany declared war on France.
   Germany invades Belgium as directed under the Schleiffen Plan, drawn up in 1905.
   The British foreign secretary, Sir Edward Grey, sent an ultimatum to Germany demanding their withdrawal from neutral Belgium. This did not happen.

August 4th 1914
   Britain declared war on Germany. The War begins.

August 5-16th 1914
   The Battle of Liège was the first battle of the war, heavily outnumbered Belgians held out against the German Army for 12 days.

August 22nd 1914

The British Expeditionary Force (BEF) encountered the German Army for the first time north-east of Mons, Belgium. The British inflicted heavy causalities on the superior German force but were forced to retreat as far as the outskirts of Paris before joining the counter-attack with the French at the battle of Marne.

September 6 - 10th 1914

Battle of the Marne (*Première Bataille de la Marne*) – French and British armies stopped the German advance towards Paris, causing a German retreat to the Aisne River, the failure of the Schleiffen Plan and beginning of a stalemate and trench warfare for the next four years.

September 1914

The *Kriegs-Journal*, produced by the Wiener Kunstfilm-Industrie is launched and from October national newsreels are produced supporting the Austrian and German war aims.

October 29th 1914

Turkey entered the war on the side of the central powers, helping with a German naval bombardment of Russia.

November 5th 1914

Russia's allies, Britain and France, declared war on Turkey, because of the help given to the German attack on Russia.

December 8th 1914

Battle of the Falkland Islands was a naval action between the British Royal Navy and Imperial German Navy. The British destroy the German East Asia Squadron with a disproportionate amount of damage and death – Germany lost six ships 1,871 men and, the British lost no ships and ten men.

December 16th 1914

German Navy bombard Hartlepool, Scarborough and Whitby killing 137 men, women and children.

Christmas 1914

Books for children explaining the war were published including, James Yoxall's (1914), *Why Britain Went to War: For Boys and Girls* and Elizabeth O'Neill's (1914), *The War 1914: An Explanation for Boys and Girls*.

Charlie Chaplin, Harold Lloyd and Bronco Billy Anderson all had popular comedy shorts released in 1914. At the end of

December the popular serial, *The Exploits of Elaine* – a crime thriller is shown in American cinemas.

December 25th 1914

The Christmas truce (*Weihnachtsfrieden*; *Trêve de Noël*) was a series of widespread but unofficial ceasefires among the frontline soldiers, along the Western Front – in some sections of the line combatants from both sides met and exchanged greetings, sang carols and played football. British retailer Sainsbury's used the truce as their 2014 Christmas television commercial causing controversy.

1915

January - February 1915

Poster 'Remember Scarborough' published.

January 15th 1915

Der Golem is shown in German cinemas – a horror film.

The Wireless World publishes the article, 'The Wireless Spy' (January).

February 8th 1915

The Birth of a Nation is released in America – commercial success but controversial due to its racism and sexual aggression.

Radio-telegraphic time and weather signals are transmitted from the Eiffel Tower.

April - August 1915

Dardanelles and Gallipoli Campaign (Turkish - *Çanakkale Savaşı*). The Allies (Britain, Australian, New Zealand, India, Newfoundland, France and Russia) successfully land in the Gallipoli region of the Dardanelles, aiming to capture the Ottoman capital Constantinople (now Istanbul). The mission was a failure. The campaign was the only major Ottoman victory of the war. This battle became a popular part of a computer game called Battlefield 1 in 2016 focusing on the Australian Army.

The Children's Story of the War, by Edward Parrott is published.

May 7th 1915

RMS Lusitania, owned by The Cunard Line, sailing from America to Britain was sunk by a German submarine (U-20). The ship sank in 18 minutes, with the deaths of 1,198 passengers and crew, including 128 American citizens.

May 12th 1915

The Committee on Alleged German Outrages (commonly known as the Bryce Committee after its chair, Viscount James Bryce) published 'The Report of the Committee on Alleged German Outrages' in every European language. It aimed to inform the world about German autocracies – some of which lacked evidence. The report and the autocracies it reported were reproduced world-wide in newspapers and magazines.

May 24th 1915

Four Feathers is shown in American and British cinemas – a story retold numerous times about a British officer deemed to be a coward who has to redeem himself through sacrifice and bravery in battle.

July 1915

In British cinemas, *The Man Who Stayed at Home*, is shown – about enemy spies in Britain.

1916

Austria-Hungary, Bulgaria and Germany defeat Serbia at the end of 1915, and the Austro-Hungarian army attacks Montenegro.

January 7 - 10th 1916

The 47th *Infanteriedivision*, firmly backed by naval artillery, conquered the Montenegrin positions at the Lovćen, which the *Lovćenski Odred* had defended. In the Bay of Kotor, Mount Lovćen was extremely important for both the Central Powers and the Entente. The mountain was a symbol of Montenegrin statehood and national identity.

January 27th 1916

Conscription introduced in Britain by The Military Service Act.

February - November 1916

Battle of Verdun Germany mounted an attack on the French at Verdun designed to 'bleed the French dry'. Although the fighting continued for nine months, the battle was inconclusive. Casualties were enormous on both sides with the Germans losing 430,000 men and the French 540,000.

Molly Angel's Adventures: A Tale of the Occupation of Belgium, by Bessie Marchant, is published.

May 31st - June 1st 1916
   Battle of Jutland. This was the only truly large-scale naval battle of the war. This was the German High Fleet's attempt to break the British naval blockade by luring out part of the Grand Fleet and causing sufficient damage that the German mercantile shipping could operate. The statistics suggest a German success in that the Royal Navy lost 115,025 tons of ships against 61,180, and 6,097 British sailors were killed compared to 2,551 German sailors. Within a matter of days, however, the Royal Navy's strength had been restored, and the status quo had been re-established.

July 1st - November 18th 1916
   Battle of the Somme. The battle was preceded by a week-long artillery bombardment of the German line which was supposed to destroy the barbed wire defences placed along the German line but only actually succeeded in making no 'mans' land a mess of mud and craters. In five months 420,000 British soldiers (60,000 on the first day), 200,000 French soldiers and 500,000 German soldiers were dead. The Allies had gained only 25 miles.
   Bei unseren Helden a der Somme ('With Our Heroes on the Somme' - 1917) was released in Germany in 1917 in response to *Battle of the Somme*.
   The Spy Hunter, by William Le Queux, is published.

August, 1916
   Battle of the Somme was a feature-length seminal British documentary film, shot during the battle (June and July 1916) with additional scenes added – was shown at over 2,000 British cinemas and probably reached an audience in excess of 10 million. It went on to attract large audiences in allied and neutral countries.

November 28th 1916
   First Aeroplane air raid was in London. The Germans hoped that by making raids on London and the South East, the British Air Force would be forced into protecting the home front rather than attacking the German air force.

December 7th 1916
   Lloyd George becomes British Prime Minister.
   England and the War: A Book for Boys and Girls, by Herbert Strang is published.

1917

February 1st 1917
   Germany resumes unrestricted submarine warfare. This act, more than any other, draws the United States into the war and causes the eventual defeat of Germany.

1917
   The Service cinématographique des armées participated directly in the creation of a new newsreel called *Les Annales de la Guerre*.

April 6th 1917
   The U.S.A. declares war on Germany. The United States enters World War I on the side of France and Britain.

April 13th 1917
   Committee on Public Information (CPI) is created by President Wilson and chaired by journalist George Creel - hence the bureau was known as the Creel Committee. The CPI had 21 agencies covering all media including Film, Photography and News.

July 28th 1918
   The Sinking of the 'Lusitania' (1918) by Winsor McCay's released. Silent animated short is regarded as a classic example of propaganda.

August
   Mickey, a comedy-drama grosses over $8 million in the U.S.A., in addition to the royalties from the song of the film that was also released separately in 1918.

November 1917
   Battle of Cambrai in France - the British took a large force of tanks across the barbed wire and machine gun posts at Cambrai. This battle became a popular part of a computer game called *Battlefield 1* in 2016.

December 18th 1917
   Universum-Film established in Germany as a direct response to foreign competition in film and propaganda.

1918

October 30th 1918
   Armistice with Turkey. The allies had successfully pushed the Turkish army back, and the Turks were forced to ask for an

armistice. The terms of the armistice treaty allowed the Allies access to the Dardanelles.

November 9th 1918

Kaiser Wilhelm II abdicated.

November 11th 1918

Armistice signed. At 11am the fighting came to an end. The official end was not until the 29 April 2018 when Germany paid the final £59.5 million remaining from the reparations sum agreed at the Treaty of Versailles in 1919.

A Patriotic School Girl, by Angela Brazil, is published.

U-Boote Heraus! Mit U-Boot 178 gegen den Feind (trans. 'U-Boats Out! With submarine 178 against the enemy') – a documentary style film with a narrative.

Post-war – 1919

January 4th

Peace conference met in Paris to determine the terms of the peace, reparations, redrawing of national boundaries and more.

June 21st

The surrendered German naval fleet at Scapa Flow was scuttled. Among them SMS Derfflinger – one of the battlecruisers that bombarded Scarborough in December 1914.

June 28th

The Treaty of Versailles was signed by Germany.

Two Daring Patriots: or Outwitting the Huns, by W. P. Shervill is published - continuing the use of the war in fiction.

Introduction

The chapters in this volume have their origins in the conference *World War I: The Media, Entertainments & Popular Culture* held at the University of Chester between the 2nd - 3rd July 2015. The organisers and chairs of sessions were, including me, Jim Aulich, Manchester School of Art, Craig Horner, Manchester Metropolitan University, Carole O'Reilly, University of Salford, Nick Mansfield, UCLAN, Gaynor Bagnall, University of Salford, and Vera Slavtcheva-Petkova, University of Liverpool.

The papers presented at the conference were: Jane Chapman, *Social Movement Comic Strips as Citizen's Journalism, Humour and Cultural Record;* Pip Gregory, *Humorous Adaption and Recollection in War Cartoons;* R. J. Wilson, *'Over the Top': The legacy of the First World War within British Political Cartoons;* Eneko Bidegain, *Basque Writers' Reportages in Eskualduna, during World War I;* John Dilley and David Penman, *Market Harborough Advertiser and the Ashbourne Telegraph;* Jesus Jimenez-Varea and Antonio Pineda, *"And Yet They Tell Us not to Hate the Hun": Popular Media, Atrocity Propaganda and War Patriotism in Winsor McCay's The Sinking of the 'Lusitania';* Claudia Sternberg, *The Enduring Appeal of Edith Cavell;* Sonja Andrew, *Dichotomies of Representation and Interpretation: A Pacifist's Story;* Martin Bayer, *From Propaganda to Pacifism: German Art and the First World War;* Andrijana Rabrenović, *The Role of Political Posters in Montenegro and Serbia during World War I;* Maria Rikitianskaia, *Transnational Perspective on Radio Amateur Movements During the First World War;* Federico Montanari, *The Memory of the Great War Remixed;* David Goldie, *Romance by other Means: Scottish popular newspapers and the war;* Tom Roberts, *Sir Keith Murdoch, father of Rupert, during World War I;* Alex Jackson, *'Practical Patriotism': Domestic Football on the Home Front in England, 1914-1919;* Robert Dean, *Recruitment as Entertainment in Music Hall Performance,* and Melanie Gall and Nicol Hammond, *Knitting All the Day: World War I Knitting Music in Britain and America.*

Academics from four universities in the North West of England co-produced this conference and related events. This conference had two main themes. The first was to discuss popular mass entertainments (e.g. singers, music, magazines, newspapers, and radio) that existed before the war and which were adapted as the war progressed that promoted the war and national identity. The second is how the war furnished the narratives for popular mass consumed productions (e.g. films, posters, story books, and fiction).

This conference did not try to trivialise the First World War. Whether it was civilian, serviceman or servicewoman popular mass entertainments had a part to play in their lives. This conference did not, therefore, aim to examine artistic production during and immediately after the war. Works by artists such as Gertler, Wadsworth, Wyllie, Bone, Lewis and Munnings, and many others, may have been popular amongst some sections of society and have become the stock knowledge for scholarship but they did not attract a mass audience. Along with contemporary sculpture, poetry and opera, they were the preserve of a minority and were relatively unknown to the masses. There are exceptions such as McCrea's 'In Flanders Fields' and possibly a few poems by Owens and Sassoon. Plus, the great composers, such as Beethoven, Brahms and Humperdinck were globally known.

The conference was about the relationship between popular and mass entertainments during the war and the use of the war for mass audience productions. It aimed to examine the role, form and development of entertainments created during and related to it post-1918. The music hall, the singers, performers, the cartoons, romantic novels, and cinema all had a place and role to contemporaries. By 1915 many of these may have relayed the experience of war, and some provided the means to maintain morale and patriotism. Not all, however, supported the war. After one year of the initial war, optimism was confronted with the realisation that this war was different to others - the number of wounded and killed was shockingly high. English coastal towns were bombarded by German battleships, while other cities were bombed by German airships. Given the reality of the war, the kinds of questions discussed include the following. How did popular entertainments react to the war? What were the dynamics, politics and reception of different positions? In what ways did the form of mass entertainments change as the war progressed? What role did technology have in disseminating entertainments? How did commercial entertainment enterprises use the war to attract audiences? What differences and conflicts emerged between regions, classes and genders?

The complexity and dynamics of historical and contemporary methodological issues relating to mass popular entertainments during the war and since 1918 are challenging.

Not all of the papers presented have been published here and nor were all the papers submitted for consideration presented to the conference. Published in this volume is a selection of papers that represent and span several nationalities, generations and subject disciplines. In particular and in keeping with the general ethos of the conference several younger social scientists have been included in this volume.

Media, entertainments and popular culture

At the onset of the First World War in August 1914 the technologies, facilities and channels of distribution of mass entertainment, information and education were firmly established throughout most parts of North America, Europe, Australia and New Zealand.

Educational reforms (throughout Europe and North America) beginning in the 19th century meant literacy, even if basic, was common in most European populations, in North America and Australasia. Here was the market for the popular newspapers with stories of daring deeds, scandal and murders. Picture based periodicals provided photographs and artist drawn illustrations to satisfy viewer interests. Events from home and abroad were shown at the cinema depicting the heroes, political leaders and events of the day.

There was no shortage of media from which to choose. From the newsstands, booksellers, and high street stores such as Boots (now the chemist and beauty retailer) and WH Smith, books could, for a subscription, be borrowed.[1] Public libraries had also been established in many countries. In America, libraries began around 1747 with the first public library being founded in 1854. The same pattern of civil provision could be found in Great Britain, Australia, Canada and across Western Europe.[2] In Britain municipal libraries were opened in the industrialised towns and cities such as Salford, Manchester, Liverpool and Bolton from the 1850s onwards. The aim was to encourage self-improvement of the masses, reduce crime rates and make the working classes better citizens. Fundamentally, the public library was free to use.

---

[1] "1903, when there were 300 Boots stores across the country, 143 had a Booklovers' Library, with six libraries in London and 8 in Nottingham. By 1920 there were 500,000 subscribers and by 1938 books were being exchanged at the rate of 35 million each year, with light romance and whodunits being the most popular." infosciencetoday.org/library-science/boots-booklovers-library.html.

[2] See, Barnett, G. K. (1973). *The History of Public Libraries in France from the Revolution to 1939.* London: Library Association; Sturges, P. (1996). 'Conceptualizing the public library 1850–1919', in Kinnell, M. and Sturges, P. (eds.). *Continuity and Innovation in the Public Library: the development of a social institution.* London: Library Association

It was in the library that fiction and non-fiction could be read, and sometimes borrowed, newspapers read each day and lectures on social, economic and technical issues listened to.

Being able to read was also an advantage when watching a film at the local cinema. The silent films used captions to communicate the essentials of the dialogue being said by the characters on the screen. Aided by the in-situ organist or pianist, the events on the screen were explained using frames inserted into the film containing the dialogue or commentary. In Britain by 1914 many of the major studios had been established such as Gaumont, Lime Grove, Ealing, Cricklewood and Elstree; not being overtaken by American studios until the early 1920s.[3]

By 1914 cinema audiences were familiar with most genres including documentaries, historical dramas, adventures, chases, and comedies. The genres of a film being made mirrored the books being published and available from Boots. The heroes, heroines and villains from history and fiction could be had through reading and watching. Names such as Dorothea Baird, Elizabeth Risdon, Fred Groves, William S. Hart, Johnston Forbes-Robertson, and many more are now mostly unknown to post-1945 generations. But in 1914 these actors were the stars of their day. Their images could be seen in the popular periodicals, newspapers and specialist magazines such as *Picturegoer, The Stage, Variety* (from 1914), and *Il Maggese Cinematografico: periodico quindicinale*. They were known throughout the world for their film appearances and in the U.K. for their work in theatres, often playing roles from Shakespeare and Dickens.

By 1914 cinemas, both purpose-built and adapted from music halls could be found throughout the U.K. In London; it was not uncommon to have between 3 to 6 cinemas per square mile. The same was also the case for other major cities.[4] Know formally as Electric Theatres, Picture Palaces, Gems and Bijous or colloquially some as 'Flea pits' or 'Flicks', literacy was not a prerequisite but advantageous, to enjoy a roster of

---

[3] See, Curran, J. and Porter, V. (1983). *British Cinema History*. London: Weidenfeld & Nicolson; Higson, A. (1995). *Waving the Flag: Constructing a national cinema in Britain*. Oxford: Oxford University Press.

[4] McKernan, L. (2007) 'Diverting Time: London's Cinemas and Their Audiences, 1906–1914', *The London Journal*, 32:2, pages 125-144. Also, there were approximately 5,000 cinemas in the U.K., 10,000 in the U.S.A. and 1,200 in Russia in 1914 – see Youngblood, D. J. (2000). 'A War Forgotten: the Great War in Russian and Soviet Cinema', in, Paris, M. (ed.). *The First World War and Popular Cinema 1914 to the Present*. New Brunswick: Rutgers University Press, page 173.

films. The cinema was new, cheap and many luxurious, an utter contrast to the dark dredge of daily work. Audiences did not go to see just one film but a programme of shorts and a feature. As places to be entertained, informed and educated they were also dark allowing for intimate relations not typically allowed in daylight.

Reasons for going to the cinema were before the war much the same as during the war. It was about entertainment and escapism. And studios provided the content to meet these wants with a fast-changing menu of comedy, drama, documentaries and suspense films; each would often be accompanied with a newsreel. The newsreels were not neutral reports but compilations of exciting and topical events and happenings. Several newsreel producers, such as *Gaumont Graphic*, *Topical Budget* and *Warwick Bioscope Chronicle* in the U.K. and France, *Pathé-Journal*, *Éclair-Journal*, *Éclipse-Journal* and *Gaumont-Actualités* competed with each other. In America, *Pathé* was often the reel shown. Subjects ranged widely from the mundane to bizarre. *Pathé's* reel for week 65, 1913 started with news on the New York's new bus corporation, followed by Hallowe'en games being played by children, then a film of a battle between striking miners and police in Trinidad. Visits to places by the powerful and famous were staples often afforded a few minutes of film-time.

Newsreels were part of the entertainment, part of a menu of films shown at the afternoon matinée, and at the early evening and late night programmes. There purpose was to bring the local, regional, national and occasionally international goings-on to the screen. Coverage of events were short, a few minutes, and never intentionally controversial. There were some exceptions such as *Pathé Frères* film of the funeral of Archduke Ferdinand that lasted approximately four minutes and tried to make sense of the event, or the death of Suffragette Emily Davidson at the 1913 Derby, that was filmed as it happened and subsequently attracted world-wide media coverage. Where the filming of the funeral of Archduke Ferdinand was planned in advance the 'unexpected' capture on film of Emily Davidson being trampled to death was equally political. So much so her funeral was also filmed and shown in the newsreels.

The newsreels like other cinematographic productions relied on an established technology that was being used by entrepreneurs such as Charles Morand Pathé – founder of *Pathé* with branches all over the world (Belgium, Russia, America, Britain, Italy, Holland, Germany, and so on) by 1914. From re-selling phonographs at fairs Charles Pathé capitalised on the invention of the cinématographe, (motion picture camera) and in 1896 formed 'Compagnie Générale de Cinématographes, Phonographes et Pellicules' that would develop into making films, establishing studios, manufacturing film and equipment for cinema photography and cinemas and establishing distribution channels for their products.[5]

With the war the international scope of the newsreel and film industry narrowed as the combatant nations instigated mechanisms to control content and to use the media of film for national purposes. In Britain, *Topical Budget* became the official source for government information and propaganda (called, *War Office Official Topical Budget*). In Germany, the *Kriegs-Journal* (produced by the Wiener Kunstfilm-Industrie) produced newsreels for German and Austrian audiences. In America, newsreels tended to be anti-war until the sinking of RMS Lusitania and the subsequent declaration of war against Germany.[6]

The significant change was in the format of the newsreel from short to more extended documentary-style feature; lasting up to an hour the new feature-length films used the existing technology to provide insight into conditions and experiences. Some of the most popular were, the British *Battle of the Somme* (1916), the French, *La revanche des Français devant Verdun* (1916) and the Italian, *Battaglia da Plava al mare* (1917). With a mix of live action showing troops marching to re-enacted scenes, showing troops 'going over the top', these films did not provide information, as most of the facts even through censorship were known – lists of the dead were widely distributed. Nor did they aim to bolster recruitment. For example, the handbill promoting *Battle of the Somme* to the citizens of Briggate, Leeds quoted Lloyd George saying, "If this exhibition of this picture all over the world does not end War, God help civilisation!" These features took film-making forward and whatever the reasons for them being made they were shown in cinemas as entertainment. The Philharmonic Hall, Oxford Street, London advertised, "Last Two Weeks. The Battle of the Somme. Official Pictures of the British Army in France. Submarine Pictures. Full Orchestra."

The same audiences for the cinemas were also the readers of the many newspaper and periodical titles being published. In Scotland, *My*

---

[5] The dominance of European cinema, notably by French and Italian producers, was radically changed by the end of the war with British and especially American production companies overwhelming all others.

[6] Anti-war and pacifist films shown in America included, *The Battle Cry of Peace* (1915), *Civilization* (1916), and *Intolerance* (1916).

Weekly began publication in 1910 offering a magazine of stories and features for women - romance stories, advice, reader contributions, knitting and clothes patterns, and gossip on the stars of the cinema and Royalty. Semi-serious and practical features were popular, entertaining and informative. In Britain *Woman's Weekly* offered a similar range of offerings that focused on the home, beauty, fashion and health advice.

In America, *Adventure*[7] was one of the most popular mis-labelled pulp-magazines. Attracting established and up-and-coming writing *'Adventure'* also had a membership scheme that included Theodore Roosevelt Jr. Membership cards were issues and details taken on the skills and abilities of the card-carrier. Adventure stories both fiction and based on real events were published alongside advice from experts on a wide range of social, political and ethical issues.

Adventure was joined by other activity periodicals such as *Boy's Life* - a magazine aimed at the scouting movement in America. Similar annuals for scouting were published in Britain. With a full-colour cover *Boy's Life* was an attractive magazine.

The colour cover could also be found in periodicals such as *Photoplay*, the first American film fan magazine. Covers were painted by leading contemporary artists, featuring the stars of the day, and were often visually striking. Though after the War the *Photoplay* awards for best film as voted by its readers preceded the now famous Academy Awards. In 1930 *Photoplay's* award for best film went to 'All Quiet on the Western Front'.

The same could not be said of periodicals like *Cartoons Magazine* that aimed to caricature world leaders and nations of the world. *Cartoons Magazine* took already published cartoons from newspapers and other periodicals (from America and Europe) and grouped them according to themes such as fashion, crime and world affairs. From moderate humour through irony to critical satire the short-lived *Cartoons Magazine* nonetheless had an audience among the growing numbers of politicised citizens in America.

In 1915, the politicisation of Americans was, it could be argued, shown in the hit song and sheet music score was 'I Didn't Raise My Boy to Be a Soldier'. One of the first anti-war songs it connected the pacifist and suffragist movements in America. It also had a moderate amount of success in Britain and Australia. Causing controversy in 1915 the song

---

[7] Bleiler, R. (1990). 'A History of *Adventure* Magazine', in *The Index to Adventure Magazine*, Maryland: Borgo Press, pages 1-38.

has lived on in popular politics, often being symbolised in contemporary works such as *'Oh what a Lovely War'*, in the song, 'Hanging on the Old Barbed Wire', that describes officers as being miles away from the front while the boys of working-class families 'Hang on the Old Barbed Wire'. In the style of *Cartoons Magazine*, there were many parodies of the song. *Puck* (October 9, 1915) magazine published a cartoon of women's suffrage with the caption 'I Did Not Raise My Girl to be a Voter'. Other parodies included, 'I Didn't Raise My Dog to Be a Sausage', 'I Didn't Raise My Boy, He Had the Joker',[8] 'I Didn't Raise My Boy to Be a Soldier, But I'll Send My Girl to Be a Nurse', and 'I Did Not Raise My Boy to Be a Coward'.[9]

Music in many forms and genres was a significant part of popular and national cultures before the war. The technology of recording sound and playing what had been recorded back in the home was widespread.

In 1913 you could play 'My Heart Still Clings to You' by Albert Ketèlbey or Arnold Safroni-Middleton's 'Imperial Echoes'. Ketèlbey would go on in 1915 to sell over one million copies of his 'In a Monastery Garden', an orchestral piece in a classical style. The buyers of popular as well as classical music may also have purchased Henry Lauder's 'It's Nicer To Be In Bed' (1913). Lauder was, in 1911, the highest paid singer-comedian in the world performing in many countries, and would, from the outset of the war raise substantial amounts of money for the war effort.

Best selling gramophone recordings and sheet music was often the result of live performances at the local music hall. In the same year, Albert Ketèlbey had his million best-sellers George and Felix Powell had the hit, 'Pack Up Your Troubles in Your Old Kit-Bag', and 'Smile, Smile, Smile'. This was the result of a competition to write marching songs and went on to be popular with music hall singers. Often associated with 'It's a Long Way to Tipperary', both songs resonated with the aims of the war possibly because their lyrics were directed towards the working-classes. 'Pack Up Your Troubles' went on to

---

[8] Parker, B. S. (2007). *World War I Sheet Music Volume I*. Jefferson, North Carolina: McFarland & Company, Inc, page 4.

[9] Zeiger, Susan (1996). 'She Didn't Raise Her Boy To Be A Slacker: Motherhood, Conscription, and the Culture of the First World War'. *Feminist Studies*, 22 (1), 7-39.

feature in the 1916 musical 'Her Soldier Boy' and continues to this day to be widely known.[10]

The handbills and posters advertising who would be on at the local music hall and what would be showing at the local cinema were usually simple print using two colours. Printed on cheap paper, these were ephemera. Magazine covers, however, would employ the much more expensive full-colour printing. These, as were book covers, were mostly done by artists working in a commercial capacity applied their skills to make the subject look exciting, glamorous or mysterious. The book covers tended to have the same purpose as magazine covers but lacking the now familiar wrap an image was embossed onto the boards (book cover) and was often framed with an ornamental scroll. The 1914, 'Three Hundred & One Things a Bright Girl Can Do' was bright red with yellow infill used on the images – a cat, bird cage, hockey stick, flower vase, sawing basket and tennis racket. Published by Sampson Low these types of book were popular as presents for nieces of the middle-class. The idea lives on; Sally Nicholls's (2018) 'Things a Bright Girl Can Do' is a fictional account of suffragettes and suffragists.[11]

Photography was fully established before the war, and even colour was possible but never used commercially until the 1930s.[12] But by 1913 most high streets often pharmacies and chemist shops offered photographic services at affordable prices. Portraits could be done of whole families or members of a family leaving home for other countries. This, of course, became a major element for the families of members recruited into the army or navy (and later in the air force). Precious images of loved ones taken using the official photographer, usually the local chemist. Portraits could also be had of famous politicians, members of the Royal family, interesting 'foreigners' (Native Indians from America, for example) or stars from the cinema and music hall.

---

[10] The song was translated into many languages including German, has featured in popular carton such as 'Snoopy', Laurel & Hardy's (1932) *Pack Up Your Troubles*, Mervyn LeRoy's, *High Pressure* (1932), and H.C. Potter's (1938), *The Shopworn Angel* (1938) staring James Swart and Margaret Sullivan. It is also featured in Busby Berkeley's (1942) *For Me and My Gal*, starring Judy Garland and Gene Kelly, and was the referent in Wilfred Owen's poem, 'Smile, Smile, Smile' (1918). For more information see Tyler, D. (2016). *Music of the First World War*. Connecticut: ABC-CLIO/Greenwood, page 19.

[11] Nicholls, S. (2018). *Things a Bright Girl Can Do*. London: Andersen.

[12] For a fascinating insight into early uses of colour, photography sees Mervyn O'Gorman's photographs of Christina Bevan taken in 1913 - scienceandmediamuseum.org.uk/about-us/press-office/christina-mystery-beautiful-102-year-old-colour-portraits-solved.

Images of Julia Marlow, Betty Blyth, Mary Nolan, Theda Bara and Maud Fealy, were all popular, with men and women.[13]

Similar media, the cigarette card (and postcards), often used colour images of famous persons. Cinema stars, footballers, cricketers, baseball players, adventurers, and regimental uniforms were, among other topics, offered as collectables by tobacco brands. A card was placed inside the packet of cigarettes. Each set could run to 15 or more cards. Many images were produced by artists except for cinema and sporting stars. These images tended to be black and white (monochrome) photographs or colourised photographs - the equivalent of Photoshop in 1913. This was a process of physically painting onto the printed photograph to make it appear as if done in colour, then using mechanical reproduction to print copies of the image, using colour inks.

For the development of photography (and the graphic arts[14]) it needs to be acknowledged that the 'photo-magazine' and 'picture storybook' were the main drivers in developing the use of illustrations over the copy. Picture storybooks helped establish the concept that a narrative could be told just as well, if not better, using a sequence of images accompanying the text.[15] The popularity of children's picture books and photo-magazines meant there was a demand for photographers and illustrators. Typical of the photo-magazine was 'The Sphere'; its sub-title was, 'An Illustrated Newspaper for the Home', and later, 'The Sphere: The Empire's Illustrated Weekly'. Printed in black and white, in the U.K. it was part of a category of illustrated newspapers including 'The Graphic' and 'Illustrated London News' that brought photographs and illustrations of world events to the public. From its onset, the 'Illustrated London News' declared it would bring its readers, "the very form and presence of events as they transpire, in all their substantial reality" (1842, page 1). Once the war began the illustrated papers had images of all the main events using photographs when possible and alongside them graphic illustrations[16] to explain things such as the

---

[13] See, Menefee, D. W. (2004). *The First Female Stars: Women of the silent era*. London: Praeger.
[14] For more on graphic arts and the war see, Aulich, J. (2014). 'Graphic Arts and Advertising as War Propaganda', in, *1914-1918-online. International Encyclopedia of the First World War*, (ed.). Daniel, U., Gatrell, P., Janz, O., Jones, H., Keene, J., Kramer, A. and Nasson, B. issued by Freie Universität Berlin, Berlin,
encyclopedia,1914-1918-online.net/article/graphic_arts_and_advertising_as_war_propaganda.
[15] See Heiting, M. and Jaeger, R. (eds.), (2012). *Autopsie: Deutschsprachige fotobücher 1918–1945*, vol.1, Göttingen, pages 302-9.
[16] All the illustrated newspapers used a technique called end-grain woodblock engraving. Ironic, as the periodical press would have to abandon metal for wood to print illustrations at scale.

trajectory of artillery shells, maps of Europe and pictures of world leaders. The illustrated newspaper was not restricted to Britain; they were popular in many countries. In Germany, there was 'Die Wochenschau' (The Newsreel), a weekly review of newsreels released for showing in German cinemas.[17] Others published before and during the war included, the *Berliner Illustrirte Zeitung, Life* (USA), and newspapers, *The Daily Mirror* (London) and *The New York Daily News*.

Media, entertainment, and popular culture - frame of reference for the war years

This book is based on five propositions. The first is this. Entertainment as a topic for study is not trivial, inconsequential or irrelevant. To understand any culture look at what its members do for their entertainment. This includes looking at such things as, in 1914, jokes and humour, songs and music, drama and plays, cartoons and caricatures, films and animation, fiction and gossip, photographs and illustrations, advertising and posters, and newspapers and magazines. This proposition will be discussed in more detail once the other four propositions have been stated.

The second position is this. The core activities that are taken as entertainment, such as the cinema, books, music and newspapers, are surrounded by the institutions, industries and crafts which bring the entertainments to the marketplace.[18]

The third position is the recognition people read, sing, watch, listen and laugh not just for leisure but also when doing work and other activities. Entertainment does not always have to be separate from the workplace or from time doing work-based tasks; it can be incorporated into most aspects of life.

The fourth position follows on from longstanding debates about hierarchical schemes of entertainment regarding differentiated cultural value. Notions of high culture and low culture, popular culture and elite

---

[17] See, Fyfe, P. (2016). 'An Archaeology of Victorian Newspapers'. *Victorian Periodicals Review* (Winter), pages 546-577; Thomas, J. (2004). *Pictorial Victorians: The inscription of values in word and image*. Athens: Ohio University Press; Sinnema, P. W. (1998). *Dynamics of the Pictured Page: Representing the nation in the Illustrated London News*. Aldershot, Hants: Ashgate.

[18] In a contemporary context, the following among others have proposed an industrial frame of reference to understand entertainment and the cultural industries, see, Hesmondhalgh, D. (2002). *The Cultural Industries*. London, England: Sage; Towse, R. (2003). 'Cultural industries', in Towse, R. (Ed.), *A Handbook of Cultural Economics*. Cheltenham: Edward Elgar Publishing, pages 170-176.

culture are overworked dichotomies that distract attention from the entertainment under study, as a thing in itself, and lead to prejudice against one of the classes of entertainment on the scale. If classical music performances are elitist, exclusionist and class-based it does not entail they are 'bad' and things should be otherwise. It is not the music or musicians that are excluding anyone. It is the instructional arrangements that bring such performances to the marketplace, a lack of education provided about the value of the experience and, possibly, snobbishness of some audiences.

The fifth proposition is entertainment is about audience experience. This can take multiple forms for the same audience of an entertainment. Bosshart and Macconi (1998)[19] include the following in a list of possible experiences an audience member can take from consuming a particular media - obtaining relaxation, being distracted, seeing something different to the norm, seeking excitement or a thrill, wanting to laugh, sharing the joy and enjoying a place.

*****

At the conference that initiated this book, Melanie Gall and Nicol Hammond, presented a performance session called, *'Knitting All the Day: World War 1 Knitting Music in Britain and America'*.[20] That session and Melanie Gall's stage performances are convenient starting points for discussing the propositions listed above.

Melanie performs, most beautifully, songs sung by women who were encouraged to knit during the war. Her work on knitting songs from the First World War, she performs, entertaining audiences with a slice of life of mostly women[21] who were unseen and unacknowledged but who had a common activity, of knitting and in many sung alone or together in their knitting group.

The knitting song has attracted very little attention from academics. This may be due to the activity not been seen as necessary, something too lowly to be worthy of academic research. It maybe knitting is regarded as 'what women do in the home', and not *really* about the war. Or how could these songs compete with those sung by men in the

---

[19] Bosshart, L. and Macconi, I. (1998). Defining 'entertainment'. *Communication Research Trends*, 18, pages 3-6.
[20] Gall, M. (2012). *Knitting All the Day: knitting songs from WW1*. Audio disk CDBaby.
[21] School children, both girls and boys, were encouraged to knit garments for the troops during the war, especially in America.

trenches? There is, of course, substantial literature and numerous archives on and of trench songs. The strange irony here is that Gall's performance work could, in contemporary terms[22] be said to be middle-class art. That irony being, the original singers of the knitting songs were, from what can be extracted from the available literature, working-class women, and therefore, under the same classification lowbrow entertainment.[23] As art Gall's work informs, reminds and recounts the themes present in the knitting songs. As entertainment, her performances give musical enjoyment, humorous lyrics and opportunities to sing along. Therefore, we can say that from our summary of Gall's work defining entertainment is no easy matter.

If the knitting songs are categorised in a broad sense as mass culture, something that was enjoyed by a large section of the populace, then they were also part of popular culture. But if the songs are categorised as requiring work and effort to produce, i.e. sing, and required discipline, attention and practice then they are examples, by accepted definition, of elite culture. The knitting was being done for a purpose, to contribute to the war effort by providing garments for the troops. As work, though unpaid, it was skillful and to sing at the same time, sometimes in harmony with others would be, for this author, daunting.

The broad definition taken in this volume for entertainment and popular culture is, based on our discussion of Gall's performances, broad. It is based, in the first instance, on Irwin and Gracia (2007) and Shusterman's (2003)[24] claims that entertainment has functions above mere subsistence, which it sustains, refreshes, distracts and provides relief from monotony. Entertainment, whatever we take it to be, has a value to the consumer. It is not usually by mere chance someone encounters entertainment. This is, based on the discussion above, to be able to be entertained the industries of entertainment need to be active, accessible and have content that is desirable in return for payment.

Entertainment *could* be classified as art but if paid for it is still entertainment; it is the outcome of organised effort directed towards offering a product people will pay to see and listen to. Taking Sayre and

---

[22] Fiedler, L. (1955). 'The Middle Against Both Ends', *Encounter* 5, pages 12-23; Gans, H. (1975). *Popular Culture and High Culture.* New York: Basic Books.
[23] Meyersohn, R. (1969). *Sociology and Cultural Studies.* Birmingham: CCCS.
[24] Irwin, W. and Gracia, J.E. (eds.). (2007). *Philosophy and the Interpretation of Pop Culture.* Maryland pages 135-6: Rowman; Shusterman, Richard. 'Entertainment: A Question for Aesthetics'. *British Journal of Aesthetics*, 43.3 (2003), pages 289-307. Also see Davison, P., Meyersohn, R. and Shils, E. (1978). *'Culture and Mass Culture'.* Cambridge: Chadwyck-Healey.

King's (2003)²⁵ characterisation of entertainment we can say Melanie Gall's performances of World War I knitting songs is entertainment. As a performer, Gall has undergone training as a singer, and she is experienced. She uses a range of technologies to maximise her performance, organises, arranges, produces and writes her act, employs symbols of the war era to add to the audiences experiences and contextualisation of the songs, and undertakes marketing communications to advertise and promote her appearances in particular venues.

It was not so different during the war. In August 1916 the film 'The Battle of the Somme' opened in cinemas across the U.K. In just one week an estimated 1 million Londoners had paid to see it; over the next six weeks, the audience across the country exceed 10 million. The film was distributed worldwide, but in the U.K. a third of the population viewed it on release. There is no doubt the film was technically and socially groundbreaking, placing a landmark for the history of documentary film-making; becoming almost immediately a historical document itself. But the fact remains, the horrors of the front line, even if some scenes were re-created (faked), attracted paying audiences. 'The Battle of the Somme' was a commercial success breaking U.K. box office receipts.

The notion of infotainment had not in 1916 been conceptualised as a category to label media production. Nonetheless, 'The Battle of the Somme' was and still is a sobering experience that informs and entertains the watcher. Contemporary audiences are different from those of 1916 as they can watch the film for free, probably would not attend a cinema to see it or be shocked by the scenes of death and suffering.²⁶ But in 1916 this kind of content was new for the motion picture goer. Some illustrated periodicals had carried images of the troops and damage to buildings and ships but not in such a graphic and life-like way as 'The Battle of the Somme' did.

But 'The Battle of the Somme' did not come into existence by accident; it was planned. Filmmakers Geoffrey Malins and Benjamin

---

[25] Sayre, S. and King, C. C. (2003). *Entertainment and Society: Audiences, trends, and impacts*. London: Sage.

[26] Except some did. The First World War Heritage project, Great War Huts (Suffolk) showed the film on the 29th October 2016 advertising it with the copy, "Don't miss this unique opportunity to see the groundbreaking 1916 film, which made cinema history, as it was originally seen – with live piano accompaniment... refreshments available." Tickets, £8. Similar showings and prices occurred throughout the UK in late 2016.

McDowell were professional commercial filmmakers; they knew what kind of content would attract audiences and went out to capture it on film. With some risk to themselves and good fortune in being in the right places and the right time, they applied their craft. The cinema-going paying public had seen photographs and artist illustrations of battles in the illustrated papers and little on newsreels except for long distance shots of battlefields[27] Malins and McDowell changed all of this. Their film had a narrative and was different to everything so far shown on the popular newsreels. The use of the close up was particularly harrowing. One scene shows a soldier in a trench, he looks exhausted, carrying an unconscious comrade on his back.

* * * * *

Whether national newspapers, local newspapers, handbills, illustrated periodicals, music hall songs, children's books, romance stories, classical compositions, animated films, posters or comedy, all are experiences available to the masses regardless of their social position, having been produced by an institutionalised set of industries that aim to bring experiences to an audience in exchange for a fee. [28]

The theme running through the contributions in this volume are the links being made between experiences, entertainment and value creation.[29] The writing of reports of battles, framing romance stories around soldiers and sailors, showing the sinking of ships, explaining the war o children, illustrating events with diagrams and photographs, publishing letters from homesick soldiers, and claiming classical composers for national identity were the heightened routine of entertainment producers during the war.

Are about creating emotional value to meet diverse needs of consumers. Those needs cannot be classified in ways that are simple or singular. The emotional value derived could be a combination of

---

[27] Even as late as mid-1918 battlefield films released as newsreels were still vague on details, relying on long-distance shots. The 1918 film, 'Battle of Arras' an example of a newsreel feature showing tiny figures in the distance, smoke on the field, and one scene of distant cavalry being hit by an exploding shell.

[28] Classical composers were and still are readily available in 1914 via the gramophone record, but more so in music halls and as accompanying motion pictures.

[29] Nijs, D. (2003). 'Imagineering: Engineering for imagination in the emotion economy', in Peeters, P., Schouten, F. and Nijs, D. (eds.), *Creating a Fascinating World*. Breda, Netherlands: Breda University, pages 15-34.

excitement, thrill, information, awareness, sympathy, escapism, aestheticism and amusement.

There are various conceptual frameworks that try to encapsulate the diversity of entertainment experience[30] but it is Schmitt (1999)[31] that gives a sequence of concepts (derived from contemporary marketing communications) that aid understanding and appreciation of mediated entertainments during the war. Schmitt's (1999) basic premise is that the media industries exist to provide experiences; they are in effect, experience providers, in business to create engaging and entertaining experiences that attract audiences. His scheme, somewhat reduced is, entertainment products aim to provide an audience with the narrative to 'sense, feel, think, act and relate'.

There are many examples of popular media entertainments produced during the war. 'The Battle of the Somme' (1916) is an example discussed above. Another multi-faceted example is the genre of espionage and spying. Stories of spies and spying had been popular before the war, but during the war, the genre offered opportunities to consolidate existing and take on new purposes in pursuit of the war effort. And there was no shortage of stories and characters with which to tell of, and contrast, the bad and good spy. A popular example was Mata Hari who has often been contrasted with Edith Cavell.

The interesting point about Mata Hari and Edith Cavell is not that they were real persons, women and were both executed; it is the enduring use of their stories long after the war. Both women received considerable media attention when executed; Edith Cavell by the Germans and Mata Hari by the French. Not only do the contrasts made between the two women provide for a rich resource for story-telling and propaganda but bring to the fore the concept of media entertainment value, that extended well beyond the war years, of these two tragic executions.

---

[30] For examples see, Berridge, G. (2007). *Events Design and Experience*. Oxford: Butterworth-Heinemann; Hill, E., O'Sullivan, T., and O'Sullivan, C. (1995). 'The arts: The market and the environment; Audiences; Product; Making the Arts Available', in Hill, E., O'Sullivan, T. and O'Sullivan, C. (eds.), *Creative Arts Marketing*. Oxford, England: Butterworth-Heinemann, pages 1-54; 101-141; 222-249; Schmitt, B. H., Rogers, D. L., and Vrotsos, K. (2004). *There's No Business that's Not Show Business; Marketing in an experience culture*. Upper Saddle River, NJ: Financial Times Prentice Hall.
[31] Schmitt, B. H. (1999). *Experiential Marketing: How to get customers to sense, feel, act and relate to your company and brands*. New York: The Free Press.

Mata Hari (as Rosie White discusses in this volume) was the stage persona of Margaretha Zelle MacLeod (1876-1917). From a middle-class Dutch family Margaretha developed the image of the exotic dancer not afraid to cross societally ascribed boundaries and constraints placed on women. Having had various relations with high-ranking officials and military officers and performed her sexualised dancing routine across Europe, she had attracted media attention before the war. During the war was accused of spying for the Germans. Her public persona of the Oriental temptress expressing decadence was a threat to the allied establishment an opportunity for them to exploit. Mata Hari as the 'other', different from expectations expected of women and portrayed as the 'savage' was an easy target for conveying the message of the threat of the female spy to the Allied war effort. Arrested, tried and convicted of espionage Margaretha Zelle MacLeod was executed on the 15th October 1917 by the French.

Edith Cavell (1865-1915) was utterly unknown before her execution on the 12th October 1915. Edith was a nurse, working in occupied Belgium and assisting with the escape network for Allied soldiers. As Rosie White says, Edith was a martyr-in-waiting. Edith could be and was portrayed as a typical middle-class white English woman, doing good deeds in the face of danger. She was arrested, and like Margaretha found guilty of espionage and executed by firing squad.

There is a lot more to each of these women and the events leading up to their executions, but the purpose here is to highlight the substantial amount of media productions created based on each of them.

Edith Cavell and entertainment value

Beginning with Edith Cavell a sense of the entertainment produced along with the moral message of what male definitions of womanhood was about can be glimpsed through a short survey of the productions.

Cavell's execution, given her moral value set, was a major resource for British and allied propaganda.[32] But she was not a simple tool for propaganda. Other atrocities had happened, and more was to come, but these would, once the war ended, fade as the war generation aged and European governments tried to suppress reminders of atrocities.

---

[32] For more on the propaganda generated by Cavell's execution see, Shane Barney, (2001). 'Edith Cavell - Wonder Women: Propaganda, Legend, Myth, and Memory'. Master's Thesis, University of Vermont, USA.

The bombardments of the English seaside towns in 1914 (discussed by Hart in the volume) are now assigned mainly to history books. Cavell, in contrast, attained a celebrity status that has endured to the present day.[33] This enduring status and awareness of Cavell has been attributed to her devotion to the sick, her refusal to be bound or wear a blindfold, wearing her nurses uniform in front of the firing squad, and what is seen as her martyrdom, as she was not afraid to die. Just before facing the firing squad she is reported as saying, 'Jesus told us to forgive everyone who hurts us and he told us to love everyone'.[34] In this list, there is a strong sense of strong women, with purpose and determination but at the same time feminine. Cavell was a challenge as was Mata Hari to male dominance. Whereas Mata Hari can be seen as having been exploited by men, Cavell was not. She was a beacon for women who had struggled for suffrage against male ignorance (ironically sacrificing herself for the institutions that had oppressed and committed violent acts against suffragists) and for generations of women through the 20th and into the 21st centuries.[35]

The immortalisation of Cavell into popular consciousness began almost straight away. While the allied governments had done little, in practical terms, to intervene in her plight, newspapers articles, periodical features, films, poems, postcards, biographies and posters were produced, and there were eager audiences keen to consume them. The ephemera of newspaper reports[36] were followed with more lasting memorisations of Cavell.

Cavell's story was converted to film by the end of November 1915, with *Nurse and Martyr*, (English silent) directed by Percy Moran, Cora Lee playing Cavell and written by Edgar Wallace.[37] The following year,

---

[33] For example, on the 12th October, each year, women dressed as nurses from 1915 meet and lay flowers at Cavell's memorial in London.

[34] Johnson, J. (1978). *The Secret Task of Nurse Cavell: A story about Edith Cavell*. Minneapolis, MN, page 29.

[35] See, for example, Anderson, Bonnie S. and. Zinsser, Judith P. (1988). *A History of Their Own: Women in Europe from prehistory to the present*. Oxford: Oxford University Press, page, 366; and Speck, C. (1996). 'Women's War Memorials and Citizenship', *Australian Feminist Studies* 11, pages 140-41.

[36] See for example, *The Times*, October 16, 1915, page 8; *The Times*, October 22, 1915, page 1; *The Times*, October 23, 1915, page 7; *The Daily Mirror*, October 16, 1915, page 3; *The Daily Mirror*, October 23, 1915, page 4; *The Morning Post*, October 23, 1915, page 6; and most other daily and weekly newspapers between the 16th and 30th October, 1915 in the U.K. and worldwide.

[37] There was a memorial service in St Paul's Cathedral on 29th October 1915 that was filmed. The memorial service can be watched at, britishpathe.com/video/nurse-cavell-tribute-at-st-pauls-1915-aka-a-nation/query/wildcard.

Figure 1 Poster advertising *Nurse Cavell*

The Martyrdom of Nurse Cavell[38] (English silent) Directed by John Gavin and C. Post Mason[39], Vera Pearce as Cavell and *The Story of Nurse Cavell, England's Joan of Arc* (English silent) (also known as *Edith Cavell* and *Nurse Cavell* and advertised as 'England's Nurse and Martyr, Edith Cavell') directed by W. J. Lincoln, with Margaret Linden as Cavell. Both of these were Australian feature-length films. Next came 1918 *The Woman the Germans Shot* (English silent) (also known as, *The Cavell Case*) directed by John G. Adolfi, with Julia Arthur as Cavell. Most of these early films

---

[38] Vera Pearce was often described as Australia's most beautiful actress.
[39] John Gavin took legal action against Lincoln and his *'The Story of Nurse Cavell'* for breach of copyright. Gavin's legal action led to *'The Story of Nurse Cavell'* being advertised with the disclaimer "patrons are reminded that this picture is in no way connected with any other bearing the same name" (see 'Advertising' *Cairns Post* (1909–1954). National Library of Australia. 5 April 1916, page 1.

are now lost, recorded in newspaper reviews and listing for show times from cinemas.[40] The two films to endure are both by Herbert Wilcox, 1928 *Dawn* (English silent) with Sybil Thorndike as Cavell, based on a play by Reginald Berkeley and the 1938 *Nurse Edith Cavell* (English) with Anna Neagle as Cavell.

Biographies, plays,[41] music and souvenirs followed, plus calls were made for donations for a monument to be built to Cavell.[42] The main outputs in 1915-16 were from, as would be expected, Britain but unusually, also Australia. *The Martyrdom of Nurse Cavell* and *The Story of Nurse Cavell* were Australian. The British Library has a superb collection of material published between 1915 onwards about Cavell. Between 1915-1918 at least 27 publications (including poems and songs) were printed in Great Britain. Other national libraries and archives also have lists of publications. Many publications were produced by publishing houses and did not, in many cases, have an author. For example, 'Nurse Cavell: the Story of Her Life and Martyrdom' (1915), published by C. A. Pearson, is credited to Edith herself. Other publishers used illustrations to enhance reader reception of outrage[43] such as 'The Martyrdom of Nurse Cavell. The Life Story of the Victim of Germany's most Barbarous Crime with Illustrations' (1915), published by Hutchinson & Co and written by William Thomson Hill. Since 1918 there have been a further 55 publications about Cavell, 18 of which published after 2000. The interest in Cavell is, even in the new millennium, unabated. Between 2015-2016 there was three plays dedicated to and telling the story of Cavell as a British Hero and woman. The memorisation and commemoration of Cavell in such a range of media cannot be mere propaganda. There is, in the Cavell narrative a number of human virtues that were personified in Cavell and the decisions she made. These can be seen in an extended treatment of what we propose is the film that consolidated the popularisation of these virtues, the 1938 *Nurse Edith Cavell*.

---

[40] *Nurse and Martyr* (1915) survive in the collection of the British Film Institute. It can be watched via, bfi.org.uk/free/film/watch-nurse-and-martyr-1915-online.

[41] A reasonable, but not complete, a source of plays and films about Cavell is Kelly, V. (2015). 'A Sweet Tribute to Her Memory': Wartime Edith Cavell Plays and Films', in Maunder A. (eds.) *British Theatre and the Great War, 1914–1919*. London: Palgrave Macmillan.

[42] The *Daily Telegraph* led the call for public subscriptions for a memorial statue of Cavell. Unveiled on the 17th March 1920, the statue stands opposite the National Portrait Gallery, in London.

[43] See, Pickles, K. (2007). *Transnational Outrage: the death and commemoration of Edith Cavell*. London: Palgrave Macmillan, pages 16-39 for a treatment of outrage.

Mata Hari and entertainment value

Mata Hari is complemented by a number of representations following her death that has continued to the present day. A film, fiction, biographical and photographic representations of Margaretha, as Mata Hari that appeared after her execution followed on from the fairly extensive newspaper reporting of her behaviour while she was alive. Mata Hari was the persona invented partially by Margaretha and, as female 'foreign' spy, was amplified by the media after her arrest. As a spy, exotic dancer, mother, and victim, Mata Hari's story provides a rich resource for factual and fictional accounts of the place, role and expectations placed on women. The four main films representations associated with her life and the story are, *Mata Hari, die rote Tänzerin* (trans. *Mata Hari: the Red Dancer*), (1927 film) directed by Friedrich Feher (Silent, German),[44] *Mata Hari* (1931 film) directed by George Fitzmaurice, (in English), *Mata Hari, Agent H21.* (1965 film) directed by Jean-Louis Richard, (in French and Italian), and *Mata Hari* (1985 film) directed by Curtis Harrington, (in English) portray the female spy as irresponsible, treacherous and sexually loose. In contrast, women spies working for the Allies are depicted as pure, white and feminine, particularly in films such as *Nurse Edith Cavell* (dir. Herbert Wilcox, 1939, U.K.).

In 1927 there were, however, three films made and released about female spies - Friedrich Feher's *Mata Hari, die rote Tänzerin* (trans. *Mata Hari: the Red Dancer*), Sinclair Hill's *Return of Mata Hari: A Woman Redeemed*, and Alfred Hitchcock's *Notorious*.[45] These alongside magazine stories and books could be seen as extending the public appetite for 'spy stories' - fiction or biographical.[46]

---

[44] See, Kreimeier, K. (1999). *The Ufa Story: A History of Germany's Greatest Film Company, 1918-1945*. California: University of California Press that discusses the Staaken Studios, where Feher made his film. The studios were on the outskirts of Berlin, in a zeppelin hangar converted to filmmaking following the First World War that in 1923 it was the largest studio in the world.
[45] See, Nora Gilbert, (2011). '"She makes love for the papers": Love, sex, and exploitation in Hitchcock's Mata Hari Films' *Film & History: An Interdisciplinary Journal of Film and Television Studies*, 41:2, page 6.
[46] The appetite is exemplified by, John Buchan's *The Thirty-Nine Steps, Greenmantle and Huntingtower* - and the readership memoirs published by former Secret Service personnel such as Basil Thomson, who as head of the Criminal Investigation Department in 1913, was twice charged with interviewing the alleged spy, Mata Hari.

A Woman Redeemed, for example,[47] was adapted by Mary Murillo from Frederick Britten Austin's *Strand* magazine short story, 'The Fining Pot is for Silver'. The film features a secret organisation of foreign spies, seeking to steal secrets about a new pilotless aeroplane, designed by a young pilot who distinguished himself in the war yet desires peace. The new aeroplane is meant to keep Britain strong against its enemies and maintain peace. But the foreign agents order their female agent, Felice, to use her beauty, charm and sexual attractiveness on the young pilot. An added twist a second female agent threatens to expose Felice if she is unsuccessful. But the British are not to be outwitted. After a pursuit from France to London, taking in some erotic scenes of women entertaining an audience by bathing and lavish hotel rooms, the foreigners are thwarted.

As an aside, it is often claimed that the first Mata Hari film was *Die Spionin* (commonly known as Mata Hari) in 1921, directed by Ludwig Wolff. This film does not, probably, exist because it was never made. It is included here because the reference to this non-existent film has itself become part of the mythology of Mata Hari. Most of the movie databases[48] reference *Die Spionin* but have no details and no copy seems to exist. There are some films similar in title and story, but none are titled, *Die Spionin*. There is *Die Rache der Spionin* (made in 1921), directed Richard Eicherg and did not feature Asta Nielsen - the actress said to have played Mata Hari in *Die Spionin*. Similarly, Ludwig Wolff, although difficult to pin-down everything he was involved in, did not make a film called, *Die Spionin*. He did, however, make and direct three films with Asta Nielsen in them; and these can be verified. They were *Steuermann Holk* (1920), *Die Tänzerin Navarro* (1922/23) and *Der Absturz* (1922). It is

---

[47] See, Amy Sargeant, (2010) 'The Return of Mata Hari: A Woman Redeemed (Sinclair Hill, 1927)', *Historical Journal of Film, Radio and Television* 30:1, pages 27-54. 'The fining pot...' is from the *Bible* Proverbs 17-3.

[48] The source for this is the blog of Ivo Blom - ivoblom.wordpress.com/2017/03/11/more-myths-and-facts-on-mata-hari-on-film/. Following through this it was found that it is probably the case as IMDb, unreliably lists *Die Spionin* as do the following: English and Dutch Wikipedia; James Monaco's *The Movie Guide*; David Thompson's *The New Biographical Dictionary of Film*; Michael R. Pitts's *The Great Spies Pictures*; James Robert Parish's *Prostitution in Hollywood films*; Jerry Vermilye's *More films from the thirties*; Léon Schirmann's *Mata-Hari: autopsie d'une machination*; Georg Seeßlen's *Filmwissen: Thriller: Grundlagen des populären Films*; Valeria Palumbo's *Le figlie di Lilith: vipere, dive, dark ladies e femmes fatales: l'altra ribellione femminile*; Rüdiger Dirk and Claudius Sowa's *Paris im Film: Filmografie einer Stadt*, and many others. The English version of Wikipedia indicates *Mata Hari* (1920) and *Die Spionin* (1921) as two separate films, both about Mata Hari.

most likely that *Die Tänzerin Navarro* (1922/23)[49] is mistaken for the non-existent *Die Spionin*. It is because the narrative of *Die Tänzerin Navarro* has elements that could be said to have come from the biography of Mata Hari. Asta Nielsen plays a Spanish dancer called, Carmencita Navarro. The story tells of Carmencita losing a child due to the revenge of a Javanese man against her husband. Mata Hari was thought to have connections to Java. Carmencita flees Java to Germany, goes into performing in vaudeville, has an affair with her late husbands business partner, is suspected of espionage and condemned to be executed; she is saved from the firing squad at the last minute. Visually there are also scenes echoing the oriental erotic performances of Mata Hari.

It is not surprising the *Die Tänzerin Navarro* used the narrative of a women spy with intrigue, sex and sexuality. This narrative was now commonplace in the popular imagination following the post-execution stories about Mata Hari; her real-life story (as reported at the time with its propaganda standpoint) contained everything needed for a gripping yarn. Other films followed the formulae - *The Mysterious Lady* directed by Fred Niblo (1928 silent film) was based on a novel by no other than Ludwig Wolff, *Der Krieg im Dunkel* (trans. *War in the Dark*, 1915). It tells the tale of Tania Fedorova, a Russian spy tasked with stealing secret plans from Captain Karl von Raden. Tania tries but fails to seduce the Captain, but the plans are nonetheless stolen. The Captain is imprisoned but is released, takes on a different identity as a musician, and by accident comes across Tania at a private party he has been asked to play at. She is with General Boris Alexandroff, head of Russian Military Intelligence and she recognises but does not betray Karl. Alexandroff suspects Tania loves Karl and sets a trap for them. The trap backfires on Alexandroff who is killed by Tania, who recovers the secret documents, escapes with and marries Karl. The interesting thing about *The Mysterious Lady* is the lead being played by Greta Garbo.

Three years later Garbo would play Mata Hari in George Fitzmaurice's 1931 film *Mata Hari*.[50] This film, alongside *The Mysterious Lady*, could be considered as providing the template for the narrative that is most commonly associated, regardless of the facts, with Mata Hari. By 1931 there was a rush to bring espionage films to English speaking audiences. When MGM announced it would be making Mata

---

[49] Only still prints of *Die Tänzerin Navarro* exist and these are in the Danish Film Archive at, dfi.dk/faktaomfilm/film/en/41888.aspx?id=41888.
[50] See, Williams, M. (2017). 'Idols and Idolatry: Greta Garbo and Ramón Novarro in *Mata Hari* (1931)', in Williams, M. *Film Stardom and the Ancient Past*. London: Palgrave Macmillan.

Hari with Garbo, its rival Paramount Pictures rushed *Dishonored* (1931) into production, starring Marlene Dietrich as a Mata Hari-like spy. *Dishonored* opened in March, and, Mata Hari in December 1931. *Dishonored*, directed by Josef von Sternberg, is not about Mata Hari, but uses the female spy as the device to tell a story about the dangers of female spies. Set against the backdrop of the First World War, the female spy has a code name, X27, has relationships with a German and Russian, and is executed by firing squad, like the real-life Mata Hari.[51]

That Garbo and Dietrich were 'foreign' could be overlooked, but the roles each played in their respective espionage films were about foreign women as dangerous spies. Garbo being Swedish and Dietrich German their accents, it could be suggested, would have fitted the expectation that female spies were foreign. *Mata Hari* (1931) was certainly tailored to use Garbo's public persona, exotic, sophisticated, confident and sexual. In the opening scene of *Mata Hari* Garbo performs a quasi-Oriental dance to the sound of Moorish pipes and citars (played by a band of men all in turbans with long white beards). In the background is a figure resembling a male pastiche of the female deities' such as Durga (Hindu) and Quan Âm Nghìn Mắt Nghìn Tay (Buddhist affiliation); the dance (such as it is) ends in long shot with Garbo apparently semi-naked. The audience is composed of men and women in formal evening dress, but the focus is on two Russian officers (father and son). Both look transfixed by the eroticism being performed for them, especially the younger officer who receives a curious glance from the other.

Garbo is playing Mata Hari but not as she was; Garbo is bejewelled and swathed in silks. After the dance she goes with the young Russian officer to his home; luxurious rooms with artworks hanging from the walls, including a picture of the Madonna (Virgin Mary or 'Madonna'). This was to prove controversial.[52] The plot is Mata Hari is an erotic

---

[51] *Dishonoured* (1931) has many similarities to the earlier 1926 film *Mare Nostrum*. Also set in World War I, the story revolves around an Austrian spy called Freya. With some interesting uses of Greek mythology, Freya falls in love with a Spanish man (called Ulysses living in neutral Spain) who is bent on revenge against the Germans for killing his son. Her Austrian masters find out about Ulysses and his quest for revenge, arrest Freya and execute her. Ulysses enacts revenge by sinking the U-boat that had killed his son but not before the U-boat has torpedoed his ship the *Mare Nostrum*. Ulysses descends in the sinking *Mare Nostrum* into the ocean depths, where Amphitrite (Goddess queen of the sea) embraces and kisses him.

[52] The picture is visible in the seduction scene when the lights are turned down. In the British version of the film, the picture of the Madonna seems to be some one's mother. And pre-1934 in the USA, after the Hays Code was introduced scenes were shorted and others cut out. The opening dance scene was too erotic for the American Hays Code censors who cut out most of it.

dancer and German spy. She is instructed to use her beauty and sexual attractiveness to obtain secret documents. By coincidence, she meets and falls in love with a Russian aviator who, initially unknown to her, happens to have the classified documents. She sleeps with him (in a darkened room) while other agents steal the documents, copy them and then return them unnoticed. Meanwhile, another female spy, who also fell in love with someone, is killed on the orders of the German spy chief for being a threat to the secret organisation. The spy chief finds out about Mata's love for the Russian and puts in place a trap. Telling her ex-lover about the Russian, he intends that Mata will be exposed as a traitor. Mata tries to convince her ex-lover she is not in love with the Russian; he does not believe her, so she kills him. Unbeknown that she was set-up Mata is told by her spy chief her Russian lover is in hospital, having crashed his aeroplane, and is now blind. She goes to him and after declaring her love for him is arrested, tried for murder and espionage. She pleads guilty hoping her Russian lover will not find out the truth about her. In prison awaiting execution, she looks for a reprieve, but it does not come. Her Russian lover does, however, come to see her, believing she is in a hospital awaiting an operation (remembering he is blind). She tells him not to grieve if her operation kills her. Shortly afterwards outside the firing squad is preparing as Mata is led towards them.

Garbo's Mata Hari is fictional. She is an exaggerated caricature of what the real Mata was assumed to be like, as portrayed in popular publications. Women were not just spies they were, in 1930s popular culture, fascinating, and dangerous aliens, unlike their male counterparts who were calm, decent and handsome. Mata was referred to by the French as 'Mademoiselle Doctor'; 'super-sexed women' able to seduce all men using their sexual 'art'. Mata was never going to be portrayed as normal, everyday woman because she was not this. This would not make for good storytelling. As cocaine snorting, gun carrying dominatrix, skillfully displaying sexual adventure beyond the experience of most 'respectable' gentlemen (circa 1916) then the deviant women, Mata, becomes a dangerous weapon in the employ of the enemy.[53]

For more on the pre-Hays Code, era see, Vieira, M. A. (1999). *Sin in Soft Focus: Pre-Code Hollywood*. New York: Harry N. Abrams, Inc.

[53] There have been many other fictional portrayals of Mata Hari including The 1964 - *Mata Hari, 'Agent H21'*; 1972 - *Up the Front* with Zsa Zsa Gábor, as Mata Hari, a minor character in the film; 1985 – *Mata Hari* with Sylvia Kristel; 2003 - *Mata Hari, la vraie histoire*, is a French movie about the interrogations of Mata Hari, directed by Alain Tasma, and starring Maruschka

In the early twentieth century, the female spy thus came to represent modern femininity that was either eroticised (and demonised) as exotic or fetishised (and exalted) as the epitome of 'pure' English womanhood, often for a potential American audience.[54]

To conclude this section the productions using Mata Hari and Edith Cavell employed diverse media and formats over a number of decades. Some, in the case of Cavell, were artist drew and painted illustrations depicting her life and death, presented on postcards, others were plays and films. For Mata Hari, there are many photographs of her, in person and actual domestic life. There are also the plays, books and films. The use of their lives and deaths lent a raft of contrasting symbolic messages that were consumed en masse as popular entertainment by the fee-paying public. Having universal appeal the morality tales comparing sacrifice with deceit, was not trivial or ephemeral, especially during the war. A substantial amount of creative and technical effort went into most of these productions; they did not simply appear. The regret is that some of the portrayals of Mata Hari were too focused on serving Allied propaganda and bolstering the anti-suffragist position done through thinly disguised eroticism as the entertainment offering. Ironically, Margaretha Zelle MacLeod's 'Mata Hari' was the entertainment of elite demographics throughout Europe before her execution and something; it can be argued, is mostly glossed over in the films about her life, as is the weakness of men she allegedly seduced. Nonetheless, it was a man that is seen as having caught her, men who tried her and men who executed her.

Hence, no matter the subject and however serious it was, such as an execution, death of thousands of sailors or drowning of mothers and their children, the creative industries took these events and repackaged them as entertainment to bring information, explanation and persuasion to the masses during the war.

* * * * *

Detmers. Plus musicals, the most recent being *One Last Night with Mata Hari* (2017); and novels such as, Michelle Moran's (2016) *Mata Hari's Last Dance,* Touchstone Books and Dan Sherman's, (2014) *The Man Who Loved Mata Hari*, Open Road Media. There are even tourist attractions based on Mata Hari – Leeuwarden calls itself the 'city of Mata Hari'.

[54] See, Bade, P. (1997). *Femme Fatale: Images of evil and fascinating women*, New York: Mayflower Books and White, R. (2007). *Violent Femmes: Women as spies in popular culture*, New York: Routledge.

Chapters in this volume

In chapter 1 Michael Paris's *'What Shall We Tell the Children? The Great War, Propaganda, and British Children'* shows how living with the knowledge their country was at war was nothing new to children in 1914. Paris points out that children born in the late 1890s had lived through a succession of international conflicts, many of which became stories in the canon of children's popular literature. He argues that Darwinian notions of superiority provided a convenient justification for British colonial administrator to call on force to bring peace to unruly indigenous people. The exploits of British soldiers and sailors, in bringing 'civilization' to rebellious tribes, provided ample material for a succession of storytellers. The popularity of the adventure story, telling tales of heroic actions, sacrifice and glory, was aimed mostly at boys. Through the media of books, posters, illustrated magazines and battle paintings the glamour of war, the ideology of empire and superiority was the message consumed by a willing readership. Paris notes that the British army was voluntary and with poor conditions for soldiers and sailors there was the need for a constant supply of willing recruits. For working-class boys the possibility of adventure must, Paris argues, have looked far more attractive than the grind of heavy manual labour on poverty wages. Focusing in on the British publishing houses Paris, therefore, takes us on a fascinating journey through some of the landmark books aimed at explaining and justifying the war to children. The need for more and more volunteers and then to give impetus to conscription encouraged, shows Paris, the greater use of illustration, to explain through a story the reason Britain was fighting the war. Why it was patriotic parents and teachers to encourage male youth to join the cause in defending civilisation against the German barbarians.

In chapter 2 Christopher Hart's *'Remember Scarborough. Re-Active Propaganda as Natural Ethics'* takes a popular and often reproduced poster called 'remember Scarborough' to propose the use of moral philosophy to recover the deeper meaning this and similar posters would have had following the German naval bombardments of towns on the North East English coast in December 1916. Hart asks, How did the official propaganda published following the bombardment of towns on the North East Coast of England, in December 1914, express deeply held moral outrage, and as such represented a real morality and not mistreatment of truth? At the core of his argument is that the poster 'Remember Scarborough' is not naïve propaganda or an exaggeration.

Surveying the reasons given by the German high command and reporting of the bombardments in German newspapers, Hart argues there was no strategic justification for the attacks. Turning to deviancy theory and moral philosophy Hart proposes that the bombardments were an action of a German Navy, humiliated in a previous sea battle. They had to gain face with their high command and the German public that despite their attempts to justify the attacks, they expressed disregard for the Hague Convention (1906) and turned to revenge as a tactic, and as such, abandoned any claim to morality. The words and the images on the poster 'Remember Scarborough' are, according to Hart, much more than a call to arms; they express deeply held outrage that the attacks were an assault on humanity.

In chapter 3 Guy Hodgson's *'Causing Unnecessary Anxiety? British Newspapers and the Battle of Jutland'* examines the breakdown in communication between official British government sources and popular British newspapers. That breakdown, Hodgson shows through a meticulous examination of reports in the *Daily Express*, the *Daily Mirror*, and the *Manchester Guardian* led to an accurate reporting of the considerable British losses compared to those of the German Navy at the Battle of Jutland. The expected role of the British newspapers was not, as the reporting of Jutland reveals, a one of acting as the mouthpiece of the Government; from initial reports beginning on the 3rd June, the newspapers provided the facts as reported to them in Admiralty communiqué. Following the honest reporting of the Battle of Jutland, in an attempt to control what was reported, the Naval Publicity Department was established a month after the battle. Its purpose was to deal with the press; reporting of the facts was to be strictly controlled. And this was, Hodgson, shows, effective for when 400,000 British and Empire soldiers died, in the 141-day battle of the Somme that began on July 1st, 1916, the scale of loss was hidden by reports of heroic advances and territorial gains. Hodgson concludes that this degree of information control was a harbinger of more serious threats to press freedom in the Second World War. Ironically the honest reporting of 6,000 British sailors killed at Jutland, even as a mistake, gave credibility to subsequent reports in ways that would have seemed unbelievable otherwise.

In chapter 4 Maria Rikitianskaia's *'Listening to 'Concert of Europe'. Pioneering Radio Amateurs During World War I'* addresses the question of how the amateur radio movement continued and developed during the War. Rikitianskaia looks at an aspect of a hobby that became, for many 'hams' secretive during the war yet helped most nations involved in it to develop their military radio communications. Rikitianskaia adapts the transnational approach to telecommunication history and to the early history of the Telegraph Union to analyse the records of communication and listening done by radio amateurs during the war. This approach allows Rikitianskaia to bring together a detailed examination of the political, economic, social and technological to show the important role radio amateurs played by establishing an international method of communication. The keenness of the amateurs was, Rikitianskaia argues, quickly assimilated into the communications of the opposing forces and allowed these militarised amateurs access to restricted resources to develop radio communications technology. The military potential of radio as a medium of communication came of age during the war; the result was by 1918 a much more formal and controlled media emerged that within a decade would be commercialised, regulated and globally popular.

In chapter 5 Andrijana Rabrenović's *'The Role of Political Posters in Montenegro and Serbia during World War I'* looks at an unusual form of a political poster, the poster that is without images. Typical of the political and propaganda poster of Montenegro and Serbia was they were unlike those produced by other combatants in that they were often issued by the respective King of the country as a personal message and were nearly always text-based.

Rabrenović takes as her starting point the practice of propaganda as a generalised form of media into which she places the posters produced by Montenegro and Serbia during the war. Rabrenović argues that this is reasonable given that whether the purpose of the posters was to recruit, mobilise, call for the defence of the country or seek assistance in 'case it' was the dominant means which resulted in the creation of a positive image of allies. At the same time a negative image, or demonising the enemy in the war. Hence, the text-based Montenegro and Serbian posters fulfilled the same ends as the more visual and graphic posters often associated with images we have of what propaganda is.

A key feature of Rabrenović's chapter is the detailed historical context she provides as a frame of reference with which to understand the nature and role of these posters. The backdrop to this is appreciating Montenegro and Serbia were Kingdoms in this period and had just come out from the Balkan Wars. Due to these circumstances, the poster above all had a role in encouraging the 'people' to oppose the Central Powers knowing their armies were weakened. It is important to note about the posters used in Rabrenović's analysis that are mostly unknown in the general literature and were made available with the kind assistance of National Library of Serbia, Archives of Montenegro and the National Library of Montenegro.

In chapter 6 Eneko Bidegain's in *'Basque Writers' Reportages in Eskualduna, During World War I'* analyses the vision disseminated by the writers of the Basque weekly magazine *Eskualduna*, during World War I. *Eskualduna* was the most important newspaper in the Basque region of France. With a general circulation of around 7,000 copies, the *Eskualduna* became the major media vehicle available to Basque soldiers longing for their homes. Before the war, the *Eskualduna* was a convenient outlet for young writers wishing to express themselves in the Basque language. With war, many of these writers joined the French army; being posted to Charleroi, Aisne and Verdun. Every week, they wrote very personal reports and letters, about the life at the front that were published in *Eskualduna*. Based on a reading of 3,422 reports and letters, written between the end of July 1914 and January 1915, Bidegain shows how these soldiers cherished their Basque culture while identifying themselves as French.

In her research Bidegain shows how content analysis can make visible how the remembered details of 'the small homeland' dominate the thoughts of these Basque soldiers. In their letters and reports published in the newspaper, while allegiance to their French 'the big homeland' as soldiers gives them a sense of pride. Their pride, Bidegain argues, is anchored in recognising their Basque culture within the larger French army. The letters provide a rich set of longings, laments and wishful emotions about Basque landscapes, their villages, their mother's cooking, Basque songs, games and, of course, the Basque language.

In chapter 7 John Dilley and David Penman's *'Market Harborough Advertiser and the Ashbourne Telegraph'* provide a fascinating insight into the daily reporting of two local newspapers that served two small towns in Britain. Based on the weekly online blog, Dilley and Penman give us an insight into the details and peculiarities of choice of stories, the choice of sources, the tone, the language, the pagination, and the advertising. As the war progressed Dilley and Penman's initial analysis reveals a distinct difference in all these areas between the pre-war period and the August to December period, particularly in language, tone and story choices. At the same time, they show a comparison with national newspaper coverage, the two local newspapers, had differences in language and story sourcing, particularly concerning censorship and the official War

Department's Press Bureau. An enduring feature of Dilley and Penman's work is how they reveal that among the big stories were many sensational stories of violent crime, freak accidents, and bizarre events that happened locally and abroad. There was, show Dilley and Penman, a concern not to report what was happening in much the same way as the national newspapers but to record with an entertaining twist. Dilley and Penman's main finding, however, is that for national newspapers 'truth is the first casualty of war' along with 'journalism' but not for local newspapers.

In chapter 8 David Goldie's *'Romance by other Means: Popular Scottish Newspapers and the War'*, offers a reading of a range of popular Scottish newspapers, with a focus on the weekly papers, *The People's Journal* and *The People's Friend*. Known popularly in the late 19th century as the 'ploughman's bible', *The People's Journal*, had a circulation of 250,000 copies and a readership of 1 million, making it one of the U.K.'s best-selling weekly papers. *The People's Friend*, it's sister paper, was aimed largely at the women's market carrying more serial fiction, features, and humorous stories. Taken together they form a comprehensive picture of how the war was figured (and ignored) in Scottish popular culture. Goldie brings to the fore the role and place of popular story-telling, often based on a real event or person, showing both the demand for these stories was widespread while identifying the structures used for pre-war story dramatisations worked to tell war stories.

Of particular interest are how the forms of journalistic reportage developed before the war in the People's Journal to deal with interesting issues such as crime are adapted, sometimes only very lightly, to deal with stories of both heroism and horror in the war.

Similarly, the advice columns and serial fiction of the People's Friend show a marked similarity to their pre-war configurations, suggesting continuity with, rather than a break from pre-war forms. The tentative conclusion of the paper is that the modes of popular journalism proved to be highly resilient and that the trauma experienced in more highbrow articulations of the war is largely absent from these forms of mass-circulation writing.

In chapter 9 Jesús Jiménez-Varea and Antonio Pineda's *"And Yet They Tell Us Not to Hate the Hun" Popular Media, Atrocity Propaganda, and War Patriotism in Winsor McCay's The Sinking of the 'Lusitania'*, examines the way in which animation was used, and used effectively, to demonise the German's as perpetrators of autocracies. Through their work on the life Winsor McCay, the American animator and illustrator, Jiménez-Varea and Pineda show how he developed the drawing of cartoons into a popular medium of storytelling for adults and children. Finding acclaim for his inventiveness in the narrative, Jiménez-Varea and Pineda argue, that McCay created a style that conveyed fluidity with the power to transform characters in ways that traded on a much more 'serious' art form, that of poetry. McCay's imaginative, and sometimes dark, cartoons were popular with adult readers of *The New York Herald* as was his adaptation of the same themes when re-drawn for children. Jiménez-Varea and Pineda show, however, that McCay's skills and imagination was not limited to drawings in newspapers. He developed, toured and performed live shows with animated stories. At the outbreak of the war McCay was working for William Randolph Hearst's *New York American* and, as Jiménez-Varea and Pineda point out, McCay expressed his employer's isolationist stance. But this changed with the sinking, first of 1917, when merchant ship *Vigilancia* and then of the *Lusitania*. McCay, Jiménez-Varea and Pineda show form contemporary sources, the outrage he felt and how he applied his skills to tell the story of the sinking of the ship and the horror of those killed. McCay's animated film *The Sinking of the 'Lusitania'* was very popular. But as Jiménez-Varea and Pineda argue, it was pure propaganda. So much so that it can be regarded as a model of the form, having a density in images, story and message it effectively establishes the framework for subsequent examples of autocracy narratives.

In chapter 10 Tom Roberts's '*The Murdochs and Gallipoli: Entertainments in Service of Myth*' focuses on the actions of the Australian journalist, Sir Keith Murdoch, (father of Rupert), during World War I. Popular culture and received history portrays Keith, as the plucky colonial who evaded the Censor and so halted the Gallipoli campaign. This paper challenges the mythology that has been fostered since, not least by his descendants, adding nuance to the account. It argues that far from remaining a thorn in the side of the existing order, Keith's famous 'Gallipoli letter' helped propel him into the very heart of the new Establishment where press and politics met. We learn how inspired by his mentor Lord Northcliffe, Keith sought to elevate the reputation of the Australian forces not only through his stirring writing on their heroic deeds but by commissioning cartoons and drawing attention to powerful imagery and photographs. Keith's promotion of his censor-evading co-conspirator, the English war correspondent Ellis Ashmead-Bartlett, is also explored. The circumstances behind and motivation for Ashmead-Bartlett's music hall tour of illustrated lectures on the Gallipoli campaign are revealed. Long overdue attention is then turned to Keith's political machinations and role as a propagandist during the rest of the War - activities ignored by the previous, family-commissioned biographies. We learn how Keith secretly organised and directed the propaganda campaigns to persuade Australian soldiers in Europe to vote for the re-election of Prime Minister Billy Hughes and his 'Win the War Party'; and to approve the conscription of their compatriots to join the Western Front action - a theatre of conflict that was to prove far deadlier than Gallipoli.

In chapter 11 Dietrich Helms's *'All Quiet on the Musical Front? German Music Production as the Source for a History of Attitudes of the First World War'* takes on a journey into the music business in Germany looking, at how at the beginning of the war it produced music based on the changing emotions of the German people. Using lists of published musical scores, Helms gives detailed analysis topics, lyrics and music produced from 1914 to 1918. The foundation for Helms's work is the proposition that the music industry has a highly developed sense for changes in the general feelings and the mentalities of its customers. As an industry that sells emotions producers of music adapt their products to the topics of their times to address issues that they hope may concern and move their customers. Consumers of music choose the music they feel that touches them most in the context of their current social and psychological situations. Popular songs in particular string together metaphors, which at that time everyone, may associate a meaning with according to his or her experiences and knowledge. They use catchwords that are on everybody's lips and have a high power to inspire associations. This makes music an interesting measure of changes in the feelings and the mentality of its consumers. Metaphors repeatedly used in the titles, lyrics and sounds of some songs, may be interpreted as of importance for their audience. Helm's explores these assumptions and finds that the summer of 1916 was a decisive moment for the feelings and the attitudes of the German population towards the war. Sometime around the end of the battle of Verdun and the beginning of the battle at the Somme it must have dawned upon the producers and publishers of music in Germany and Austria that compositions relating to the war neither in a positive nor in a sentimental way were no longer in demand. The machinery of war ceased to be a novelty and disappeared from the titles of pieces of music. The realities of war, death, suffering and mourning had reached many German families and households. Who, Helms askes, wants to sing songs of heroic death and heroes' graves on the battlefield, if he or she is mourning a father, a brother or a husband? Who wants to buy songs on the funny side of soldiers lives, if he or she knows, how sad the situation in the trenches is? Moreover, what is heroic about death if death becomes normality? Helms work shows that musical theatre had turned its productions from propaganda back to popular variety entertainment in late 1915 and that in summer 1916 the rest of the music business followed.

In chapter 12 Rosie White's, *Englishness and the 'Other'. Mata Hari and Edith Cavell on Celluloid* considers the contrast between Edith Cavell and Mata Hari - two women executed as spies, the former by the Germans and latter by the French. Edith Cavell's role as an agent for the Allied resistance in occupied Belgium and her execution in October 1915 was caught up in the propaganda war between Britain and Germany. The martyred Cavell was contrasted with that of Mata Hari, with Cavell epitomising all that was best in English womanhood while Mata Hari became the orientalised *femme fatale*. Both women are still remembered unlike many of their contemporaries who were also executed having been convicted of espionage. Substantial amounts of media were produced on Cavell and Hari following their executions, with books and films being made about them until the present day. White draws our attention to the power of media representations arguing both entangled in contemporary discourses regarding gender, sexuality and race, offering opposing accounts of the female spy which continue to inflect representations of women and espionage.

In chapter 13 Lucy Church's *Defining Musical 'Germanness': The Reciprocal Influences of Music and National Identity Formation* takes a close look music and the ways in which it both flows from and contributes to the formation of national identity - in this case German national identity. There can hardly be a better era to examine issues of national musical identity, Church argues, that in the years surrounding World War I, where the broadly European canon of Western art music collided with a wartime mentality, and issues of nationalism, morality, and musical expression became inseparable. Germany was at the time a relatively new country with a nevertheless long and distinct cultural history, and its art music was nearly unanimously thought to be the finest in the world, both aesthetically and morally. It is for this reason that Church looks at German national identity formation as a primary topic of study.

Church asks, how did certain music and composers come to be associated with national identities? And how did notes on a page become symbols of a country? How did German musical style come to be known as 'German'? And how did this type of music come to be favoured above all others, not to mention seen as morally superior? In this chapter Church brings her musical scholarship to examine how music cooperates in and sometimes transforms national identity formation by looking at the ways that critics and writers in the 19th century perceived musical national identity and by looking at the ways in which Germany itself used the great composers as a resource to consolidate and promote allegiance to 'Germanness'.

In chapter 14 Sonja Andrew's *Dichotomies of Representation and Interpretation: A Pacifist's Story* looks in detail at the case of John Edgar Bell who held firm on his conviction now to be a combatant in the war. From drawings made by conscientious objectors on the walls of their prison cells enabled translation of John Edgar Bell's conscientious objection story into visual form via a series of textile panels as installations in public spaces. This chapter places exhibition within a communication paradigm, considering cloth as a narrative form and examining the relationship between authorial intention and viewer interpretation. The panels in the exhibition attempted to tell the narrative of the consequences of his beliefs for himself and his family. The narrative textile panels within the series aim to communicate the different stages and situation of the family at the start of the war, the objector's imprisonment, and the post war hostility the family endured.

Taking the contemporary approach Sonja Andrew's work on this telling of John Edgar Bell considers the personal and cultural experiences that inform making and viewing, and the influence of content and context on viewers' interpretations of the work in a range of public spaces. Readings of the individual images and narrative sequences are examined, revealing areas of collective cultural understanding on war, religion, family and loss, and the projection of personal memory on audiences' construction of meaning from the work.

Chapter 1

What Shall We Tell the Children? The Great War, Propaganda, and British Children[1]

Michael Paris
Emeritus Professor of Modern History,
UCLAN

Introduction

For British children of the early twentieth century, war was a very familiar experience. In 1914, for example, a child born at the end of the previous century had lived through the Anglo-Boer war (1899 - 1902), the Boxer Rebellion in China in 1901, the Russo Japanese War of 1904 - 1905, the Italo - Turkish War of 1911, and the two Balkan Wars of 1912 - 1913. There were numerous other war scares and alarms, and any number of punitive expeditions by European armies in Africa or Asia as they dealt with minor rebellions or dissident leaders within their empires. War was indeed an everyday occurrence. Inevitable really, in a world dominated by a handful of rival empires each seeking security and an advantage over their competitors. Most Britons had come to accept that it was the Empire on which British power, prestige and wealth depended, and regarded the Empire on which the 'Sun Never Set', as their greatest asset. In return, it was claimed, the Motherland had a great responsibility towards the citizens of that empire - to improve their lives through good administration, through education and through the maintenance of peace. The 'white

---

[1] Parts of this chapter were given in an address to the *Approaching War: Childhood, Culture and the First World War* Conference, University of Newcastle, March 2013, and in a paper to the *1914/2014 - Erster Weltkrieg: Kriegskindheit und Kriegsjugend, Literatur, Erinnerungskultur* Conference at the Institute of Children's Literature, Goethe University, Frankfurt, September 2014.

man's burden' was indeed a hard taskmaster, but how could those aims be accomplished without sometimes resorting to force. Often likened to naughty children by colonial administrators, the subjects of the Empire occasionally needed a firm hand to bring them into line. Thus, the punitive column, the skirmishes with rebellious tribes, the village burnings and the executions were ultimately for their own good. Only in stable conditions could Britain's civilizing mission be achieved. It was a fine and noble argument which did much to undermine the stark brutality of the imperial mission; but the reality was that what had been taken with the sword could only be held by the sword, and was essential to the nation's interest.

War was even believed by some to be an inherent part of the human condition. By the end of the nineteenth century, the legitimation of conflict had been powerfully reinforced by the emergence of so-called 'scientific' explanations of war. In 1859, Charles Darwin had published *The Origin of the Species*. Although few had read the book, most educated Britons thought they had grasped its essential meaning. But it was not long before evolutionary theory was being applied to human societies as well, and under the banner of 'Social Darwinism,' it was crudely argued that nations, like animals, were equally involved in the struggle for survival. As historian Bernard Semmel has pointed out, it was widely believed that human progress was the "result of an evolutionary struggle between groups of men, between tribes or nations or races, the fittest group predominating in the ceaseless warfare which constituted the evolutionary process."[2] By the end of the nineteenth century, Britain's leading exponent of Social Darwinism, the mathematician, and biostatistician Karl Pearson, could suggest that national progress depended on national fitness to win the battle for survival, and the supreme test of fitness was war, 'the fiery crucible out of which comes the finest metal'. For Pearson, war was the ultimate challenge for the nation and, he claimed, "when wars cease, mankind will no longer progress for there will be nothing to check the fertility of inferior stock."[3] War, then, served another vital function for the nation: in Cecil Eby's felicitous phrase, it "functioned rather like well-managed pruning shears, eliminating the weak and undesirable shoots and allowing the

---

[2] Semmel, B. (1960). *Imperialism, and Social Reform*. London: George Allen & Unwin, page 30.
[3] Pearson, K. quoted in Semmel, (1960), page 41.

development of luxurious blossoms."[4] War ensured that only the strongest would survive and procreate, and in a climate where fear of racial deterioration and national decay was widespread, war ensured the survival of the fittest and stiffened the sinews of society. As Brigadier-General R. C. Hart argued in the pages of *Nineteenth Century and After*,

> The means of [physical] improvement must be the same as in the past, namely war, relentless war extermination of inferior individuals and nations. The process will be slower than in the past because natural selection is hindered and thwarted by 'civilized man'.[5]

If war was inevitable, then, it was essential that the nation is prepared for these conflicts.

Peace loving British

In the nineteenth century, it was a commonly held belief among the English that they were a peace-loving people, interested only in

Figure 1.1 *Scouting for Boys*, 1908 and 1815

commerce and in extending their trading empire. Their great Empire, the manner in which it had been created and the ferocity with which it

---

[4] Eby, Cecil, D. (1987). *The Road to Armageddon: The martial spirit in English popular literature.* London: Duke University Press, page 2.
[5] Hart, Brigadier R. C. (VC). (1911). 'A Vindication of War', *The Nineteenth Century and After*, 3rd September, page 347.

was defended demonstrate just how empty this belief was. Nevertheless, considering how vital the Empire was perceived to be, it is surprising how loathed successive governments were to spend money on the agency that defended the frontiers of that empire and kept it secure - the army - and a constant problem was finding enough men to serve. Seeing themselves as peaceful, liberal and progressive, successive governments steadfastly refused to countenance any form of compulsory military training, and alone of all the Great Powers, the British continued to rely on a purely voluntary army. Curiously, however, they were even reluctant to spend money improving the conditions of soldiers but relied on the conscription of poverty that drove men to enlist and sort of unofficial propaganda campaign that might hopefully attract a better class of patriotic youth. This suggested that war was not only morally justified but romantic and glamorous: through war, a young man could find adventure and glory. Such beliefs, although perhaps sometimes less forcibly expressed, were common in all forms of popular culture, in the press, the illustrated magazines, in popular prints and battle painting, in spectacular theatricals and, above all in the popular literature aimed at boys and young men - the heroic novels and stories written by authors like G. A. Henty, Gordon Stables RN, Captain F. S. Brereton, Herbert Strang and many others. War, then, was essential to the continued wellbeing of the nation, and could even be a valuable experience for the individual. With these methods the army muddled through, switching its regiments from trouble spot to trouble spot as where as required. In times of crisis, of course, the nation could rely on the popular patriotism of some men that would ensure some volunteers of the 'better-sort' swell the ranks, as during the Second Boer War of 1899, for example. But while most educated middle-class males might admire the idea of the soldier-hero, few were anxious to share the realities of the military life, except in dire emergencies. Thus, on the eve of the Great War, the British Government prepared to commit its army, numbering less than 300,000 men, to a European war against the highly trained millions of the German Empire.

 Britain and Germany were in many ways similar, their Royal Houses were closely related, and they had many interests in common, yet by 1914, a war against Germany should not have surprised any Briton. Since the 1890s, there had been a growing antipathy between the two nations. Based on German desire for a 'place in the sun,' the British saw German ambitions as envy and rivalry. And when the Kaiser embarked on grandiose naval expansion, the British saw only a blatant challenge to the supremacy of the Royal Navy. The press in both countries fanned the flames and heightened the tensions, and many believed that a war between the two nations was inevitable. Some began to prepare for the coming struggle. In 1908 R. S. S. Baden-Powell, the hero of Mafeking, published his *Scouting for Boys*, an instruction book specifically to prepare British boys for manhood and the inevitable struggle. The Boy Scout movement, which followed, was, like the other paramilitary youth organisations, intended to instill discipline, a sense of duty and the basis of military training. Academics published succinct explanations of the problems between German and Briton, and the gutter press dived into character assassination of the bullying, arrogant Prussian *Junkers*. Adventure writers came up with endless imaginative stories of how Germany invaded Britain and how the British fought back, and by 1914 many boys, like Robert Roberts of Salford had come to believe that the long-expected war couldn't come soon enough.[6]

1914 and the excitement of war

A hundred years after the event, popular opinion mostly regards the Great War as a prime example of a futile struggle in which a generation of young men were needlessly sacrificed in a war of attrition in which achieved very little and which led inexorably to another and even more brutal struggle twenty years later. But in 1914 the war against Germany was an immensely popular cause. Perhaps not as popular as was once believed,[7] but among many young men, it was seen as a noble and righteous cause, and most could hardly contain their excitement. Here was romance and drama and a sense of purpose; as the Nation's favourite poet, Rupert Brooke proclaimed,

> Now, God be thanked Who has matched us with His hour,
> And caught our youth, and wakened us from sleeping,[8]

---

[6] Roberts, R. (1971). *The Classic Slum*. Manchester: Manchester University Press, page 85. And see, for example, Cramb, J. H. (1914). *Germany and England*. London: John Murray; Blatchford. R. (1914). *Germany and England*. London: Harmsworth; Westerman, Percy, F. (1914). *The Sea-Girt Fortress*, London: Blackie; Le Queux, W. (1906). *The Invasion of 1910*. London: Nash.
[7] See Gregory, A. (2008). *The Last Great War: British society and the First World War*. Cambridge: Cambridge University Press.
[8] Brooke, R. (1965). 'Peace,' in *Rupert Brooke*, London: Studio Vista, page 44.

Brooke spoke for many men who, influenced by a popular culture that had glamourised and romanticised the experience of battle, saw only the glory of war. No one, of course, expected a long war, 'Over by Christmas' was the rallying cry, and over 470,000 men volunteered for military service in the first month of the war alone. But very few had any conception of the devastating power of modern weapons; what hideous damage high explosives and machine guns bullets could do to the human body. There was little realisation that this was to be a very different kind of war from the usual colonial skirmishes that the nation had engaged in where the superior technology and discipline of the British Army eventually won the day. Now Britain faced one of Europe's most technologically advanced and military prepared nations, and some wondered how long this popular support would last if the war weren't over by Christmas, if it lasted for perhaps a year, or even longer? How could a steady flow of recruits be maintained? Britain's position was unique among the Great Powers for she had rejected compulsory military service in favour of a purely volunteer army. Certainly the British were accustomed to war, and many thought of it as exciting, romantic even, but a ready supply of young men willing to fight was the key factor in Britain's ability to wage war. It would equally be a war in which the nation had to supply the largest army Britain had ever put into the field - could the enthusiasm and productivity of the industrial front be sustained? Consequently, within the first few weeks the government, concerned organisations and private individuals, anxious to maintain support for the war and the sympathy of neutral nations like the United States of America, began to create a system of mass persuasion that would sell the war to the British people and the world at large, and maintain the morale of the nation. As historian Philip Taylor has noted, for the first time the government "deployed the twin weapons of censorship and propaganda to impose a rigid control over public perceptions... about how and why the war was being fought."[9] In the event over 2.5 million volunteers were accepted in the period between 4th August 1914 and April 1916, creating the largest volunteer army of the modern age.[10] Notwithstanding these impressive numbers, however, by the end of 1915, it was realised that the voluntary principle was not providing sufficient manpower for the mincing

---

[9] Taylor, P. M. (1999). *British Propaganda in the Twentieth Century: Selling democracy*. Edinburgh: Edinburgh University Press, page 1.

[10] Simkins, P. (1988). *Kitchener's Armies: Raising and training the new armies, 1915-1916*. Manchester, Manchester University Press, page 75.

machine of the Western Front and, albeit reluctantly, conscription was finally introduced from April 1916.

Government communications to the people

Yet in 1914, with almost no experience in such matters, a government-controlled propaganda machine was created that was by and large remarkably effective. For despite over four years of brutal warfare, despite casualties on an unprecedented scale, despite all the hardships and restrictions at home, the British people remained largely committed to the war and to fighting on until victory was achieved. The main thrust of official propaganda was directed at a foreign audience because of the effectiveness of German propaganda in undermining Britain's cause, particularly in America. The government was seemingly so confident of the support of the people, that initially at least, they were content to leave domestic propaganda to the press and various unofficial committees and individuals. This was not as haphazard as it appears. While the press was often critical of government policy in domestic matters, they were largely uncritical of the government's foreign policy - a sort of 'Johnny Foreigner is always wrong' concept. Besides which the Foreign Office was adept at manipulating news reports through personal contacts with the elite of Fleet Street.[11] Equally, the press had long ago discovered that popular patriotism sold papers. And the public had a seemingly inexhaustible appetite for tales of imperial adventures, deeds of daring, and other patriotic fare which were dispensed through literature, the music hall, theatre, and even the fledgling cinema, all of which whipped up jingoist sentiment among the public. Even recruiting propaganda - seemingly vital for a nation that relied on the voluntary principle, was left to the War Office and the Parliamentary Recruiting Committee, which despite its impressive name was little more than an informal grouping of Members of Parliament and public figures working on a voluntary basis to produce posters, leaflets, organise parades and pageants, and address meetings.[12] Equally effective were the many individuals and organisations determined to get men into khaki either through persuasion or accusation. Organisations like the author Baroness Orczy's 'White Feather' campaign - a group of

---

[11] Messenger, G. S. (1992). *British Propaganda and the State in the First World War*. Manchester: Manchester University Press, pages 11-12.
[12] Ferguson, N. (1998). *The Pity of War*. London: Allen Lane, page 205.

determined women who presented a white feather, the mark of a coward, to apparently fit young men, not in uniform. But a most effective channel for propaganda was literature, and this was exploited by the government's Propaganda Bureau at Wellington House and organised by the Liberal politician Charles Masterman.

Masterman, a close friend of Prime Minister H. H. Asquith, was invited to take responsibility for refuting German propaganda and justifying Britain's cause. On 2nd September 1914, Masterman organised a conference of leading writers and academics - those who were considered the most influential on public opinion. Twenty-five leading figures attended the first meeting including, G. K. Chesterton,

Figure 1.2 Best selling in 1915, *A Hero of Liège*

John Galsworthy, Thomas Hardy, H. G. Wells, Gilbert Murray and A.C. Benson. Rudyard Kipling and Arthur Quiller-Couch were unable to attend but pledged their support. Masterman's idea was that these pillars of the literary establishment should produce leaflets, pamphlets, books, and articles explaining why the nation was at war and justifying British policy. These would be distributed through commercial publishers such as Hodder & Stoughton, Macmillian or Thomas Nelson as if they were personal responses from concerned individuals and not in anyway orchestrated or directed by a government agency. All those recruited were sworn to absolute secrecy about their government connections, and their material would be handled by the literary agent A. P. Watt. A few weeks later, another tranche of writers were recruited including Jerome K. Jerome, Mrs. Humphrey War, and Arthur Pinero. Wellington House, then, became the,

> Principle production and distribution centre of official British overseas propaganda and working so effectively beneath its blanket of secrecy that even Parliament was largely unaware of its existence.[13]

However, it was not until 1935, when the historian J. D. Squires published his history of British wartime propaganda, which the connection between these writers and official government was made public. Masterman tried to ensure that all work produced for Wellington House was based on accurate information and attempted to present a measured argument rather than the rhetoric of hate that was the staple ingredient of the popular press.

The documentation relating to Britain's propaganda effort has, unfortunately, not survived, it was either destroyed in the 1920s or lost in the years that followed. Thus, while there have been several credible attempts to reconstruct the propaganda war, it is likely the whole story will never be known. It is not known,[14] for example, what material was commissioned and targeted at particular groups on the home front, or if other lesser authors were invited to join the great and the good of Wellington House, or the National War Aims Committee, formed in 1917 to combat war-weariness and apathy at home. However, as Britain relied on the voluntary principle until 1916, we know that recruiting was a particular concern, and this meant targeting young men, not just those approaching 18 but also younger boys who would be needed later. They needed to be told why Britain was at war, how the

---

[13] Sanders, M. L. and Taylor, Philip. M. (1982). *British Propaganda during The First World War*. London: Macmillan, page 40.
[14] *Ibid*. Page 30.

war was being fought, and what part they might play in securing the final victory. Thus, heroic and inspiring fictions for younger readers, which both fostered the martial spirit, and the desire to 'beat the Hun' could play a vital part in the war effort. Many of the authors associated with Wellington House were popular with young male readers - Henry Newbolt, John Buchan, Anthony Hope, A.E.W. Mason, Rider Haggard, and H.G. Wells, for example. Newbolt and Buchan did produce work for younger readers during the war. We know that several authors that wrote for specifically juvenile readers were recruited by Masterman because some of their work appears in the list of Wellington House Publications made public in 1919[15] (which unfortunately is not complete). But no evidence has survived for how many other writers were recruited, or how, or what they were instructed to do. It seems likely, though, that there were many lesser literary figures connected with Wellington House or inspired by Masterman's authors to take a patriotic stand on the war and produce their own unofficial propaganda following the parameters established by the Propaganda Bureau. This chapter, then, examines some of the literary propaganda directed at boys and young men to encourage recruitment in the armed forces.

The publishing industry and war stories

In 1914, the publishing industry, like most other commercial concerns, was encouraged by the government's policy of 'business as usual', and there was certainly no decline in the demand for printed material of all kinds, especially war-related material. As historian Peter Buitenhuis has noted, "The public appetite for stories about the war was very strong; people had a craving to know about the fighting and to see their faith in the moral and physical strength of the Allies reflected in an accessible form."[16] And this was particularly true of young male readers. Agnes Blackie, of Blackie & Sons, one of the most prolific publishers of children's literature, later noted that despite paper shortages and other problems, the demand for children's books saw the greatest demand year after year.[17] Adventure stories about the war written by writers of juvenile fiction were popular with both children and adults alike, and

---

[15] See, *Schedule of Wellington House Literature*, copy available at The Imperial War Museum.
[16] Buitenhuis, P. (1989). *The Great War of Word: Literature as propaganda, 1914-1918 and after*. London: Batsford, page 102.
[17] Blackie, Agnes, A. C. (1959). *Blackie & Son: A short history of the firm*. London: Blackie, page 53.

interestingly, the boy's adventure story *The Hero of Liege* (Herbert Strang) and William Le Queux's *Secrets of the German War Office*, were among W.H. Smith's best-selling war books in October 1915.[18] As the memoirs of veterans reveal, the predominant aim of almost every young

Figure 1.3 G.A. Henty's 1902, *To the Herat and Cabul*

man was to enlist and take part in the 'Great Adventure'. But for those too young for soldiering reading about the war was the next best thing. As Huntley Gordon later remembered, "our curiosity to know what it would be like to be under fire had to be satisfied from the novels of G.A. Henty and Captain F.S. Brererton."[19] War stories, then, not only tried to explain what it would be like in combat but also why Britain was at war. These often contained long sections of historical explanation and interpretation, often to the detriment of the narrative, but authors saw

---

[18] Orel, H. (1992). *Popular Fiction in England, 1914-1918*. Lexington: University Press of Kentucky, page 157.
[19] Gordon, H. (1967). *The Unreturning Army*. London: Dent, page 11.

themselves as patriots and educators with a moral duty to their readers. Before the war they had continually demonstrated their patriotism, valorising the military, justifying the empire, decrying foreigners and attempting to instill a sense of duty and the need for sacrifice in their young readers. Now their first duty was to justify the conflict and prepare readers to play their part in the coming struggle. They were joined in their endeavours by the publishers and authors of some factual works specifically written to explain the underlying causes of the war and why Britain had to fight to younger readers. While these were never as popular as novels by established authors, they sold well and were often gifts from relatives or given as prizes in schools.

Most writers considered their purpose was to educate and instruct as much as entertain; moulding the character of their young readers and guiding them to become good citizens of the Empire. The model here was G. A. Henty, the most influential writer of juvenile fictions in the late nineteenth century. Henty had clearly expressed his purpose in some novels. He wanted to 'teach patriotism', inspire faith in the destiny of the Anglo-Saxon race, and offer examples of personal morality; he wanted to show boys how to behave. According to his friend and biographer, George Manville Fenn, Henty wanted his boys to be 'bold, straightforward, ready to play a young man's part, not to be 'milksops.'[20] His successors subscribed to the same principles. W. E. Johns, who would begin his own writing career in the 1920s, clearly expressed this intent when asked why he wrote by fellow-author Geoffrey Trease,

> For the entertainment of my reader... I teach at the same time, under camouflage. Juveniles are keen to learn, but the educational factor must not be obvious... I teach a boy to be a man... I teach sportsmanship according to the British ideal... I teach that decent behaviour wins in the end as the natural order of things. I teach the spirit of team-work, loyalty to the Crown, the Empire, and to rightful authority.[21]

Clearly, with ideals such as these, the writers of juvenile fiction, patriots to a man, could be counted on to support Britain's cause and the armed

---

[20] See, Richards, J. (1989). 'With Henty to Africa', in Richards, J. (ed.). *Imperialism and Juvenile Literature*. Manchester: Manchester University Press, pages 75-76.
[21] Trease, G. (1948). *Tales Out of School*. London: Heinemann, pages 94-95.

forces, and do all they possibly could to encourage young men to do their duty. Setting the lead was an almost official explanation for the young written by Sir James Yoxall, a Liberal MP, a friend of Masterman, and an ex-president of the influential National Union of Teachers. *Why Britain Went to War* of 1914 is worth quoting at length, for its imagery, which might have come directly from R.S.S. Baden-Powell's *Scouting for Boys*,

> In all this war there is nothing for us to be ashamed of: we fight for honour. You know what honour is among schoolboys - straight dealing, truth speaking, and 'playing the game.' Well, we are standing up for honour among nations, while Germany is playing the sneak and the bully in the big European school. Germany must be taught to 'play cricket,' to play fair, to honour a 'scrap of paper.' A boy who behaved as Germany has done would be 'sent to Coventry' by all the school.[22]

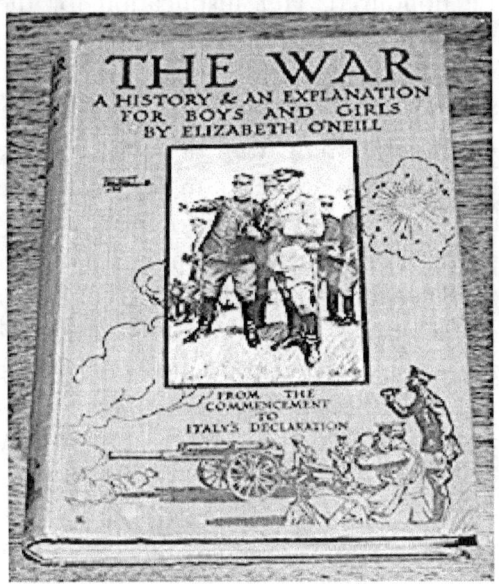

Figure 1.4 O'Neill's book for boys and girls explaining the war

---

[22] Sir James Yoxall. (1914). *Why Britain Went to War: For boys and girls*. London: Cassell, page 2.

But the first commercial publication to be published was Elizabeth O'Neill's *The War 1914: An Explanation for Boys and Girls*, which appeared in November 1914.

O'Neill, a well-known author of books for young children, specialised in histories for the very young - the very popular *A Nursery History of England*, first published in 1912, remained in print until the 1950s. Her history of the war, which eventually ran to five volumes, began with a simplified explanation of the events of the July Crisis and emphasised how Germany had persuaded a weak Austria into declaring war on Serbia and thus precipitated the European war. For O'Neill, the major cause of the war lay in Germany's belief that it was England that had denied her a place in the sun. Thus the war was the climax of German hostility towards England. The British, she explained, had always been peace-loving and in 1914 were desperate to preserve the peace, but echoing Prime Minister Asquith, she stated that honour demanded that once German armies invaded Belgium, Britain's promise to protect the Belgians had to be honoured. Her justification for the war is worth quoting at length for it neatly summarises how most authors dealt with war origins at the time - as a chivalric struggle against the forces of evil.

> The war of 1914 was different from other wars in this, that no one but the Germans can say that Germany was in the right. The Allies as all the world knows were fighting for justice and right against a country and an emperor who seemed almost mad with pride. The soldiers of the allies went out to battle, not as soldiers have often gone to war, because it is business to be done, but rather like the knights of old, full of anger against an enemy who was fighting unjustly; and full, too, of a determination to fight their best for justice and right. This is one more reason, which has made the Great War of 1914 so wonderful a thing.[23]

But for O'Neill, this was not simply a conflict about Britain's honour; it was a crusade against barbarians who had committed the most appalling atrocities on innocent citizens. Throughout the first months of the war, the popular press had carried numerous reports of the crimes committed by the German army as it advanced through Belgium. Most of these stories were later discredited, but at the time they provided

---

[23] O'Neill, E. (1914). *The War 1914: An explanation for boys and girls*. London: T.C. & E.C. Jack, page 15.

vicious but effective propaganda and incited many Britons to seek vengeance against the 'Huns.' O'Neill and her fellow authors were more than happy to provide suitably censored accounts for their young readers. Of the destruction of many fine churches in Flanders, of town halls and libraries razed to the ground; peasants burned to death in their own homes; others made homeless. Women and children treated horribly - many parents, in fact, forced to watch their "little children killed by the half-mad soldiers."[24]

Picking up on pre-1914 ideas about war, O'Neill even suggested that the conflict could have beneficial effects on Britain. The suffragettes, she noted, had settled their differences with the government in the cause of national unity, and even "Irishmen have forgotten their quarrels and sent their bravest men to fight for the country they all love." Like many others, O'Neill almost welcomed this 'wonderful thing' as a regenerating factor for British society. For those who had begun to believe that Edwardian society had become over-indulgent and hedonistic, war might well be the agent of purifying, cleansing and rejuvenating the nation as a whole. As Michael Adams has explained,

> Throughout the period, some people prescribed a little bloodletting as good for the body politic as well as for the individual. War scrubbed clean national arteries clogged with wealth and ease and produced a trimmer, fitter culture.[25]

A typical spokesman for these Social Darwinist views was Sir Edmund Gosse, the influential literary critic, biographer, and Librarian for the House of Lords. Gosse believed that the war was the,

> greatest scavenger of thought. It was the sovereign disinfectant that... cleans out the stagnant pools and clotted channels of the intellect. War was the agent that would cleanse the present: not just culture but the self-indulgent hedonism that had infected society.[26]

---

[24] *Ibid.* Pages 35-36.
[25] Adams, M. (1990). *The Great Adventure: Male desire and the coming of World War 1*. Bloomington: Indiana University Press, page 51.
[26] Gosse, E. quoted in Samuel Hynes. (1992). *A War Imagined, the First World War and English Culture*. London: Pimlico, page 44.

O'Neill, then, was simply reflecting a train of thought that was widely held; the war was a golden opportunity for national regeneration, and the young seized it with both hands. In this context, it is something of a cliché to mention Rupert Brooke and his enthusiasm for an adventure, which believed would save him from tedium of everyday life. But the simple truth is that Brooke did speak for a number of his generation. After his first experience of combat, Julian Grenfell, eldest son of Lord

Figure 1.5 Popular periodical for children on the war

Desborough, wrote home, "It"s a great war, whatever. Isn't luck for me to have been born to be just the right age and in just the right place."[27] Grenfell was unusual in that he continued to enjoy the war right up to the minute of his death in 1915, but most young men, of all classes, certainly shared his excitement until they experienced the Western Front. Only then, when they saw the waste, the futility and the horror of modern combat, did they become disillusioned. George Coppard, for example, in 1914 a 16-year-old at a Brighton elementary school, later recalled, "The newsagents' placards screamed out from every

---

[27] Grenfell, J. (1986). 'Letter to his Mother', quoted in Mackenzie, J. *The Children of the Souls*. London: Chatto & Windus, page 157.

corner, the military bands played martial music, and, as if drawn by a magnet, I knew I had to enlist right away." Lying about his age, he enlisted on the 27th August.[28]

The first volume of Nelson's magisterial history, *The Children's Story of the War*, by Sir Edward Parrott MA, LL.D, did not appear until early 1915, but it then became a running commentary on the events of the conflict with new volumes appearing at regular intervals until Volume 10 in 1919, which dealt with Germany's collapse. Aimed at an older demographic than O'Neill's readership, a reviewer in the *Athenaeum* referred to the series as a readable and inspiring narrative of the war, pointing out that, "a connected and sufficiently well-explained narrative is a useful thing to put before a child - much more intelligible than newspapers."[29] Parrott, an editor at Thomas Nelson & Sons, had written some schoolbooks and was active in the Liberal Party, specialising in education. In 1917 he was elected to Parliament for an Edinburgh constituency. He was almost certainly known to Masterman and, although there is no real evidence, it seems likely that his *Children's Story* was written at the latter's suggestion. Parrott offered a detailed and well-illustrated serial history of the unfolding conflict, but he devoted the whole first volume to an examination of the causes of the war, tracing them back to the Napoleonic wars. Like O'Neill he put the blame squarely on the Kaiser but introduced a new factor, the malignant influence of the Prussian Army,

> Feeling sure that Russia would not fight, that France would not resist, and that Great Britain would not interfere in what seemed to be a far-off quarrel, the Kaiser decided that 'THE DAY,' so long hoped for and prepared for, had come. In July of the present year, he was ready to 'let slip the dogs of war.'[30]

A whole chapter was devoted to 'Deeds of Shame and Horror' - the 'Rape of Belgium'; and we are told of babies slaughtered, old men hanged and burnt alive, and young women and girls 'tortured in the most horrible ways.' But by early 1915 when this volume appeared, the veracity of many of these stories was in doubt - and at least Parrott did introduce a cautionary note, "Perhaps all these terrible stories are not

---

[28] Coppard, G. (1969). *With a Machine Gun to Cambrai*. London: Imperial War Museum, page 1.
[29] The *Athenaeum Christmas Supplement*, December 1917, page 689.
[30] Sir Edward Parrott. (1915). *The Children's Story of the War*. London: Nelson, Vol. 1, page. 154.

true, but no one can deny the gross cruelty of the Germans in Belgium."[31]

Serial histories proved enduring but, one suspects were more popular with parents and school prize committees than with young readers. They were still being commissioned as late as 1916 when the popular adventure authors Herbert Strang (George Ely and James L'Estrange) entered the field with a series of factual books for young readers, published by Hodder & Stoughton. The most interesting of these was *England and the War: A Book for Boys and Girls*. Strang was commissioned by Wellington House to produce the series, apparently the first author of juvenile adventure stories to be enlisted in the official propaganda campaign. The booklet proved popular and was later reissued as *Great Britain and the War*. It was on sale at just three old pennies, but copies were distributed free to schools and libraries. The copy in John Rylands Library in Manchester was presented by the News Department of the Foreign Office to Manchester University - part of a general mailshot and not, one hopes, a comment on what the Foreign Office thought of the standards in provincial universities! Strang followed the general argument that the war had come like 'thunder from a clear blue sky'; that Britain had not wanted war but had to do their duty to Belgium. In doing so had 'performed an act of friendship to France.'[32] It also reiterates the idea that the British hated war. Strang, of course, was writing in early 1916 when it had become more difficult to represent the war in the same romantic terms as it had been used in 1914. Faced by enormous casualty lists and the walking wounded seen on the Streets of British cities it was difficult to write of chivalric young Britons riding of to glory when the reality was a bloody conflict which had dreadful consequences for those who fought.

Strang's version offered at least a little more reality,

> No one in the United Kingdom wanted war. For sixty years Great Britain had been at peace in Europe, and she desired that peace should continue. The people had grown to hate more and more the horrors of war - the waste of young lives, the ruin of happy homes,

---

[31] *Ibid.* Page 257.
[32] *Op. cit.* Strang, H. (1916), page 11.

the sorrow and suffering which war inflicts upon women and children.[33]

But where Strang's books differ from the earlier explanations is that it includes a specific section on war aims – 'What Britain is Fighting For.' The authors list three principle aims: the restoration of Belgium and Serbia; the right of small nations to determine their own affairs, and finally 'for honour' - not simply that the Nation's honour demanded involvement, but to teach Germany the meaning of the word, and here the authors explain that the Germans must learn that,

> Honour is as necessary among States as among individual men, and she will only learn that lesson by suffering defeat in war, the British Empire is pledged to fight on until Germany is beaten.[34]

Strang concludes with a survey of what Britain's armed forces have achieved at sea and on land and how the home front had rallied to the cause. His final admonition is that Britain is spending the lives of her 'finest manhood' and her treasure so that "her children and the children of her allies may be free from the terror that German ambition and German ruthlessness have imposed on the world."[35]

In 1918, an extended version was issued which included the events of 1917-1918. However, in 1916 Strang still found time to write a further three short, books for young children, *The War on Land*, *The War at Sea*, and *Our Allies and Enemies*. Intended for nursery age children these profusely illustrated volumes have reverted to the heroic and romantic view of war with line drawings of cheerful Tommies and Jolly Jack Tars laughing at danger. The recurring theme throughout these volumes is German militarism as the cause of the war, thus in *The War on Land* the author tells us, while the whole world has come to hate war,

> Germany alone has cherished the opposite view. Her historians and philosophers have taught for generations that war is necessary and military service the noblest occupation. All her organising powers have been devoted to the perfection of war as a science. The result is

---

[33] *Ibid.* Pages 1-2.
[34] *Ibid.* Page 16.
[35] *Ibid.* Page 26.

lamentable. Conscious of her strength, she has become the bully of the world.[36]

Strang interestingly ignores the many British writers who, as we have seen, equally argued that war was a social necessity, of the importance of honour and duty to King and Empire, and the many, many occasions over the past hundred years when the British, militarily superior forced submission on weaker peoples throughout Africa and Asia.

However-excitingly written, however well illustrated, these factual titles could never have the appeal of the adventure story that would excite and involve readers and make them want to share the heroic world of war inhabited by their fictional heroes. Adventure fiction as a recruiting agent was not new, and the inherent patriotism of British authors had, throughout the nineteenth century, ensuring that their stories had often acted as unofficial recruiting propaganda for the nation's imperial wars and prepared boys for future service. This seems to have been remarkably successful, and the most enthusiastic volunteers in August 1914 were young, middle-class suburbanites, [37] exactly the kind of young man who had been raised on Henty's novels and patriotic magazines like the *Boy's Own Paper*. Thus it was inevitable that authors of adventure fiction would respond to the crisis of 1914 in exactly the same way.

Adventure stories were dominated by a handful of prolific authors who wrote very much in the Henty style. Often hanging the fictional adventures of their young heroes on the coat tails of famous military figures *Fighting with French* (Herbert Strang), *With Joffre at Verdun* (Captain F.S. Brererton) or *With Haig on the Somme* (J. H. Parry). Most were remarkably similar and usually involved two patriotic young men, who can't wait to 'get into the fight,' get to the front and after various adventures distinguish themselves. Before 1916, most stories began with some explanation of how the war had come about because, of course, the British had no 'warlike' intentions at all! This usually provides the opportunity for a diatribe about Germans and Germany. For Example, in Escott Lynn's In *Khaki for the King* of 1914, the author tells us that,

---

[36] Strang, H. (1916) *The War on Land*. London: Hodder & Stoughton.
[37] See, Hughes, C. (1990). 'The New Armies', in Beckett, I. F. W. and Simpson, K. *The Nation in Arms*. London: Tom Donovan, pages 102-104.

The civilised world is threatened by a barbaric invasion. What Attila, the Ancient Hun, was to the world in the fifth century, that would Wilhelm, the Modern Hun, be in the twentieth century.[38]

Lynn also dwells at length on 'Robotic' Germans who have been 'drilled into submission,' who are 'swaggering, bullying and insolent' when in command but cowed and submissive when faced by an authority figure.[39]

The prolific Captain F. S. Brereton, despite returning to service as a doctor in the Royal Army Medical Corps, maintained his literary output throughout the war. In his first novel about the war, *With French at the Front*, tells us that the Germans had been planning this war for years, a 'war that would make them masters of the world.' But it is when he describes the sack of the Belgian city of Louvain that he lets rip,

At Louvain, the seat of Belgian universities... the Prussian hosts executed a deed as terrible as ever committed by Attila and his barbarian Huns. They burned and destroyed the city, slaughtered civilians on every side, and committed nameless atrocities.[40]

And like many another author, Brereton reminds his readers that there will be retribution for these 'Hunnish' acts, honour demands it. 'Honour' carried great significance in explanations of what Britain was fighting for. In *Two Daring Patriots*, W. P. Shervill explained, that the nation had begun the war because of her honour and, whatever the cost, must see it through, for 'Life without honour, even for nations, is not worth living.'[41]

Conclusion

Before 1914, the world of adventure writing was almost wholly dominated by male authors. But as the new century dawned, several women had entered the field finding locations within the Dominions locate their adventurous heroines, L. T. Meade's *A Sister of the Red Cross:*

---

[38] Lynn, E. (1915). *In Khaki for the King: A tale of the Great War*. London: W. R. Chambers, page iii.
[39] *Ibid*. Page v.
[40] Captain F. S. Brereton. (1915). *With French at the Front*. London: Blackie, page 125.
[41] Shervill, W. P. (1919). *Two Daring Patriots: or outwitting the Huns*. London: Blackie, page 130.

A Tale of the South African War - the adventures of a young English nurse during the conflict, for example. The war, however, opened up new areas where girls and young women might serve the nation in nursing; munitions work, as refugees, and even, after 1916, as military personnel in the armed forces. The authors of the very popular girls' school stories tailored their stories to suit the times, with their heroines on the trail of suspicious German masters and spies. Angela Brazil's *A Patriotic School Girl* is a useful example here.[42] But some authors went further and located their protagonists in the war industries or the war zone. Several of the early war novels addressed the issue of why the nation was at war. These, however, generally lack the wild anti-German rhetoric and viciousness of male authors. In Bessie Marchant's *Molly Angel's Adventures* (1915), for instance, the story of a young English woman caught up in the German invasion of Belgium, and the author relies on press reports of the chaos and confusion of the German advance. But interestingly, here the Germans of the novel are arrogant and single-minded but not bestial or intentionally cruel. Molly herself is compassionate, calm, and courageous in dangerous situations - a perfect role model for young women suffering from the hardships of war.[43] In *The Cub*, the author Ethel Turner is less concerned with the events than with the tragedy of war. It is that rare thing for 1915 a book for young readers that dares to ask if the human cost of war can ever be really justified.[44] Surprisingly the reviews were positive even if a reviewer in The Times did gloomily note "war kills off the most promising lads and leaves mothers childless."[45]

Before 1914, the authors of adventure fiction for the young believed it their duty to support the King and Empire; to uphold the nation's imperial mission, support the Army and Navy and encourage young men to play an active role in promoting the national interest. They had portrayed war as a romantic adventure, an exciting rite of passage through which boys became men. When the Great War came, they helped promote what they genuinely believed to be a just and honourable war - perhaps even a war of national survival. Their strategy was to explain what Britain was fighting for and the wicked

---

[42] Brazil, A. (1918). *A Patriotic School Girl*. London: Blackie.
[43] Marchant, B. (1915). *Molly Angel's Adventures: A tale of the occupation of Belgium*. London: Blackie.
[44] Turner, E. (1915). *The Cub*. London: Ward Lock.
[45] *Times Literary Supplement*, December 9, 1915.

nature of their enemy to encourage the young to enlist for what they saw as a moral crusade for the nation's honour. They certainly succeeded in helping create a patriotic 'mind-set', which sent young men in droves to the recruiting offices. And even after conscription was introduced, some young Britons did not wait for the official notification, but volunteered, many lying about their age in their eagerness to get to France. These stories of pluck, endurance, and derring-do in the trenches resonated with much of the British public even after 1918 for many of these stories remained in print until the late 1930s. Many were given as parental gifts, or class or Sunday School 'rewards' by parents and teachers - men who had fought the war and who thought that what these stories had told an earlier generation of children was worthwhile passing on.

Chapter 2

Remember Scarborough
Re-Active Propaganda as Natural Ethics

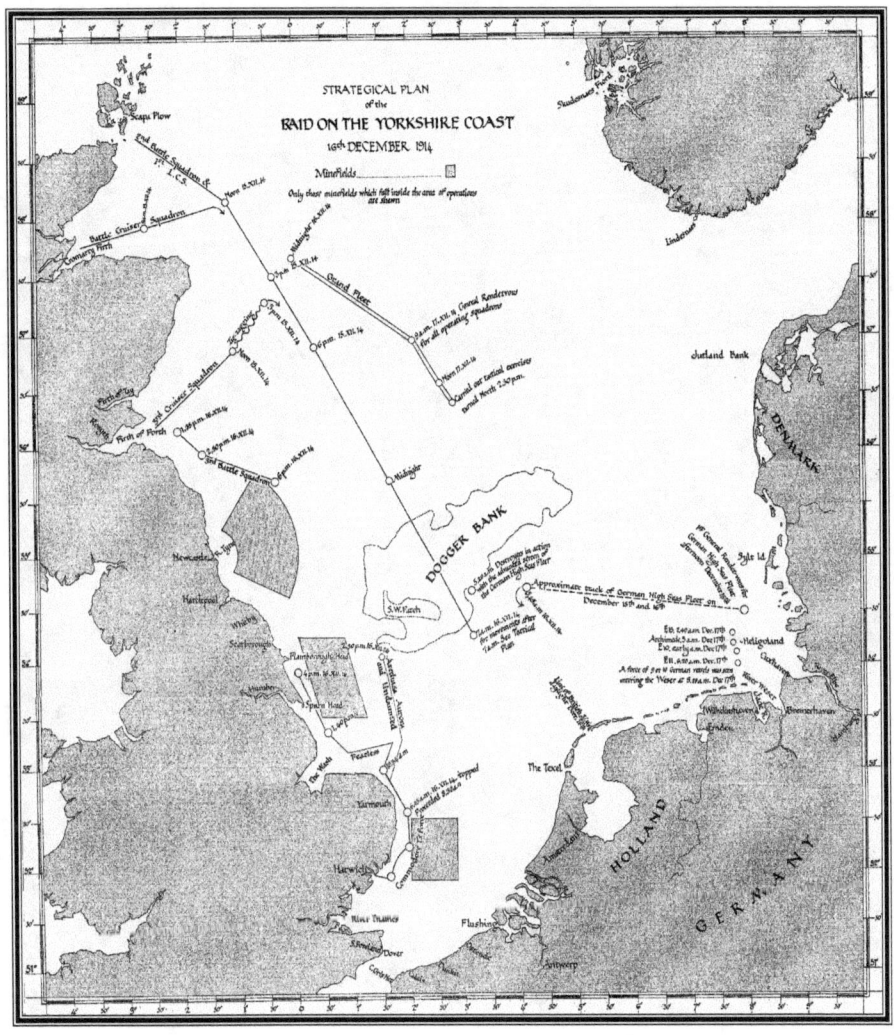

Chapter 2

Remember Scarborough
Re-Active Propaganda as Natural Ethics

Christopher Hart
University of Chester

Introduction

On August 4th 1914, a warm Friday, Great Britain and its commonwealth declared war on Germany.

On December 16th 1914, a cold misty Wednesday morning, just after 8am two battle groups of the Imperial German Navy bombarded towns along the North East coast of England - Scarborough, Whitby and the Hartlepools. 137 men, women and children were killed (18 from Scarborough, 3 from Whitby others from Hartlepool) 592 were injured, many seriously maimed. Over 1,100 shells were fired from 8 and 6-inch guns by the five battle-cruisers, damaging hundreds of buildings.

This chapter is about a media commonly discussed when it comes to looking at the First World War - the propaganda poster. In this case I will look at a series of reactive propaganda posters, articles and images (alongside other media) that was issued immediately after the bombardments.

The treatment of the posters, newspaper, and journal articles that were published in the days and weeks immediately after the attacks could be approached using the usual standpoint and approach. The literature 'on propaganda' is well known.

This chapter does not, however, look at propaganda but at a broader set of theories that I want to propose as an explanatory account of the nature of the posters and newspaper articles. This proposition begins by placing these texts, and their usual frames of analysis, to one side to ask of this material a series of 'morality' questions.

Research Questions and Methodological Problems

The leading question for this research was,

> How and why did the official propaganda published following the bombardment of towns on the North East Coast of England, in December 1914, express deeply held moral outrage, and as such represented a real morality and not a mistreatment of truth?

The focus of this research question is the recruitment posters and newspaper articles published between December 1914 and April 1915 mentioning and reporting on the bombardments. The question aimed to investigate the proposition that the moral standpoint they took reflected widely held opinions and were not, in the conventional sense, top-down, motivational rhetorical exaggerations and falsehoods.

A related question is,

> Given this was war, why were the citizens of the U.K. and many other countries morally outraged at the attacks?

What this related question is attempting to find out is 'why' did the survivors, the British government, newspapers and magazine editors react with surprise to the attacks and focus reporting on the immorality of the German Navy.

Both of these questions are about morality and how different moral standpoints became visible after the bombardments. The questions are about media responses reflecting contrasting national moral boundaries. In this case, the different moral position held by the British public and that of the German Navy.

We now have a different problem than explaining the working of what we have called propaganda.

Let us, for the sake of definitional clarity call the posters, newspaper, and journal articles 'reactions' to the bombardments. As reactions they may embody some of the features of what is generally labelled propaganda and these should not be overlooked. But the main point is that the sentiments and morals expressed in this reactive material have other features rooted in public morality. They are not expressing, I argue, government manipulation but public expressions of right and wrong, of what is ethical and what is not, even in war. In short, I am asking the reader to consider the reactions as deeply felt morality and that this stance was not restricted to the victims of the bombardments

Figure 2.1 'Remember Scarborough' published in early 1915

but felt throughout the world, with the exception of Imperial Germany.

Methodologically these questions are problematic. At the centre of the methodological problem is the question, how, if at all, can we explain the reactions in terms of moral philosophy given that this event happened over 100 years ago? The postulate is that the poster *Remember Scarborough* is not another example of propaganda, with all the derogatory connotations now associated with the category but is part of a much broader narrative that made visible the morality of the British public in December 1914. If this postulate is to be methodologically adequate, there is an anthropological problem to address. That this event was experienced by people over 100 years ago possess an interesting sub-question; can we, living today, understand the moral attitudes of those living a century ago? This seemingly simple question may not be, on closer consideration, as simple as it seems. This is because if we go back to December 1914 could we live as those living then lived? Would we hold or even be able to understand their moral position? For example, if we as critical analysts were transported back in time to Scarborough, following the bombardment, in December 1914 what would we make of the posters, newspaper articles and handbills condemning the attacks? Would we see them as government propaganda? As attempts to manipulate public opinion and encourage more young men to join the army or navy? Or would we 'read' them as symbolising something much more complex, say a moral dichotomy between 'us' the British and 'them' the Germans? Similarly, if a resident of Scarborough were transported to our time would they look back and think they had been subject to government falsehoods or would they challenge this interpretation? Would they argue that the posters embodied and reflected the opinions and views of the public in 1914, and that we, the academics of media, need to understand morality before we make judgements on their intellectual capabilities?

This research aims to bring together historic events, post-event reactions and moral theory to produce an explanatory framework and methodological approach that pays respect to historic contemporary reactions.

To navigate the argument this chapter will look at what happened when, where, to whom, and by who followed by the reactions in the general media and then at the official responses. Using contemporary accounts, attention will the turn to exploring a sociological framework and philosophical principles to evaluate the reasons for the attacks and to ask if the messages in the posters that followed, were a case of straight forward propaganda.

The bombardment of Scarborough

It was just another Wednesday morning in Scarborough. The weather was cold with a mist. The inhabitants of Scarborough were going about their usual early morning routines. The following account gives some idea of the normality, routine and sense of safety the people of

Scarborough felt on that misty morning. The following[1], although fictional, gives a sense of that morning.

Lily Bain was in the back room of her home at 51 St John's Road, lacing up her winter boots ready for another day at school. Lily was fourteen, soon she would leave books and homework to find a job, but not just yet.

Around the corner at 2 Wykeham Street, nine-year-old Jack Ward was in the gas lit kitchen of his grandparents' house. It faced across the Whitby railway to Gladstone Road School where one or two children had arrived early. On a grey morning in 1914 their thoughts were of Christmas and the holidays...

At Westlands School in Westbourne Grove, at Queen Margaret's School in Filey Road, and at other school dormitories emptied as breakfast bells rang.

Shop workers took down shutters as postmen and milkmen went from house to house. Cream and maroon trams from Hampton Road (now Harley Close) clanked through the streets and travelers heading to the railway station for trains to York, Hull, Whitby or Pickering, looked at the clock tower to check their watches. It was eight o'clock on Wednesday 16th December and daylight was just breaking.

In St Martins Church, a small congregation gathered for Holy Communion, and near the Spa a few early morning bathers swam in the cold waters of the North Sea.

The ships shelling Scarborough were the battle cruiser *SMS Derfflinger* and *SMS Von Der Tann* of the Kaiserliche Marine (Imperial Navy[2]). *SMS Derfflinger* was relatively new in 1914 having been launched in 1913. Nicknamed the 'iron dog' by the British, the *Derfflinger* was heavily armoured with eight 12-inch guns and twelve 5.9-inch guns. The *SMS Von Der Tann* was older being launched in 1909. At the time of her construction, *SMS Von der Tann* was the fastest dreadnought-type warship afloat, capable of reaching speeds in excess of 27 knots. With eight 11-inch guns, ten 5.9-inch guns and sixteen 3.4-inch guns *SMS Von der Tann* was a major gun platform capable of inflicting and taking serious

---

[1] From, scarboroughsmaritimeheritage.org.uk/article.php?article=27 by Bryan Berryman. Also see Reed, L. (2005). *Thunder In The Morning Fictional Account of Scarborough Bombardment 1914 WWI*. Family Reed Publications.
[2] Kaiserliche Marine was created at the same time of the German Empire in 1871.

damage. While the two battle-cruisers shelled the town, the light cruiser *SMS Kolberg* laid a minefield, of 100 mines, off the town.

Is a 'technicality' sufficient as a moral excuse?

Witt and McDermott (2016)[3] conclude that the bombardments of Scarborough, Whitby and Hartlepool were, in retrospect and at the time, not a "reckless or indiscriminate act of terror." They add in support of this claim that,

> indeed, it is very clear that in neither the intention nor the outcome could the Scarborough raid be considered to have been a war crime. Rather, it was an unsuccessful attempt by the German High Seas Fleet to break the strategic stalemate in the North Sea... as a direct result of this, the civilian dead and wounded of Scarborough, Whitby and Hartlepool became unintended casualties, albeit taken into account as part of the strategic errors of the German Admiralty. But they were not victims of a German terror attack.[4]

The problem with this claim is the words 'reckless' and 'indiscriminate'. Taking Scarborough as our focus, the German Admiralty made the decision to attack the town based on poor, incomplete and non-verified information about the defence of the town. The battle cruisers set out on their mission with the wrong ammunition. The gunner crews had no experience of coastal bombardment. The targeting crew could not see the primary targets. The guns could not use steep trajectory targeting but used instead flat trajectory that caused a wider spread of shells. Plus, they would have been fully aware that Scarborough was a small town, with densely packed housing and at 8 am in the morning most people would still be at home getting ready for the day. On the day, the visibility was poor and there was a heavy swell making targeting and shooting more difficult.

In all technical respects, the bombardment of Scarborough was reckless, primarily due to the use of secondary targets such as a church and railway station clock, and also due to the lack of detailed and

---

[3] Witt, J. M. and McDermott, R. (2016). *Scarborough Bombardment: Der Angriff der deutschen Hochseeflotte auf Scarborough*. Berlin: Der Palm Verlag, page 163. Written in English and German.
[4] *Ibid.* Page 163.

reliable information. The attack was indiscriminate due to the lack of appropriate ammunition, angle of firing and number of shells fired.

However, if, we accept that in 'spirit' the decision and orders to attack included concern to minimise civilian deaths and damage to buildings, then there is only one technical point to support this position. This is the order not to use, unless fired upon, the main armaments; to use the 15 cm and 8.8cm guns. Technically, then firing 776 number of shells[5], from 15 and 8.8cm guns, onto the residents of Scarborough could be seen as enacting the 'spirit' of the order and in all likelihood did not kill, injure and damage buildings as much as the main 30cm and 28cm guns would have[6]. But with shells striking the homes of the residents such a concession was wholly irrelevant.

Facts such as the calibre of the guns, the weight of the shells and the weather conditions have relevance to a post attack rationalisation. But the human experience of being shelled in closely packed housing, from whatever calibre of cannon, is what really matters. Being shelled, without warning, with no protection, morally outweighs the 'spirit' of the order to restrict the calibre of gun to 15cm, regardless of the intent.

On balance the argument that technically the number of deaths, injuries and levels of destruction in Scarborough could have been worse has, nonetheless, some purchase. Dropping 405kg shells fired from 30.5cm guns would have caused more 'collateral damage'.[7] But, when offered up as part of a basket of reasons (gunnery crews lacking the necessary skills, had the wrong shells and could not see their primary targets) they fall short of a valid argument[8].

---

[5] The following number, 333 x 15cm and 443 x 8.8cm explosive shells having been fired, comes from, Der Krieg in der Nordsee, 83-84. Für den Kurs der Derfflinger und der Von Der Tann siehe Karte Nr. 10, 10 (Beschießung von Scarborough and Whitby 16. XII).

[6] This is the point made by Witt and McDermott (2016), page 157, "where the fall of a 15 cm shell in a densely-packed housing area tended to result in damage to a specific building, the outcome of a main armament shell falling in the same place would have been to destroy it completely and at the same time inflict severe damage on all other buildings surrounding it, as well as killing a far greater number of people."

[7] This is the term used by Witt and McDermott (2016), page 163 when they claim the dead of Scarborough "were what is now referred to as collateral damage, i.e. the bitter, but unintended, side-effects of a military operation."

[8] That attacks from 1915, and more so in the 2nd World War, were on civilian populations is irrelevant unless the claim is this was one of the first. Until December 1914 indiscriminate bombing of civilians was not only unheard of but also generally regarded as morally abhorrent.

The targets

A key tenant of the German justification for the attacks was the claim the towns had military installations and were defended. Therefore, in this section the following question is the main concern: was the attacks meant to damage British military installations? The short answer is no. Hartlepool was defended, if by 3 old guns. Scarborough and Whitby had no defences. In terms of damaging or disabling the British military little was achieved by the bombardments. But if we take a charitable approach to the legitimacy of attacking military targets then we have an interesting debate.

Hartlepool has two-gun batteries. The 'Heugh Battery' had two BL 6-inch MKVII naval guns and the 'Lighthouse Battery' that had one BL 6. Some 11 officers and 155 local men of the Durham Royal Garrison Artillery manned the guns. In the harbor were two light cruisers (*HMS Patrol* and *HMS Forward*) and a submarine (*HMS C9*). Hartlepool also had major iron and steel making, ship building, docks, large stores of props (wooden beams) for the coalmines and railways. Hartlepool was, therefore, a much larger town with major engineering industries, supplies for the coalmines in Durham and docks used by the Royal Navy.

Scarborough had no industry other than fishing and tourism. It did, however, have one of the first Wireless Telegraphy Stations (radio station). First set up in 1912 by Signal Intelligence (Sigint), in 1914 there were three such stations on the outskirts of the town[9]. Their purpose in 1914 was to intercept and monitor radio transmissions of the German High Seas Fleet. The existence, of at least one, of these stations was known to the Germans.[10] Hence, the one that was definitely known to exist was a target. But so too was the water-company, gasworks, railway station and coast guard station.

---

[9] In 2014 the latest incarnation of the station, GCHQ Scarborough, celebrated their centenary and the station is considered to be the longest running of its type in the world.
[10] In August 1913 a party of German delegates from an international conference visited Scarborough. The *Scarborough Pictorial* 30 December 1914 reported the delegates visited the ruins of the castle; saw the obsolete cannons and the wireless station. The article claims these Germans were on a recognisance mission. See,
scarboroughsmaritimeheritage.org.uk/article.php?article=37.

Worldwide condemnation of the bombardments as moral outrage

On the evening of the 16th December 2014 MPs in the British Parliament listened to Mr. Iain Wright MP for Hartlepool.[11] He opened his talk with the following observation, that the bombardments, "forever altered civilian life and the way in which modern warfare is conducted." Wright also notes the effect on recruitment on the army and navy and raising of funds from Hartlepudlians for the war effort,

> The effect on the people of my constituency following the bombardment was astonishing. In the weeks and months after the attack, 22,000 men from the Hartlepools signed up for the war effort, something like one in two of the towns' adult male population. The Hartlepools received the award for raising the most money per head of the population for the war effort of any place in the British Empire, a modern equivalent, in a town of 100,000 people, of £545 million.

Mrs. Helen Grant, Parliamentary Under-Secretary of State for Culture, Media and Sport, followed Wright. She reinforced the human aspects of the attacks by saying,

> The raids by the imperial German navy on Hartlepool, Scarborough and Whitby 100 years ago today are justly remembered this evening for the devastating effect they had on normal people going about their daily business.

Similarly, the anniversary of the bombardments was covered by most of the current popular media. The *Mail Online* (30.11.2014), reproduced a list of those killed, and featured contemporary photographs of SMS Derfflinger, damaged buildings and recruiting posters headed 'Remember Scarborough!'. The *Mirror* (16.12.2014), had the headline, 'The baby killers of Scarborough' - an extract from a recently discovered letter from Winston Churchill. The article includes images of the damage done and stories about individuals killed. *Historic England* took the perspective of Mr. George Rowntree, portraying his experience in an animated narrative. The *BBC News* included video interviews with survivors of the bombardment, including Mrs. Violet Muers, along with other first-hand accounts and images of the damage. *ITV News* broadcast

---

[11] Hansard: 2014: V.589

a series of short films with archivists and of commemoration services in the three towns. *The Independent* (18.04.2014), recounts how the bombardments "shocked the nation." While the *Express* (16.12.2014), focused on Churchill's branding the German's the "baby killers" and his view that the German Navy was desperate; that, according to Churchill, the bombardment showed they had,

> lost their sense of proportion; of schemers, who have ceased to balance loss and gain.
> Practically the whole fast cruiser force of the German navy, including some great ships vital to their fleet and utterly irreplaceable, has been risked for the passing pleasure of killing as many English people as possible, irrespective of sex, age, or condition, in the limited time available.

Of all the coverage *The Scarborough News* (22.12.2015), is the most sober with curious facts. While having reported on the centenary in 2015 *The Scarborough News* reported on the first anniversary of the attack, finding in the event some humour and odd facts. Reporting on the first anniversary, the correspondent 'Jottings', noted,

> that the group of Scarborians who had best cause to remember the Bombardment were the brewers, publicans and licensed victuallers. Had readers not noticed that not a single public house in the town had been damaged by German shells, whereas many of its places of worship had received direct hits? "The publicans were saved but not the patrons."

In the period between December 1915 to January 1916 the reporting of the attacks was less cordial.

From mid-afternoon on the 16th December the nationals and local evening papers were quick to print what was known and assumed to have happened to Hartlepool, Scarborough and Whitby. While initial details were sketchy by late evening the details of what had been done, where and when, and how many dead and injured there were began to be published. Within days all newspapers carried photographs of the dead, damage to houses, hotels and lighthouses and diagrams showing the trajectory of the shells. The common theme framing all of the stories was these attacks were an outrage against civilians and in many cases, that the German Navy had committed a crime of war. Initially no distinction was made between the three towns. It mattered little if the children were killed in Scarborough or Hartlepool; they were still children and were dead because of the bombardment.

Many of the London based papers sent reporters and photographers to King's Cross Station. This is where trains from the North East arrived in the capital. Injured victims fleeing from the bombed towns would make for good copy. The most extreme reports were in *The Daily News* (somewhat opposed to the War) that reported the Northern train arrived full of injured civilians who said hundreds of houses in Scarborough were in flames when they left for London. Neither of these claims was true. They were a few injured on the train and there were no fires consuming Scarborough.[12] More sober and factual was *The Star*. The evening edition (printed at 7pm) on the 16th dedicated its front-page to

Figure 2.2 Photographs and names of children killed

the attacks. Carrying a postcard picture of Scarborough in peacetime, it showed the town as a visitor destination. Through this the frame of reference for reading Scarborough as sea-side resort was set. The picture postcard showed Scarborough as a spa-town, with pleasure craft in the bay and in the distance the ruins of a castle. The copy was dominated by multiple large headlines, statements from the Admiralty and snippets of witness accounts.

---

[12] Mr. Arthur Wood as reported in *The Daily News*, 17 December 1917. Mr. Woods was bookkeeper with the Scarborough Electric Supply Co. and had sustained minor injuries.

On Thursday the 17th December newspapers worldwide had copy reporting the attacks. The *North-Eastern Daily Gazette* (p:6) ran a column with five heading, 'Hartlepools Victims', followed by, 'Inquests Held To-Day in both Boroughs', 'Heavy Death Toll', Hartlepool 40; West Hartlepool 37', and bold font 'Many Infants & Young Children Dead'. Similarly, on the same day *The Newcastle Daily Journal* printed a special edition reporting the attacks. Even with scant details the Journal reported (pp:5-6) on 'Serious Loss of Life', 'Absence of Panic', 'Shells at Holy Communion', 'Ladies' Experience in Scarborough', 'Miraculous Escapes', and eye-witness accounts of explosions and shells falling in Scarborough 'half-a-dozen at a time'. They also report on the arrest of German residents in Tynemouth. On page 5 a map was reproduced of the North East showing the locations of the towns including Newcastle and Tynemouth. One of the few papers to carry a photograph on the 17th was *The Northern Echo*. Its front page showed a badly damaged Grand Hotel in Scarborough with, curiously, some 'prim and proper' looking women sitting on benches outside. The *Echo* also mentioned the damage to the ancient church of St. Hilda in Hartlepool. Like many of the other newspapers the *Echo* had some interesting juxtapositions in the adverts on pages reporting the bombardments. The *Echo*, for example, had an advert on its front-page saying, 'Brighten your Xmas, by trying pure Jam. The name must be Whittakers'. For the survivors in Hartlepool Christmas would be anything but bright or warm as the gasometer[13] had been destroyed.

Some papers had photographs for the morning editions of the 17th. *The Daily Mirror* printed two editions. The first showed a photograph of pre-war Scarborough with visitors on the promenade and of ships birthed in the docks at Hartlepool. The later edition was more graphic; front page was taken up with photographs showing the extent of damage to buildings. Its headline was, 'Great Britain Bombarded. German Navy Shells Three English Towns and Makes Its Escape'. The early edition of the *Daily Sketch* on the Thursday also carried a pre-war photograph of Scarborough and one of the railway yards in Hartlepool. It carried the headings, 'Another 'Sacred Memory' of the Keiser for Archbishop Lang', and 'German Effort to Create Panic In England'.

Papers in the U.S.A. had reports printed by the evening of the 16th but most lacked accuracy and details. One of the first to report was *The Evening World* (New York) in its final edition on the 16th. The heading

---

[13] A gasometer was a large container that stored and supplied gas to towns and cities.

was, 'Two of Kaiser's fleet reported sunk after raid on British Coast Towns'. *The Evening World* also reproduced, as did other papers, a familiar postcard image of Scarborough used to promote the town as a sea-side spa resort. Other sub-headings were similarly inaccurate, 'British Destroyers, Called By Wireless, Attack the Raiders which Dashed Out of the German Naval Base and Slipped Passed the Mine Fields'. Nonetheless, like other American newspapers the basic information was reported - 'Many Persons Killed, Churches Damaged and other Buildings Wrecked by Shells in Scarborough, Hartlepool and Whitby...'. Even by the next day, when matters had become clearer,

Figure 2.3 Scarborough pre-war

American papers lacked information. *The Herald* (Washington D.C.) 17th dedicated half of its front-page to the attacks. The main heading, 'German Raiders Escape; British Cities Wrecked' was followed by the sub-heading, 'Hundreds Free Coast Towns Following Attack from the Sea'. The facts, as reported by papers like the Herald, were thin and couched in cautious terms. For example, 'The death toll is heavy among non-combatants... Probably more than 100 civilians were killed'. The point about what was and what was not fortified was, however, made in the leading paragraph, 'Only one attacked town was fortified – hospitals, churches, and houses wrecked by projectiles'.

One of the most interesting American articles was on the front page of the *Chicago Tribune* (17th December). It had a double cartoon showing John Bull declaring to Germany, 'Hey! Can't You Read? Britannia Rules the Waves' - John Bull is looking over his shoulder at men running towards a recruiting station, with the caption, 'Anyway, That Raid Will Help Recruiting'. The *Tribune's* report was largely composed of reproducing the official releases by the German High Command and the British War Office. Other parts of the article were from the *Newcastle Chronicle*.

The Morning Leader (Saskatchewan, Canada) on the 17th December reported, 'German Shells Crash Into English Homes', 'English Towns on Yorkshire Coast Bombarded By Raiding German Fleet; Buildings Wrecked and People Killed'. The article makes the point, that the 'Attack Was Without Any Warning...'.

By Friday 18th December the details were clearer. *The New York Herald* had photographs of the destruction, lists of public buildings that were damaged such as churches, including Whitby Abbey and incomplete lists of the dead. Among the multiple reports in the paper was one headed, 'Outrage Results in Great Rush of Recruits'.

From Friday 18th and Saturday 19th the full extent of what had happened became clear, especially in the British newspapers. Nearly all titles had a range of photographs some with odd headings. *The Daily Mirror* on the 18th declared, 'English Towns Bombarded: Wonderful Photographs'. The photographs were of damage to a range of buildings in Scarborough and Hartlepool. Next day, however, matters were more sombre. *The Daily Mirror's* front page announced, 'Portraits of Women and Children Murdered By The Kaiser'. The whole page showed photographs – 11 were of young children and 2 of women. The names and ages of each were given underneath each photograph. For example, 'Stanley Walker and Albert Walker, killed'. The emotive force of the *Mirror's* piece were the photographs of the Dixon family – George (14 years), Margaret (8 years), Joseph (13 years), and Albert (7 years) – all killed. On the same day German newspapers were reporting the heroism of their sailors; a point not missed by *The Mirror*. Above the photographs of the dead children the heading was, 'Berlin Rings Joy Bells Over The Butchery Of These British Babes on England's East Coast'.

The previous day (Friday 18th) the *Daily Sketch* had one photograph covering their front page; it was what had once been the inside of a house, now completely destroyed. The headline was, 'A Whole Family Wiped Out Causes Joy In Berlin'. Next day, the Saturday edition of the *Daily Sketch's* front page had photographic portraits of some of the dead children arranged around a picture of the Keiser, as a child and adult. The headline was, 'With His Victims All Around Him', 'The Keiser Was Once An Innocent Child'. And above the papers heading was, 'Our Own Murdered Women And Children Now Call On You To Join'.

From Monday 21st onwards the funerals began. The *Daily Sketch* once again had photographs on its front page; Mrs. Merryweather and Mr. Beale's funerals were shown, accompanied with the headline, 'The Stigma of The Bay-Killers Will Stick To Them'.

Popular periodicals such as *The Tatler, The War Illustrated* and *The Sphere* provided the British public with more photographs and artists impressions of the attacks. Two days before Christmas (23rd December) *The Tatler* stated, 'Enemy's Shells Damage Undefended British Towns for the First time in the History of Our Country', and with it a photograph of a devastated house in Wykeham Street, Scarborough where a Mrs. Barnett and two children were killed. On the 26th December *The Illustrated London News* and *The Sphere* both carried multiple page spreads full of photographs showing the damage to buildings. One page of *The Illustrated London News* showed photographs of damage to Scarborough ancient castle, with the heading, "Fortified' by Castle Ruins - Scarborough After Bombardment'. There was also a photograph of the Merryweather's shop with its windows and door blown out, with the caption, 'Where Mrs. Merryweather Was Killed...'. *The War Illustrated* had a double-page illustration showing the bay of Scarborough being bombarded, with shells exploding in the air and building on fire, and people running for their lives. Part of the detailed caption read, 'an audacious and futile raid on unprotected towns...', followed by, 'an armoured cruiser attacked defenceless Scarborough...'.

While we could expect British newspapers and periodicals to express outrage the same feelings were expressed elsewhere. One of the most straight forward was from *The Independent* (28th December, Toronto, Canada),

IT IS MAGNIFICENT - BUT IT IS NOT WAR

It is not enemy ships that they have attacked, not fortresses that they have bombarded, not soldiers that they have killed. Three quiet, peaceful towns have felt the rain of shells; almost five score non-combatant.

Men, women, children perhaps, have met death from the hurtling missiles.

This is not warfare, it is murder.[14]

German jubilation

While the newspapers around the world were outraged by the attacks German newspapers rejoiced. The *Nürnberger Zeitung* (Nuremberg Newspaper) 17th December had the headline,

Figure 2.4 *Lustige Blatter* in January 1915.
Artist W. A. Wellner

A New Courageous Deed By Our Naval Forces. Bombarding of English Resorts. Panic in Scarborough, Hartlepool And Whitby.

---

[14] *The Independent,* December 28, 1914, pages 494-5.

The article made it clear the German Navel defeat in the Falklands had been avenged,

> The joy of victory of the English after their success in the Falkland Islands has been short lived. On Wednesday morning parts of our naval forces appeared off the English east coast and started a surprise cannon attack of Scarborough, Hartlepool and Whitby, where a lot of damage was done.
>
> This bold strike by our brave 'Blue Boys' is felt in the whole of Germany as a fantastic revenge for our unavoidable defeat at the Falkland Islands.[15]

The *Hamburger Nachrichten* made the attacks more a of a personal revenge for the death of German sailors killed in the Falklands defeat,

> The German ships approached with daring courage. They practised retaliation for what English squadrons did to us at the Falkland Islands and at the Cocos Islands. A great mourning-salute for Count Spree, his two young sons and the many faithful men who found their graves in the ocean along with them, or previously from the cruiser Emden, boomed over English soil and English homesteads, and carried with voice of thunder the message to Great Britain, that the spirit of the fallen and the drowned of the Falkland Islands is living and can prove itself formidable.[16]

The *Berliner Neuesten Nachrichten* (Berlin Latest News), *Berliner Tageblatt* (Berlin Daily Paper) and *Hamburger Nachrichten* (Hamburg News) similarly praised the bravery of the German navy. The also emphasised the official line that the towns were 'fortified'. Both papers used the phrase 'fortified places'. These and other newspapers churned the copy from the official report from Von Pohl, Chief of the Admiralty Staff,

> BERLIN, Dec. 16th. Official. Parts of our High Sea forces made an attack on the English east coast and early on December 16th the two fortified coast-places Scarborough and Hartlepool were bombarded.[17]

---

[15] Gowans, A. L. (1915). *A Months German Newspapers. Being representative extracts from those of the memorable month of December, 1914.* London and Glasgow: Gowans and Gray Ltd, page 175.
[16] *Ibid.* Page 175.
[17] *Ibid.* Page 175.

Next day the evening edition of the *Berliner Lokal-Anzeiger* (Berlin Local Advertiser) thought the news made a dull day splendid,

> How splendid is this dull rainy day! In the morning we had news of the bold exploit of German cruisers against the coast of England. And now we know that their guns, when they sent their iron hail hurtling into Scarborough and Hartlepool, were at the same time firing a salute for the great victory in the east.[18]

The reasons Germany attacked the British coastal towns

There are some obvious reasons the German Navy made the decision to attack the East coastal towns of England, and there is a sociological one. The obvious reasons include the following. The ships of the German Navy were within 24 hour striking distance from Germany. It was simply a case of the ships sailing through two minefields, shelling the towns and making good their escape before the Royal Navy could catch up with them, either from their Scottish base at Rosyth, or from their south-east base at Harwich. Such a quick 'victory' would raise morale in their own Navy after their humiliating defeat by the British Navy in the Falklands.[19]

Rear Admiral Franz Hipper, commander of the German battle cruiser squadron, had done some reconnaissance; presumably to check his battle-cruisers would not be destroyed. Submarine U-17[20] was sent to investigate the area near Scarborough and Hartlepool.[21] Its purpose was to assess the power of coastal defenses in the two towns. Hipper learnt from U-17 that neither town had much in the way of onshore defense, that minefields could be navigated and from both town harbours there was a steady stream of shipping.

---

[18] *Ibid*. Page 175.
[19] On the December 8, 1914, in the South Atlantic, near the Falkland Islands the British destroyed the German East Asia Squadron. The Imperial German Navy lost five ships, the *SMS Nürnberg, Leipzig, Gneisenau, Scharnhorst* and *Dresden*, with 1,871 killed, compared to 10 British killed, with no ships lost. See, Prommersberger, J. (2016). *Battles at Sea in World War I - Falkland Islands*. Published by, Jürgen Prommersberger, also see, Massie, R. K. (2004). *Castles of Steel: Britain, Germany and the winning of the Great War at sea*. New York: Ballantine Books.
[20] Compton-Hall, R. (1991). *Submarines at War 1914-1918*. Penzance: Periscope Publishing.
[21] *The Hamburger Nachrichten*, December 17, 1914 praised the use of submarines, "Our fleet does not only send submarines in advance, but it also appears with its large fighting ships, when it seems to it to be the right moment, and then it knows how to make itself intelligible to the English."

This would be an opportunity to embarrass the British Navy for their failure to prevent an attack on the British mainland. Outrage from the British public would force the embarrassed Royal Navy to seek revenge and pursue the German ships. The force that would attack the coastal towns would be substantial - with four battle-cruisers, an armored cruiser and four light cruisers and eighteen destroyers. The Royal Navy would, it could be assumed, send nothing less than a group led by battle-cruisers in pursuit. With 85 German ships positioned East of Dogger Bank[22] Hipper's squadron would lead the British into a trap.

The final reason for the attack was to send a clear message to the British public; that they were not safe, that this was not a war being fought overseas, on someone else's land. If British harbours could be so easily bombarded then so too could others, including the important ports of Hull and Grimsby, and the iron and steel making plants in around Middlesbough. The *Hamburger Nachrichten* made this clear, explaining to their readers that[23], "Hartlepool and Scarborough lie in the north-east of England between the important economic centres of Newcastle and Hull."

The attacks as deviant rebelliousness vice

In the normal course of naval warfare, the expectation is that opposing fleets face off, too lesser or greater degrees, and slug it out. The means to this expectation is the combination of warships, technology, materials, skills and leadership application of intelligence to strategy and tactics. It may have been, as the Battle of Jutland shows, a face-off is not predetermined; the opponent with the largest fleet is not necessarily the winner. A sea battle is not an end in itself but the means for achieving other outcomes such as the control of maritime trade, with access to the resources needed to wage war. The British Navy aimed, therefore, to achieve and maintain general control of radio communications. As such general control of the North Sea, English Channel, Mediterranean, North and South Atlantic was combined with blockades of ports used by the German Navy.[24] This strategy by the British was evidently a cause of resentment to the German newspapers. The *Hamburger Nachrichten*, for example, wrote on the 17th December,

---

[22] Admiral Friedrich von Ingenohl in command.
[23] *Hamburger Nachrichten*, December 17, 1915.
[24] Mahan, A.T. (2012). *The Influence of Sea Power upon History, 1660-1783*. London: Rare Book Club.

What was it they said so often and so reassuringly for British minds in London newspapers'? That the North Sea was swept clean, that the German fleet was penned up in the 'German Bight' and blockaded by the British giant-fleet. The thunder of the cannon at Hartlepool and Scarborough, falling chimneys, exploding gasometers, tumbling railway-stations, dying cries of wounded, the mad anxiety of the fugitives, tell a somewhat different story... Even on the open sea the German fleet does not allow its rights to be prescribed by Englishmen...

As bad as they were to the victims, the bombardments achieved little in terms of altering British Navel strategy. As a means to achieve specific objectives the attacks largely failed. The British Navy was not diminished and recruits to Kitchener's Army increased; the only objective to be achieved, and this had unintended negative consequences, was the fact an attack was made on the British Mainland. This in itself was cause for rejoicing by the *Frankfurter Zeitung* that on December 31st sought to address the outrage expressed by newspapers around the world.

> the superiority of the English fleet looks very questionable. We have waited in vain for more than four months for the English 'bull-dog' that was to force our ships to fight. Only last week there was proof furnished once more of the fact, that the German fleet is not afraid to search out the enemy in his hiding-places, and it was bound to cause the impression, even in England, that the German attack on Scarborough and Hartlepool signified a brilliant success. Not only did the German ships sink two torpedo-boat destroyers, and damage a third severely; they also silenced the coast-batteries of Hartlepool and destroyed various coastguard stations. Of course, this time again hypocritical complaints were raised, that our ships had bombarded what were alleged to be 'open places'.
> ... the fact that it can hardly be maintained that hostile shore batteries fall under the definition of 'open places'. The fact nevertheless remains, that at the decisive moment the English coast was without protection against the German Attack...

Two points stand out from this report. One is the reference to there being a coastal battery in Hartlepool, with no mention of any in Scarborough. The second is the reference of 'open places'.

By January 3rd 1915 the *Berlin Lokal Anzeiger*, on the defensive, insisted Scarborough had fortifications and that the towns attacked were not 'open places'. Referring to old maps 'Scarborough Castle' it was claimed, had a battery 'fitted with 15cm. (6in.) quick firing guns.' Scarborough had no such battery other than obsolete cannons on the battlements of the ruined castle. The article also mentions the

Figure 2.5 German newspaper report of attacks

coastguard station at Whitby but says nothing about its purpose. The *Berlin Lokal Anzeiger* was trying to re-frame the criticisms Germany had been subject to regarding the view the attacks were an autocracy committed on civilians. The key to the defence is the claim that the three towns were militarised. Hartlepool certainly was a military town; of this there is no argument against, and it did have defences. Including the other two towns in the same class is a reference to the Second Hague Conference of 1907 stated that, 'The bombardment by naval forces of undefended ports, towns, villages, dwellings or buildings is forbidden'. The German view was that the three towns came under Part II of the convention that states,

> Military works, military or naval establishments, depots of arms or war material, workshops or plant which could be utilised for the needs of the hostile fleet or army, and ships of war in the harbour, are not, however, included in this prohibition. The commander of a naval force may destroy them with artillery, after a summons

followed by a reasonable interval of time, if all other means are impossible, and when the local authorities have not themselves destroyed them within the time fixed.

The claim then being made by The *Berlin Lokal Anzeiger* is that there were defences and all three towns had military significance. But none of the towns were given 'a reasonable interval of time'. Nonetheless, there is a sense here that The *Berlin Lokal Anzeiger* is attempting to say the German Navy had conformed to the Hague Convention. But there is another way to look at this claim of conformity.

Merton's paradigm of possible behaviours

If the attacks achieved, as I have claimed, little except to galvanise opinion against Germany and motive more men from Britain and the Empire to sign up, then we may need to look elsewhere for an additional frame of reference to understand the rationale for the attacks. In the *Berliner Tageblatt*, of the 31st December 1914 a hint is given of the challenge being made to acceptance of the assumptions about what naval warfare is about.

> Amazement at the peculiar method of warfare increases from week to week, from month to month. If one pictures to oneself the events, which have happened in the war up till now on the seas, one cannot repress an ironical smile at the prophecies of the naval strategists. Fundamental principles have been shaken, many a theoretical assumption has been swept away, and we now see the completely unexpected become a fact.[25]

By 'unexpected' the reference to the bombardment of the three coastal towns would certainly fit with this. But why? The *Hamburger Nachrichten*, on the 17th December

> What was it they said so often and so reassuringly for British minds in London newspapers"? That the North Sea was swept clean, that the German fleet was penned up in the 'German Bight' and blockaded by the British giant-fleet.
> ... England has tried to restrict our room and to assume the

---

[25] *Op. cit.* Gowans, (1915), pages 264-268.

sovereignty over all seas. Now German shots have swept over her own country from the sea and destroyed houses, thrown down lofty factory-chimneys, slain men.

With the British, American, French and Italian Fleets aided by minefields blockading merchant and military shipping there is a distinctively sociological way of looking at the claim, the German Navy challenged fundamental principles and did the unexpected. According to Robert K. Merton (1938) if we conceptualise any society, like the German Empire, as a social system with a particular social structure and culture, comprised of a set of institutions such as the polity, military, transport, exchange and so on, underpinned by a German 'Kultur'.

According to Merton (1938)[26] each social system will have a set of goals that are in normal times, in the main, shared and accepted by its citizens and espoused by its institutions. In uneventful times and with properly functioning institutions such as education, politics and the arts the most common form of behaviour is that of 'conformity'. Individuals accept the cultural values of the system and institutionalise the means for pursuing those goals. Within the paradigm of possible responses to the goals there are other alternatives. For some individuals and organisations this may mean they accept and aspire to the goals but look to circumvent the institutionalised means. These individuals, therefore, are willing to use whatever means are available to realise the goals of their society; they 'innovate' the means (e.g. tax avoidance). There are two other possibilities in this paradigm: 'ritualism' and 'retreatist' The ritualist has, for whatever reason, given up on the cultural goals but, nonetheless, goes through the motions and continues to follow (or at least not challenge) the culturally prescribed means (e.g. the disillusioned teacher). The 'retreatist' rejects both the goals and the means, essentially dropping out of conventional society (e.g. Bohemian). The fifth possible course of behaviour is the 'rebellious'. The rebellious rejects the goals and the means; often, substituting alternative goals and means to follow a life-style different from and often in contrast to the rest of society (e.g. nudism, flappers).

Even in normal times the demands of the social system can exert pressures on individuals and organisations. The result being that different adaptations can be seen across most sections of a society, even

---

[26] Merton, R. K. (1938). 'Social Structure and Anomie', *American Sociological Review*, Vol 3: 5, pages 672-682.

the rebellious will be present. But during unusual times the strains can be amplified where once the outsiders such as the innovator or the rebellious become the focus for popular support. The sub-cultures that develop in reaction to a problem come to express wider problems; soon the small sub-cultures become larger collectives, offering apparent solutions, to the wider society.[27] For this to gain momentum opportunities must exist that can, in some way, be legitimised to the wider collective.[28]

Empirically in late 1914 the German Empire had achieved a number of spectacular victories on land that contrasted with defeats at sea and the inability to break the blockades. The German army had already shown a new kind of approach to warfare with its neighbouring countries. The destruction of the university library of Louvain and the cathedral of Rheims were strictly unnecessary and can be regarded as signs that Germany's leadership and intellectuals had a problem with understanding morality.[29] Rather than having the goal of disabling an enemy to prevent further engagement the new strategy was one of annihilation through complete destruction regardless.[30]

The concept of annihilation was, for the German High Command, present from the beginning of the War. By late 1914 the blockade, defeat in the Falklands and failure of the Schlieffen Plan quickly brought the concept into the mainstream. So much so that by the time of the bombardments this concept, once the preserve of the military, moved into popular culture, the media and intellectual life - literature[31], school text-books[32], newspapers (as we have seen), poetry[33], film[34],

---

[27] This argument is based on the work of authors such as Cohen, A. K. (1955). *Delinquent Boys: The Culture of the Gang*. New York: Free Press.

[28] This position is based on Cloward, R. A. and Ohlin, L. E. (1960). *Delinquency and Opportunity: A theory of delinquent gangs*. New York: Free Press.

[29] This is ironic given the status of Emmanuel Kant's work on morality in German culture.

[30] The strategy of pursuing a 'war of total annihilation' was developed by Alfred von Schlieffen between 1891 – 1905. The concept was based on another misunderstanding, a one Schlieffen seems to have of Clausewitz's statement of the purpose of war, being the "annihilation of the enemy armed forces always as the purpose that stood above all others pursued in war." Quoted in Howard, M.E. and Paret, P. (1984). *Carl Von Clausewitz on War*. Princeton: University of Princeton, pages 226-229. These claims are not uncontroversial, for the wider debate see, Winter, J. and Prost, A. (2005). *The Great War in History: Debates and controversies, 1914 to the present*. Cambridge: Cambridge University Press.

[31] For example, Hermann Bahr (1863-1934), Rudolf Borchardt (1877-1945), and Gerhart Hauptmann (1862-1946).

[32] See for example, Bendick, R. (1999). *Kriegserwartung und Kriegserfahrung. Der Erste Weltkrieg in deutschen und französischen Schulgeschichtsbüchern* [trans. *War expectancy and war experience. The First World War in German and French school history books*]1900-1939/45. Pfaffenweiler: Centaurus-

photographs[35], post-cards, cartoons[36] and paintings[37] were used to defend the individual acts of destruction regarded as autocracy by Allied and other nations.

Rather than focusing in on the goals of war, Germany seemed to have got caught up in regarding the means as ends in themselves. From 1914 notions about Germany being exceptional (*deutscher Sonderweg*) and its 'kulture' needing to be defended against Western capitalist individualism became widespread. Institutions in Germany propagated these goals (see footnotes 23 to 29 for example)[38] with messages about the need for national coherence and harmony, the need for Gemeinschaft (society based on community and comradeship) in place of Gesellschaft (impersonal society based on individualism).[39] The means needed for defending the German *Heimat* (home) and their *Sonderweg* (exceptionalism or special way of life) against Western societies based Gesellschaft capitalism was to direct all cultural and economic resources to the efficient and rational organisation of the necessities of war. With such powerful institutional backing the German military it could, it can be argued, do whatever it liked in the knowledge that those institutions would provide the necessary justification to legitimise their actions.

Verlagsgesellechaft; also see, Demm, E. (2002). 'Zwischen Propaganda und Sozialfürsorge – Deutschlands Kinder im Krieg', [trans. 'Between propaganda and social welfare - Germany's children in the war'] in: *Idem, Ostpolitik und Propaganda im Ersten Weltkrieg* [trans. *Eastern policy and propaganda during the first world war*]. Berne and Frankfurt: Lang, pages 71-131. Aslo in this volume, 'Agents of propaganda: German teachers at war', pages 61-70.

[33] For example, Bab, J. (1920). *Die deutsche Kriegslyrik 1914-1918* [trans. *German War Poetry*]. *Eine kritische Bibliographie* [*A critical bibliography*]. Stettin: Norddeutscher Verlag.

[34] For example, Erich Ludendorff (1865-1937).

[35] For example, Avenarius, F. (1915). *Das Bild als Verleumder. Bemerkungen zur Technik der Völkerverhetzung* [trans. *The image as a Slanderer. Remarks on the technique of incitement of the people*]. Munich: Georg D. W. Callwey; and Kessel, M. (2012). 'Talking War, debating unity: order, conflict, and Exclusion in 'German Humour' in the First World War', in, Kessel, M. and Merziger, P. (eds.), *The Politics of Humour. Laughter, inclusion, and exclusion in the Twentieth Century*, Toronto: Toronto University Press, pages 82-107.

[36] For example, Schwalbe, H-H. (1935). 'Die Grundlagen für die publizistische Bedeutung der Karikatur in Deutschland'. [trans. 'The basics of the journalistic importance of caricature in Germany']. (thesis), Berlin.

[37] For example, Max Slevogt (1868-1932) and Hugo Vogel (1855-1934).

[38] The *Zentralstelle für Auslandsdienst* (Central Office for Foreign Service) organised and coordinated activities and the *Kulturbund deutscher Gelehrter und Künstler* (Cultural Association of German Scholars and Artists) was established with the purpose to influence public opinion abroad.

[39] See, Tönnies, F. (1887). *Gemeinschaft und Gesellschaft*, Leipzig: Fues's Verlag. An English translation of the 8th edition 1935 by Charles P. Loomis appeared in 1940 as *Fundamental Concepts of Sociology (Gemeinschaft und Gesellschaft)*, New York: American Book Co.

Germany's problem with understanding morality

This suggestion that the German high command decided on a strategy to avenge the Falkland's defeat, to show contempt for the British Navy and arrogant jubilation at attacking soft targets, takes us to Kant and moral philosophy. Kant's work on vice is particularly relevant here.[40] A starting point for understanding Kant's scheme is with the following working definition of virtue - "a disposition or kind of character that makes rational but embodied agents do what they ought to do, because it is what they ought to do, even when it conflicts with their self-interests."[41]

By the notion of virtue Kant is referring to 'moral strength of the will', and 'a firmly grounded disposition to fulfill one's duty strictly'. This does not mean conforming habitually to the accepted behaviours of one's culture, for acting virtuously is doing, despite sometimes having feelings to the contrary, what is morally right, out of a commitment to and recognition of the essential morality of human kind. In Merton's paradigm (1938) of possible responses to a situation the institution (government, media, armed forces etc.,) may negate their will to act virtuously by habitually conforming to or retreating from the accepted institutional means and ends within the frame of reference. With habitual conformity there is a lack of a principled commitment to morality. Such a person or institution 'goes through the motions' and while appearing to be virtuous could, because they are not committed to the principle itself, be tempted to do the opposite. The 'banker', for example, may find acting virtuous a practical thing to do; to do otherwise would be imprudent, risking reputation and thereby the confidence of customers that is crucial to the success of their business. To be virtuous, however, the 'banker' would need to have a commitment to morality for the right reasons that genuinely have the best interest of their customers in mind. To do so 'the banker' would also need the strength of will to try an act virtuous, despite temptations and conflicts of interest.

---

[40] Kant's moral philosophy is complicated and no claim is being made here to fully represent the details and sophistication of his arguments and of successive interpretations of his work.
[41] von Platz, J. (2015). 'The Metaphysics of Vice: Kant and the Problem of Moral freedom', in, Munchnik, P. and Thorndike, O. (Eds.). *Rethinking Kant*. Volume 4. Newcastle: Cambridge Scholars Publishing, pages 157-183.

Figure 2.6 'Enlist Now' published early 1915

There are then, three elements to morally correct behaviours - understanding of what morality requires (moral understanding), the principled commitment to do it because it is what morality requires (a good will), and strength of will to do it (self-mastery). Each of these is a matter of degree and inevitably subject to counter-interests, and can create conflict with instincts and a struggle with the 'rabble element'.

This is because the ideal of virtue is an ideal; it can never be achieved. This is because behaviour is contextual, being contingent of a whole range of unique circumstances. Nonetheless, to act within what is possible accepting the ideal is not achievable, while committed to the principle is what being virtuous is about. To do otherwise is what Kant calls 'vice'; this is lacking understanding of what morality requires (moral understanding), and / or lacking the principled commitment to do it because it is what morality requires (a good will), and / or lacking the strength of will to do it (self-mastery). Behaviours that Kant classified as virtuous include, self-respect, honesty, thrift, self-improvement, beneficence, gratitude, sociability, and forgiveness. Behaviours Kant classified as vice include, malice, lust, gluttony, greed, laziness, vengefulness, envy, servility, contempt and arrogance.

Framed in this way, the loose interpretation of the Second Hague Conference of 1907, the contempt for the British, the vengefulness expressed for the Falkland's defeat, and arrogance in praising the risks faced by the German sailors are all measures of a moral problem with the German high command. The evidence for each of these vices is written in numerous German newspapers such as the *Hamburger Nachrichten* (17th December, 1914), the *Frankfurter Zeitung*, (31st December, 1914), *Berliner Tageblatt* (31st December, 1914), and the *Berlin Lokal Anzeiger*, (3rd January, 1915).

Conclusion

Some such as Witt and McDermott (2016) have concluded, with the power of hindsight, that the bombardments of Scarborough, Whitby and Hartlepool were not a "reckless or indiscriminate act of terror" (2016:163). There is an argument that can, to some degree, support this position. There are the technical issues that if taken into account show the German battle-group to have been unprepared for land bombardment. And if taken into account the damage and scale of death could be seen as accidentally indiscriminate. But this was the German Navy, the second largest and as professional as any other including the British. Another line of defence is that all three towns had military significance and were defended. Hartlepool certainly did have military significance with British naval vessels in the harbour, heavy industry and it was defended, but by old cannons. But the attack on Hartlepool did more damage to civilians and domestic properties than to the military resources. Plus, it has been argued the attacks were not about achieving the destruction of military resources; they were about revenge. Hence, the choice to bombard Scarborough and Whitby. Both towns were undefended even if an old map showed obsolete cannon in the ruins of Scarborough Castle. Up-to-date intelligence was available to the German High Command; they just did not use it. This was turned to an advantage in official communiques from the German commanders and repeated by German newspapers - that maps showed defences in Scarborough. Nothing of the kind was claimed for the small fishing village of Whitby.

Hence, taking into account rationalisations furnished by Germany in 1914 (and into 1915) and those at the beginning of the centenary of the attacks, and finding these wanting in substance, an alternative

Figure 2.7 'Men of Britain', published early 1915

explanatory framework was explored. Strategically the attacks made some sense; they may have shown the British what Germany was capable of and they may have enraged the British Navy, goading them to follow the attacking battle-group that would have taken them into a trap. The former is accurate but the latter did not happen. The result was outrage that led to more British men volunteering for Kitchener's Army and moral disgrace for a Germany already morally compromised. The posters that followed the attacks were clear - the attacks were a moral outrage. Posters declared, 'REMEMBER SCARBOROUGH', 'The Germans who brag of their 'CULTURE' have shown what it is made of by murdering defenceless women and children at SCARBOROUGH. Great Britons resolve to crush the GERMAN BARBARIANS'. The argument for this reaction has been sociological and philosophical. The sociology of Robert K. Merton's work on deviance was used to explain how the German Navy found itself in a situation that demanded it 'save face'; that it did so by turning to an extreme course of action. A position the Canadian newspaper, *The Independent* claimed was, 'not warfare, it is murder'. As the attacks had no measurable strategic goal, the argument is that they were, in effect, ends in themselves. In rejecting the conventional goals of warfare, the moral philosophy of Emanuel Kant was discussed. The relevance of Kant resides in that he gives us a framework with which to understand morality itself. And applying the principles laid down by Kant, the evaluation of the bombardments as behaviour, concluded it failed to meet any of them.

The poster, therefore, 'REMEMBER SCARBOROUGH!' has only four words and one picture but it embodies a set of principles regarding morality that, regrettably, human kind moved further away from as the 20th Century passed, and that movement had a watershed moment on the morning of the 16th December, 1914.

Chapter 3

Causing Unnecessary Anxiety? British Newspapers and the Battle of Jutland

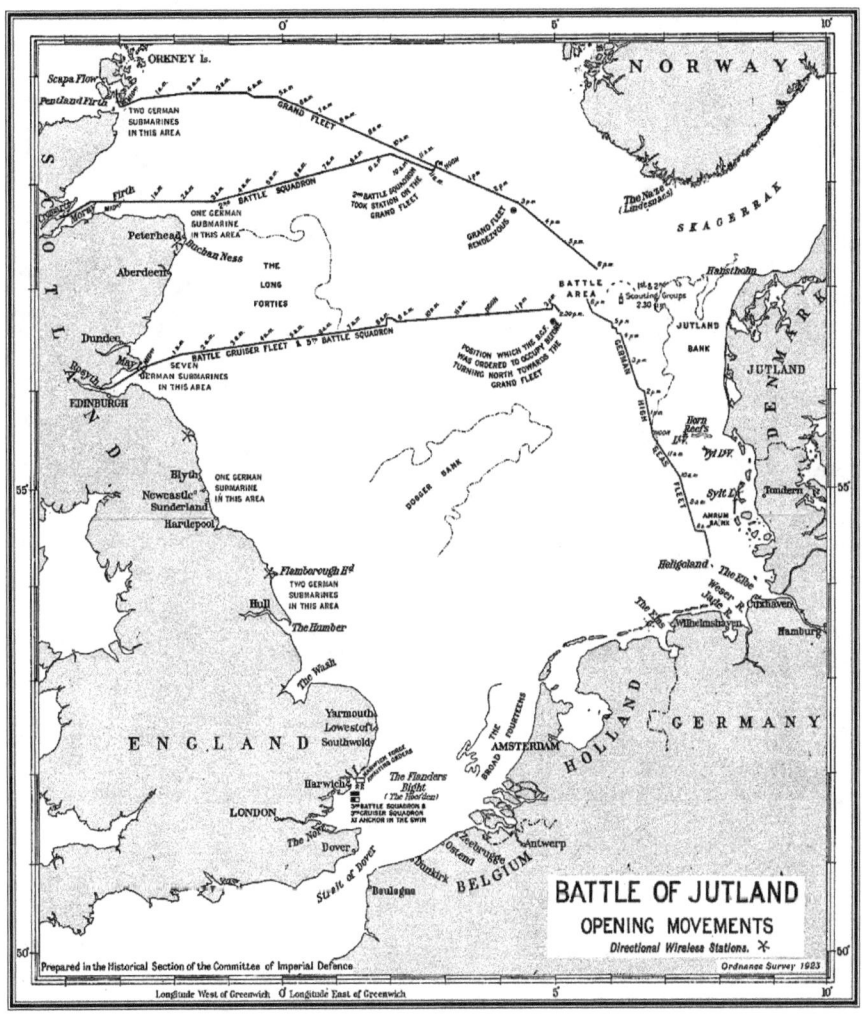

Chapter 3

Causing Unnecessary Anxiety? British Newspapers and the Battle of Jutland

Guy Hodgson
Liverpool John Moores University

Introduction

Jutland was the largest naval engagement of the First World War and, according to Mordal (1959), "the greatest naval battle ever fought." The scale of the action that took place approximately 60 miles off the coast of Denmark on May 31 and June 1, 1916, is underlined by the statistics: 151 Royal Navy vessels against 99 German; 96,000 men; 25 admirals; and 9,000 deaths. By comparison, at Trafalgar a century earlier, the decisive sea battle of the Napoleonic Wars, Nelson commanded 27 ships of the line against a 33-strong Franco-Spanish fleet.[1] Jutland, put simply, was the German High Fleet's attempt to break the British naval blockade by luring out part of the Grand Fleet and causing sufficient damage that the German mercantile shipping could operate. The statistics suggest a German success in that the Royal Navy lost 115,025 tons of ships against 61,180, and 6,097 British sailors were killed compared to 2,551 German sailors.[2] Within a matter of days, however, the Royal Navy's strength had been restored and the status quo had been re-established. As the *New York Times* put it: "The German Navy has assaulted its jailor, but is still in jail."[3]

The sheer size of the battle would have guaranteed Jutland historical debate, but, as Halpern (2012) noted, its inconclusive result has

---
[1] Thirteen smaller ships (six British) also took part in the battle.
[2] Mordal, J. (1959). *25 Centuries of Sea Warfare.* London: Abbey, page 265
[3] Kennedy, P. (2014). 'The War at Sea'. In Jay Winter (Ed.), *The Cambridge History of the First World War.* Vol. 1, Cambridge: Cambridge University Press, page 335.

provided an impetus for "endless discussion."[4] Much of it has focused on the British commander, John Jellicoe, who ordered the Grand Fleet to turn around and head for port when confronted by a rear guard of destroyers armed with torpedoes when a leader in the Nelson mould, according to critics, would have instinctively brushed them aside and pressed home the advantage to destroy the retreating German High Seas Fleet. Armchair strategists in the 1920s called for his court-martial, although others have been more supportive including Winston Churchill who argued that circumspection was appropriate as Jellicoe was the only man who could have lost the war in an afternoon.[5] More recently, Kennedy (2014)[6] defended the admiral on practical grounds:

> It is easy to be critical of Jellicoe's 'turn away' order but how exactly does an admiral command all his warships if they were no longer sailing in parallel lines at four knots and in fine weather… but steaming at 20 knots in the fogs of the North Sea, with cruiser squadrons scattered forward for reconnaissance, destroyers trying to keep up and a battered battle-cruiser squadron either advancing into trouble or returning?

While the debate about the battle has raged for a century, the consensus about the national press's role in the First World War has been consistent in its criticism. In 1928 Ponsonby (1928) was scathing when he asserted: "There was no more discreditable period in the history of journalism than the four years of the Great War",[7] and more recently Knightley (2004)[8] estimated that "more deliberate lies were told than in any other period of history." Both were commenting on the coverage of the Western Front where the industrial scale of the slaughter ensured that Britain embarked on a campaign of information suppression and manipulation.

Jutland was a sea battle, however, a theatre of the war in which Britain "ruled the waves." The Royal Navy was a part of the national

---

[4] Halpern, P. G. (2012). 'The War at Sea', in Horne, J. (Ed.), *A Companion to World War One* Chichester, West Sussex: Blackwell, page 48.
[5] Arthur, M. (2005). *Lost Voices of the Royal Navy* (3rd edn.). London: Hodder and Stoughton.
[6] *Op. cit.* Kennedy (2014), page 336.
[7] Ponsonby, A. (1928). *Falsehood in Wartime*. London: Allen and Unwin, page 134.
[8] Knightley, P. (2004). *The First Casualty: The war correspondent as hero and myth-maker from the Crimea to Iraq* (3rd edn.). London: Hopkins, page 84.

identity, a measure of Britain's position in the world. Gordon (1996) wrote:

> The Navy occupied a unique place in the national sentiment; ordinary people could recite the vital statistics of the latest battleships, children were dressed in sailor suits, posters of bearded Jack Tars sold cigarettes.[9]

A second Trafalgar was anticipated and this was reflected in the reporting, which differed significantly from the despatches from the trenches. This was partly due to the expectation, but also to other, practical, factors that will be discussed later. This chapter will explore whether the coverage was an anomaly in the press narrative, that instinctively responded to persuasion from the British government to manufacture support for the war or a continuation of the hegemonic imperative. Was it the messengers, the newspapers, that changed or the message? It will do so by examining three daily newspapers, two national and one regional: the *Daily Express*, the *Daily Mirror*, and the *Manchester Guardian*.

Methodology

The empirical part of the research is the newspapers that were chosen because they represent a range of political views, proprietors, and target audiences. The *Daily Mirror* was first published in 1903 and was originally written by women for women, but by 1916 the editorial team had been "defeminised" in the "slaughter of the guilty"[10] and the audience had become wider, being pitched at the middle and lower classes of both sexes. Launched by Alfred Harmsworth (the future Lord Northcliffe), the *Mirror* was sold for £100,000 to his brother, Harold (Lord Rothermere), in 1914 and, from a circulation of 630,000 in 1910.[11] Its readership increased substantially so that in July 1915 it declared an average daily sale of 1,053,000.[12] Politically, argues

---

[9] Gordon, A. (1996). *The Rules of the Game: Jutland and British Naval Command*. London: John Murray, page 250.
[10] Hagerty, B. (2003). *Read All About It: 100 Sensational Years of the Daily Mirror*. Lydney, Gloucestershire: Corpus, page 14.
[11] See, Butler, D. and Sloman, A. (Eds.). (1975). *British Political Facts 1900-1975* (5th edn). London: Macmillan.
[12] *Op. cit.* Hagerty, (2003).

Haggerty (2003), it initially aligned itself to the Labour Party but distanced itself as Rothermere - "politically naïve and ultra-conservative on social issues"[13] - took a greater interest in what appeared in its pages. The *Daily Express* was founded by Sir Arthur Pearson in 1900, but by Jutland was surviving on loans, including from Max Aitken (Lord Beaverbrook), a Canadian-born MP who purchased the newspaper outright in November 1916.[14] It had a circulation of 400,000 (Butler and Sloman, 1975) and, politically, thanks to Aitken, was aligned with the Conservatives and Unionists. The proprietor and editor of the *Manchester Guardian*, C. P. Scott, also had connections in Parliament where he had been a Liberal MP between 1895 and 1906. Consequently, he carried influence in the ruling governments from 1906 to 1922 even though the *Guardian* was based in northwest England and had a circulation of only 40,000.[15]

This is a qualitative study underpinned by the methodology outlined by Richardson (2007)[16], by which newspaper reports and headlines are evaluated in the knowledge they can carry value judgements as well as dictionary meaning. The research comprises a study of the newspapers from 3rd June, 1916, the first day in which news of the battle appeared, to 16th June, two weeks later. All significant reports were studied, in conjunction with editorials, readers' letters and advertisements, totalling more than 150 extracts. The findings are divided into two parts, the first concentrating on the coverage in the first two editions, Saturday 3rd June and Monday 5th June, 1916, when the reporting waivered between describing a defeat or victory, and the second on subsequent reports which accommodated a period long enough to allow for more measured journalistic reflection.

Censorship and Propaganda

The First World War from the start was, according to Finn (2010),[17] a "media event", and the British government's approach to newspaper coverage of the First World War was typified by the cutting of the direct

---

[13] *Ibid.* Page 27.

[14] A condition attached to Aitken's loans was that reports about his Parliamentary work should appear in the *Daily Express*. See, Taylor, A. J. P. (1972). *Beaverbrook*. London: Simon and Schuster.

[15] *Op. cit.* Butler and Sloman, (1975).

[16] Richardson, J. E. (2007). *Analysing Newspapers*. Basingstoke: Palgrave.

[17] Finn, M. (2010). 'Local Heroes: War News and the Construction of 'Community' in Britain, 1914-18'. *Historical Research*, 83(221), pages 520-538. Page 520.

subterranean cables between Germany and the United States within hours of the declaration of hostilities.[18] Transatlantic communication was restricted, and so was the traffic of information between the armed forces and the public via the national press. Successful mass mobilisation required social consensus and political leaders were, argues Carruthers (2011), convinced that "esprit would shatter if people perceived the brutal realities of trench warfare too vividly" and, as a consequence, no casualty figures were issued until 19th May, 1915. Even after that date, official lists were circulated only on a "for private information of editors" basis.[19]

This was a reflection of the influence of the popular press that had grown significantly at the start of the century. Hopkin (1970)[20] noted that the new press had created a new readership that was "more impressionable" than the traditional newspaper public and the authorities quickly realised that, to sustain morale, the press had to be controlled. 'D' notices, official requests not to publish material that could endanger national security, defined what could be printed and an official Press Bureau was established in August 1914 with two main functions: to control the supply of information from the War Office and the Admiralty; and to monitor every cable and telegram going to and from newspaper offices. National newspapers, the *Manchester Guardian* included, adopted an approach to news from the Western Front summed up by Lloyd George's much-quoted quip to C. P. Scott:

> If people really knew, the war would be stopped tomorrow. But of course, they don't know and can't know. The correspondents don't write and the censorship would not pass the truth.[21]

As the quote implies, the censorship restricted the flow of news, but would have been unworkable without the co-operation of newspaper proprietors and editors and as early as July 27th, 1914, a week before the outbreak of war, the major national newspapers had agreed, according to Hopkin (1970), not to publish details of military dispositions. Even as

---

[18] See, Taylor, P. M. (2003). *Munitions of the Mind: A history of propaganda from the Ancient World to the Present Day* (3rd ed.). Manchester: Manchester University Press.
[19] See, Carruthers, S. L. (2011). *The Media at War* (2nd edn.). Basingstoke, Hampshire: Palgrave Macmillan, page 46.
[20] See, Hopkin, D. (1970). 'Domestic Censorship in the First World War'. *Journal of Contemporary History*, 5(4), pages 151-169. Page 152.
[21] *Op. cit.* Knightley, (2004), page 116.

late as August 7th, 1914, three days after the declaration of war, Scott, the editor of the *Manchester Guardian*, was expressing his opposition to the war to a local trades council, but added "we have no choice but to do the utmost we can to assure success."[22] Patriotism is a default position for the press in times of war, but news management was also provided by, according to Marquis (1978),[23] a "tight-knit group of 'press lords' who (over lunch or dinner with Lloyd George) decided what was 'good for the country to know'." Why were journalists suppressing news?

> The obvious answer is that they all belonged to the same club, whose membership also included the most powerful politicians. Publishing a casualty list (or a letter from a wounded corporal about military bungling) would have meant expulsion from the club; social ostracism apparently meant more to the newsmen than their professional duty to inform the public.[24]

Allied to the censorship was propaganda designed to bolster the war effort. The British form focused on demonizing the enemy, an objective hugely advanced by the German invasion of Belgium and the fact that much of the war was fought on Belgian soil. Taylor (2003) argued that no matter how much the Germans attempted to justify their actions, "Poor Little Belgium" remained a "rallying cry for their enemies throughout the war."[25] Tales of barbarity became commonplace - less than four weeks after Britain declared war, *The Times* ("Atrocities in Belgium", 28th August 1914, p:7) reported that a witness saw "German soldiery chop off the arms of a baby which clung to its mother's skirts" - and Demm (1993) wrote that the German soldier was depicted as a murderer who regularly committed acts of wickedness. It was, according to Taylor, a lasting impression:

> Images of the bloated 'Prussian Ogre'... the 'Beastly Hun' with his sabre belt surrounding his enormous girth, busily crucifying soldiers, violating women, mutilating babies, desecrating and looting

---

[22] Wilson, T. (Ed.). (1970). *The Political Diaries of C. P. Scott 1911-1928*. London: Collins, pages 99-100.
[23] Marquis, A. G. (1978). 'Words as Weapons: Propaganda in Britain and Germany during the First World War'. *Journal of Contemporary History*, 13(3), pages 467-498. Page 476.
[24] *Ibid*. Page 478.
[25] *Op. cit.* Taylor (2003), page 176.

churches, are deeply implanted in the twentieth century's gallery of popular images.[26]

For the war at sea, there was little need for propaganda - the British public had been demanding more Dreadnought-class battleships for a decade - but censorship ensured that newspapers demurred from reporting important losses.[27] This included the sinking of the battleship *Audacious* in 1914, which hit a mine off the coast of Ireland in October 1914 but was included in Royal Navy lists until the end of the war.[28] Only on 14th November 1918 did *The Times* report the loss ('HMS Audacious', p:7), adding: "This was kept secret at the urgent request of the Commander-in-Chief, Grand Fleet, and the press loyally refrained from giving it any publicity." The Battle of Jutland occurred in a news vacuum and the only civilians who were aware of it were the Prime Minister, Herbert Asquith, and the Foreign Secretary, Sir Edward Grey, who "happened to call. "[29] No information was issued because, as the First Lord of the Admiralty Arthur Balfour told George Riddell, the chairman of the *News of the World*, it "would have occasioned unnecessary anxiety."[30]

The news blackout ensured that the Admiralty did not issue a communiqué until 7pm on 2nd June and it did so, in part, because it had no choice. Damaged ships were returning to east coast ports and wounded men were filling hospitals, so evidence of a battle was overwhelming. There was also a need to respond to German reports claiming victory earlier in the day. The German fleet had a shorter distance to travel and this, according to Steel and Hart (2003)[31] gave them an advantage in the "war of words that was to follow." They applauded a great triumph and, in terms of ships lost, were fully justified in doing so, while the Admiralty had to face selling a strategic success to a public for whom only the complete destruction of the German fleet would have been acceptable. As Steel and Hart (2003)[32] noted: "They

---

[26] Demm, E. (1993). 'Propaganda and Caricature in the First World War'. *Journal of Contemporary History*, 28(1), pages 163-192. Page 180.
[27] The popular demand was "We want eight, and we won't wait." See, Brooks, J. (2005). *Dreadnought Gunnery and the Battle of Jutland*. Abingdon: Routledge, page 2.
[28] See, Haste, C. (1977). *Keep the Home Fires Burning: Propaganda in the First World War*. London: Penguin.
[29] *Op. cit.* Marquis, (1978), page 478.
[30] McEwen, J. M. (Ed.). (1986). *The Riddell Diaries 1908-1923*. London: Athlone, page 158.
[31] Steel, N. and Hart, P. (2003). *Jutland 1916: Death in the Grey Wastes*. London: Cassell, page 417.
[32] *Ibid.* Page 418.

simply expected the Germans to be soundly thrashed. In the harsh light of this view what actually happened... fell far short of expectations." Balfour, the naval censor Sir Douglas Brownrigg and others crafted a "brief but completely truthful" press communiqué that admitted to heavy British losses even though, as the latter later admitted, it would be a "frightful staggerer."[33]

The First Reports: "Unsatisfactory for Us"

Because of the Admiralty's delay, the first news of the Jutland did not appear until 3rd June and the newspapers, usually dealing with heavily censored dispatches from the Western Front, had a rare freedom, to be frank. The front page of the *Daily Express*, for example, carried a sub-head under the main headline ("Fleets meet in the North Sea in a gigantic battle") that stated "Heavy British losses - three battle-cruisers sunk" and a smaller report analysing the losses to the Royal Navy was remarkably close to what is now accepted as the accurate statistics: "108,000 tons and over 5,000 men." The frontpage headlines also listed the destroyed British ships including the battle-cruisers *Queen Mary*, *Indefatigable* and *Invincible*. There were no attempts to demonize the enemy; on the contrary the lead story was even-handed in that it comprised the simple repetition of the statements from the Admiralty and the German Navy. The only propaganda was contained in a single column story to the right of the lead that reported the Germans had 'claimed' a success. The report, from Amsterdam, included:

> The German Admiralty staff's communiqué naturally excited the most intense interest in Holland, but people, knowing by innumerable experiences the untrustworthy character of German news, awaited for the British Admiralty communiqué all day. ('Mafficking in Germany', p:1).

The *Manchester Guardian* also carried the enemy statement in full under the headline 'German story of success' (3rd June, p:7) and reported the lost British ships, the word "story" suggesting the possibility of exaggeration and fabrication. It differed from the *Express* in that it

---

[33] Messinger G. S. (1995). *British Propaganda and the State in the First World War*. Manchester: Manchester University Press, page 116.

offered analysis. The Germans, its lead story read, "say they sank the British super-Dreadnought *Warspite*... and omit the *Invincible* from their list. Beyond doubt they are wrong; possibly they innocently mistook one vessel for another" ('Great battle in North Sea', p:7).

The word "innocently" was surprising given that the British press

Figure 3.1 Six of the main battle-ships lost listed in 3rd June *The Daily Mirror*

had been drawing up a list of German crimes, including the alleged bayoneting of babies, since the start of the war.[34] The tone, too, lacked the normal condemnation, the claims about the *Warspite* (which was hit 13 times by shells) being attributed to error rather than malice. On page 6 there was the more familiar theme of understated bravery in the "Our London Correspondence" column that reported: "He would have been a very superficial observer who did not see in every man he met on that great fleet the same quiet readiness and resolution." The report went on to diminish the Royal Navy's losses, describing the *Queen Mary* as "far from our last word in guns and in speed" even though it acknowledged she had been "the show ship of 1914-15." On page 8, however, a column headlined 'A week of the war' conceded the Jutland "result was unsatisfactory for us."

---

[34] See, Kinghtley, (2004).

The *Daily Mirror*'s headlines on 3rd June, like that of the *Express*, listed the Royal Navy's losses but went further in claiming German casualties. "2 German Dreadnoughts sunk" one sub-head claimed, and another announced that three enemy battleships had been "hit repeatedly" ('Greatest naval battle in history in North Sea', p:3). The doubling of the *Express*'s one German battleship could have been due to edition times because the *Mirror* included a 1am communiqué from Jellicoe that reported that one Dreadnought had been "blown up in an attack by British destroyers" and another was believed to have been "sunk by gunfire" ('Admiral Sir John Jellicoe's estimate', p:3). Both claims, it transpired, were wrong as the High Seas Fleet lost the battle-cruiser *Lutzow* and the pre-Dreadnought battleship *Pommern*, but no Dreadnoughts. Lower down on the front page, in a story headlined "Foe admiral's version of the battle" there was a report of a speech in the Reichstag that stated: "Our young navy has gained a great and splendid success." "Foe" and "version" were words imbued with subjectivity.

Those words might have been weighted but it mattered little because the coverage overall read like a defeat to a British public used to a diet of successes. Lloyd George summed up the norm when he told Riddell in September 1916: "The public knows only half the story. They read of victories; the cost is concealed",[35] and as a consequence the stark news that three battle-cruisers and at least eight other vessels being sunk was greeted with dismay in Britain. Steel and Hart (2003)[36] wrote of "stunned and horrified disbelief" and that some naval personnel suffered verbal abuse from "wilder spirits." Gordon (1996)[37] wrote that the crew of HMS Malaya received a "mixed reception" from dockworkers at Invergordon. Arnold Ridley, the playwright and actor best remembered for his part of Godfrey in *Dad's Army*, was in Devonport recovering from a shrapnel wound received while serving near Arras.[38] He noted:

> Not only did the first reports suggest a major defeat, but also most of the sunken ships were Devonport commissioned. Union Street seemed full of women - some hysterical, some crying quietly and

---

[35] *Op. cit.* McEwen, (1986), page 168.
[36] *Op. cit.* Steel and Hart (2003), page 421.
[37] *Op. cit.* Gordon (1996), page 499.
[38] *Dad's Army*, a television programme about the British Home Guard in the Second World War, was broadcast on the BBC from 1968 to 1977.

others, grey-faced with staring unseeing eyes and leading small children by the hand. They had no illusions, these women - they knew only too well that, when large ships were sunk in battle in the North Sea, there could be but few survivors.[39]

The Royal Navy was furious that the Admiralty had made no attempt to explain the strategic significance of the battle.[40] The government, too, felt that reports had been too gloomy and Balfour persuaded Winston Churchill, who was "sulking in 'retirement'," to write a "semi-official précis… based on official documents" that was released at 7pm on 3rd June.[41]

This and a further statement on 4th June boosted German losses and marked a change in mood in Fleet Street. The *Daily Express*'s front page of Monday, 5th June, included a headline "We won the action" by Lord Beresford, a former MP and admiral, in which he accused the press of "pessimistic views" about the battle, although a sub-editor had added in brackets "not in the *Daily Express*". To underline the point, the next sentence - "There is no justification for them." - was set in bold. The lead story was also heavily influenced by the propaganda message, the headline reading "18 German warships (compared to 14 British) lost in great battle. " The copy, too, was more condemnatory.

> That the accounts they have given to the world are false is certain… The Admiralty entertain no doubt that the German losses are heavier than the British - not merely relative to the strength of the two fleets, but absolutely.

Alongside the lead, another story ('We know better', p:1) stated that the German sailors also discounted the alleged triumph. "When the men were shown yesterday's mad 'victory' reports from Berlin they smiled and said, 'Unfortunately, we know better'." At the top of the page, a headline claimed: "The *Hindenburg*, Germany's greatest warship, lost." The *Hindenburg* was not at Jutland. On page 4 an editorial headlined 'Victors do not run away' stated: "Our allies and neutral nations agreed in ridiculing the German boast that their fleet has, in any sense of the word, defeated the British."

---

[39] Van Emden, R. and Piuk, R. (2014). *Famous 1914-1918*. Barnsley: Pen and Sword, page 61.
[40] *Op. cit.* Gordon, (1996), page 498.
[41] *Op. cit.* Marquis, (1978), page 478.

Readers of the *Daily Mirror* on 5th June, 1916, had to go inside the newspaper to discover more optimistic news about Jutland. Page one was devoted entirely to photographs under the headline 'Women who mourn and the men who have died', the largest picture being reserved for Grace Clark, who had been due to marry a naval chaplain that day, but on page 3, it announced that enemy losses had exceeded those of the Royal Navy, claiming that the Germans had lost at least 18 ships ('German losses are heavier than the British'). The story began: "Officers who landed at an East Coast town... were astounded to find that the public thought the British Navy had suffered defeat." The *Mirror* also carried an interview on page 2 with Lord Beresford under the headline "I declare it a British victory", but an editorial on page 5 ('Questions') suggested the newspaper had not been persuaded entirely:

> The third question that many bereaved but brave people asked was in the nature of a supplication, a hope, that the Admiralty will refrain from excuses, and official people from the absurdity of trying to pretend that we have won a big victory in disguise.

The *Manchester Guardian* also reflected the confusion in its 'Our London Correspondence' editorial column on 5th June (p:4). "The more we learn about the great sea battle," it read, "the more people are puzzled and even indignant about the first official report on the subject." It added: "The navy - and it is not given to boasting – considers that it has won what victory there was in this admittedly indecisive action." The lead story on page 5, the main news page, was more forthright in claiming victory, its headlines stating 'German losses the heavier.' This was inaccurate, although it reflected the Admiralty's exaggerated estimates, but the *Guardian* cast doubts on the German reports rather than the British, a sub-head reporting "Berlin reports known certainly to be untrue." Under another headline on page 5, 'Story of the battle', it was stated the men who had fought in the battle were sure that "the enemy received a most salutary lesson before they slunk away into their haven of refuge." 'Slunk' was chosen to denigrate the enemy and could be compared to the report from Edinburgh that described the Royal Navy's return to port in glowing terms. "I watched the mighty ships pass out; I watched the victorious ships one by one come home. I emphasise the word victorious" ('How the fleet sailed and came back', p:5).

Kitchener Lost, the Battle 'Won'

The ephemeral nature of news was underlined in the editions of 7th June when Jutland, four days after first entering the national consciousness, was supplanted as the lead story. Lord Kitchener, the Secretary of State for War, had been killed, going down with 600 others when the cruiser *Hampshire* struck a German mine close to the Orkneys. The death of the field marshal the *Daily Express* described as "The man who prepared the way for victory" (7th June, 1916, p:1) dominated the news agenda, and the focus of the coverage of the North Sea battle moved away from the outcome and on to a debate over how the initial Admiralty reports had been so downbeat. According to Steel and Hart (2003), it was the German confession that they had concealed the loss of the battle-cruiser *Lutzow* and the light cruiser *Rostock* that eradicated any doubts that Jutland had been a qualified British success. This allowed the newspapers licence for anti-German rhetoric and to conduct a debate about the merits of the initial dispatch from the Admiralty.

All the newspapers asserted the Germans had distorted the facts about Jutland, the *Daily Express* almost on a daily basis. Thus on 7th June there were headlines 'Nailing down the German Lies' and 'More fabrications' (p:1), and a report stated: "Germany's glib stories of victory in the naval battle are now disbelieved by the whole world"; on 9th June headlines read 'Tearing the truth out of Germany' and 'Admission of Falsehood by German's naval staff' (p:1); on June 12 'Covering up the facts' and 'German efforts to hide the naval losses' (p:5); and on 16th June 'Still unable to tell the truth' (p:5). The *Daily Mirror* carried an editorial on 9th June ('Their way and ours', p:5) that compared the communiqués from the Admiralty and the German Navy, an exercise in linguistic criticism that also allowed the paper to excuse its own initial, pessimistic, reports. "British way - to claim defeat and then find victory," it read. "German way - to claim victory, then find defeat." The leader also asserted: "If you are a British official you let your public frankly - and rightly - know about losses sustained", which was disingenuous given that the newspaper was aware that the number of casualties on the Western Front was being withheld by the War Office. The editorial was part of a campaign to undermine the authenticity of reports coming from Germany and was underlined by a cartoon on 15th June (p:5) that had a caricature of the Kaiser. "There's only one thing that troubles me," he says. "That is, that if we have many more great naval victories, I shan't have any navy left!" The following day, 16th

June, one *Mirror* headline read "Hun lie factory's finest output" (p:2), a phrase that used the derogatory term Hun that became a feature of British newspapers between 1914 and 1918 while implying that there was a industrial-scale conveyor belt of disinformation emanating from Berlin. The *Manchester Guardian*'s disparaging of German news releases was less strident than that of the *Mirror* and the *Express*, but was there, nevertheless, in the headlines "Enemy's false claims" (7th June, p:5) and "Why false news was spread" ("Not a victory", 10th June, p:7), all of which were a departure from the "innocent" mistakes they reported initially.

The anti-German narrative coincided with analysis of Admiralty's first communiqué, and none was complimentary. An editorial in *Daily Express*, under the headline 'That message!' (8th June, 1916, p:4), read: "If ever an official dispatch was calculated to cause the gravest misgivings in the public mind it was this communication." It was a theme touched upon by a reader's letter on 9th June, from H. C. F., ('Mr. Balfour's excuses', p:5) that stated:

> The Admiralty had only to phrase their announcement more correctly, while utilising precisely the same information, to have avoided the unpleasant and unsatisfactory incident which marked the return of our victorious seamen to their home.

The letter would have had to pass editorial gatekeepers (if, indeed, it was a genuine letter from the public and not a journalist in disguise), and was likely to conform with the newspaper's view, a notion that was confirmed the following day when the *Express* printed what it believed should have been announced on 2nd June. It read:

> A great naval action was fought in the North Sea on Wednesday the 31st. Though only a portion of our Fleet was engaged by the whole, or almost the whole, of the German High Sea Fleet, we defeated the Germans and sent them back to their ports in confusion. Their losses were exceedingly heavy ('How to tell the news', 10th June, p:5).

The *Manchester Guardian* ('The test of naval success', 8th June, p:5 reported a speech by Balfour in which the First Lord of the Admiralty agreed first newspaper reports about Jutland had struck a "tragic note." He added: "If my candour, if my desire immediately to let the public know the best and the worst was in any way responsible for that result, I can only express my regret." An accompanying editorial ('The naval battle', p:4) carried a censure: "We are not quite satisfied with the statement." The *Daily Mirror* also reported Balfour's speech under the headline 'The 'whole truth' of naval fight' (8th June, 1916, p:2) The report noted: "Totally erroneous inferences were built on the first message, and those papers who jumped at conclusions should have a little passing prick of conscience." What could have followed, and did not, was "including the *Daily Mirror.*"

The condemnation of the Admiralty's first communiqué had an element of self-interest as newspapers needed to explain why their reports had been misleading, but perspective was available during the study period, albeit in another newspaper, the *Observer* "There is too much of the 'frantic boast and foolish word' going about," a comment piece ('The sea-battle and its lessons', 11th June, p:8) read. It continued:

> Especially cheap is the taunt that the Germans ran away from the Grand Fleet. They were not out for suicide… When that day comes it is not likely that the German Navy will shrink from any sacrifice and we have learned enough from this battle to make sure that we will find German sailors tough and skillful foemen.

This thoughtful critique differed strikingly from the heavily censored propaganda coming from the land war.

Conclusion

In his otherwise excellent book about Jutland, Gordon (1996) was scathing about the press, ascribing the Royal Navy's "pathological mistrust of the media"[42] to the coverage of battle. He also wrote of the "mendacious constructions of journalists."[43] This conforms to the historical judgement of the national press in the First World War, a verdict summed up by Knightley (2004) who described the conflict as a "disaster for journalism."[44] This chapter has tried to challenge this orthodoxy, at least in terms of the reporting of the Battle of Jutland, while acknowledging the motivations behind that coverage conformed to the template set on the Western Front. This research has shown that

---

[42] *Op. cit.* Gordon, (1996), pages 498-9.
[43] *Ibid.* Page 505.
[44] *Op. cit.* Knightley, (2004), page 532.

the reports of the battle did not subscribe to the normal propaganda model. Instead, there was no attempt to diminish British losses - the casualty figures were extraordinarily accurate on 3rd June, 1916, given that the Grand Fleet had not reached port by print deadlines - and the painting of the Germans as ogres in uniform was watered down to accusations of vainglory and distortion. Even that had a sub-motive because the press had reasons to explain why its original reports were being challenged.

This is not to assert that the press coverage of Jutland marked a new zeal by newspapers to the cause of independent reporting. Rather it was a breakdown in the propaganda machine. The Admiralty, unable to easily hide its losses as its ships returned to port, simply told the truth and, in a war where obfuscation was the norm, the bare un-spun facts were taken as a major reverse. This was acknowledged by Gordon (1996) who wrote that the Admiralty's initial statement on Jutland, was "strictly honest about British losses" and "would make things worse. "[45] The Admiralty, too, acknowledged its public relations shortcomings by creating a Naval Publicity Department a month after the battle in an attempt to "avoid the sort of presentational mistakes which had been made in dealings with the press after Jutland."[46] The Navy made no attempt to put a gloss on the battle, admitted its losses and Fleet Street, just as it did on the Western Front, reported what it was given. It was business as usual.

For once, to paraphrase Lloyd George, the people really knew thanks to national newspapers and, although Finn (2010), Bourke (1999)[47] and Schneider (1997)[48] have asserted that local newspapers, soldiers' letters and Red Cross dispatches ensured that the British public were not wholly ignorant of conditions on the Western Front, this was exceptional. Yet, the same chain of news supply after Jutland operated a month later when correspondents reported the Somme, it was the reaction of generals, the War Office and the information being emitted from them that differed, and with it the reports that appeared in Britain's newspapers. As a consequence, the death of 400,000 British

---

[45] *Op. cit.* Gordon, (1996), page 498.
[46] Rudyard Kipling and John Buchan, the author of *The Thirty-Nine Steps*, were considered as consultants for the new department before Julian Corbett (a historian at the Naval War College) and Filson Young, a journalist, were employed. See, Gordon, (1996), page 507.
[47] Bourke, J. (1999). *An Intimate History of Killing: Face-to-face killing in Twentieth-Century Warfare.* London: Granta.
[48] Schneider, E. F. (1997). 'The British Red Cross Wounded and Missing Enquiry Bureau: A Case of Truth-Telling in the Great War'. *War in History*, 4(3), pages 296-315.

and Empire soldiers in a 141-day battle that began on 1st July, 1916, was hidden by reports of heroic advances and territorial gains to the extent that even on 15th November the *Manchester Guardian* printed the headline proclaiming 'The British Victory'. It was not alone and the effect of this distortion, once the full scale of the military disaster became known, damaged the reputation of British journalism. This chapter has shown that the reporting of Jutland can largely be exempted from that historical verdict.

Nevertheless, the coverage of the battle had effects beyond fuelling the subsequent historical debate. Surprisingly, given its scale and importance, the battle was not debated in Parliament until 22nd June, 1916, when, during a short exchange a Conservative MP, Ronald McNeill called for the suspension of the *Daily News* and condemned newspapers generally. The Home Secretary Herbert Samuel, dismissing the call for suppression, replied: "I am afraid a great many people when they received the first news of the battle took a somewhat depressed view of the facts."[49] This partly exonerated the press, but nevertheless was a harbinger of more serious threats to press freedom in the Second World War. There was also a hint of criticism of the Admiralty as the suppliers of the first news, but in the long term it benefitted from its honesty. Brownrigg, the naval censor, wrote:

> Whatever the rights or wrongs of the first Admiralty communiqué… our reputation for telling the truth was re-established, and from that time onward, I believe it is fair to say that what appeared in our communiqués was accepted as fact.[50]

The most enduring consequence of the Admiralty's frankness, however, is that it played a part in placing the dead of Jutland in the litany of First World War memories. More than 6,000 British sailors died in the North Sea and, while that was overshadowed by the 19,240 killed at the Somme on 1st July, 1916,[51] it was still a disaster in human terms to compare with the darker days of the Western Front. Yet, stripped of the censorship and propaganda that hid the horrors of the trenches, and because strategic victories lack the poignancy of

---

[49] *Hansard*, HC Deb, Vol 83, cc. 302-3, June 22, 1916.
[50] *Op. cit.* Messinger, (1995), page 116.
[51] *Op. cit.* Carruthers, (2011).

catastrophic military miscalculation, Jutland's casualties have receded in the ranks of commemoration. Steel and Hart (2003) wrote:

> The Somme and Passchendaele still weave their grim fascination, but, while the deaths of the men in the 'Pals Regiments' are morbidly 'celebrated', the sacrifice of the hapless crews of the *Indefatigable*, the *Queen Mary*, the *Invincible*, the *Defence*, the *Black Prince*, the *Shark*, the *Ardent* and the *Broke*… are commemorated mainly by a few dramatic photographs that linger round the edges of folk memory.[52]

On 15th June, 1916, the *Manchester Guardian* printed a report on a memorial service to the servicemen killed at Jutland in which the Bishop of Liverpool said they would be 'forever immortal' ('Liverpool's memorial service to sailors', p:6). He was a right, but only to a degree.

References to sources

Anon. (1916). 'Fleets meet in the North Sea in a gigantic battle', *Daily Express*, June 3, page 1.
Anon. (1916). 'Mafficking in Germany', *Daily Express*, June 3, page 1.
Anon. (1916). 'We won the action', *Daily Express*, June 5, page 1.
Anon. (1916). '18 German warships (compared to 14 British) lost in great battle', *Daily Express*, June 5, page 1.
Anon. (1916). 'We know better', *Daily Express*, June 5, page 1.
Anon. (1916). 'The *Hindenburg*, Germany's greatest warship, lost', June 5, page 1.
Anon. (1916). 'Victors do not run away', *Daily Express*, June 5, page 4.
Anon. (1916). 'K. of K., the man who prepared the way for victory', *Daily Express*, June 7, page 1.
Anon. (1916). 'Nailing down the German Lies', *Daily Express*, June 7, page 1.
Anon. (1916). 'That message!', *Daily Express*, June 8, page 4.
Anon. (1916). 'Admission of Falsehood by German's naval staff', *Daily Express*, June 9, page 1.
Anon. (1916). 'Mr. Balfour's excuses', *Daily Express*, June 9, page 5.
Anon. (1916). 'How to tell the news', *Daily Express*, June 10, page 5.
Anon. (1916). 'Covering up the facts', *Daily Express*, June 12, page 5.

---

[52] *Op. cit.* Steel and Hart, (2003), page 7.

Anon. (1916). 'Still unable to tell the truth', *Daily Express*, June 16, page 5.
Anon. (1916). 'Greatest naval battle in history in North Sea', *Daily Mirror*, June 3, page 3.
Anon. (1916). 'Admiral Sir John Jellicoe's estimate', *Daily Mirror*, June 3, page 3.
Anon. (1916). 'Foe admiral's version of the battle', *Daily Mirror*, June 3, page 3.
Anon. (1916). 'Women who mourn and the men who have died', *Daily Mirror*, June 5, page 1.
Anon. (1916). 'I declare it a British victory', *Daily Mirror*, June 5, page 2.
Anon. (1916). 'German losses are heavier than the British', *Daily Mirror*, June 5, page 3.
Anon. (1916). 'Questions', *Daily Mirror*, June 5, page 5.
Anon. (1916). 'The 'whole truth' of naval fight', *Daily Mirror*, June 8, page 2.
Anon. (1916). 'Their way and ours', *Daily Mirror*, June 9, page 5.
Anon. (1916). 'Hun lie factory's finest output', *Daily Mirror*, June 16, page 2.
Anon. (1916). 'Our London Correspondence', *Manchester Guardian*, June 3, page 6.
Anon. (1916). 'German story of success', *Manchester Guardian*, June 3, page 7.
Anon. (1916). 'Great battle in North Sea', *Manchester Guardian*, June 3, page 7.
Anon. (1916). 'A week of the war', *Manchester Guardian*, June 3, page 8.
Anon. (1916). 'Our London Correspondence', *Manchester Guardian*, June 5, page 4.
Anon. (1916). 'German losses the heavier', *Manchester Guardian*, June 5, page 5.
Anon. (1916). 'Story of the battle', *Manchester Guardian*, June 5, page 5.
Anon. (1916). 'How the fleet sailed and came back', *Manchester Guardian*, June 5, page 5.
Anon. (1916). 'Enemy's false claims', *Manchester Guardian*, June 7, page 5.
Anon. (1916). 'The naval battle', *Manchester Guardian*, June 8, page 4.
Anon. (1916). 'The test of naval success', *Manchester Guardian*, June 8, page 5.
Anon. (1916). 'Not a victory', *Manchester Guardian*, June 10, page 7.
Anon. (1916). 'Liverpool's memorial service to sailors', *Manchester Guardian*, June 15, page 6.

Anon. (1916). 'The British victory', *Manchester Guardian*, November 15, page 6.
Anon. (1916). 'The sea-battle and its lessons', *Observer*, June 11, page 8.
Anon. (1914). 'Atrocities in Belgium', *The Times*, August 28, page 7.
Anon. (1918). 'HMS Audacious', *The Times*, November 14, page 7.
Arthur, M. (2005). *Lost Voices of the Royal Navy*. (3rd edn.). London: Hodder and Stoughton.

Chapter 4

Listening to 'Concert of Europe' Pioneering Radio Amateurs During World War I

Maria Rikitianskaia
Università della Svizzera, Italiana

Introduction

World War I is frequently claimed to be the turning point in radio development that provoked the boom of professional radio broadcasting and amateur radio. The aim of this chapter is to argue against this assumption and show that radio amateurs existed in Europe before and throughout the war, and played an important role in radio development. The history of amateur radio, in general, is often written from the 1920s and the antecedent period is widely understood as only pre-history. This chapter's goal is to show that this pre-history, taken from the transnational point of view, shows significant trends in European radio development.

This chapter aims to revise the literature about European radio amateurs, using a transnational approach identified by media scholars as relevant because radio transcends national borders and often exceeds national frameworks. The concept of radio as an instrument of constructing national identity often obscures the transnational nature of radio propagation.[1] Enlarging the focus from national history to a bigger European picture, highlighting trends and similarities in the different national contexts. Moreover, World War I also represents an event of transnational nature, where phenomena transcended national

---

[1] Badenoch, A., Fickers, A., and Henrich-Franke, C. (2013). 'Airy Curtains in the European Ether: Introduction', in Badenoch, A. and Henrich-Franke, C. (eds.), *Airy Curtains in the European Ether. Broadcasting and the Cold War*. Baden-Baden: Nomos.

borders and impacted different parts of the European world in different ways.² Therefore, the main goal is to identify the common trends and similarities of European radio amateurship in World War I that is characterised by its nature with the transnational exchange of information, experts, and communication.

In research about the role of pioneering radio amateurs, the works of Haring (2007) and Douglas (1989)³ are followed that showed how hobbyists in the USA played a decisive role in applying and re-inventing the technology of radio communication at the beginning of the 20th century. In Europe, this aspect was overlooked because the scholarship was more focused on the national histories that naturally developed after the war within the birth of public broadcastings. The history of radio amateurs is typically presented through landmarks and heroes meaningful for national history.⁴ Here I suggest bringing into focus the ordinary users of the radio technology - curious amateurs, experimenters, hobbyists. The sporadic examples of ordinary radio amateurs in the 1910s were examined rather as an exemption in each European country, although all altogether they represent valuable material for describing the general trends of radio communication in Europe. With amateurs developed the idea of using the radio in a ludic, unpredicted and new scope, which was not considered before by governmental or military organisations.

In other words, based on the findings on national literature, the aim to build a transnational understanding of European amateurs in World War I. This chapter is structured in five sections: the formation of the radio amateurs' community before the war, governmental measures taken after the start of the war, the response and confrontation of amateurs, forms of collaboration between governments and hobbyists, and the aftermath of the war and a new institutionalisation of amateurs.

---

² Neiberg, M. S. (2012). 'Toward a Transnational History of World War I'. *Canadian Military History*, *17*(3), pages 31-37.

³ Haring, K. (2007). *Ham Radio's Technical Culture*. Cambridge MA, London: The MIT Press. Douglas, S. J. (1989). *Inventing American Broadcasting, 1899-1922*. Baltimore: The Johns Hopkins University Press.

⁴ Clarricoats, J. (1967). *World at Their Fingertips: The Story of Amateur Radio in the United Kingdom and a History of the Radio Society of Great Britain*. London: Radio Society of Great Britain. DeSoto, C. B. (1936). *200 Meters and Down. The story of amateur radio*. West Hartford, Connecticut: American Radio Relay League, Inc.; Körner, W. F. (1963). *Geschichte des Amateurfunks: seine Anfänge (1909-1963)*. Hamburg: FT-Verlag Rojahn and Kraft.

We conclude with an explanation of the most important characteristics of the transformation of the radio during this period.

Formation

In Europe, transnational communication was never considered an extraordinary accomplishment. In contrast to the history of the United States and Canada, where radio amateurs were described as 'distance fiends', because of their specific intention to transmit messages the farthest possible distance and connect to different part of the world.[5] In European countries, where the territories were reasonably small and boundaries were close the transnational nature of communication appeared in a natural way and accompanied radio development. Radio amateurs frequently followed the news of their colleagues in different countries and exchanged information about the latest inventions.

The major part of European radio amateurs operated on an individual basis. They were forced to follow the professional societies, mainly addressed to telegraph operators. For many years, the difference between ham radio and professional radio service was not tangible on the institutional level. For instance, in France, both radio amateurs and wireless telegraphists engaged with organisations like The French Society of Wireless Telegraphs and Telephones (Société Française De Télégraphes And Téléphones Sans Fil) founded in 1901, or The Union of the Societies of the Wireless Telegraphy in France (Union des Sociétés de TSF de France) formed in 1914.[6] The wireless organisations were rather unusual phenomena for expanding radio amateurship at that time, but the first attempts to consolidate into the communities are noticeable from 1910 onwards. One of the first societies specifically organised for amateurs was the Derby Wireless Club formed in 1911.[7]

The main exchange of information occurred through personal correspondence and publications, such as monographs and articles in technical journals. In 1914, in France, some amateurs from the Society of the Wireless Telegraph in Juvisy-sur-Orge published a review *TSF*. In the U.K., one of the first wireless magazines was issued in 1911 by the Marconi Company, *Marconigraph*, which within two years was

---

[5] *Op. cit.* Douglas, (1989), page 53.
[6] La Télégraphie Française sans Fil. (1903), August 19. *Supplément Du Galois*.
, *The Year - book of Wireless Telegraphy and Telephony*. (1923). London: Marconi Company, page 8.
[7] 'Wireless station for 30s'. (1913), February 6. *Daily Sketch*.

superseded by *Wireless World*. In Russia, the first radio journal emerged in 1912, *Vestnik telegrafii bez provodov* (transl. '*Herald of wireless telegraphy*'). It was mainly based on translations from foreign journals and lobbied the interests of the British Marconi Company because it was edited and managed by Semen Aisenstein, who negotiated all the deals of the Russian government with the Marconi Company and who, after the Revolution, had to immigrate to the U.K. for work at this commercial empire.

Radio amateurs mostly evolved from technical hobbyists of all kind, from the play with thousands of different devices. The report of the establishment of Derby Wireless Club was accompanied in newspapers with the following description of radio amateurship:

> If you possess a few empty jam jars, a roll or two of copper wire, a rubbish drawer and 30s you can erect a wireless receiving station, and by spending another 30s you may also signal through space to anybody who has a similar installation within a radius of six miles.[8]

This means that the first radio equipment was relatively weak, but affordable, and most readily obtainable.

Equipment allowed the transmission of messages over a short distance, meaning mainly coverage of a local community. Amateurs were handling messages between each other. The regularity and intensity of this communication is unknown because there was no system yet established to prove that contact actually happened like a later QSL-system[9]. In many European countries, communities formed on a regional or even local level and are known only by significant records or inventions, such as the case of Arthur F. Carter of Aylesbury, UK, who in 1911 set his first receiver to exchange messages with the five other stations up to a distance of seven miles.[10] Another example could be a Portuguese amateur Fernando de Medeiros who in 1914 delivered one of the first music broadcasts in Europe by linking a phonograph to the microphone and transmitting the 'Festival of

---

[8] *Ibid.* 'Wireless Station for 30s', (1913). The 's' stands for shillings in British currency of the period.
[9] QSL Card system is a system, which was widely accepted in the late 1920s and has been used until nowadays, that compels amateurs after establishing a wireless contact to exchange postal cards by regular post to have material confirmation of this contact.
[10] *Op. cit.* Clarricoats, (1967), page 13.

Wagner'. The listeners were three other amateurs.[11] Regularly such groups later formed themselves into local societies.

In general, amateurs were already quite experienced in the 1910s. For instance, to get full membership of the Wireless Society of London, one had to prove that they had operated for at least two years or to demonstrate a necessary qualification. By the end of the first year, the club included 151 Full Members, which means that it mostly gathered advanced experimenters, in contrast to only 11 unskilled Associate

Figure 4.1 Wireless World responds to the war

Members.[12] This fact shows that the formation of the first societies was not the first step in the birth of amateurship, but only the start of the institutionalisation process. No qualification was required to hold a

---

[11] Silva, A. P. (2010). 'From Point-to-Point to Cass Communication: the radio in Portugal from 1898 to 1939'. Lisbon: Unpublished manuscript.
[12] Richards, E. (2013). *Centenary. 100 Years Working for Amateur Radio*. Bedford: Radio Society of Great Britain.

license; the sets were almost exclusively Morse-operated; equipment was often not available for sale. Nevertheless, despite the lack of choice in the sets and the problems of electrical interference, the amateurs became skilled at calling one another.[13] The radio amateurship was slowly rising.

The vast majority of radio amateurs were not aware of the others' existence in European space and rarely got a chance to communicate via radio waves over a long distance. The ether was very chaotic; the call signs were randomly self-assigned. Harlow, (1971) referred to this period as 'state of virtual anarchy'.[14] The structuring of the community started from the local to national level gradually with the amateurs and small local societies that published the first call-books based on their records. One of the first centralised collection of call-signs on a national level was a 'Directory of Experimental Wireless Stations' published by A.W. Gamage in 1913 in the U.K., which contained information about 250 licensed amateurs and hints about receiving messages.[15]

The exact number of amateurs during the war is not known. Even in the U.K., where the radio community was the most institutionally developed, there is no evidence. This is because the publication of the national *Wireless World* Directory of Amateur Wireless Stations was postponed to keep secret all the names, addresses and all significant information related to amateur stations.[16] In other countries, such as Germany and France, societies and clubs preferred to operate autonomously and regionally and did not aim to cover the whole nation.

State monopoly

With the outbreak of war in Europe in August of 1914, the advantages and risks of wireless communication became extremely clear. On the one hand, to establish a wireless communication, little investment was needed: receiving and transmitting devices, without cable infrastructures such as wired telegraph or telephone systems, could provide a mobile

---

[13] Juniper, D. (2004). 'The First World War and Radio Development'. *History Today, 54*(5), pages 32-38.
[14] Harlow, A. F. (1971). *Old Wires and New Waves*. New York: Arno Press and the New York Times.
[15] Gamage, A. W. (1913). *Directory of Amateur Wireless Stations in the United Kingdom Licensed for Experimental Purposes by the Postmaster-General*. London: A.W. Gamage, Ltd.
[16] 'The Notes of the Month'. (1914). *The Wireless World, September*, pages 372-373. Page 372.

communication channel which was convenient in combat. However, the pitfalls of this communication were huge in a martial environment – being heard by any station around, including those of an enemy. Therefore, the governments had to restrict access to this communication in an attempt to cut off all unfavourable agents. Radio amateurs quickly fell into disgrace for two reasons: firstly, they could intercept a secret message and, secondly, even a small and unintended mistake in the construction of a radio receiver could turn it into a transmitter and would be of benefit to a spy.

To ensure the control of the transmission of the messages in the country, European governments, one by one, issued orders requesting the dismantling of radio amateurs' stations for the war effort. In the U.K., the Defence of the Realm Act was passed in August 1914 and gave exclusive powers to the government to suppress published criticism, imprison without trial and to commandeer economic resources. Amateurs in possession of wireless sets were being arrested as early as two days later.[17] The Italian government suspended all licenses to set up and run wireless stations given to private citizens and companies in 1914 even before the country joined the conflict.[18] Some states did not pursue new laws because existing legislation was already in favour of state monopoly. For instance, in Russia, legislation implied such strong bureaucratic restrictions on the installations of amateurs stations, that de-facto almost prohibited any amateur activity and left radio communication in the hands of military authorities.[19]

This ban influenced not only hobbyists but also some professional workers. The countries had to deal with businesses that relied on the wireless telegraph. In Switzerland, clockmakers relied so much on wireless time signals, that the precision in adjusting clocks was no longer achievable. The Swiss government had to employ wired telegraph and telephone to transmit time signals for clockmakers during the war. It meant that the Swiss state took responsibility to control transnational communication, and restricted the opportunity to get international time

---

[17] Joly, N. F. (1990). *The Dawn of Amateur Radio in the U.K. and Greece*. London: Project Gutenberg.
[18] Balbi, G., and Natale, S. (2015). 'The Double Birth of Wireless: Italian Radio Amateurs and the Interpretive Flexibility of New Media'. *Journal of Radio and Audio Media*, 22(1), pages 26-41. Page 32.
[19] Шамшур, В. И. (1954). *Первые годы советской радиотехники и радиолюбительства*. Москва, Ленинград: Госэнергоиздат, page 12.

signals sent from the Eiffel Tower and other radio stations, replacing it with a new national limited service.[20]

In practice, the restriction on wireless communication came in force shortly after each country entered the war. In the USA, for instance, it happened three years after the start of the war, in April 1917, after the country entered the war. American radio amateurs even predicted this scenario months before.[21] In some countries, like in the U.K., some radio equipment was held in custody and was returned to the amateurs only when they re-applied for the licences after the war. Governmental monopoly and restrictions hit radio amateurs particularly hard who were almost left without the legitimacy to practice their hobby. 'Wireless silence' was supposed to begin.

Limited activity

Apart from this widely known fact about restrictions on radio communications, there is evidence of amateurs operating during the war. The limited, and even secret, radio amateur's activity is an overlooked aspect of the restrictions during the war. The decision to leave experimenters without their hobby met strong resistance among amateurs in various places. The hobby had to transform according to new regulations, evolved into different forms, was highly repressed, but still remained in existence.

First, even though the number of publications significantly reduced, there was still literature for an amateur. In September 1914, the *Wireless World* started with the big article 'The Effects of the War'[22] which stated that a considerable number of journalists and editors responded to the call of duty. Consequently, there were problems with the creation of the issue: the volume became considerably slimmer (58 pages instead of usual 72) because of the shortage of printing paper. However, *Wireless World* was never dropped. Editors of the Russian monthly *Herald of Wireless Telegraph* in September 1914 apologised for the deferral of the issue for more than three months and expressed their hope for future productive and regular work. Unfortunately, after that forward-looking statement, the journal was permanently suspended. However, later other magazines took its place, such as 'Vestnik voennoj telegrafii'

---

[20] 'Telephonic Time Service in Switzerland', (1918). *The Wireless Age*, March 6, page 488.
[21] 'If We Are Closed Up', (1917). *QST*, April, 26.
[22] See, americanradiohistory.com/Archive-Wireless-World/10s/Wireless-World-1914-09.pdf.

('Herald of military telegraph'), which drew attention to the military usage and war effect on wireless telegraph.[23] Large communication organisations such as the International Telecommunication Union also experienced difficulties: its monthly *Journal Telegraphique* became slimmer and was printed on thinner paper, but continued to be issued and sent to amateurs and experts throughout the world. Radio did not evaporate from everyday life because of the restrictions. For instance, instructions for receiving signals from the Eiffel Tower were published in 1915 in the midst of the war, and even included a dictionary useful for an amateur unacquainted with the French language.[24] There were still amateurs who followed the news about recent inventions and were quite active in this field, though officially their activity was more theoretical, than practical.

Secondly, in all prohibitions and restrictions, there were still small loopholes that allowed amateurs to operate during the war and improve their techniques. In the U.K., the telegram about the suspension was sent only to those who used power in excess of fifty watts.[25] Some amateurs still remained in possession of transmitting and receiving equipment. There were also amateurs that moved to other countries and continued operating and keeping in contact with their native amateurs' community. For instance, one Englishmen, located in Turkey, in 1915 described his experience of listening to messages by various foreign Embassies and their sea vessels, predominately German and French, that he called the 'concert of Europe'.[26]

In general, amateurs were mainly picking up and listening in, because they wanted to remain undetected[27] and they had wireless sets that were unable to transmit.[28] In this practice of listening, when the broadcasts were not regular, chaotic and did not address the amateurs, amateurs are described as 'ether-flâneur'. The closest concept to that is actually modern idea of web surfing, meaning time-consuming and uncontrolled listening to the radio ether.[29]

---

[23] Отъ редакціи. (1917). *Вестник Военной Радіотелеграфіи И Электротехники*, 1, pages 1-2.
[24] *Wireless Time Signals. Radio-telegraphic time and weather signals transmitted from the Eiffel Tower, and their reception.* (1915). London: E. and F. N. Spon, Ltd.
[25] *Op. cit.* Clarricoats, (1967), page 36.
[26] 'Wireless amateurs in England are....' (1915). *The Wireless World, December*, 3:(33), page 595.
[27] Bruton, E. and Gooday, G. (2016). 'Listening in combat - surveillance technologies beyond the visual in the First World War'. *History and Technology*, 32(3), pages 213–226.
[28] *Op. cit.* Balbi and Natale, 2015
[29] Daniels, D. (2004). 'Interaction versus Consumption: Mass Media and Art from 1920 to Today', in Stocker, G. and Schoepf, C. (eds.), *Timeshift: The World in Twenty-Five Years*.

Thirdly, clubs and societies still held regular meetings, though fewer members were able to come because many had been drafted. These societies sometimes even got permission to work on the apparatus without actual communication, always under control. To keep up with practicing Morse code, amateurs were advised to construct a busser set for intercommunication between two operators sitting in the same house only in separate rooms.[30] The Wireless Press and the Gramophone Company produced a series of records for disc-talking machines, which played signals in Morse characters to provide amateurs with the opportunity to practice first-class Morse sending at various speeds without breaking the Defence of the Realm Regulations.[31]

But keen amateurs took the risk of operating illegally. Those journals that managed to stay published throughout the war were asking amateur communities to stop illegal activity. Wireless World even launched a special section called 'Wireless in the Courts' in the 1915-1916. The court records show the extensive activity of amateurs and represent valuable sources for historians in many countries.[32] Many amateurs were convicted because of a suspicion of espionage. For instance, a radio amateur from the southern part of Russia (currently Ukraine) Sergey Zhidkovsky was arrested in 1914 because he regularly received international broadcasts from the Eiffel Tower, transmitted weather reports by wire to Kiev, and in general communicated with foreign countries.[33] However, the prosecution arguments were weak and Zhidkovsky was convicted to only three months. In Russia, the power of wireless telegraphy was yet to be acknowledged, and the only political group aware of the significance of wireless was the revolutionary party that would come to power in October 1917. The Russian tzarist government did not massively use wireless telegraph, although they made some effort in constructing a broadcasting station to communicate with the Entente powers.[34]

Since radio devices still needed an aerial, the most important task of erecting a wireless station unnoticed was to camouflage the aerial. The most popular way of doing that was to mask it into a clothesline. It

---

Ostfildern-Ruit: Hatje Cantz.
[30] Barnard, C. C. (1914). 'A Morse Practice Set'. *The Wireless World*, November, page 528.
[31] 'Wireless Signals for the Home', (1916). *The Wireless World*, March, pages 790-792.
[32] *Op. cit.* Balbi and Natale, (2015).
[33] Добряков, Ю. (1935). Дело крестьянина Жидковского. *Радиофронт*, pages 7-8.
[34] Lovell, S. (2015). *Russia in the Microphone Age. A history of Soviet radio, 1919-1970*. Oxford: Oxford University Press.

became the main topic of many humoristic cartoons and anecdotes, like the one about the lady pretending to dry her clothes on the shorefront but was in fact sending messages to a German ship.[35] The clothesline became an object of suspicion and now attracted extraordinary attention in the neighbourhoods where people were anxious about spies. The British novel 'The Spy Hunter' issued in 1916 demonstrates the typical mindset of the time by telling the story of radio amateur and ex-wireless operator Harry Nettlefield and his fiancée Clotilde who were chasing and cornering German spies in England, who disguised themselves as ordinary English men and women and transmitted information by wireless.[36]

Amateurs were also able to spread this information in their neighbourhood, although at first their access to information channels seemed improbable. Introducing their devices to the public, amateurs were met with confusion and misunderstanding. It was not an easy task to explain how something could be transmitted a long distance without wires, by air, and it took many years and a lot of effort to convince society in these early years of radio (Лощилов, 1928)[37]. In 1914, a 21 year-old British amateur W. Kenneth Alford heard a radio message: 'Aug. 4 1914. POZ (Nauen). War is declared against France and Russia', but his friends and neighbours did not believe him until they read the newspapers the following day. Only in 1918 did they believe, and he made this entry in his logbook: 'Nov 11 1918. FL (Paris). War is over'.[38] This kind of anecdotic storytelling is representative for a narrative about the development of a new medium.[39]

In general, radio amateurs possessed unique access to the communication of military bodies of different countries. In Germany, amateurs developed their own language style, transmitted talks and music for their colleagues, and formed a their own structure in opposition to government and commercial control[40] Listening in to the 'Concert of Europe' meant that they were able to pick up the necessary

---

[35] 'The Wireless Spy'. (1915). *The Wireless World*, January, page 646.
[36] Le Queux, W. (1916). *The Spy Hunter*. London: C. Arthur Pearson, Ltd.
[37] Лощилов, М. (1928). 'С приемником у крестьянина'. *Радио Всем*, 14, page 387. Also, Отъ редакцiи. (1917). *Вестникъ Военной Радiотелеграфiи И Электротехники*, 1, pages 1-2.
[38] 'Farewell'. (1986). *Electronics and Wireless World*, 92, page 60.
[39] Natale, S. (2016). 'Unveiling the Biographies of Media: On the Role of Narratives, Anecdotes and Storytelling in the Construction of New Media's Histories'. *Communication Theory*, pages 1-34.
[40] Daniels, D. (2004). 'Interaction versus Consumption: Mass Media and Art from 1920 to Today', in Stocker, G. and. Schoepf, C. (eds.), *Timeshift: The world in twenty-five years*. Ostfildern-Ruit: Hatje Cantz, page 146.

information anywhere in the world, even in the middle of the ocean. The newspapers told the story of the radio amateur and Arctic explorer Boris Vilkitsky, who left Vladivostok and was planning to cross the Arctic passage from east to west, but decided to defer the expedition because he obtained information from a wireless receiver somewhere in the Bering Strait that the hostilities between the Allies and Germany had begun.[41]

Sometimes this illegal operation was not a deliberate form of resistance, but just a natural order. Before the war, not all amateurs were licensed, and this complicated the process of finding them in many European countries. In the UK, a pioneering country in organising hobbyists, only 69 out of 162 members of the Wireless Society of London held transmitting licenses, which means that at least a half of members knew how to operate the devices and conducted experimental work without a license.[42] Yet in the 1920s, many private individuals and institutions were broadcasting without a permit because countries did not establish a licensing system, as in Luxembourg including Radio Luxembourg.[43]

Overall, amateurs continued operating discretely and tended not to leave any traces of their activity. The main activity was to listen in and secretly improve the technology and devices. This also explains the lack of literature about their activity in the scholarship. Overall, amateurs continued operating discretely and tended not to leave any traces of their activity. In general, radio experimentation in the early days of broadcasting imposed transgressing the limits 'that would throw governmental sovereignty into question'.[44] The main activity was to listen in and secretly improve the technology and devices. This also explains the lack of literature about their activity in the scholarship.

Participation in the war and training

One of the most significant parts of operating radio amateurs in the war was their actions in combat. In different years, the majority of amateurs

---

[41] 'Wireless War News in the Arctic,' *The Wireless World*, 1915, page 412.
[42] Richards, E. (2013). *Centenary. 100 Years Working for Amateur Radio*. Bedford: Radio Society of Great Britain, page 4.
[43] Lommers, S. (2012). *Europe - on Air: Interwar projects for radio broadcasting*. Amsterdam: Amsterdam University Press, page 165.
[44] Gilfillan, D. (2009). *Pieces of Sound. German Experimental Radio*. Minneapolis, London: University of Minnesota Press, page xvi.

were called-up. Those who got into engineering and technologically equipped units could apply their knowledge to real-life tasks, and through there constant operation improved and experimented with technology.[45] Amateurs drafted into military wireless operations spread the term 'broadcast' known as sending messages to a number of naval vessels at once.[46] For instance, in Germany, Hans Bredow that held several governmental positions within the postal affairs ministry, worked as an electrical engineer and is credited with one the first experimental music broadcasts to troops on the front in 1917.[47]

There were specially organised training courses. Unless they were not professional wireless telegraphists, the amateurs' education was fragmented and consisted mainly of secondary literature and journal articles, or general physics courses in the best case.[48] The war forced a higher standard in many countries. For instance, the Royal Fighting Corps organised training, which included general discipline training, military law, and use of machine guns, the theory of flight, map reading, and nuances of wireless signalling and receiving. This comprehensive training took the usage of new technology to an entirely new level, because before the war a pilot that could fly a plane to one kilometre and land without breaking anything was already considered to be useful.[49] Even children were taught to help with telephone, telegraph and radio work. In Paris, boys from ten to sixteen years old from the scout organisation Les Eclaireurs de France were trained by the Department of War and the Department of the Navy to be ready on three hours' notice to act as messengers, to assist the post offices flooded with soldiers' telegrams and special delivery letters.[50]

Another side effect of the war was the fact that amateurs significantly improved their knowledge and experience because they got access to state-of-the-art devices. World War I is frequently considered the technology driven war[51] because governments made a considerable investment into new technologies, such as tanks or aviation. Wireless

---

[45] *Op. cit.* Bruton and Gooday, (2016).
[46] Satia, P. (2010). 'War, Wireless, and Empire. Marconi and the British Warfare State, 1896-1903'. *Technology and Culture*, 51(October), pages 829-833. Page 852.
[47] *Op. cit.* Gilfillan, (2009), page 33.
[48] Jessop, G. R. (1990). *The Bright Sparks of Wireless*. Potters Bar: Radio Society of Great Britain.
[49] 'Training aviators'. (1917). *The Wireless World*, July, pages 234-235.
[50] Felix, E. (1917). 'Department of Defence'. *QST*, February, pages 20-21.
[51] Shimshoni, J. (1990). 'Technology, Military Advantage, and World War I: A Case for Military Entrepreneurship'. *International Security*, 15(3), pages 187-215.

communication was no exception since it was a necessary communication infrastructure for these weapons of war and served many purposes.

One of the necessary changes driven by the war was the fact that in the 1920s, radio jumped from the spark transmission to continuous wave, which significantly improved the quality of signals and allowed radio broadcasting to develop in its full capacity.

First, the change of equipment from spark to crystal transmitters slowed transformation of the industry. Even at very high spark rates, spark transmitters were too noisy to transmit speech without intolerable distortion, and this change helped boost radio voice transmission. It also contributed to tuning the radio, because with the spark transmitters the signals bled across the spectrum. That was the exact reason why in 1912 the operator of the Titanic transmitted: 'Shut up, shut up, I'm working Cape Race', ignoring and suppressing the warnings of the nearby ship about the surrounding icebergs.[52] Even though crystal was invented at the beginning of the 1900s, it was hidden as a secret military innovation, and got applications in its full capacity during the war.[53] It reached the market after the war,[54] which made amateur radio devices stronger and easier to construct. Previously, they were trying to construct similar DIY devices, but they hardly worked for most amateurs living in Europe. For instance, Horace Hurm around 1914 manufactured and sold a small crystal detector 'Ondophone' in Paris, but it practically worked only around the Eiffel tower.[55] The war mobilised commercial companies, and the progress in vacuum tubes was taking place. After the production of hundreds of devices for military communication, a strong industrial base to mass manufacture radio sets for domestic use in the 1920s was prepared.[56]

There were so many amateurs and experts that benefited by getting training and access to the new devices that at some point many

---

[52] *'Titanic' Disaster: Hearings before a Subcommittee of the Committee on Commerce, Sixty-Second Congress, Second Session, Pursuant to S. Res. 283, Directing the Committee on Commerce to Investigate the Causes Leading to the Wreck of the White Star Liner 'Titanic'.* (1912). United States Senate, pages 735-740.
[53] *Op. cit.* Satia, (2010).
[54] Spohrer, J. (2008). *Ruling the Airwaves: Radio Luxembourg and the Origins of European National Broadcasting, 1929-1950.* Columbia University, New York City, page 40
[55] Wythoff, G. (2013). 'Pocket Wireless and the Shape of Media to Come, 1899-1922'. *GreyRoom*, 14(51), pages 40-63. Page 43.
[56] Balbi, G. (2017). "Wireless's 'Critical Flaw'. The Marconi Company, Corporation Mentalities, and the Broadcasting Option'. *Journalism and Mass Communication Quarterly*, 1(22), page 16.

technically knowledgeable amateurs were not needed anymore in the army. Hams showed their dissatisfaction in the letters:

> I naturally thought that my knowledge would be of some little use in some sphere or other at the present time, and made several enquiries, but only to receive the 'cold shoulder' at every attempt.[57]

Overall, the war had become an opportunity for some amateurs to progress beyond typical peacetime restrictions, using military equipment, national resources and the vast necessity for getting information. Mainly it was with the proper experience and the spread of the crystal detector for wireless receivers, that the amateurs gradually became interested in radio primarily for the sake of communication. It enabled them to converse pleasantly with each other, and shifted the focus from the mere pleasure of putting the device to work to being included into the community. It became more social a practice, and therefore more notable.

New institutionalisation

Many of the radio amateurs who were deployed didn't survive the war. Others were trained to be radio engineers and grew from hams to professionals after the war. After a demonstration of the practical application of radio and serving the needs of the country, the hobbyists became more knowledgeable and apparently made the basis of the radio industry that experienced a boom afterwards.

After the war, the landscape of radio communication became more organised and at the same time, met more restrictions.[58] Hobbyists reapplied for licences, new journals and new societies appeared, using new techniques and equipment. Many countries went through an immense political, economic, and social transformation, and the process of the institutionalisation of radio amateurs coincided with the total restructuring of the country, as was seen in Russia. All Russian radio magazines and societies were entirely replaced with other controlled bodies, because the new political power understood the importance of radio broadcasting, and started propagating the ham radio to a broader audience in 1918. In addition to the serious academic journal

---

[57] Lewis, J. R. (1916). 'Correspondence'. *The Wireless World*, July, page 215.
[58] *Op. cit.* Richards, (2013), page 6.

'Telegraphy and Telephone without Wires' that replaced the earlier 'Wireless Telegraph Herald', the Bolshevists started issuing the humorous and entertaining 'Radiotechnician' which was addressed to a broader audience.

From the transnational point of view, the war practically equalised the development of radio in Europe, bridging the gap between higher achievements and slow progress in different countries. In 1918, UK amateurs expressed their gratitude for improvements in the radiotelegraphic equipment of the French installations, because it made signals more regular and vigorous to get from abroad.[59]

European amateurs started forming national associations, following the

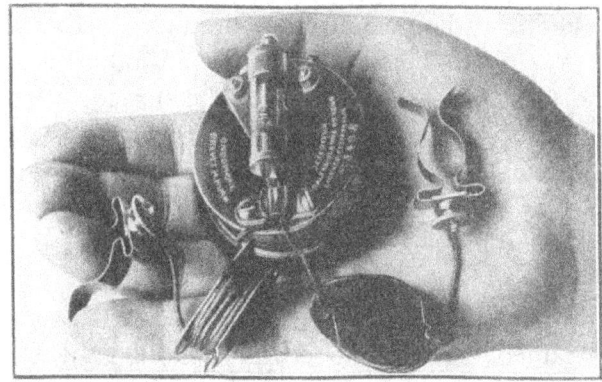

Compact Wireless Receiver.

Figure 4.2 Horace Hurm's 'Ondophone'

successful example of the local communities. It was no longer small radio clubs in towns, but big national leagues that collected information about hams in the centralised mode, published call-books and acted as a QSL-bureau for sharing contacts.

The London Wireless Club took other clubs under its patronage and transformed into the Radio Society of Great Britain in 1922. The same year, Ireland similarly formed its national association, the Radio Society of Ireland. In 1925, the first German Radio Technical Association was founded (Deutsche Funktechnische Verband, DFTV), which assembled many regional associations. In 1925, an association of radio amateurs Reseau des Emetteurs Français succeeded its predecessor Union des Sociétés de TSF de France. Portugal opened Network of Portuguese

---

[59] 'Progress in France'. (1918). *The Wireless World*, May, page 91.

Transmitters (Rede dos Emissores Portugueses) in 1926. In 1927, the first national society of radio amateurs in Italy was founded, Associazione Radiotecnica Italiana. In 1929, The Union of Swiss Short Wave Amateurs opened in Switzerland.

This enlargement of amateur communities from the local to a national level reached its peak in 1925 when the representatives of 23 countries in Europe, North and South America, and Asia established the International Amateur Radio Union (IARU).[60] The original constitution of the union provided radio hobbyists with individual membership because national societies did not exist in all of the countries, but already in 1928, the members acknowledged the federative model as a more productive one. The IARU focused on supporting the national societies, which it does to the present day.

Main characteristics of the turn

Although the years of the war are usually viewed as having a 'lack of amateur radio experimentation', the restriction did not mean that radio amateurs did immediately drop their interest.[61] Firstly, some of them operated illegally. Secondly, the society still functioned and shared the knowledge about the latest inventions and news, thereby stimulating intellectual work. Thirdly, many amateurs were deployed in the wireless units of the Navy, Army and Air Forces, where they could show their talents and promote radio communication thanks to government investment into the communication equipment and proper training.

Radio amateurship significantly changed during World War I, because it finally took place in opposition to a professional. Prior to the war, the borderline between amateurs and experts was very thin because specific radio education was not widespread. In fact, even Gugliemo Marconi was just an amateur inventor at first.[62] Any amateur also had to play the role of inventor and constructor, applying different details from other mechanisms to a radio transmitter or receiver, and sharing this knowledge with other hobbyists. Some of them, like Horace Hurm with the Ondophone[63], also made a fortune in selling these

---

[60] *Op. cit.* DeSoto, (1936), page 107.
[61] *Op. cit.* Richards, (2013), page 5.
[62] Weightman, G. (2003). *Signor Marconi's Magic Box: How an amateur inventor defied scientists and began the radio revolution.* London: HarperCollins.
[63] See, *Electrical Review and Western Electrician,* April 11 1914, page 745, for a description of the 'Compact Wireless Receiver - the Ondophone'.

devices to other enthusiasts, and therefore made radio their professional activity.

When radio turned to broadcasting in the 1920s, ham radio finally crystallised as a non-profitable activity for leisure time among hobbyists, in opposition to radio professionals who held certificates of specifically completed training, earned money and concentrated on radio mainly in their working hours. Since many radio amateurs had received military training and were well familiar with the devices, they were frequently employed by radio stations, and therefore formed this first generation of professionals of radio broadcasting.

Amateur radio has also become a mainly communicative activity between members of amateur communities, which was driven by regular publications, meetings of national societies, and other appropriate institutions. The institutional affiliation was not necessary for amateur activity but expressively facilitated the process. It provided courses for beginners and introduced hobbyists to the rules of communication, providing them with the lists of call signs of the known amateurs, useful techniques and handbooks with appropriate abbreviations. Furthermore, the material change from spark to crystal facilitated communication via radio waves.

Moreover, during World War I amateur radio became more nationally focused. It coincided with the general trend of nationalisation of radio through public radio stations, and also was caused by the institutionalisation of the community. With the formation of the Amateur Radio Union in 1925, national organisations took the responsibility of serving also as QSL-bureaus that collected information about amateurs in the country, exchanged information and QSL-cards with other QSL-bureaus, and issued call-books. This institutionalisation and segregation of the field also brought about new international regulations that were approved at the 1927 conference in Washington.[64] The international and national regulations towards the ham radio most likely were implemented as a direct consequence of the First World War. Radio had proved itself as a weapon of war, and enthusiast who had served in the forces used their skills to great effect, proving that these trained communities, if properly organised, would be invaluable to the nation.[65]

---

[64] *Op. cit.* Schroeder, (1954).
[65] Wood, J. (1992). *History of International Broadcasting*. London: Peter Peregrinius Ltd. and The Science Museum, page 15.

Conclusion

World War I did not provoke the birth of professional and amateur radio but rather stimulated its segregation into different fields within the institutionalisation, nationalisation and extensive development of radio.

The 'birth' of radio broadcasting after World War I was not a revolutionary process but rather an evolutionary one. Before the war, radio amateurs consolidated into small local societies and attempted to construct devices to transmit the clearest signal possible because the equipment was quite weak. They were exchanging news about the inventions and devices in journals and through correspondence.

During the war, wireless telegraphy had been used for espionage, and governments were eager to maintain this control. Most European governments had drawn up regulations for using airwaves to establish the 'wireless silence'. The wireless technology was considered an instrument of national power politics that should remain out of the hands of private individuals. The international climate was too fragile to be threatened by experiment with wireless technology that may hinder government employment of wireless telegraphy and telephony for national defence.

Even though amateurs experienced high restrictions and crises during the war, they nevertheless continued operating. They exchanged information and followed the news, practised without exceeding tolerated scopes, attended meetings of the societies and clubs, and, finally, operated illegally. Under circumstances of individual and mostly hidden work, experimenters made significant progress in the technology. Many were suspected of espionage because they operated illegally despite the obligations to dismantle the stations. The 'concert of Europe' was listened to by hundreds of hobbyists in different European countries. The movement grew phenomenally during the war and procreated a generation of radio professionals and first institutions of amateurship.

Many amateurs were deployed and worked as technical experts in combat, studied the technology professionally and applied their knowledge to real-life tasks. The main reasons for the significant boost to radio after the war lay in the fact that governments invested in the development of radio for military reasons. In particular, it had to deal with the technological change from spark to crystal and the extensive practice of radio amateurs during the war. New equipment significantly raised the performance of the amateur stations and stimulated the boost to radio communication in the 1920s.

All of this could also explain why there are fewer studies of European cases in contrast to studies of American amateurs. Firstly, European history was predominately written in the national framework, and the similarities in the radio development and amateurs' response were overlooked and excluded from the national framework. Secondly, because many European countries introduced a ban or restrictions on amateur work at the beginning of the war, their activity was mainly hidden and secret.

During the years of the war, radio use was significantly transformed. An amateur of the early 1910s listened to rare chaotic messages, mainly intended for technical communication, while an amateur of the late 1920s had to deal with flows of regular communications from all over the globe. The chaos was gradually abolished. Technical messages, radio broadcasting and radio amateur's communication were completely separated and limited to particular frequencies. Radio amateurs were controlled. They were obliged to get licenses, were institutionalised in the national amateurs' societies, which became members of the International Radio Amateur Union. The development of the institutional structure was intensive, but it only organised already existing trends in radio technology and development.

Amateur radio clubs and industry lobbied their activities and performed numerous experiments for these four years of the war. The war changed society's perception of radio. It was finally proved to be useful, and underwent institutional changes. The war suggested social, commercial and political applications of radio communication, brought in powerful new equipment and turned radio hobbyists into a powerful community of engineers and enthusiasts. Radio came completely under the control of national and international regulation and was formed into institutions.

By showing that radio amateurs existed before the war, operated under different circumstances in the martial and civil society, reshaped the technology and became widely recognised experts in the 1920s, we claim that the development of radio during World War I should be understood as a transnational process that provoked a high mobilisation of already existing resources. Taken with its premises and aftermath, the war boosted radio development as the continuation of then current trends and suggested political and social applications of radio techniques. World War I pushed radio amateurs towards a new phase of development that was a natural continuation of the growing technology and stimulated new regulations and institutionalisation.

Chapter 5

The Role of Political Posters in Montenegro and Serbia during World War I

Andrijana Rabrenović
Editor in Chief Radio Bijelo Polje, Montenegro

Introduction

In World War I both sides, the Triple Entente Powers and the Central Powers were using all the then known propaganda tools as part of their war efforts, and one of the most effective means was political poster. Regardless of whether the purpose of the posters was to recruit, mobilise, call for the defence of the country or seek assistance in cash it was the dominant means which resulted in the creation of a positive image 'of their side', and at the same time projected a negative image, demonising the enemy. This paper will attempt to determine what the role of a political poster was in Montenegro and Serbia during World War I. Two countries in the Balkans that were Kingdoms in this period have just come out (military weakened) from the Balkan Wars. Due to these circumstances, the poster had an important role - to encourage and motivate people to oppose the Central Powers. In order to understand the then position of the Montenegro and Serbia on the international political scene, I will briefly describe the socio-political context in which they found themselves, and their political aspirations and relationship with the great powers of the period. Then with the help of the descriptive method I will look at the most representative political posters from the two kingdoms. The political posters used in this analysis are those that have been published in the literature and in the collections of the Central National Library of Montenegro and National Library of Serbia.

Why do we believe in the power of propaganda and posters?

There are numerous definitions of propaganda and political propaganda. The word and general meaning of 'propaganda' is well known; it is etymologically derived from the Latin word 'propagare' and means to spread something widely.[1] The same author emphasises that "the first institution that contained the term 'propaganda' in its name was the *Sacra Congregatio de Propaganda Fide*, which was founded in 1597 by the Pope Clement VIII." While, he claims, the notion of political propaganda appeared later, at the end of the 18th century, with the formation of the *Propagande* association. The definition used as the foundation for this research is from Slavujević (1999) propaganda is "... a planned and organised activity on shaping, presenting, spreading political content to win people and provide their support, for the certain political content and their bearers."[2]

Notions and assumptions about propaganda are not equivocal or unproblematic. In his book *Propaganda: the Formation of Men's Attitudes*, Jacques Ellul, states that propaganda is not something perpetrated by evil propagandists on a helpless society. Ellul (1963) claims:

> One can lead a horse to water but cannot make him drink; one cannot reach through propaganda those who do not need what it offers ... To understand that propaganda is not just a deliberate and more or less arbitrary creation by some people in power is, therefore, essential. It is a strictly sociological phenomenon, in the sense that it has its roots and reasons in the need of the group that will sustain it.[3]

Propaganda, Moore (2011) argues, is a reciprocal activity; a continuous dialogue between the giver and receiver, long recognised by historians as a faithful and sensitive index to changes which occur in society. One of the most successfully used techniques used by the propagandist, is according to Moore (2011), content repetition. Moore (2011) gives the following as an example of this,

---

[1] Slavujević, Z. (1999). *Politički Marketing* (Political Marketing). Beograd: Fakultet Političkih Nauka, Čigoja.
[2] *Ibid.* Page 12.
[3] Ellul, J. (1963). *Propaganda. The formation of Men' attitudes.* New York: Random House, cited in Moore, C. (2011). *Propaganda Prints: A history of art in the service of social and political change.* London: Hardcover, A. & C. Black, page 8.

Only constant repetition can finally bring success in the matter of instilling ideas into the memory of the crowd. The most important thing is to paint your contrasts in black and white.[4]

Simplicity, clarity and the use of images, including graphical design seem to be attributes giving some posters the power to communicate more effectively than others. In *The Posters: 1,000 Posters from Toulouse-Lautrec to Sagmeister*, de Jong (2010) highlights the role of the visual:

For more than ten thousand years we have felt the need to express ourselves with writing and drawing. Since the Neolithic period, we have communicated not only through gestures and sound but also by means of a visual language.[5]

According to de Jong (2010) in the last hundred and thirty years of poster design, it is typography and illustration rather than text dominates. The purpose of the poster has always been to deliver a message. De Jong (2010) notes that this mean requiring a vision of how things should be, of how others should behave and think.[6] Moore (2011) is of similar thinking, which emphasises that people "throughout history have used art to influence the beliefs and behaviours of others."[7] Moore also notes that a picture, song, sculpture or building can be used for the purposes of influencing opinions. About the significance of art, Moore (2011) adds that it, among other things, "used to educate us, to mould our opinions, to confirm us in our nationhood and to persuade us of the existence of many gods." He concludes, "the art created for these purposes – art in the service of social and political change – is propaganda art."[8]

Nikolić (2012)[9] also speaks about the connection between posters, art and propaganda, noting that the illustrative value and function of art

---

[4] *Ibid.* Page 11.
[5] de Jong C. W., Purvis A. W. and LeCoultre, M. F. (2010). *The Posters: 1,000 posters from Toulouse-Lautrec to Sagmeister*. New York: Abrams, page 7.
[6] Here we note that the author of this work also studied the predecessors and the creation of posters. See more in: Rabrenović, R. (2008). *Plakat kao sredstvo političke propagande: magistarski rad* (trans. Plakat as a Mean of Political Propaganda: master's thesis), Univerzitet u Beogradu, Fakultet političkih nauka, UDC: 32.019.5(043) COBISS.SR-ID 512869719.
[7] *Op. cit.* Moore (2011), page 7.
[8] *Ibid.*
[9] Nikolić, K. (2012). *Nemački ratni plakat u Srbiji: 1941:1944* (trans. German War Poster in Serbia: 1941-1944). Beograd: Zavod za udžbenike.

has been co-opted by the propagandist in the form of posters. The propaganda poster is rightly to be taken as an historical document, as an artefact made for a purpose at a particular time. Yet they are also creations that exhibit particular aesthetic and artistic values. Speaking more specifically of the political poster, Nikolić (2012) believes that the aesthetic and artistic values cannot be separated from the political message or the context in which the poster was produced. Not least because, he notes, that "the poster is a symbol in itself" adding that some posters enter the conscience collective as symbolic of much larger historic events and attitudes.[10]

This follows de Jong (2010) about the effective poster is one that "instantly grasp the attention of the onlooker and maintain it until the communication has been conveyed."[11] How effective a poster will be, it is determined by a number of qualities, including distinctiveness, lucidity, and, without exception, a striking design. In particular, it emphasised that this was especially important during the latter half of the nineteenth century when posters were often displayed together with other designs in 'hoardings', so the poster had to be conspicuous among its competitors.

Turning to the First World War, Calvocoressi and Wint (1987) in *Total War*[12] point out that the contemporary notion about the political poster emerged during World War I, when it gained a new place in politics, being used to communicate the views of the political elite, to the population of a country. Calvocoressi and Wint (1987) identify the focus on patriotism and national morals, with calls to help the 'homeland'. Through appeals, flattery but also threats the modern political poster gained power from playing on emotions, morality and nationalism. In and as a part of this was, Calvocoressi and Wint (1987) argue, the use of contrast; evident in depicting the enemies as evil beings, as opposed to their own being the personification of goodness.

De Jong (2010) also points out the widespread use of posters and describes them as vital propaganda tools, both by the Allies and Central Powers, during World War I.[13] As part of all war events, they served for "fund-raising, recruitment, increasing industrial production, the conservation of resources, and volunteer initiatives." In the USA alone,

---

[10] *Ibid.* Page 10.
[11] *Op. cit.* De Jong (2010), page 11.
[12] Calvocoressi, P. and Wint, G. (1987). *Total War: Causes and courses of the Second World War*. Harmondsworth: Penguin, in *Op. cit.* Nikolić, (2012), page 20.
[13] *Op. cit.* De Jong (2010), page 63.

more than 2,500 designs and 20 million posters were produced. Political communication was then, to become part of the political-military machine. The forces of Triple Entente saw unprecedented investment in political communications, and in the deliberate control of information during World War I. Mihailović (1984) points out that agencies on both sides of the Atlantic achieved such a spectacular success in the manipulation of public opinion that the practice of propaganda would be treated from then on as indispensable for all subjects of public life.[14]

Terminological differences and language dilemmas regarding posters

Given that this chapter is about the role of political posters in Montenegro and Serbia, it is especially important to explain how in this region (not just the territorial, but also the spoken one) the idea of a poster was understood. The dilemma of understanding the poster was discussed by Rikards (1971) who says the English language meaning; to 'post up' (in the sense of put on the pole or pillar) can be found throughout Europe during this time.[15] In French and German to these findings, *affiche* and *Anschlag* respectively point out, as he states, to 'sticking' or 'pinning'. What was pinned up was a proclamation, meant to be seen and read by those who could read who lived in a particular area. The idea of mass communication was for limited to those who could read or have the poster read to them. A more effective means of communication was to use images, symbolising the meaning in metaphor or analogy or narrative. In this chapter these will be looked at alongside Rickards' notion of the political poster being for the use of making a proclamation. The focus will be, however, looking at the poster as a 'technique of action', that through acclamations, proclamations, and declarations, a population is called upon to do something they are being told is for the greater good.

---

[14] Mihailović, V. (1984). *Propaganda i rat* (trans.Propaganda and War). Beograd: Vojnoizdavački Zavod, page 22.
[15] Rikards, M. (1971). *Uspon i pad plakata* (Rise and Fall of the Poster). Beograd: Thames and Hudson.

Methodologically, Slavujević (1990) provides two useful criteria: the type of presentation of the message and the way of presenting the content of the posters.[16] According to the first criterion, he distinguishes the leaflet (written message), the poster (picture message), and the poster

Figure 5.1 Nikola I Petrović-Njegoš was the ruler of Montenegro from 1860 to 1918

in the narrow sense (a combination of the text and the picture). To these he adds a division between a personalised poster and a non-personalised poster, as counter-poster.

History of Montenegro and Serbia on political posters before the Great War

As a basic material for the analysis of political posters related to Montenegro in the period before and during World War I, we will use the capital edition of the *National Library of Montenegro 'Đurđe Crnojević'*

---

[16] *Op. cit.* Slavujević (1990), pages 169-170.

entitled Orations and Declarations of King Nicholas I (originally, *'Besjede i proglasi Kralja Nikole'*) that was published in 2010 on the occasion of 100 years since the restoration of the Kingdom of Montenegro. This volume contains a total of 58 King's addresses to the people. Almost half are proclamations, declarations and decrees of King Nicholas I (1841-1921), who was the last ruler of the Petrović Njegoš dynasty. The earliest published proclamation in this special edition dates back to 1876 when the war on Turkey was declared. The King also addressed the people through a proclamation when Austro-Hungarians annexed Bosnia and Herzegovina in 1908.

The proclamations were not concerned only with the foreign policy but also important internal issues. Thus, for example, in 1879 King Nicholas addressed the people in Podgorica and Zeta, on the occasion of incorporation to Principality of Montenegro. He also called on all the displaced inhabitants of Islamic faith to return to Montenegro and live peacefully in it (1881). Also, through the proclamation of 1905, the introduction of the Constitution[17] and the convening of the National Assembly were announced. The most important of the then political and historical events is the proclamation of the restoration of the old Kingdom of Montenegro and King Nicholas I as its hereditary King in 1910.

King Nicholas addressed to the people through 'proclamation' when he went on official visits to e.g. Russia, Austria-Hungary and other countries (1882 and 1908, 1909, 1912, 1914) or when he was absent in 1906 for treatment in Vienna. The last proclamation relates to 1918, when King Nicholas addressed the Montenegrin people and said he was against the entry of Montenegro into Yugoslavia.

A special group is made up of proclamations inviting the people to war. The King called Montenegrins to war in the Balkan War in 1912, and thus mobilised soldiers. He also spoke through the proclamation to the soldiers, intending to strengthen their morale and faith in victory – as an example, we cite the messages sent to the Dečanski detachment that fought with the Serb army and participated in the fighting with Bulgaria.

---

[17] With it the Prince announced the introduction of constitutionality 18/31, October 1905. He addressed the people with the intention on electing representatives who would adopt a way of governing. The proclamation states that he has decided to 'bestow' to representatives of the people the rights and duties in administration of the country.

After the end of the Second Balkan War, the King informed all citizens of all religions by the proclamation of the outcome of this conflict and the substantial territorial expansion of the state.

Within the Digital National Library of Serbia there is a collection of posters and documentation, consisting of: theatrical posters, address books and directories, guides, old securities, literary announcements and proclamations of royal dynasties. According to NBS (National Library of Serbia), this collection is made up of digital copies of old posters from the collection of posters and documentation material of the special funds of the National Library of Serbia.

For this work, the last category in this collection is significant: the announcements and proclamations of the royal dynasties, more precisely Obrenović (26 proclamations), Karađorđević (65 proclamations) and Petrović (19 proclamations). Within this collection, there are more than a hundred digital copies of the decrees, proclamations, orders and announcements of the mentioned royal dynasties. This documentary material of significant historical and cultural value, according to the NBS data, dates from the time of the Kingdom of Serbia, the Kingdom of SCS and the Kingdom of Yugoslavia.

As we analyse the social and political context in which Serbia finds itself before the Great War in this section, it is important to point out that the most important events of the period were presented on political posters by each of the dynasties.

The first dynasty included in the collection, is the Obrenović dynasty. The collection includes a number of announcements (proclamations) including changes to the Ordinance of the National Assembly by Milan Obrenović (1854-1901), then the Serbian Knights, from 1876, then the protocol events, e.g., the reception of King Alexander to Cetinje, in Montenegro, from 1897. The publication from 1888 is also significant for the researchers, which states that the next year of 1889 is the anniversary of five centuries, as alleged, the collapse of the Serbian state in Kosovo. The history of Serbia and Montenegro are, from these documents and posters, clearly intertwined. Notions of nationalism, shared history and freedom are common themes. Some of these can be seen in the Karađorđević dynasty posters and proclamations. Some are about the reign of King Alexander I (1888-1934), Peter I (1844-1921) and Peter II (1923-1970). Work by Prince Peter I, about John Stuart Mills' 'On Liberty' (1867) sits among declarations about the marriage of the Princess Zorka and Peter I in 1883.

The relationship with Serbia is fully evident with the war proclamation of June 25, 1913, in which Peter I Karađorđević calls "courageous army" to the fight against Bulgaria, which was in war with Serbia, as he said, without the announcement of the war. This proclamation highlights friendship and good relations with Montenegro because it is said that they will defend against "the pests" together with the "knight brothers, Montenegrin falcons."[18]

Montenegro and Serbia in World War I: the role of political posters in the socio-political context

World War I, the global conflict that spread across continents, was the conflict between the two alliances of states - the Triple Entente and the Central Powers. Montenegro sided with the Triple Entente Forces. Rastoder et al. (2006) explains that war originated from so called 'July Crisis' of 1914, triggered by the assassination of Austrian Crown Prince Archduke Franz Ferdinand of Austria in Sarajevo. After that, Austria-Hungary declared the war against Serbia. Montenegro immediately sided with Serbia. King of Montenegro Nicholas Petrović Njegoš announced a declaration on mobilisation, and on August 6, Montenegro officially declared war against Austria-Hungary. Montenegro did not accept the call or the offer of Austro-Hungarians to remain neutral in the war, and thus even extend its territory (primarily to Shkodër)[19].

Before entering the war, King Nicholas addressed the people with a proclamation, while Radonjić (2006) observes the manner of King Nicholas' address:

On that platform, and with the promise that the blessing of their 'old King' will follow them in their feats, 35,000 Montenegrins went to

---

[18] Within the National Library of Serbia, there are posters, both for World War I, and relating to the period after its completion, i.e., the reign of Peter II, but they are not within the focus of this chapter and will not be included in the analysis.

[19] Since gaining independence at the Berlin Congress in 1878, Montenegro has received, inter alia, numerous diplomatic representatives of permanent character. Among them was the representative of Austria-Hungary, through whom diplomatic relations were established through Cetinje's representative office. After Montenegro declared the war against Austria-Hungary in 1914, its last diplomatic representative Edward Oto leaves Cetinje. See, Rastoder, Š. Andrijašević, Ž, Papović, D, Folić, Z, Šabotić, S, Drobnjak, S, Selhanović, J, Drinčić, Ž, Prekić, A. (2006). *Istorijski leksikon Crne Gore* (Historical lexicon of Montenegro, (books 2, 3). Podgorica: Daily Press, pages 551-554.

war unprepared and under the command of the Serbian Headquarters.[20]

On the basis of the Army Structure Act, i.e. Article 212, on July 15, 1914, King Nicholas mobilised the entire Montenegrin army, along the border, through proclamation. The King called them "a brave army", which means he expects and invites them to fight[21] for the 'motherland'[22] and

> ...if you are heroes, take up arms! If you are heroes, follow in steps of Two Old Serbian Kings - to die and spill our blood for unity and golden freedom!
>
> God is on our side, justice is on our side. We wanted peace, they wanted war. Take it as you always did, take it as Serbs and as heroes. Blessing of your Old King will follow you in every battle.
>
> Long live my dear Montenegrins!
> Long live our dear Serbdom!"

The ruler believes in the strength of the army and in this way wants to strengthen the morality among them, considering it was recently in the war. Calling the army 'brave' aims to make such a message a driver for war operations and a positive influence on the situation among the soldiers[23].

---

[20] *Ibid.* Page 249.

[21] Due to the complete precision in the work, first of all the way of presenting the content of posters, both Montenegro and Serbia equally apply the domination of war invitations, which are exclusively textual. If we compare posters calling for war in the United Kingdom or the United States, we see a huge difference in relation to these two Balkan states. Among the poster's theoreticians the most famous posters were designed by Alfred Leete 'Your Country Needs You' in the United Kingdom, featuring only the head of General Lord Horatio Herbert Kitchener with a pointed finger and a later poster by James Montgomery Flagg, also with the pointed finger of Uncle Sam in the U.S.A.

[22] Đurović, J., Vračar, M. and Lompar, D, (2010). *Besjede i proglasi Kralja Nikole: 100 godina od obnove Kraljevine Crne Gore: 1910-2010* (trans. Orations and Declarations of King Nicholas I: 100 Years since the Restoration of the Kingdom of Montenegro: 1910-2010). Podgorica: Centralna narodna biblioteka Crne Gore 'Đurđe Crnojević', DPC, Cetinje, page 139.

[23] Montenegro entered the First World War politically and militarily exhausted. The outcome of the First and Second Balkan Wars in 1912 and 1913 had a devastating impact on the future of Montenegro.

Наредба ОБр. 8676

Врховног Команданта Његовог Краљевског Височанства

Престолонаследника АЛЕКСАНДРА

својој српској војсци

за 15. децембар 1914. год. у Крагујевцу.

Јунаци!

Већ се навршио пети месец како је на нашу милу Отаџбину напао непријатељ. Истрошени у два славна али тешка рата, ми смо га ипак мушки и јуначки дочекали. И пошто смо га једном потукли на Церу и Јадру, ми смо му после толиких других крвавих али славних бојева, сада задали удар тежи од свих досадашњих. Хиљаде заробљеника, стотине топова и силна опрема војна што је од непријатеља задобисмо сведоче о његовом поразу и нашој слави.

Јунаци!

Ја сам поносит да објавим да на земљишту Краљевине Србије нема више непријатеља. Изагнали смо га крваве главе.

У том свечаном тренутку (када се на поноситом српском Београду вије поново победна српска застава) ја хоћу пре свега другог да испуним један дуг захвалности.

У редовима вашим, раме уз раме с вама, ратују у овом трећем рату и браћа наша коју од Турака ослободисмо. Ви сте сведоци њиховог јунаштва и њихове љубави према Отаџбини. Косовци и Вардарци, Жеглиговци и Брегалничани, Битољци и Поречани показали су се достојни своје браће Шумадинаца и Дунаваца, Подринаца и Мораваца, Тимочана и Ужичана. Показали су се достојни Потомци јунака Милутинових и Душанових, што некад далеко пронесе славу српског имена и оружја.

Ја хоћу да вам дам видан знак признања Отаџбине. Пред овако несумњивим доказом свога великог пожртвовања и пред тако јуначки проливеном својом крвљу за своју Србију; пред таквим стварним доказом вршења своје најтеже грађанске дужности и то са таквим одушевљењем, — Ја објављујем њихово право на све политичке и уставне тековине Ослободитељке Србије. Прва редовна Народна Скупштина по закључењу мира решиће све потребне мере, те да се то потпуно и у живот уведе.

Јунаци!

Гвоздени обруч наших моћних савезника стеже се све више око нашег заједничког непријатеља. Осећајући се пред поразом и страхујући од његових тешких последица он се бори очајно али упорно. Али узалуд. Број његових војника све је мањи, а наши савезници уводе сваког дана све нове војске у борбу. Крај тој џиновској борби већ је данас јасан и ако она још није завршена.

Ми морамо још неко време вршити нашу тешку дужност и стојати уз наше велике и силне савезнике који се боре и за вас, докле ови не сможде нашег заједничког непријатеља на њиховим пространим пољима, а тада ће настати мир, и то дуги мир, који ће достојно наградити жртве за нашу Велику Србију — тада ће наша Отаџбина бити много већа, силнија и срећнија но што је икада била.

А за то ће, Витезови, Србија бити вама благодарна.

Врховни Командант
Престолонаследник
Александар с. р.

Figure 5.2 Order No. 8676 from 1914, of the Supreme Commander of His Royal Majesty the Crown Prince Alexander, to his Serbian Army for 15 December

After the mobilisation, another proclamation[24] followed from the King, (July 24, 1914), in which the War was declared against Austria-Hungary. Since Montenegro has only just emerged from the Balkan Wars, the King starts the proclamation with the words that he has to call the Montenegrins to arms for the third time in two years, and as he emphasises, "in the holy war for the freedom of Serbdom and Yugoslavism." We can see the use of the techniques of action through striking words, and that is *freedom*.

What we also notice in this proclamation that the enemy – Austria-Hungary is described as a 'black-and-yellow flag' that is leaning over Serbia and Montenegro as a nightmare, and it must be 'overrun'. The association is obvious because it alluded to the colours of the monarchy, using the symbol to explain who the enemy is and what purpose it has. Although the war has only been declared, the King uses the word 'overrun', which should serve as a demonstration of the power of the adversary, but also to persuade the Montenegrins in the significance of the struggle against Austro-Hungarians. Then the King remembers that the Slavs, by defending from the Ottoman invasions, adapted to Christian Austria and helped on several occasions in various battlefields, especially in the preservation of Vienna, from which they now issue an order for the destruction of Serbs. In the central part of the proclamation, the King, referring to the Montenegrins, states that Austria has declared war on 'our beloved Serbia, declared it to us, declared it to Serbdom and all of Slavianism'. This is in fact shows the political connection between these two countries and the readiness to fight against the enemy. It also points out the alliance with Russia, for which he says is with France, the protector of Montenegro. The message is the people wanted peace but war was imposed on them, hence, Montenegrins have 'God and Justice' on the side, against the aggressors. This was, of course, a feature of many propaganda posters used by all sides from the beginning of the war. Gallo (2001), notes, "Each side insisted that it was right, that and its army fought with God's help" (2001).[25] The proclamation ends with cries "Long live my beloved my Montenegrins!, Long live our beloved Serbdom!", as well as expressing the faith in Russia and its allies.

Germany and its allies did not see the map in the same way as the King of Montenegro. A contemporary German cartoon mocked the

---

[24] *Op. cit.* Đurović, Vračar and Lompar (2010), No: 54, page 141.
[25] Gallo, M. (2001). *The Poster in History*. London: Norton, page 203.

Allies as 'bandits', showing Montenegro as small and fat. Nonetheless, the King was convinced of a victory over Austria-Hungary, as evidenced by his speech[26] published in *The Voice of Montenegrin* (originally: Glas Crnogorca) on December 29, 1914, (No 71), describing it as an oppressor who "for no reason at all assailed our dear Serbia" and further "...this horrible war is prolonging, and it is unknown how long it will last, but it is known, that our victory is obvious and reliable!"

In the second year of war, the King addressed the Montenegrin army and the people through a proclamation[27]. By the winter of 1915 a change in his opinion on the course and the outcome of the war becomes evident. In the proclamation, it is clear that the King admits that Serbia is powerless, for neither "the help of Montenegro... was not enough for a great wave of enemies to be deterred or stopped." As a point of the King's address, it is stated that for both Montenegro and Serbia the same things will occur, but that the state enjoys freedom rather than slavery. And here we can observe the use of words as a powerful propaganda tools, because emphasises is on the importance of freedom, to which both the people and the army will strive because they do not want to be slaves.

Yet it is claimed that the enemy has not yet conquered Montenegro and that there is belief in the final victory and the aid from the allies. No matter how much the King was sure of victory, there was a suspicion in his address because he says if the people hear that the enemy has conquered any part of the territory, it is only temporary. Also, if they hear that his throne is not in the place where it previously was, and then it will be in place wherever he is. Believing in the courage of his people, at the end of the proclamation, the King says that he knows that they are fearless and he does not need to shout out 'do not be afraid'. In fact, the aim was to encourage the people and the population by mere lexicology to believe in victory, which is one of the key words to trigger emotional reactions to those targeted by the propaganda message.

After almost a year and a half of fighting, and after the Serbian army withdrew to the island of Corfu, as a result of the great offensive that commenced in October 1915, the General Attack of the Third Army of Austria-Hungary commenced on Montenegro on January 5th, 1916. Although Montenegro won a victory at Mojkovac on January 7th, after only a few days, the Austro-Hungarian main attack was devastating for

---

[26] *Op. cit.* Đurović, Vračar and Lompar (2010), No: 54, page 143.
[27] *Ibid.* Page 145.

Montenegro. Montenegro requested a ceasefire on January 10th, but the Austria-Hungary sought unconditional capitulation[28]. As early as January 19th, after the commanding officers of the Supreme Command from Serbia withdrew, King Nicholas left Montenegro for Nei in France (near Paris). Only a few days later, on January 25th, Montenegro capitulated. After the King's departure, an occupying military administration was established in the occupied area, and the *truncated government* was abolished. This caused the constant resistance and conflict to the occupying forces from August 1916. At the very end of the war began the breakthrough of the Thessaloniki Front on September 14th, 1918. Montenegro was occupied by the troops of French, British, Italian and American Army, and also by the Serbian troops that were under the command of the General Louis Franchet d'Espèrey Živojinović (2002).[29]

Figure 5.3 German cartoon mocking the Allied countries as a rag-tag of bandits

According to the data from the History Lexicon of Montenegro (book 2),[30] in World War I, Montenegro lost about 20,000 soldiers, or 10% of the total population. About 15,000 people went through the camps, while the material losses were estimated at 723 million francs,

---

[28] After Austria-Hungary, Bulgaria and Germany had defeated Serbia at the end of 1915, the Austro-Hungarian army attacked Montenegro. Between 7 and 10 January 1916, the 47th*Infanteriedivision*, closely backed by naval artillery, conquered the Montenegrin positions at the Lovćen, which the *Lovćenski Odred* had defended.
[29] Živojinović, D. (2002). *Kraj Kraljevine Crne Gore: mirovna konferencija i posle 1918-1921* (The End of the Kingdom of Montenegro: Peace Conference, 1918-1921). Beograd: Službeni list SRJ.
[30] *Op. cit.* Rastoder, et al. (2006).

which was the war damage claim filed at the Paris Peace Conference (1919). In the fourth year of war, the signing of the Corfu Declaration (July 20th, 1917) took place, which defined that the Serbs, Croats and Slovenes would form a common state, the Kingdom with the Karađorđević dynasty at the helm. As one of the testimonies of these historical moments and events there is a proclamation[31] (dated December 24th, 1918) in which the ruler of Montenegro, King Nicholas from Paris opposes the entry of Montenegro into Yugoslavia. It was also signed by members of the emigrant government: Evgenije Popović, Milo Vujović, Niko Hajduković and Pero Šoć.

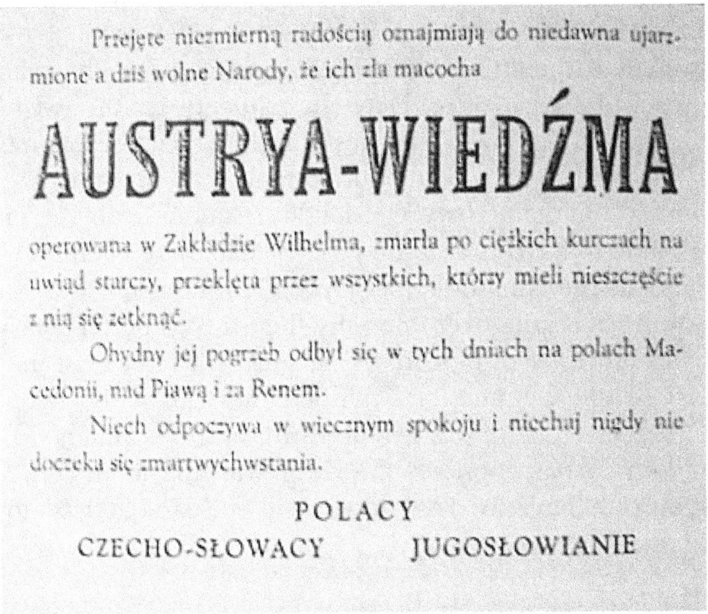

> Przejęte niezmierną radością oznajmiają do niedawna ujarz-
> mione a dziś wolne Narody, że ich zła macocha
>
> # AUSTRYA-WIEDŹMA
>
> operowana w Zakładzie Wilhelma, zmarła po ciężkich kurczach na uwiąd starczy, przeklęta przez wszystkich, którzy mieli nieszczęście z nią się zetknąć.
>
> Ohydny jej pogrzeb odbył się w tych dniach na polach Ma-cedonii, nad Piawą i za Renem.
>
> Niech odpoczywa w wiecznym spokoju i niechaj nigdy nie doczeka się zmartwychwstania.
>
> POLACY
> CZECHO-SŁOWACY   JUGOSŁOWIANIE

Figure 5.4 The defeat of Austria was an opportunity to mock them

In that proclamation, the King addresses the Montenegrins and reminds that he was separated from the people for three years, "them in slavery, and him in exile." Essentially, this proclamation also reveals the socio-political context in which Montenegro found itself after the King emigrated because it describes how he, in the name of the people, decided to be allied with Serbia when the Austria-Hungary declared the war. After this agreement and battles on the battlefield, primarily defending the retreat of the Serbian army, Montenegro became a

---

[31] *Op. cit*. Đurović, J., Vračar, M. and Lompar, D, (2010), No: 58, page 148.

victim. The King is openly convinced that someone will have to answer for his defamation. It is the case of open King's propaganda, because he makes accusations of those who turned back to Montenegro during the war. We note that it is here that he is accused of maintaining ties with Austria-Hungary, which means that he was also under attack by propaganda campaign, and he fought back to it with as little political power as he had at that moment. The King further in the proclamation claims that although he was aided by the allies, he had to obey, leave the country and go to exile, and the position in which he and the country found themselves he does not accuse 'the heroic and fraternal people of Serbia', but official Serbia. The King becomes even more direct, and states that 'certain politicians from Belgrade' have been leading, as he says 'the most disgusting' campaign, using the principle – the goal justifies the means. Here he alluded to the well-known Machiavellian learning. He even states that the official Serbia has given money to the Allied press to announce that both he and other state representatives "maintained secret friendly relations with the enemy." As the war came to a close, and the allies defeated the enemies who left the homeland, as the King describes further, Montenegro was occupied on behalf of the Serbian government by the army. The Great National Assembly was established, that the King stated did not exist under the Constitution of the Country and falsified the will of the people and destroyed the sovereignty of Montenegro and its statehood. Such unification with Serbia, considers the King, was not on an equal terms. Montenegro would be treated as "one or two Serbian districts" to which they would rule.

1918 War's End

Thus, the delegation of the People's Council of Zagreb sent in 1918 to the Crown Prince Alexander, an Address which states that Slovenes, Croats and Serbs who have been in the territory of the former Austro-Hungarian Monarchy have overturned it and temporarily constituted an independent state - want to unite in a unified people's state of Serbs, Croats and Slovenes, which would refer to the ethnographic territory of Southern Slavs. They note that parts of their territory were occupied by the kingdom of Italy and sought the Crown Prince of the throne to take up for the return of their ethnographic boundaries. In response to this Address, the Crown Prince Alexander proclaims the unification of Serbia with the countries of the independent state of Slovenes, Croats and Serbs in the Kingdom of Serbs, Croats and Slovenes, while on pleading for demarcation with Italy, he hopes the Allies will 'fairly assess' the point of view on this issue.[32]

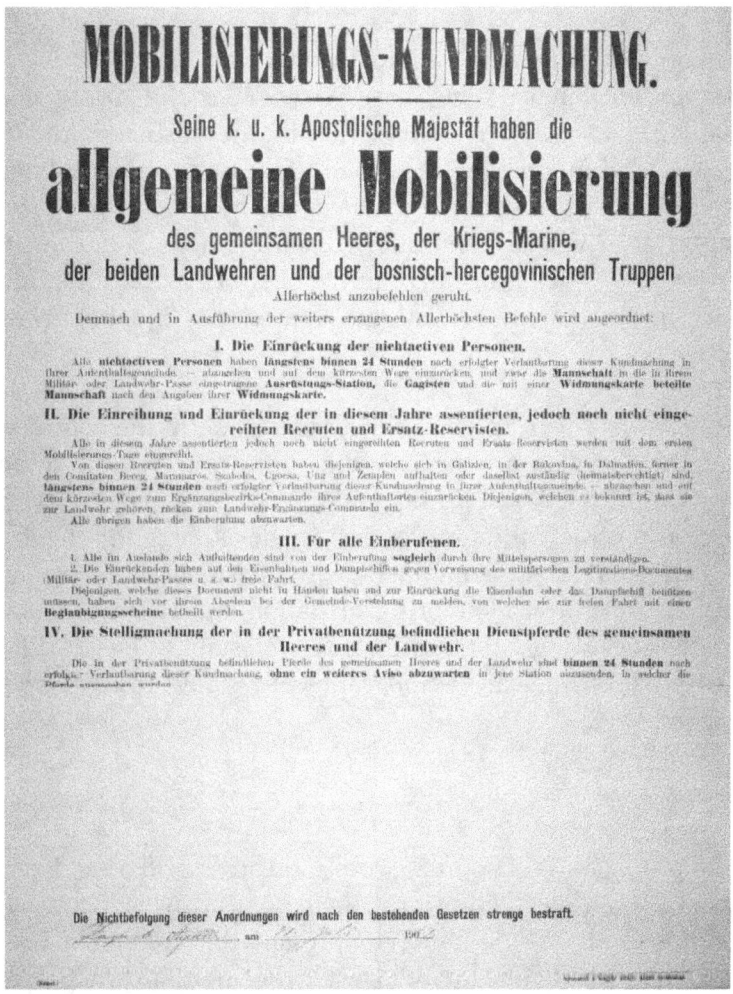

Figure 5.5 Mobilisierungs-Kundmachung, 1914

From the court in Niš on December 24th, 1918, King Alexander says that everyone is happy to welcome liberation and unification in an independent state, and that the government formed will have the task to

---

[32] Source: A ceremonial proclamation of the state unity of Serbs, Croats and Slovenes, 1918 digitalna.nb.rs/wb/NBS/Plakati_i_dokumentacioni_materijal/Objave_i_proglasi_srps kih_kraljevskih_dinastija/Karadjordjevici/PL-153-016#page/0/mode/1up, COBISS.SR-ID: 113564684.

apply all rights and freedoms to every citizen, as the citizens of Serbia previously had. The following is an extract of a letter from the King of Montenegro to the President of the United States of America, (Paris, January 7th, 1919).

> The union of Montenegro with its Jugoslav brothers.
> But all my life I have been the most resolute and most listened to partisan of it! Only, I have always felt that it was necessary to leave my people and independence, which they have so dearly bought by five long centuries of strife, and I have always proclaimed that in the formation of a Jugoslav community each member ought to preserve its autonomy. This I restated in October 1918. No Jugoslavia is possible, in my opinion, without liberty and equality among its members.

After a four-year war, the King cites main goals in the coming period as: feeding the population, especially the poor, 'restoring the ruined and devastated country', establishing land and sea traffic, which is considered as a basic condition for proper development. This is where internal propaganda is combined with participation propaganda, because the people are called for participation in certain actions. As the highest task, the King emphasises that in establishing world peace, borders of a nation that are ethnographically suited to its people must be established.[33]

Conclusion

Numerous propaganda resources were used in World War I, with the intention to encourage members of their own army or people for the conflict, and on the other hand, to present the enemy in the worst possible context. A significant role in all the then known propaganda tools has a political poster. Aulich (2007) in the *War Posters – Weapons of Mass Communication*, one chapter, which is referring to posters in World War, is entitled 'Selling the War and the Peace', because it is precisely the essence of propaganda activities.[34]

---

[33] See, 'To my people: Serbs, Croats, Slovens', velikirat.nb.rs/items/show/4270, COBISS.RS ID108176652
[34] Aulich, J. (2007). *War Posters - Weapons of Mass Communication*. London: Thames & Hudson, Imperial War Museum.

It was equally used by the powers of Triple Entente and the Central Powers, trying to direct propaganda in the desired direction. Political posters remained as permanent archives, testimonies and documents about the course and the outcome of this global scale conflict.

Propaganda activities were not just features of great powers, either of Triple Entente forces, or the Central Powers, which were the major carriers of war actions and strategy for the win in the war, but the other participants of the war diligently engaged in propaganda, including Montenegro and Serbia.

Both states, in this historic period of the kingdom, entered the Great War totally weakened by the just finished Balkan wars. However, the political circumstances were such that these wars had to be continued with the fights in this, because Serbia was the one to which Austria-Hungary declared the war, on the occasion of the murder of the Crown Prince Franz Ferdinand in Sarajevo on June 28th, 1914 committed by Gavrilo Princip and Montenegro immediately sided with of Serbia.

In those war events, Montenegro and Serbia used a political poster for various purposes. In order to fully understand its role, it is important to understand that this is the period when the dominance of the press has been recorded in the classical mass media. Both Balkan states had – when we talk about the press, already recognisable newspapers that followed the domestic and international issues.

However, under war conditions, there is an undeniable significance that political posters have had in these countries, precisely because of its ubiquity and the availability to masses. Both Kings, Nicholas I Petrović and Alexander Karađorđević informed the people through proclamations that the conflict with Austria-Hungary and the countries that were their allies had begun. In the first months of the war, through political posters, both countries ordered general mobilisation, as the enemy was more numerous and every soldier was important for defending the country. As the war progressed, and the fighting moved from front to front, the contents of political posters changed. In the beginning it was believed that the Austro-Hungarians, though with the numerous troops, would soon be overcome with the help of the Allies. However, as the war continued, we can find in posters the perceived strength of the enemy and conclude that without the help of great powers, neither Montenegro nor Serbia can defeat the enemy.

In the analysis of political posters that were available to the author of this work, it is evident that Montenegro is represented mostly by 'direct propaganda'[35] by King Nicholas towards the people and negative propaganda directed at the enemy, while in Serbia, in addition to proclamation of King Alexander, political posters that were produced and published by the members of the Central Powers are archived. When we sum up the messages that these posters have transmitted, we conclude that Serbia tried to intimidate the local population through them, for example, if anyone in any way helps the forces of Triple Entente, or in any way harms the soldier-member of the Central Forces, the death penalty was imposed. The Austro-Hungarians claimed that the Serbian army was forcibly and reluctantly fighting the war and invited soldiers to surrender.[36]

In the current sense, specifically when we only analyse the text, the political posters of Montenegro and Serbia were similar in message to those in other countries. But, in artistic, graphic sense, they were not like posters of Great Britain or Germany. When we talk about the influence of political posters, one should not forget that it is equally important to look at the verbal component of text.[37] The posters produced in World War I in these Balkan states were exclusively focused on the power of the message they send. It is not possible to draw direct parallels with posters from other countries in World War I, where the visual elements of the political poster are dominant. Here we note that, for example, for Serbia, posters were created and produced in the USA. These posters were completely different from those produced at that time in Serbia.[38]

In World War I, Montenegro and Serbia, did not have the industrialised methods of political communication readily available to Britain, France or the USA. They did have methods such as the 'proclamation' that propagated motivational communication with the army and the population at large, and this was from the start essentially an ethnically motivated political struggle *par excellence*.

---

[35] *Op. cit.* Slavujević, (1999).
[36] About the use of posters in political propaganda see more in: Rabenović, A, (2012), 'Posters as Mean of Political Propaganda' (Plakat kao sredstvo političke propagande), *Meda Dialogues (Medijski dijalozi)*. ISSN 1800-7074. Year 5, No. 13-14, pages 159-179. UDC 32.019.5:659.132.22. COBISS.CG-ID 21769744.
[37] Rabenović, A. (2010). Vizuelni i verbalni elementi političkog plakata (Visual and Verbal Elements of Political Posters), *CM*. ISSN 1452-7405. Year. 5, No. 17 pp. 95-118. UDC 32.019.5:766. COBISS.SR-ID 261171975, page 95.
[38] For more see: Rabenović, A. (2013). (February), Political Posters in World War I (Politički plakat u Prvom svjetskom ratu), Media dialogues (*Medijski Dijalozi*). ISSN 1800-7074. Year 6, No. 15, pages 323-344. UDC 32:659.22 '1914/1918'. COBISS.CG-ID 22127888.

Sources for political posters

Đurović, J., Vračar, M., and Lompar, D. (2010). Besjede i proglasi Kralja Nikole: 100 godina od obnove Kraljevine Crne Gore: 1910-2010 (trans. Orations and Declarations of King Nicholas I: 100 years since the restoration of the Kingdom of Montenegro: 1910-2010), Centralna narodna biblioteka Crne Gore 'Đurđe Crnojević', DPC, Cetinje, Podgorica, page 139, No: 53, page 141, No: 54, page 143, No: 55, page 145, No: 56, page 148, No: 58.

Objave i proglasi srpskih kraljevskih dinastija (Announcements and proclamations of the Serbian royal dynasties), n. d., viewed 19 July 2017. Available from: digitalna.nb.rs/sf/NBS/Plakati_i_dokumentacioni_materijal/Objave_i_proglasi_srpskih_kraljevskih_dinastija.

Veliki rat (Great War), n.d., viewed 19 July 2017, available from: velikirat.nb.rs & velikirat.nb.rs/onama.

Throne speech, which His Majesty Crown Prince Alexander opened the session of the extraordinary Session of the National Assembly, convened in Niš on 14 July 1914. Available from: velikirat.nb.rs/items/show/4288, n.d., viewed 19 July 2017.

Order No. 8676 from 1914, of the Supreme Commander of His Royal Majesty the Crown Prince Alexander, to his Serbian Army for 15 December. Available from: digitalna.nb.rs/wb/NBS/Plakati_i_dokumentacioni_materijal/Objave_i_proglasi_srpskih_kraljevskih_dinastija/Karadjordjevici/PL-153-071, COBISS.SR-ID: 114522124), n.d., viewed 19 July 2017.

It is reported to the Serb people and the military, 1915. Available from: velikirat.nb.rs/items/show/6192, COBISS.RS ID 96284684, n.d., viewed 21 July 2017.

Mobilisierungs-kundmachung, 1914. velikirat.nb.rs/items/show/6197, COBISS.RS ID 196986380, n.d., viewed 21 July 2017.

Placard about readiness, 1914. Available from: velikirat.nb.rs/items/show/6193, COBISS.RS ID 118149644, n.d., viewed 21 July 2017.

Serbian soldiers!, 1914?. Available from: velikirat.nb.rs/items/show/4282, COBISS.RS ID 105856012, n.d., viewed 21 July 2017.

Commander in chief General of the Austro-Hungarian Army in Serbia, 1915 Available from: velikirat.nb.rs/items/show/4259, COBISS.RS ID (105784076), n.d., viewed 21 July 2017.

Serbian soldiers. Available from: velikirat.nb.rs/items/show/1054,

COBISS.RS ID196957452, n.d., viewed 22 July 2017.

A ceremonial proclamation of the state unity of Serbs, Croats and Slovenes, 1918. Available from: digitalna.nb.rs/wb/NBS/Plakati_i_dokumentacioni_materijal/Objave_i_proglasi_srpskih_kraljevskih_dinastija/Karadjordjevici/PL-153-016#page/0/mode/1up, COBISS.SR-ID: 113564684, n.d., viewed 22 July 2017.

To my people: Serbs, Croats, Slovens. Available from: velikirat.nb.rs/items/show/4270, COBISS.RS ID108176652, n.d., viewed 22 July 2017.

Chapter 6

Basque Writers' Reportages in *Eskualduna*, During World War I

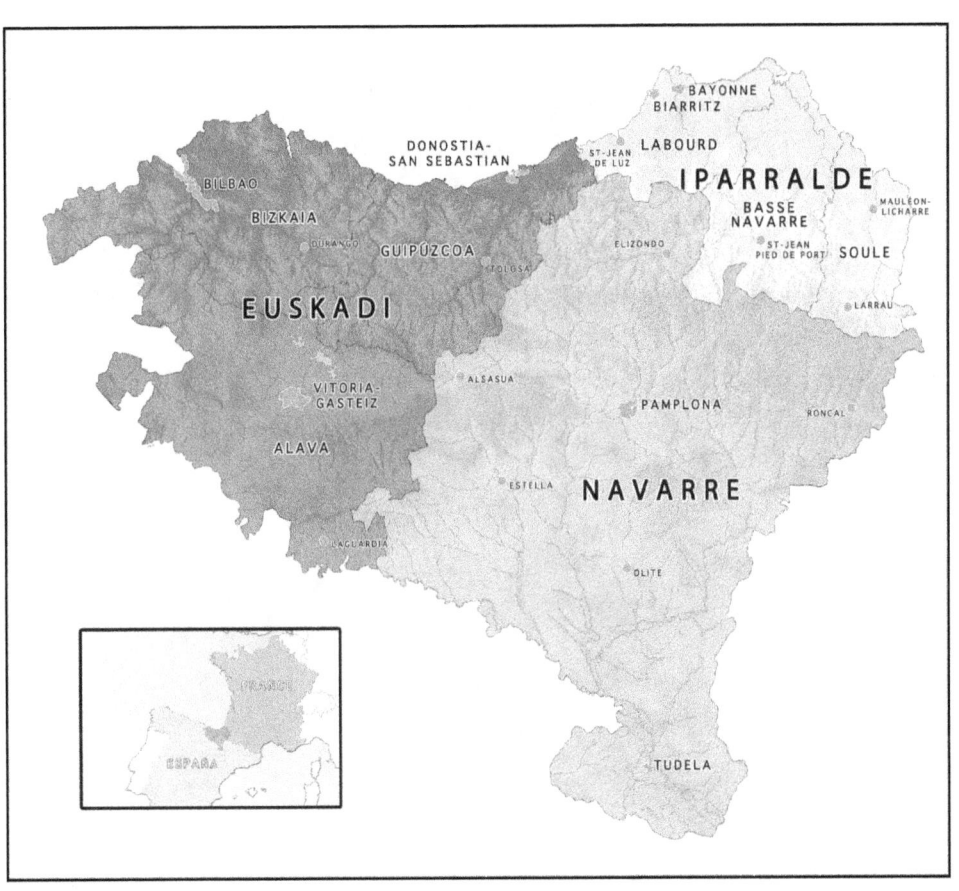

Chapter 6

Basque Writers' Reportages in *Eskualduna*, During World War I

Eneko Bidegain
Mondragon Unibertsitatea

Introduction

This chapter based on my doctoral thesis (Bidegain, 2013) and aims to analyse the vision disseminated by the writers of the Basque weekly magazine *Eskualduna*, during World War I (1914-1918). Created in 1887 by the Bonapartist politician Louis Etcheverry, *Eskualduna* was the most important newspaper in the continental Basque Country (France), with a circulation of 7,000, in a region where the population was 187,775. It was a Catholic newspaper, written in Basque, essentially by priests. It was not a professional journal, but many people contributed on a voluntary basis.

The French Basque Country was very rural, except for the coast, and especially Bayonne. The population did not speak French or only a little. At the end of the XIX century, the Government of France made a great stride in education, and schooling became compulsory, with the result that children started learning in French. Also, the goal of the education system was not limited to the language: teachers taught the territoriality of France, patriotism and military movements, with the intention of preparing the population for a war of revenge against Germany, after the defeat of 1870.[1] World War I was launched in this

---

[1] See, Sohier, A. (2010). 'L'enfant et la guerre à l'école primaire: en Bretagne 1871-1914', in Denis, G. *Mémoire et trauma de la Grande Guerre. Bretagne, Catalogne, Corse, Euskadi, Occitanie*, pages 11-30 and Thiesse, A.M. (1997). *Ils apprenaient la France: l'exaltation des régions dans le discours patriotique*. Paris: Éditions de la Maison des sciences de l'homme.

context, in 1914. The entire population of France was united, suppressing political divisions. 20,000 Basque men were mobilised as were all French men aged between 20 and 49 years old.

Within a few days, all the villages of France and the French Basque Country were emptied of the majority of the adult male population. It was the same for *Eskualduna*: the youngest writers were sent to the front lines at Charleroi, Aisne, and Verdun, as soldiers. This situation could have been a handicap for the newspaper. Paradoxically, this handicap became a great opportunity to create a unique newspaper, as these writers wrote weekly, personal reportages, about life on the frontline.

It is interesting to analyse their discourse, taking into account that they were French soldiers, in spite of their Basque identity. This contradiction constitutes the originality of our research. There is very little research into the Basque people in the First World War, and their relationship to French identity; such research, is limited to military history[2] such as Ansoborlo, (1995), Garat, (1983) and Rocafort, (1997) and a handful of articles such as Charriton, (1988, 1992), Elissalde, (1995) and Saint-Pierre 'Anxuberro', (1998). Apart from this, there are some theses on press discourse during the Great War including, Brandenberger, (1964), Dalbin, (2007), Eglezou, (2009), Falcomatà & Nunnari, (2004), Farrar, (1998), Venturelli, (1991) and Wolfs, (2001).[3] All these studies are relevant to our subject in terms of the methods and

---

[2] For example, Ansoborlo, J. (1995). *Histoire militaire de Bayonne: 1789-1940*. Bayonne: Société des Siences Lettres et Arts de Bayonne; Garat, J. (1983). *Insoumissions et désertions en France pendant la Grande Guerre: Le Cas des cantons basques* ([tesina-memorioa, zuz. Jacques Julliard]). EHESS, Paris; Rocafort, J. (1997). *Avant oubli: soldats et civils de la côte basque durant la grande guerre*. Biarritz: Atlantica. And articles by, Charriton, P. (1988). *Jean Etchepare mirikuaren idazlanak. III. Kazetaritza (A) (1903-1915)*. Donostia: Elkar; Charriton, P. (1992). *Jean Etchepare mirikuaren idazlanak. IV. Kazetaritza (B) (1916-1935)*. Donostia: Elkar; Elissalde, J. (1995). *LVII.a gerlan*. (P. Urkizu, Ed.). Zarautz: Alberdania; and Saint-Pierre "Anxuberro," J. (1998). *14eko Gerla Handia*. (P. Xarriton, Ed.). Donostia: Euskal Editoreen Elkartea.

[3] Brandenberger, D. (1964). *La presse parisienne et les buts de guerre: (septembre 1916-février 1917)* ([tesina-memorioa, zuz. Pierre Renouvin]). Université de Paris. Faculté des lettres et sciences humaines; Dalbin, S. (2007). *Visions croisees franco-allemandes de la premiere guerre mondiale: étude de deux quotidiens: la Metzer Zeitung et L'Est Republicain*. Bruxelles: Peter Lang; Eglezou, G. (2009). *The Greek media in World War I and its aftermath: the Athenian press and the Asia Minor crisis*. London, New York: Tauris Academic Studies; Falcomatà, I., & Nunnari, D. (2004). *Il Corriere di Calabria e l'opinione pubblica nella grande guerra (1914-1918)*. Ravagnese: Città del sole; Farrar, M. J. (1998). *News from the front: war correspondents on the Western Front, 1914-18*. Thrupp: Sutton Pub; Venturelli, G. (1991). *La grande guerra in prima pagina: la stampa cattolica italiana tra neutralità e intervento*. Firenze: Atheneum; Wolfs, G. (2001). *La Russie en guerre (1914-1918) vue par les périodiques occidentaux: relation des événements, nationalismes et propagange* ([doktorego-tesia, zuz. Paul Dumont eta Vladimir Claude Fišera]). Strasbourg: Université Marc Bloch.

political analysis they employed. However, this research differs from identity, the subject of analysis being articles written in a regional language (in Basque, in this case).

The methodology

Considering that the articles of Basque writers on the First World War have not been analysed until now, this paper intends to highlight one aspect of these testimonies. The writers who contributed most frequently were Jean Saint-Pierre (1884-1951), Jean Elizalde *Zerbitzari* (1883-1961) and Jean Etxepare (1877-1935). The first two were clerics and the third a doctor. They wrote an almost weekly chronicle between 1914 and 1918. A fourth journalist, Jules Moulier Oxobi (1888-1958), started describing his adventures, until 1917, when he was sent to the front, after having been exempt for three years due to health problems.

The texts composed by those soldiers are interesting for several reasons, developed in my doctoral research.[4] Firstly, they gave the readers their point of view on the causes of the war, with their political opinions and their hatred of the Germans. Secondly, they related life very vividly on the front or behind the lines. They glorified the acts of war by the French army, omitting details banned under censorship law. Thirdly, they consistently exhibited their Basque identity. That is the particularity of this subject, so we shall focus on this point. What was the strongest sense of identity of those Basque correspondents fighting in the French army? The main proposition is that these writers felt French, in spite of their Basque identity and the fact that they were homesick.

The research method used to demonstrate this proposition is content analysis: following the method proposed by Bardin (2007)[5] and used by Dalbin (2007).[6] 3,422 articles were examined, redacted between the end of July 1914 and January 1915. The articles were classified into various themes, and correlations were made. For this chapter, passages dealing with identity (both Basque and French) were selected. The theme of identity has been subdivided into subtopics such as French nationalism, Basque nationalism, France, identity, engagement, sacrifice, homesickness, family, home and Basque culture. Associations can also be made with more general subjects, such as religion, politics, society,

---

[4] Bidegain, E. (2013). *Lehen Mundu Gerra "Eskualduna" astekarian* (Vol. 29). Bilbo: Euskaltzaindia.
[5] Bardin, L. (2007). *L'analyse de contenu* ([lehen edizioa: 1977]). Paris: Presses universitaires de France.
[6] *Op. cit.* Dalbin, (2007).

and combat. This method helps us understand what the vision of Basque combatants was during the World War I.

The finding

There is more than one aspect in the discourse of *Eskualduna* on the First World War. We can analyse the main article on the first page, which gives the political point of view of the editor of *Eskualduna*. This editorial is followed by general news of the war. The rest of the first page offers direct testimonies of Basque writers, thanks to their letters published in this newspaper. The second page presents local news, organised village by village. Due to the war, these are about soldiers who have died or been decorated.

Figure 6.1 Front page of the *Eskualduna* 7 August 1914

Before analysing the manifestation of Basque identity in those pieces of news, it is necessary to summarise the principal subjects covered every week: international politics, military events, and life at the front and Basque identity.

As regards the political opinion of the newspaper, the message was always against Germany and the German army: for the writers of

Eskualduna, the Germans were animals, and France and England represented civilisation. Furthermore, they wrote that God sustained France and England. They accused Germany of unjustly attacking Belgium and France, and they affirmed that French people needed to defend the nation and civilisation.

Military news lacked precision. They were not allowed to give any information about the location or situation of regiments. In addition, they avoided negative news about the French, English and Russian armies. They recognised their defeats weeks or months later when their armies had recovered the lost terrain. However, they described their soldiers' lives in more detail: the organisation of trenches, the poor hygiene including the presence of rats and lice, and life behind the lines. Readers could not be informed of the true military situation of the war, but they were provided with a detailed picture of the lives of soldiers.

Homesickness

After spending several months far from the Basque Country, the Basque writers and priests Jean Saint-Pierre and Jean Elizalde *Zerbitzari* show that they are missing their country keenly. For example, Saint-Pierre (1915e) wrote that when he saw the name of a Basque village on a car, his heart throbbed.[7] According to Blaise Adéma, in charge of *Eskualduna*, Basque soldiers were delighted when they received *Eskualduna*, 200 copies of which were sent to the front where Basques were fighting. The compilers of *Eskualduna* asked Basque women to send their copies to their husbands or sons. They were happy reading news of their villages:

> Lurpeko barne ilhun hetarik batean Eskualdun kazetak berehala bihotzak argitzen ditu eta arintzen:
> (Into one of those dark interiors, the Basque gazette quickly lightens hearts).[8]

In this way, for them, it was gratifying to read in Basque (Adéma, 1916a). For every copy, ten people grouped together to read news from the Basque paper. Moreover, Basques soldiers planned to create a

---

[7] Saint-Pierre, J. (1915e, March 26). 'Beskoitzeko karrosa'. *Eskualduna*.
[8] Adéma, B. (1916b, November 17). 'Berriketariak'. *Eskualduna*.

magazine for soldiers in Basque but were unable to find paper, printers or writers. However, for the soldiers, the most important item was *Eskualduna*, because they could feel "the good wind of their village."[9] They did not want only local news; they wanted news of their birthplaces.

Another aspect is referenced to the landscapes of the Basque Country, especially the mountains and the sea. Jean Saint-Pierre lauded the beauty of his country, and when he described his surrounding area, he compared the mountains that he could see to the mountains of his homeland, which he expressed a wish to return to.

> Hunat heltzeko mendietan gaindi gabiltza *Eskualduna* laster alegeratzen du mendiaren itzal nasaiak, mazela baten hegalean gordea dagon bazter etche pollitak, oihan handien pherdeak. [...] Nehun baino minago hemen dugu bihotzaren deia entzuten; hemendik bihotzak dio: Zoaz Eskual Herrira! (Basque people are soon happy seeing the shadow of mountains; the pleasant, small, hidden houses... the green of the forests. More than anywhere, we heard the hearth's call: go back to the Basque Country!)[10]

In this case, the homesickness was exacerbated by the absence of any beautiful or familiar landscapes. *Zerbitzari* wrote the same, when he returned to the front, after a week on leave in his village:

> Oraidik, nere agurra igortzen dut herritar guzieri. Agur ere, Eskual-Herriko mendi zabalak: agur, gure itsaso ederra. Milesker bihotzean emanen dautazuen gozoarentzat. Zuek utziz hunat itzultzeko, negar bat erortzen balitzaut begitik harritzeko othe litake?
> (Good-bye, all citizens. Good-bye too, large mountains of the Basque Country; good-bye our beautiful sea. Thank you for the warmth that you have given me in my heart. When I leave you to return here, is it strange if I should shed a tear?)[11]

He was not crying only for the mountains and the sea, the people from his village were important too. However, the importance of the landscape was undeniable, as we can see when considering another

---

[9] Elizalde, J. (1915e, December 17). 'Ez dakizue berri?', *Eskualduna*.
[10] *Op. cit.* Saint-Pierre (1915d).
[11] Elizalde, J. (1916a, February 11). 'Azken solasa orai'. *Eskualduna*.

article, written when he returned to the Basque Country. He was happy for the sun, the climate, the sea and the mountains.[12] Of course, the contrast between Basque landscapes and the devastated terrain of the war was clear in those parts of the text, as he wrote in September 1918.[13] Another day *Zerbitzari* was sad, and he smoked to "alleviate the sorrow."[14]

The presence of landscapes in texts about home has a deeper explanation. According to Hubert Pérès (1993), objects, landscapes and sensorial experiences are part of individual's identity.[15] Anne-Marie Thiesse (1997) thinks that landscapes, geography, history, and products from this land are elements of the 'small homeland'.[16] For Thiesse, those characteristics are the same to all small homelands or regions. There are created by the same Creator, God. So, when they lauded their mountains, we should not see a materialistic concern, but one aspect of the identity of this region and, even more so, the attachment to the land created by God.

Family in mind

The homesickness of Basque soldiers was not expressed only in references to the Basque Country or Basque landscapes. Indeed, home and family were very present in the letters of Jean Saint-Pierre or *Zerbitzari*. In this way, there was an element that was often linked to food. For example, when they wrote about Basque soldiers returning from their village after a week's leave, food played an important role, as can be seen in the article,[17] that talked about soldiers returning with ham and peppers from home. Another reference to food from home was mushroom picking; in fact, one Basque soldier was punished for picking mushrooms, as doctors suspected they might be poisonous, but Saint-Pierre (1916d) wrote that Basque people knew their mushrooms very well, remembering home food and home customs.

---

[12] Elizalde, J. (1916b, February 18). 'Izenbururik gabe'. *Eskualduna*.
[13] *Ibid.*
[14] Elizalde, J. (1917d, October 19). 'Azken hitza'. *Eskualduna*.
[15] Pérès, H. (1993). *Individus entre village et nation. Une expérience identitaire dans la formation de la France républicaine* ([doktorego-tesia, zuz. Albert Malabileau]). Université de Bordeaux I, Institut d'Etudes Politiques, Bordeaux, page 216.
[16] *Op. cit.* Thiesse, A.-M. (1997), page 34.
[17] Saint-Pierre, J. (1915i, August 13). 'Permisioneak'. *Eskualduna*.

Basque Soldiers wanted objects from home, in order to remember their homes and the Basque Country, as Blaise Adéma writes in this extract:

> Orhoitzen da bere etcheaz, hango jauntzi eta oinetako idorrez, hango ohe beroaz, hango subazter chokoaz, eta bihotza ttikitzen zaio. [...] Eta gure ganik etorriko zaioten orhoitzapenak on handia eginen diote bihotzean, lagunduko ditu hormaren, elhurraren, ichtilaren hobeki jasaiten.
> (He remembers his home, dry clothing and shoes there, a warm bed and the hearth; and his heart shrinks. [...] And the souvenirs that we send them will do them good in their hearts, and will help them to better bear the snow and the mud)[18]

Adéma asked his readers to send things that smelt of home, like sausage and ham, after killing the pig,[19] because that was a way to remember home. This phenomenon was general, according to François Cochet; home objects and food had a psychological function.[20] For Baconnier, Minet, and Soler (1985)[21], the value of food was symbolic because of the emotions embodied by the food. This example illustrates very well the link between food and family:

> Atzo, bi arroltze atzemanik, lagun batekin partitu ditut. Etzuen jan arroltze bat oraino, gerlarat joanez geroz. Huna zer erran dautan berak: "Agorrilaren bian ikusi nituen azken arroltzeak: amak: emanik partitzean, goizean goiz... Han berean utzi nituen."
> (Yesterday, I found two eggs, and I shared them with a friend. He had not eaten an egg since the start of the war. He told me: "I saw my last eggs on the second of August, cooked by my mother, in the morning... I left them there")[22]

---

[18] Adéma, B. (1916c, December 8). 'Ez ahantz'. *Eskualduna*.
[19] Adéma, B. (1916d, December 15). 'Noiz egor?' *Eskualduna*.
[20] Cochet, F. (2005). *Survivre au front, 1914-1918. Les poilus entre contrainte et consentement*. s.l., page 201.
[21] Baconnier, G., Minet, A., and Soler, L. (1989). 'Quarante millions de témoins', in Canini, G. (Ed.), *Mémoires de la Grande Guerre. Témoins et témoignages, Actes du colloque de Verdun, 12, 13, 14 juin 1986*. Nancy: Presses Universitaires de Nancy, pages 141-169.
[22] Saint-Pierre, J. (1915c, February 26). 'Kruspetak'. *Eskualduna*.

Apart from food, the hearth of the home was strongly present in texts of Basque writers, and by hearth, we should understand the kitchen and family warmth:

> Euriak euriari, hotz minenekin, tente kampoan egotea, chichpa eskuan, supazter chokoan, amacho ichtorio kondari, hain gocho litakelarik, dorphe zaiku.
> (It is very hard for us; to stay away, to stand with gun in hand, in lashing rain and the harsh cold, while it would be nice to be near the fire, with Mum telling stories).[23]

Homesickness expressed through food and hearth hides another, more important longing, for the presence of mothers or grandmothers,[24] and the nostalgia of childhood. In short, homesickness based on the love of family. According to Baconnier, Minét, and Soler (1989),[25] when soldiers wrote words in their language, for example, in Catalan, they wrote "sweet words" or "words from the heart." Languages have an emotional side, linked to love.

Furthermore, soldiers were worried about the loneliness of their wives who were left to do the farm work alone.[26] Paul Lazarsfeld and Jean-Jacques Becker (1988)[27] affirmed that farmers, (in spite of being accustomed to living and working in hard conditions) suffered more than city dwellers due to being worried about their responsibilities on the farm and not being able to do the farm work. In addition, soldiers suffered imagining the anxiety of their families:

> Baginaki gurek ez dutela sofritzen gu hemen izaiteaz, nola ari gintazken! Horko minak gaitu higatzen.
> (If we knew that our families did not suffer because we are here, imagine how we could fight! It is their grief that worries us).[28]

---

[23] Elizalde, J. (1916h, November 24). 'Permisioneak'. *Eskualduna*.
[24] Moulier, J. (1918b, March 1). 'Atso bat'. *Eskualduna*.
[25] *Op. cit.* Baconnier, G., Minet, A., and Soler, L. (1989). 'Quarante millions de témoins' in Canini, G. (Ed.), *Mémoires de la Grande Guerre. Témoins et témoignages, Actes du colloque de Verdun, 12, 13, 14 juin 1986.* Nancy: Presses Universitaires de Nancy, pages 141-169.
[26] Elizalde, J. (1917f, December 7). Zaharrak berri. *Eskualduna*.
[27] Mariot, N. (2003). Faut-il être motivé pour tuer? Sur quelques explications aux violences de guerre. *Genèses*, 53, pages 154-177 and Becker, J-J. (1988). *La France en guerre 1914-1918. La grande mutation.* Bruxelles: Editions Complexe, page 41.
[28] Elizalde, J. (1915a, January 15). 'Urtarrilaren 9an'. *Eskualduna*.

The suffering endured as a result of leaving one's loved ones behind also emerged in some cases. There was a moving article in which an old soldier described how he went home on leave on one occasion and his child, who had been two at the outbreak of the war, did not know who he was:

> […] Bi urthe eta erdi zituen ni gerlarat joaitean. Deusek ez daut hala hautsi bihotza, nola ikusteak eztuela haur gaichoak bere aita ezagutu. Egungotzat haatik adichkidetuak ginen. Damurik noa hoin fite.
> (The child was two years old when I went off to the war. I have experienced nothing more heartrending than realising that the poor child did not recognise its father. But within a day, we had become friends. Unfortunately, I have to go back far too soon).[29]

Hiriart-Urruti described this event in the form of a story as a way of transmitting that soldier's testimony. He drew attention to the suffering of those who went home on leave and who were fathers. *Eskualduna* depicted the pain and suffering endured by the soldiers and their families. That does not mean that they were complaining about the war or that they were refusing to accept the situation. Far from it. As *Zerbitzari* wrote, they were prepared to put up with the dreadful conditions, and they wanted to win the war. In that father's testimony about his two-year-old child, Hiriart-Urruti wrote that this father had refused to go beyond the mountains and become a deserter, and praised his attitude. As Annette Becker (1993) explained, they were torn between hope, sadness, suffering, and prayer.[30]

Family and friends were very important in the soldiers' hearts, and so was their village church. As regards totheir homeland, when referring to the Basque Country, the village (parish church) appeared alongside their loved ones, and that was evident among all the other soldiers, as has emerged throughout the thesis by Hubert Pérès (1993).[31] Up until that time, in terms of the concept of their identity, their village was the location and reference for those of the interior because they lived with the villagers, because they were there with them all the time and because that was their specific milieu, whereas the French nation remained an abstract concept. But he also points out that they accepted

---

[29] Hiriart-Urruti, M. (1915, July 26). 'Bortz haurren aita'. *Eskualduna*.
[30] Becker, A. (1993). 'Les dévotions des soldats catholiques pendant la Grande Guerre', in, Chaline, N-J. (zuz.), *Chrétiens dans la Première Guerre mondiale*. Paris: Cerf, page 16.
[31] *Op. cit.* Pérès, (1993), page 332.

their participation in the war as a way of opposing the threat hanging over their villages. So the fact that each one cherished the memory of his village, in particular, did not affect only the Basques but all the soldiers of the inland areas of France. Being Basque did not set them apart. What is more, according to Pérès, the war itself encouraged them to regard their villages as part of the (French) nation.

Basques together

With their loved ones far away, the presence of the Basque Country could be felt by the Basque soldiers. In particular, when we read the articles written by *Zerbitzari* we realise that the Basques in different regiments used to meet up whenever they could; he highlighted this fact. For example, he once said that he met up with the 249th regiment. Whenever the Basques met up on rest days, he wrote that they used to have 'a good time'. They played cards ['Mus': a card game similar to poker using a Spanish deck and with two opposing pairs of players; the aim is to win points] and drank wine from a wineskin bottle.[32]

On another occasion, Jean Saint-Pierre spoke about his Basque friends. One by the name of Acheriberro and his friends had returned to the Basque Country on leave, and he wrote that without them their rest days were gloomy.[33] The absence of his Basque friends made him feel homesick, too.

The regiments mostly comprised soldiers from the same area, and the regiments of one particular area used to fight in the same place. As the war progressed, regiments were reformed to replace casualties. So even though soldiers from the same area were together at the beginning, as time passed, they were mixed up with those of other areas, and it was more difficult to find people from the same area.[34] For example, A.I., a soldier from Zuberoa (Soule), reported that he did not see any Basques when he was sent to Serbia:

Jauna, galthatzen deitadazut ea badenez Zerbian soldado Uskaldun hanitch. Eztut orano bakhotchik ere ikhousi, nahiz ari nizan bethi galthatzen. Bat utzi dut hargatik nihaouren khantian ezagutu gabe igaraitera. Geroztik jakin dut Donapaleu altheko dela,

---

[32] Elizalde, J. (1917c, October 12). 'Atzoko gure berri'. *Eskualduna*.
[33] Elizalde, J. (1916c, March 17). 'Eta Acheriberro?' *Eskualduna*.
[34] Elissondo, R. (Ed.). (2006). *Mémoires de la Soule: 1914-1918: une petite vallée du Pays Basque dans la guerre*. Maule: Ikerzaleak, page 46.

Domintchaineko. Ez ta algar atzamaitia aisa; tropak orai diren lekhia hanitch zabal da.

(Sir, you asked me whether there are many Basque soldiers in Serbia. I have yet to see a single one, even though I am always asking. However, there had been one close to me, but I did not get to know him. Later I found out that he hailed from the Donapaleu (St. Palais-le-vieux) area, from Domintxaine (Domezain). It isn't easy to come across one another; the area where the troops are stationed now is quite big).[35]

A.I. also admitted that he had been looking for Basques. He also mentioned previously that he had been with Basques:

Etzen beste uskaldunik bi aphez baizik, bata herri tchipi batetako erretora, hanitch jaun pollita, bestia misionest bat Afrikatik edo Madagaskarretik jinik, biak soldado simple eta koraje handiko gizounak.
(There were no other Basques but two priests, one the parish priest of a small village, a very pleasant man, the other a missionary who had come from Africa or Madagascar. Both were ordinary soldiers and very courageous men).[36]

He did not spend very long with those soldiers, but he attached great importance to having met them. Later on, he admitted he had been looking for Basques. When he did not see any more Basques, he wrote that he was feeling lonely. Cochet (2005), says the motivation for participating in the war was intensified by the fact that each one was with people from his area or else the commander was from the same area.[37]

Language

The bond with the Basque Country also emerged when referring to the language. It is easy to understand that they spoke in Basque amongst themselves because they sang Basque songs together, and because they gathered together to read the *Eskualduna* weekly magazine. When

---

[35] A.I. (1916a, January 28). 'Zerbiatik letera'. *Eskualduna*.
[36] A.I. (1915, December 31). 'Serbiatik letera'. *Eskualduna*.
[37] *Op. cit.* Cochet, (2005), pages 155-156.

reading the reports by *Zerbitzari* it becomes apparent that the Basques spoke to each other in Basque, but in wartime, they also had to use French. However, French was not the Basques' language, and he admitted on occasions that during the war they were learning French, for example, when they were in the Somme area on one occasion:

> Oren oneko sortu ginen. Gerla huntan hoinbertze kurrida badabilkagu, urririk. Erdara, entzunaren bortchaz, guti edo aski ikasten ari gare,… errienteri sosik eman gabe.
> (We were born at a good time. In this war, we have been going on many free journeys. Through hearing French, we are learning it more or less… without having to pay any teacher any fees).[38]

This shows that the Basques who went to the war did not speak French very well. But *Zerbitzari* was happy because they were learning French, and what is more, because they were learning it without having to pay a penny. Despite speaking French, he attached particular importance to Basque.

Basque Country customs

The Basque Country was referred to in the writings of Basque soldiers in connection with other aspects, too. They often mentioned that whenever they had time, they used to sing, dance and play Basque pelota. Through these customs that they frequently used to engage in back in the Basque Country, they were bringing a part of the Basque Country to the battlefields. Previously we mentioned some songs, and in other cases they also wrote that they had been singing or had been listening to Basque songs. Jean Saint-Pierre, for example, mentioned the song by Elizanburu Ikusten duzu goizean:

> Lasterka *Eskualduna* nausi; kantuz ere, bai.
> Ikusten duzu goizean,
> Argia hasten denean…
> (The Basques win at races and singing, too.
> You see in the morning,
> When it gets light…)

---

[38] Elizalde, J. (1917a, January 12). 'Somme delakotik'. *Eskualduna*.

> Ea emanen duzuen hemen bezen ederki? Kolonela harritua zagon, Eskualdunek eman kantu ederrari. Eskualdunek bihotzeko begiez bakarrik ikusten zuten, urrun, biziki urrun, kantuak aipatzen duen etche ttipia, mendi hegalean.
> (Will you sing it as beautifully as here? The colonel was surprised at the beautiful song the Basques sang. The Basques could only see the cottage on the mountainside mentioned in the song far away, very far away, through the eyes of their hearts).[39]

In this extract the song does not appear as a single subject. That song carried a tremendous weight over hundreds of kilometers from the Basque Country, recalling the house and the surrounding area, and reminding them of their families. The homesickness was evident below that, and that is why we say that they remembered the Basque Country through songs, as it conveyed the presence of the Basque Country. The songs reminded them of the Basque Country, and that brought tears to their eyes.[40] So the songs were inspiring or expressed homesickness. More references to song appeared mostly in combination with dance.[41]

During rest times the Basques entertained themselves through dance or song. *Zerbitzari* reported that on the battlefield or behind the frontlines the Basques used to spend their free time much as they did back in the Basque Country.[42]

Nevertheless, the subject of Basque pelota appeared frequently in the articles by *Zerbitzari*. It has often been pointed out that the Basque soldiers in the First World War were good grenade throwers because they were skilled Basque pelota players. *Zerbitzari* did not mention grenade throwers. When he mentioned pelota, he was referring to a game played during rest times, and he linked the reference to pelota with the Basque Country.

> Azkaindar bat eta Itsasuar bat pilotan ikusi ditut, bidearen erdian, sagar batekin. Urruntchago lau Azkaindar elheketa zauden Ortzaiztar batekin.
> Behin batzueri eta bertzeeri agur erran-eta, ostatuari buruz abiatu denak tropan. Harat gabe, errechimenduko musika ikusi eta

---

[39] Saint-Pierre, J. (1916b, June 23). 'Oihanetan'. *Eskualduna*.
[40] Saint-Pierre, J. (1914, December 18). 'Pausu egunak'. *Eskualduna*.
[41] Saint-Pierre, J. (1916c, August 11). 'Bero'. *Eskualduna*.
[42] Elizalde, J. (1916e, July 28). 'Fandangoak gerlan!' *Eskualduna*.

hurbildu. Choratua han atchiki naute eskualdun musikariek! Nola charamelatu dituzten Bethi Eskualdun, Reverte, Kinkirri Kunkurru eta akabatzeko Arin-Arin!

[...] Ah, eta ez nuke ederrena ahantzi behar: musikari horiek eman daukutela ere fandango bat Eskualdun batek moldatua: Sencilla delako fandangoa, Vicendoritz donibandarrak moldatua.

(I saw one from Azkaine and another from Itsasu in the middle of the road playing pelota with an apple. Further away, four from Azkaine were talking to someone from Ortzaize.

After I had greeted them, they all streamed towards a bar. Before arriving, I saw the regiment band, and I approached them. I was charmed by the Basque musicians and stopped there. How beautifully they sang Bethi Eskualdun, Reverte, Kinkirri Kunkurru ending with Arin-Arin!

[...] Ah, and I must not forget the nicest part: these musicians also played us a fandango arranged by a Basque: the fandango was called "Sencilla" and had been arranged by Vicendoritz of St. Juan de Luz).[43]

In this passage, he not only mentioned pelota but also songs and fandango. In this article he gathered together the three best-known features of Basque popular culture as if they could not be distinguished from each other. Concerning pelota, it is noticeable that anything sufficed to play the game.

Even though they remembered the Basque Country through pelota, *Zerbitzari* was also heartened by the fact that they continued to play pelota in the Basque Country. When reading an article in *Eskualduna*, *Zerbitzari* was delighted to discover that in the Basque Country the young people played pelota, but more than that, he said in the next one that he had dreamt about playing pelota in the Basque Country.[44] The fact that pelota, dance, and song appeared so much on the battlefield, is not just connected with the need to forget the harsh conditions of the war during rest times. But also with the need to remember the homeland, even though it was understandable that each one should do what he knew how to do, hence the Basques engaged in song, pelota, and dance.

---

[43] Elizalde, J. (1917c, October 12). 'Atzoko gure berri'. *Eskualduna*.
[44] Elizalde, J. (1916g, August 4). '*Eskualduna*'. *Eskualduna*.

But more has to be seen behind pelota than that. *Zerbitzari* also displayed a clear cultural stance through pelota, because given the choice of either football or pelota, he would opt for pelota, because he saw that football could predominate. The Basques played pelota, whereas all the rest played football in particular. *Zerbitzari* did not find football so beautiful, even though the Basques were playing football, too; he preferred them to continue with pelota.[45] He saw pelota as a way of preserving Basque identity. Firstly, it was about playing something they were familiar with, and secondly, it was about defending their culture and, along with that, their identity. As Baconnier, Minet and Soler (1989) said, that did not happen exclusively with the Basques; the Catalans also spoke about their national games with the same passion, because it reminded them of their country.[46]

Apart from sports or physical pursuits, the soldiers enjoyed themselves in other ways, too, like playing cards. The Basques used to play the card game 'mus', according to several letters by *Zerbitzari* and Jean Saint-Pierre. Through the articles in *Eskualduna*, both *Zerbitzari* and Jean Saint-Pierre often asked Basques back home to send them 'mus' cards. In one of the latter's articles (Saint-Pierre, 1915b) he says they spent so many hours playing cards that the cards themselves would end up completely worn out. They apparently played cards while taking cover during heavy bombardments (Saint-Pierre, 1915g).[47]

Oxobi described a 'mus' game.[48] This long article about 'mus' provided no details about the war. The conversation about the time spent playing 'mus' provided neither information nor any significant details about the atmosphere. Any reader who knew how to play 'mus' also knew what these 'mus' conversations were like. In these lines Oxobi grafts on the battlefield, the memory of the Basque Country atmosphere in the bars or homes; or else he pointed out that they were making an effort to recreate that atmosphere on the battlefield.

When reading these articles and others, it becomes clear that the soldiers of the Basque Country spent much of their rest time and leisure time playing pelota and 'mus'. But is there a concern about nostalgia for the Basque Country underlying this? According to Baconnier, Minet

---

[45] Iizalde, J. (1915e, December 17). 'Ez dakizue berri?' *Eskualduna*.
[46] *Op. cit.* Baconnier, et al. (1989).
[47] Elizalde, J. (1915d, November 12). 'Gerlarien berri'. *Eskualduna*. Saint-Pierre, J. (1915b, January 15). 'Muslariak'. *Eskualduna*. And, Saint-Pierre, J. (1915g, July 23). 'Gure astea'. *Eskualduna*.
[48] Moulier, J. (1918e, March 15). 'Josteta'. *Eskualduna*.

and Soler, people from each area entertained themselves with their customs. Football and rugby were what they mostly played. The Catalans had their national customs and when one looks at these *Eskualduna* articles, we should not be surprised when it emerges that the Basques also had their customs. It was no exception, and should not be regarded as a way of remembering their country or nostalgia. Each one did what he knew how to do, and played the games he was familiar with. That is why the Basques played pelota and 'mus'.

The Basque Country, the reference

These *Eskualduna* correspondents also referred to pelota and 'mus' differently. On many occasions they used pelota as a metaphor to describe a battle. For example, before a battle began, the question most heard was who was going to attack. And Jean Saint-Pierre (1917a) compared the start of the battle in question with the start of a pelota match (court sport in which two teams face each other) referring to "serve or return to serve", for example.[49]

Zerbitzari compared the war with a pelota match and the soldiers with the pelota players.[50] On several occasions Jean Saint-Pierre also used pelota to compare some battles or the course of some of them. In this case, too, *Zerbitzari* pointed out that they would win the pelota match at some point. As a pelota match could go on for as long as one wanted, he explained that the weaker side would fall at some point, explaining that the same thing could happen in the war.[51] It appears that he was in no doubt that Germany would be the one to fall. Jean Saint-Pierre made the same kind of comparisons between the war and a game of 'mus', to explain that the war was set to go on and to make it clear that at the last moment they were sure the Allies were going to win.[52]

They also used the Basque Country as a reference to describe the places they were in, over and above the ups and downs of the war. They often compared the places where they were stationed in the Basque Country. Jean Saint-Pierre (1916e) specified that the area around them consisted of large tracts of fertile land and village clusters; in other words, he specified that they were not like those in the Basque Country. In that article, he also compared the farming practices with those of the

---

[49] Saint-Pierre, J. (1917a, February 9). 'Bota ala errefera?' *Eskualduna*.
[50] Elizalde, J. (1917e, December 7). 'Craonne-tik hurbil'. *Eskualduna*.
[51] Saint-Pierre, J. (1915d, March 19). 'Bethi aintzina!' *Eskualduna*.
[52] Saint-Pierre, J. (1917b, March 23). 'Mus partida'. *Eskualduna*.

Basque Country.[53] In another, he said he was in a city on the banks of the Aube river, and compared it with the Errobi river and its surrounding area.[54] When he went to Alsace, however, he wrote that the places there bore a resemblance to those of the Basque Country.[55] *Zerbitzari* was also in the habit of comparing any town he saw with one in the Basque Country:

> Duela zenbeit dembora, eskualde hautarat ethorri gineneko, erran nautzuen zer Itsasuko chokoaren itchura duten. Gereziak zirela bakarrik eskas. Geroztik ohartu naiz gerezirik ere ez dela eskas.
> (Some time ago when we arrived in this region, I told you how much it resembled Itsasu. Only the cherries were in short supply. Afterwards, I noticed that they weren't in short supply after all).[56]

A.I., too did likewise not far from Serbia, comparing the countryside of Serbia with that of Zuberoa-Soule. Thus, readers were able to identify the place mentioned by A.I. (1916b) through a place they were familiar with.[57]

Oxobi was not far from the Versailles area at one time, and when he described the places he saw, according Moulier, (1917)[58] he compared them with the Basque Country - the beauties of the Palace of Versailles did not strike him as being as beautiful as the Basque Country. When he mentioned mountains, he compared them with those of the Basque Country, saying that the ones in the Basque Country were more beautiful.[59] He often referred to the weather to say that the weather in the Basque Country was more pleasant:

> Churiak ez du hemen Eskual-Herrian bezalako distirarik. Iguzkia ez ditake elhurrarekin josteta har. Zerua, dena lanho kasik lurrari josia da. Papo gorririk ez oihanean ez eta sasietan chochorik. Lanho bustian bizi bakharrik beleak, ehunka. Noiz ikusiko ditugu baratze mahastietako mertchikak lore? Noiz jauzaraziko gure aintzinean papo-gorri gaichoak eta entzunen sasi gibeletik chochoaren trufak?

---

[53] Saint-Pierre, J. (1915f, June 25). 'Bazterrak'. *Eskualduna*.
[54] Saint-Pierre, J. (1916e, October 6). 'Lerroetarik urrun'. *Eskualduna*.
[55] Saint-Pierre, J. (1917c, July 20). 'Gerezi asean'. *Eskualduna*.
[56] Elizalde, J. (1916f, August 4). 'Arregak'. *Eskualduna*.
[57] A.I. (1916b, February 18). 'Zalonikatik letera'. *Eskualduna*.
[58] Moulier, J. (1917, December 21). 'Edertasun hilak'. *Eskualduna*.
[59] Moulier, J. (1918a, January 11). 'Mendien zolan'. *Eskualduna*.

(The whiteness is not as bright as that in the Basque Country. The sun cannot play with the snow. The sky full of clouds is almost sewn to the land. There are no robins in the wood, or blackbirds, either. The crows in their hundreds live in the damp fog. When are we going to see the peach blossom in the gardens and vineyards? When is our poor robin going to jump before us and when are we going to hear the mocking of the blackbird from behind the brambles?).[60]

Oxobi did not only use the Basque Country as a tool for comparison purposes to get closer to the reader; he expressed how painful it was for him to be such a long way away from the Basque Country. Emphasising that the Basque Country was a good place and the place where he was stationed was a bad one.

The desire to return to one's native country

There may only be a short distance between admiring the Basque Country and dreaming of returning there. When we read many of the articles, we notice that all those disciplined soldiers writing in *Eskualduna* could not wait to get back to the Basque Country and expressed this feeling. Jean Saint-Pierre told an anecdote about the outbreak of the war a year after it had started. In August 1914, Saint-Pierre wrote what a soldier had said during the retreat following the fall of Charleroi:

> Beljikatik gibelerat ginoazilarik, gau eta egun, gudu batean nausi izana gatik, bethi aintzina Frantzia barnerat, aintzindari bati bihotza ilhundu zitzaion nigarra begietarat jauzterainokoan. *Eskualduna* zen, eta Eskualdunekin. Soldado batek erraiten dio: Zer duzu, jauna, nigarrez? - Ez duk bada ikusten makhur handia badela nunbeit? - Bego, bego, jauna: Eskual herrirat buruz ari gira!
> (As we were retreating from Belgium, day and night, despite winning a battle, always advancing through France, someone who was in front became saddened and started to cry. He was Basque; he was with Basque men. One soldier asked him, "Why are you crying, Sir?" "Don't you understand that we have had a big setback?" "Wait, wait, Sir: we are heading back to the Basque Country").[61]

---

[60] Moulier, J. (1918d, March 15). 'Aroa'. *Eskualduna*.
[61] Saint-Pierre, J. (1915h, August 6). Eskualdunen 'sanfrela'. *Eskualduna*.

This shows that right from the very start the Basques were remembering the Basque Country and that returning to or approaching their native country warmed their hearts. It was not Saint-Pierre who had spoken, but rather he was reporting on a sentiment existing among the soldiers when telling that anecdote.

Although Saint-Pierre himself did not often speak in those terms, the desire to return to the Basque Country often appeared in the writings of *Zerbitzari*:

> Guzien gatik, bihotzak Eskual-Herria diote galdetzen. Han dire sortu. Han handitu. Han dute zahartu eta zango herrestatu nahi. Ah, Eskual-Herri maitea!
> (Because of all of this, their hearts are yearning for the Basque Country. They were born there; they grew up there. They want to grow old there and hobble along there. Oh my dear Basque Country!).[62]

He expressed the wish to return to the Basque Country on other occasions, too. He expressed the hope and desire for the war to end so that he could return to the Basque Country. That wish had been making itself felt since 1915, and particularly after the end of 1917, it was being felt more deeply. In January 1918 he once again expressed the burning desire to return to the Basque Country. What stands out is what he emphasised: to see the mountains and sea, to hear the songs, to watch pelota or to pray. In other words, what he missed were mostly locations and the culture. That was the root of his homesickness. The same in this passage:

> Beraz, *Eskualdunak*, altcha bihotzak demborak heldu dire. Uste guzien arabera, udan gure Herria, gure burhasoak, gure etcheak, gure mendiak eta gure itsasoa ikusiko ditugu. Eta agian, orduan eginen den bakeak iraunen du, gure haurrak eta gure haurren haurrak handitu arte.
> (So, Basque men, cheer up, the time has come. According to all accounts, in the summer we will see our Country, our parents, our houses, our mountains and our sea. And perhaps, the peace that is

---

[62] Elizalde, J. (1916d, June 9). 'Laborariak'. *Eskualduna*.

struck then will be one that will last until our children and our children's children have grown up).⁶³

Cultural Basque language loyalty

Simply recalling the Basque Country in terms of its mountains, sea or houses is not sufficient to conclude that these writers were Basque language loyalists. The 19th century saw the emergence of regionalism in Brittany and Provence. In the Basque Country, too, there were reflections on the Basque origin, with Cultural Festivals (Lore Jokoak), etc. The Zazpiak Bat concept (literally "The Seven are One" proclaiming that the Peninsular and the Continental Basque Country were a single country) also emerged but was restricted to the cultural sphere. Basque-language loyalty had experienced a watershed, but by 1910 the movement had lost momentum.⁶⁴ So by the period between 1914 and 1918, the Basque-language loyalty of that time was not as strong as it had been previously.

Jean Saint-Pierre's Basque-language loyalist attitude did not emerge as strongly as that of the others. It is true that sometimes he distinguished between Basques and French; for example, when casualties were mentioned, he specified whether any Basques had died or how many. There were some German bombardments on July 14th. He pointed out that there had been numerous casualties but that there had been no Basques among them.⁶⁵ He distinguished between the French and the Basques, but rather than to highlight the difference in identity; he most likely did so for reasons of proximity. But the Basque community appeared many times, for example when he mentioned that they used to attend their own mass.⁶⁶

A number of articles in favour of the Basque language also appeared among these numerous reports by Saint-Pierre. There is one anecdote worthy of mention in which a Basque who had confessed his sins in French wanted to do so in Basque because he felt he had not confessed. This served to highlight the value of the Basque language.⁶⁷

---

⁶³ Elizalde, J. (1918a, January 4). 'Urthe on!' *Eskualduna* and Elizalde, J. (1915b, April 2). Martchoaren 21ean. *Eskualduna*.
⁶⁴ Casenave, J. (2002). *De l'article de presse à l'essai littéraire: Buruchkak (1910) de Jean Etchepare*. Madrid: Universidad nacional de educación a distancia, page 154.
⁶⁵ Saint-Pierre, J. (1915g, July 23). 'Gure astea'. *Eskualduna*.
⁶⁶ Saint-Pierre, J. (1916a, May 26). 'Maiatzeko hilabethea'. *Eskualduna*.
⁶⁷ Saint-Pierre, J. (1915a, January 8). 'Eskuaraz-ko kofesioa'. *Eskualduna*.

On the whole, Jean Etxepare did not praise or mention the Basque language very much. In that coldness of his, he also emerged as being indifferent concerning the Basque Country. Nevertheless, he called for Basque to be used properly, and, among other things, he felt the language and the vocabulary linked to the war, in particular, should be studied. He was concerned about the richness of Basque and feared the language would disappear:

> Haren nahitik da gure eskuara zaharra, edo endurtuz, frantsesak emeki ithotzen duela edo apur bat aberastuz joanen.
> (That's why our old Basque language will either weaken, slowly strangled by French, or will gradually emerge a little more enriched).[68]

A similar call was issued by *Zerbitzari*, too, when asking those who had learned French not to allow Basque to be lost. In fact, he remarked that the Basques had learned French during the war. Once again in another article, he criticised those who had forgotten Basque. In his articles Oxobi also came across as a staunch Basque language loyalist. He praised Basque, and this is borne out by the fact that he asked someone who sent in the news to write in Basque:

> Bainan *Eskualduna*k nahi du eskuara. Aita eta ama *Eskualduna*k dituzu. Zuhaur garbiki mintzo zire eskuaraz. Zertako ez izkira eskuaraz?
> (But Basques love Basque. Your mother and father are Basque; you too speak Basque perfectly. Why don't you write in Basque?).[69]

In other words, he did not approve of the fact that someone who was proficient in Basque should write in French. But there was another reason for the attachment to the Basque language, as Blaise Adéma pointed out in one article. When Hiriart-Urruti died, Adéma praised his attachment to Basque, because he also saw Basque as a tool for spreading the Christian religion. In the view of Hiriart-Urruti, Basque was the custodian of Christianity; according to the person who had been the editor of *Eskualduna* for many years, Basque was a tool for saving Christianity, and that is why he wanted to save the language.

---

[68] Etxepare, J. (1916, January 21). 'Eskuaraz'. *Eskualduna*.
[69] Moulier, J. (1918c, March 1). 'Eta eskuaraz?' *Eskualduna*.

As Xabier Itçaina (2007) carefully explained, these Basques of the Continental Basque Country were Basque language loyalists, but they had only a cultural awareness, not a political one.[70] This attitude emerged in all the *Eskualduna* articles. There was no political awareness of the Basque Country in the attitude in favour of Basque; nothing of that nature ever appeared. Philippe Vigier (1977) also says that the early regionalisms had been linked to the language in the 19th century and that they somehow defended the regional language on the same level as the national language.[71]

Opposing a Basque state

We will now see that it was one thing to express oneself in favour of Basque but quite another to be politically aware. At that time different forms of patriotism or nationalism were arising in different places. Jean-Yves Guiomar (1970)[72] said that a patriotic party of Brittany was set up in 1911, even though few people joined it and the majority mocked or opposed it. The revival of Catalonia also exerted a great influence in some areas of Occitania, sparking off patriotic or regionalist sentiments. In the Peninsular Basque Country, patriotic ideas were developing through the Euzko Alderdi Jeltzalea (EAJ/PNV-Basque National Party). But according to Xabier Itçaina, (2007)[73] the ideology of Sabino Arana was exerting little influence on the Continental Basque Country because Arana was not interested in the Continental Basque Country and because the EAJ was calling for autonomy for politics and clericalism. Nevertheless, patriotism was beginning to emerge with Pierre Broussain, even though the priests watered down his message considerably.

By the time the war had broken out in 1914, Manex Hiriart-Urruti had written about the patriotism of the Peninsular Basque Country and about those who had gathered around Pierre Broussain (to point out that there were only a few of them). He wrote that there were those who were calling for the unification of the whole of the Basque Country

---

[70] Itçaina, X. (2007). Les virtuoses de l'identité. Religion et politique en Pays Basque. Rennes: Presses Universitaires de Rennes, page 97.
[71] Vigier, P. (1977). 'Régions et régionalisme en France au XIXe siècle' in Gras, C. and Livet, G. (eds.), *Régions et régionalisme en France du XVIIIe siècle à nos jours*. Paris: Presses universitaires de France, page 165.
[72] Guiomar, J.-Y. (1970). 'Régionalisme, fédéralisme et minorité nationales en France entre 1919 et 1939'. *Le Mouvement Social*, 70, pages 89–108.
[73] *Op. cit.* Itçaina, (2007), page 96.

within the Peninsular Basque Country, but that he did not like the idea, arguing thus:

> Nere burua nor nahi bezen eskualdun daukatalarik, ene hitzean nago: berech izaiteko eztela aski erraitea: Espainia bat da, Eskual herria bertze bat. Bainan hola zaiotenek hola erran bezate berentzat. Guk eskualdun frantsesek eztugu Frantziatik berechtea galdatzen: are gutiago erraiten ja bi direla Frantzia eta gure Eskual-herri hau?
> [...] Noizpeiko aspaldiko ethorkiz bat izanik ere, demborak berezi bagitu erresumaz: bi zathitan ezarri bagitu bi populu auzori eratchikiak, bien ararteko edo lokarri izaitea gu hiruen onetan ez litakea?
> (While regarding myself as being as Basque as anyone else, I assert the following: that to be separate it is not enough to say: "Spain is one thing, and the Basque Country is another. " But those who say that should go on saying it exclusively for their own benefit. We French Basques are not asking to be separated from France: even less do we say that they are already two different things, France and this Basque Country of ours.
> [...] Even though at some point long ago we were originally only one, time has divided us into kingdoms, we have been divided into two parts concerning our neighbours, would not being the intermediary or link between the two benefit all three?)[74]

Hiriart-Urruti opposed the independence of the Basque Country. He did not, however, deny that the Peninsular and Continental Basques shared the same roots and that it was the same country. He regarded the Peninsular Basques as brothers, as members of the same family. He admitted that there was a single identity, and did not deny the legitimacy of that ideal union. But the awareness of that identity was not political, as that article suggests. The awareness in *Eskualduna* was restricted to the language or the culture. When speaking of political identity, they were in no doubt that it was a part of France. Jon Casenave (2002) also says that at the time of the 1914-1918 war, there was a hiatus in the cultural movement and the division between the Peninsular and the Continental Basque Country became deeper.[75]

Conclusions

---

[74] Hiriart-Urruti, M. (1914, October 23). 'Frantzia eta Espainia'. *Eskualduna*.
[75] *Op. cit.* Casenave, (2002), page 172.

There is no denying that the Basque Country had a true place in the pens of the reporters of the *Eskualduna* weekly magazine. They were Basques, and they declared that loud and clear and with pride. But no political intentions surfaced in that love for the Basque Country. The pain of being far from home was not the same as the pain of being in a foreign country, or at least they did not express it in that way. The battlefields were apparently very harsh, the conditions there were obviously unbearable even if in the articles they were not spoken about

Figure 6.2 Monument des Basques (1928)

in such harsh terms. That being the case, it is understandable that they missed home, in particular, the warmth of the home and the affection of their loved ones. But feeling that nostalgia - or rather that homesickness – was not a political attitude.

Nor can one see any political attitude in the other references they made to the Basque Country. Comparing the surrounding places and people with those of the Basque Country can be understood as a very easy, natural resource. Their readers were in the Basque Country, the places they knew were those of the Basque Country, and therefore an effective way of explaining something was to draw a comparison with what the readers were familiar with.

They were certainly Basque language loyalists. But mere defenders of the language. They spoke out against a political union of the Basque Country; they were very critical of the Basques in the Peninsular Basque Country. So even though they had the Basque Country in their hearts, even if they were in favour of the Basque language, in no way can one deny that their political identity was associated with France, as is apparent in their writings during wartime.

A more in-depth piece of research by Bidegain (2013)[76] linked to this study confirms the attachment the *Eskualduna* reporters felt towards France, as it becomes clear during the war that they agreed with the idea of France and with the French forces. At the same time, they continually highlighted the fact that the Basques were good, exemplary French soldiers.

Additional sources not cited in the chapter

Adéma, B. (1916a, May 26). 'Soldadoak'. *Eskualduna*.
Bidegain, E. (2009). *Gerla Handia, muga sakona*. Donostia: Utriusque Vasconiae.
Elizalde, J. (1915c, May 21). 'Maiatzaren 11an'. *Eskualduna*.
Elizalde, J. (1917b, July 27). 'Hemengo jendea'. *Eskualduna*.
Elizalde, J. (1918b, September 27). 'Eskual herrian'. *Eskualduna*.
Saint-Pierre, J. (1915b, January 15). 'Muslariak'. *Eskualduna*.

---

[76] *Op. cit.* Bidegain, (2013).

Chapter 7

How Local Newspapers Scooped the National Press to Tell the Truth about the First World War[1]

John Dilley and David Penman
De Montfort University

Introduction

In an era of social media, digital, fibre optic and satellite networks it is easy to forget the ease and speed with which we now communicate, but in the early years of the 20th century the pre-eminent source of information was print; millions relied on newspapers for news from near and far.

The declaration of war in the summer of 1914 put the role of newspapers into sharp focus, as they were the principal organs of communication for a nation embarking on a military campaign.

Alongside the big guns of the newspaper world, including *The Times*, the *Daily Mail*, the *Daily Telegraph* and the *Daily Express*, there were legions of smaller, regional newspapers avidly consumed by local populations. Thanks to the developing technology of the day, newspaper publishing was a vibrant and rapidly expanding industry.

Among those titles were the *Ashbourne Telegraph* and *Market Harborough Advertiser*, both small market-town weeklies, chosen by the authors[1] to investigate the role played by local journalism in the reporting of the Great War. These newspapers were typical of independently owned

---

[1] John Dilley and David Penman embarked on the five-year project in June 2014 with the initial parameters of exploring how local newspapers reported the First World War and the differences in reportage from the London-based national press. Dilley has access to the archive newspapers of the *Market Harborough Advertiser*. He writes a weekly essay which is published every Monday on his website *newspapersandthegreatwar.wordpress.com* as well as the online platform of the newspaper's modern day successor, the *Harborough Mail*. Penman works from the microfilm archives at the Derbyshire County Records Office to investigate and publish to his weekly blog *greatwarreports.wordpress.com* that is also published in the print edition of the present day *Ashbourne News Telegraph*.

publications, across the countries, which were relied upon by their communities.

It has become apparent that factors such as censorship, propaganda and political ambition had a very different impact on the way in which the war was reported by national and local newspapers. First-hand accounts in local papers from named, known individuals carried greater impact than anodyne accounts of troop movements sanctioned by Government propaganda and relayed by press barons.

What did the Victorians do for us?

Before looking at the contemporary coverage of the First World War, it is important to contextualise the circumstances surrounding the publication and consumption of national and local newspapers in 1914. There were three defining factors in the shaping of those newspapers that go back a further half-century.

In 1855 an enlightened Victorian government abolished Stamp Duty, commonly known as 'a tax on knowledge'.[2] This had the effect of making it cheaper to publish newspapers, cut the cover price, and therefore increase circulation. As Griffiths (2006) says: "With the 'taxes on knowledge' finally gone, there now appeared a rush of would-be newspaper owners, especially in the provinces." That equated to a 60 percent circulation increase in London and a massive 300 percent across the U.K.[3]

This stampede included the establishment of the *Market Harborough Advertiser* (1855) and the *Ashbourne Telegraph* (1905). By 1914 there were two papers in each town. The *Advertiser* 'held the field' against its rival the *Midland Mail*, but in 1923 they merged and eventually became known today as the *Harborough Mail*.[4]

The *Telegraph* was up against the *Ashbourne News*, these titles, too, merged as recently as 1959 to become the present day *Ashbourne News Telegraph*.

In London, there was a similar revolution. In 1850 before the abolition of Stamp Duty, Fleet Street as a whole was selling around

---

[2] Griffiths, D. (2006). *Fleet Street: Five Hundred years of the Press*. London: The British Library, page 92.
[3] *Ibid.*
[4] Newton, M. (1977). *Men of Mark*. Peterborough: EMAP, page 78.

60,000 copies a day – by 1890 the *Daily Telegraph* alone was selling 300,000.[5]

A second significant influence was a new Education Act (1870) which brought about a huge school building programme and a massive drive to allow ALL children to 'attend school until they were 12' and learn how to read and write.

As Temple (2008) puts it "the Education Act of 1870 had introduced a new literate working class population desperate for lively reading material"[6] and they turned to newspapers.

Figure 7.1 Front page of the *Market Harborough Advertiser*

There were many other key factors. Williams (2010) says "it is claimed the (electrical) telegraph virtually created the evening press in

---

[5] Williams, K. (2010). *Read All About It! A history of the British newspaper*. Abingdon: Routledge, page 48.
[6] Temple, M. (2008). *The British Press*. Maidenhead: Oxford University Press, page 24.

the provinces" because it allowed reports to be communicated to newsrooms quickly but there was also huge growth on the railways and by the time the trains reached every corner of the country "the London papers gradually began to exert themselves."[7]

The third key factor that directly affected the Regional Press coverage of the First World War was the launch in 1896 of the *Daily Mail* by Alfred Harmsworth, who later became Lord Northcliffe and an instrumental figure in the war itself.

Figure 7.2 Front page of the *Ashbourne Telegraph*

By 1914 Northcliffe controlled roughly 40 percent of the morning, 45 percent of the evening and 15 percent of the Sunday total newspaper circulations.[8] After the success of the *Daily Mail*, he bought *The Times* in 1908, cutting the price from 3d to 1d and tripled sales to 150,000. Also among his titles was the *Evening News* and *Weekly Dispatch*, a Sunday title.

---

[7] *Op. cit.* Williams (2010), page 117.
[8] Thompson, J. L. (1999). *Politics The Press and Propaganda: Lord Northcliffe and the Great War 1914-1918.* Kent, Ohio: Kent State University Press, page 3.

The Press lord had "influence more than that of any British Press Figure before or afterward."[9]

But he also had a magazine background: he founded *'Answers to Correspondent'* which provided responses to questions such as *Can fish speak?* It was hugely popular as were many other magazines he founded which included *Comic Cuts,* which carried the slogan 'amusing without being vulgar' and *Forget-me-not,* 'a high-class penny journal for ladies'.[10] The direct influence on the magazines that are on the shelves of WH Smith today is still evident.

What Northcliffe also did with the *Daily Mail* was transfer that quirky, human interest mix and stir in hard news stories that would make people talk. As Temple (2008) says, "it was full of punchy and readable stories" and marketed as "a penny newspaper for one halfpenny", which wooed "a readership who aspired to better things."[11]

Within the space of four years, the *Daily Mail* had reached a circulation that was just shy of one million copies sold every day.[12]

Part of the success was down to the paper's coverage of crime. Northcliffe's famous rallying cry for his new paper was 'Get me a Murder a Day' - and there was no shortage of that type of story.[13]

But the magazine-style ideas of features, adventure, human interest and readers' letters with a bright and entertaining style changed the face of journalism and 'the Northcliffe Revolution' was copied everywhere, including in rural Market Harborough and Ashbourne.

There was a heavy emphasis on 'people' stories – and, in particular, plenty of gore. The assassination of Archduke Franz Ferdinand on June 28, 1914, was covered by national and local papers but the threat of war was largely ignored in those early weeks of July in favour of the regular diet of sensational content.

Both local papers carried extracts from novels serialised for the readers: a crime thriller called *At Dead of Night,* in the *Advertiser*[14] and in the *Telegraph* there was a thriller called *Double Chance* by J. S. Fletcher.[15]

In just a single summer edition of the *Advertiser,* there were many sensational stories - a bridegroom who slit his throat four days after his

---

[9] *Ibid.*
[10] *Op. cit.* Williams, (2010), page 54.
[11] *Op. cit.* Temple, (2008), page 56.
[12] Seaton, J. C. (2010). *Power Without Responsibility.* London: Routledge, page 40.
[13] *Op. cit.* Williams, (2010), page 54.
[14] *Market Harborough Advertiser,* June 5, 1914, page 2.
[15] *Ashbourne Telegraph,* June 8, 1914, page 4.

wedding; a six-year-old boy who fell from a moving train; five people injured in a 'motor omnibus' accident; and a German spy cornered in Paris.[16]

There was also an incredibly bizarre story from Russia relating the 'serio-comic accounts' to restrain a rogue elephant by poisoning it with 'orange, cake and vodka'.[17]

Although there were no marauding elephants in the *Ashbourne Telegraph*, there was a tragic story of a young man who wounded a girl and murdered her parents in Budapest and then took refuge in a church steeple from whence he fired "at all comers" and only surrendered after three had been killed and 16 injured.[18]

Politics was also hugely prominent in those early summer editions of the papers, particularly taking a dim view of the Suffragette movement and the Home Rule Bill that would later change the shape of Ireland.[19]

In the July 14 edition of the *Advertiser* despite the squabbling in the Balkans, there was still room for the salacious court story from Chester Assizes where a 72-year-old woman was sentenced to death for murdering her 66-year-old husband with an axe in a jealous rage – because he had taken a lover. "He kept saying he loved her and I lost control over myself," she told the court.[20]

The *Daily Telegraph* carried the same report and – very much in keeping with the Northcliffe revolution style – went into graphic detail. "There were 20 deep wounds on the back of the head, penetrating to the skull; one or two of the fingers were almost severed, and on the left, there was a deep incised wound almost severing it."[21]

And the *Ashbourne Telegraph's* inquest report of an accidental shooting of a young girl barred no holds: The report read: "The whole of the lower part of the left side of her face had been blown away and the skull shattered, and the brains scattered for a distance of about ten feet."[22]

This was the state of newspapers in 1914: a trusted, healthy Press – both national and regional – with readers expecting papers to record with an entertaining twist.

---

[16] *Market Harborough Advertiser*, June 9, 1914, page 7.
[17] *Market Harborough Advertiser*, June 9, 1914, page 5.
[18] *Ashbourne Telegraph*, June 12, 1914, page 6.
[19] *Ibid.* Page 6.
[20] *Market Harborough Advertiser*, July 14, 1914, page 7.
[21] *Daily Telegraph*, July 10, 1914, page 6.
[22] *Ashbourne Telegraph*, June 19, 1914, page 4.

Censorship

The Crimean War marked a turning point for journalism; it was the first conflict in which British newspapers employed professional civilian reporters as war correspondents.[23] William Howard Russell's report of the Charge of the Light Brigade has been lauded for its powerful clarity.[24]

And it was The Charge of the Light Brigade which inspired Northcliffe's *Daily Mail* to write at the outbreak of war in 1914: "Our duty is to go forward into the valley of the shadow of death with courage and faith – with courage to suffer and faith in God and our country."[25]

Yet the First World War saw unprecedented restrictions on journalists and huge amounts of misinformation fed to the public. As Knightley (1978:80) observes: "More deliberate lies were told than in any other period of history, and the whole apparatus of the state went into action to suppress the truth." Indeed Knightley's title echoes the words of Senator Hiram Johnson: "The first casualty when war comes is truth."[26]

So how was it that the freedom to report in colour and detail, as Russell did with his report of the Charge of the Light Brigade, was so rapidly eroded in 1914?

"Out of my way you drunken swabs," is how Lord Kitchener greeted journalists in the Sudan in 1898.[27] He had only contempt for the press,[28] believing his reputation had been sullied in the aftermath of the Boer War.[29]

The day after war was declared, Lord Kitchener, newly appointed as War Minister, and Winston Churchill, First Lord of the Admiralty, summoned lawyer and Conservative politician F. E. Smith and asked him to supervise the business of press censorship. Sanders and Taylor (1982) observe this was not without its irony given Kitchener's well-

---

[23] *Op. cit.* Thompson, (1999), page 25.
[24] Simpson, J. (2002). *News From No Man's Land Reporting the World*. London: Pan Macmillan Ltd, page 29.
[25] *Op. cit.* Thompson, (1999), page 25.
[26] Knightley, P. (1978). *The First Casualty*. London: Quartet Books, page 80.
[27] Paxman, J. (2014). *Great Britain's Great War*. London: Penguin Viking, page 89.
[28] *Op. cit.* Thompson, (1999), page 27.
[29] *Ibid.* Page 27.

known dislike for journalists and Churchill's previous career as a war correspondent.[30]

Such was Churchill's enthusiasm for propaganda and control of the media he urged Asquith to commandeer *The Times* and turn it into the official British gazette – a plan that never came to fruition.[31]

The Defence of the Realm Act (DORA) was rushed into law on August 8th, 1914, to restrict newspaper reporting of the conflict. It was

Figure 7.3 Ernest Dunlop Swinton 'Eyewitness'

later extended to not only make it illegal to whistle, buy binoculars or fly kites, but also to introduce shorter pub opening hours and British Summer Time, among a raft of other restrictions.

In particular, it became an offence to talk about details of troop movements and other military matters: "No person shall by word of mouth or in writing spread reports likely to cause disaffection or alarm

---

[30] Saunders, M. L. and Taylor, M. S. (1982). *British Propaganda During The First World War 1914-1918*. London: MacMillan, page 19.
[31] *Op. cit.* Knightley, (1978), page 94.

among any of His Majesty's forces or civilian population."[32]

Key to the Government's propaganda plans was the creation of the Press Bureau, set up as an official channel for news of the British Expeditionary Force, and tasked with preventing newspapers publishing anything that may help the enemy or undermine public morale. Fleet

Figure 7.4 1457 Pte. Frederick Bull killed 9 April 1915, aged 26

Street journalists, frustrated by the constraints placed on reporting, quickly named it the 'Suppress Bureau'.[33]

Within days of the Press Bureau's formation, the Prime Minister was challenged by Sir A. B. Markham in the House of Commons:

> Is the right hon. Gentleman aware that military operations have been published in French, German, and Belgian papers a week before they have been published in any newspaper in this country, and does he not think that it is in the public interest that the public here should know of these things as soon as the readers of these

---

[32] Defence Of The Realm Act, 1914.
[33] *Op. cit.* Sanders and Taylor, (1982), page 20.

Continental papers?[34]

Information restrictions took physical form too. The trans-Atlantic telegraph cable, which enabled German communications with America, was cut, rendering it impossible for an enemy perspective of the conflict to be relayed to the world.[35]

The British Press tried to maintain a presence near the battlefield, but they still relied on second-hand information from Army aides. For instance, the *Daily Mail* correspondent G. Ward Price was credited with a report of a brilliant victory for the French at Altkirch in Alsace and an encounter with mounted German troops.

He told how seven 'fearless' French Chasseurs had threatened a 22-strong German Uhlan cavalry patrol. "Instantly the Uhlans, not waiting for the charge of the handful of their foes, clapped spurs to their horses and galloped off." [36]

However, it was made clear this colourful account was not witnessed at first hand by the closing paragraph: "No indication of the German and French losses is given except that it's said they were not excessive in proportion to the results achieved."[37]

Attempts by national reporters to get first-hand accounts were frustrated at every turn. Newspapers were initially banned from sending correspondents to France and Belgium. Knightley (1978) states that "Kitchener had ordered any correspondent found in the field should be arrested, have his passport taken and expelled" and that "war correspondents were in and out of prison."[38]

The War Office also announced that rather than authorising journalists, reports would be issued by Major Ernest Swinton, the official correspondent on the Western Front. He held the role from September 1914 to July 1915.[39]

The British press was forced to accept his "unsatisfactory and unimaginative" accounts,[40] and the "uninformative communiqués"

---

[34] HC Deb 31 August 1914 vol 66 cc454-511. Also, HC Deb 26 July 1915 vol 73 cc1935-6 and HC Deb 23 September 1915 vol 74 cc549-50.
[35] Tuchman, B. (1962). *The Guns of August.* New York: MacMillan, page 112.
[36] Price, G. W. (1914, August 10). Details of The Fights. *Daily Mail*, 3. London: Daily Mail, page 3.
[37] *Ibid.* Page 3.
[38] *Op. cit.* Knightley (1978), page 88.
[39] *Op. cit.* Thompson, (1999), page 32.
[40] *Op. cit.* Sanders and Taylor, (1982), page 23.

issued by the Press Bureau.[41] Major Swinton was styled Eyewitness, although editors at the time thought Eyewash a better pseudonym.[42]

Of course, the local papers of Britain serving their local communities did not have the luxury of foreign correspondents, but they did have local men serving at the front.

A September 1915 report in the *Ashbourne Telegraph*, based on a letter from a sergeant with the 9th Battalion Sherwood Foresters, apparently contravened the censorship laws when he said they had landed on the Italian coast and gone straight to the front line and spent 11 days in action.

> We have come out of the firing line today, but everywhere here is under fire - there is no such thing as getting a comfortable safe sleep. We have 23 casualties up to date. Our worst worry is flies, and there is simply a plague of them here; I suppose it is on account of so many bodies lying about. You can see hundreds of dead Turks, and they don't half smell.[43]

Given the circumstances he had just outlined, his following lines are quite extraordinary: "I am not at all bothered, in fact I have quite settled down, but of course we have a lot to put up with. But why grumble? It is for a good cause."[44] Despite snubbing DORA he is clearly still patriotic.

In another DORA-flouting *Ashbourne Telegraph* story from September 1915, Private Harold Wynn Woodyatt, of the 11th Sherwoods, related being shelled by the Germans almost incessantly and how one shell came through the roof of their billet.

> There are other things, which worry us as well as the Germans; very large rats, which have lived on dead bodies, do not fear us and run over our faces at night when we lie down, and will actually take our breakfast out of our hands.[45]

The only photographers allowed at the Western Front in 1915 were two army officers providing an official historical record, and anyone

---

[41] *Ibid*. Page 23.
[42] *Ibid*. Page 86.
[43] *Ashbourne Telegraph*, September 3, 1915, page 6.
[44] *Ibid*. Page 6.
[45] *Ashbourne Telegraph*, September 3, 1915, page 7.

attempting to take photographs faced the firing squad.[46]

Yet in clear breach of these regulations in April 1915, the *Ashbourne Telegraph* published two pictures of the Ashbourne Territorials on active service 'somewhere in France', the only nod to strict censorship rules.

"A batch of interesting photographs has been received by Messrs. R. and R. Bull, Victoria Square, from whom copies may be obtained."[47]

The most likely explanation is that Private Fred Bull, whose family ran a photographic business in Ashbourne, had taken a camera to France and sent the images back home in direct contravention of the law. Bull was to be killed in action just a week later.

The topic of censorship of newspaper reports came to a head in October 1915 when the author John Buchan's report for *The Times* of fighting on the Western Front was redacted. It led to the Home Secretary Sir John Simon issuing a statement, reproduced in the *Market Harborough Advertiser*.

The Press Bureau, it said had been unfairly blamed for enforcing rules which it did not make and had no authority to change.

> But when the allegation is that the Press Bureau deliberately excises reference to the bravery of German troops, that it sets itself to exaggerate good news or to conceal disagreeable news, it is necessary that the real fact be known.[48]

The blame for censorship was placed firmly at the feet of General Sir John French.

> Everything that is written by accredited newspaper correspondents at the front is submitted to the censors appointed by him at General Headquarters in France and the Press Bureau is instructed to accept their censorship as final.[49]

And there is no doubt the *Ashbourne Telegraph* editor was aware of the rules when he wrote about censorship on 28th April 1916 (page 3).

> The main object of most Tommies seems to be to let their relatives know where they are, and all sorts of schemes have been discovered.

---

[46] *Op. cit.* Knightley, (1978), page 99.
[47] *Ashbourne Telegraph*, April 16, 1915, page 5.
[48] *Market Harborough Advertiser*, October 19, 1915, page 4.
[49] *Ibid.* Page 4.

A common one at the outbreak of war was to place dots under certain letters, which when read together, gave information as to the writer's whereabouts, but parents soon began to receive letters with a confused jumbling of dots placed under other letters by the censor, who is very wide awake as a rule.

Apparently, one soldier with the Mediterranean Expeditionary Force managed to outsmart the censors in a postscript to his letter. "It read 'I met Sally on the car.' Whether you see it or not depends on how you pronounce Salonica."[50]

Propaganda

The Government also started to exploit the press as a medium for propaganda. After the war one MP wrote, "there was no more discreditable period in the history of journalism than the four years of the Great War."[51]

Knightley (1978) blames,[52] at least partly, the British war correspondents whom, he says, identified themselves with the armies in the field, protected high command from criticism and kept silent about the terrible slaughter.

Northcliffe, the owner of *The Times* and *Daily Mail*, was director of propaganda in foreign countries and was characterised by the Germans as The Minister of Lying.[53] Knightley (1978) argues that, "a propaganda machine developed that became the envy of the world" and "by the end of the war had created a propaganda organisation that became the model on which Goebbels based that of the Germans some 20 years later."[54]

According to Knightley (1978): "The willingness of newspaper proprietors to accept this control and their cooperation in disseminating propaganda brought them rewards of social rank and political power. But it also undermined public faith in the press."[55]

---

[50] *Ashbourne Telegraph*, April 28, 1916, page 3.
[51] Ponsonby, A. (1928). *Falsehood in Wartime*. London cited in *Op. cit.* Sanders and Taylor (1982), page 30.
[52] *Op. cit.* Knightley (1978), page 81.
[53] *Ibid.* Page 82.
[54] *Ibid.* Page 82.
[55] *Ibid.* Page 81.

It is important to recognise that regional proprietors and editors, who had no such advantage to gain, would have been less inclined to peddle the government line. The readership of their papers was rooted in tight-knit communities in which extended families and neighbours knew the men on the front line and would not so easily be taken in by misinformation and propaganda.

The good news stories emanating from the Press Bureau gave the impression that British soldiers were doing well and this was hugely successful in establishing the Germans 'as menacing aggressors'. The Kaiser was "painted as a beast in human form," says Knightley (1978).[56]

In common with the national newspapers, the local press including the *Market Harborough Advertiser* and the *Ashbourne Telegraph* published many of these reports throughout the war.

Much of this material may well have been printed in good faith, but history was to show that much of the output of the Press Bureau was "little more than propaganda." [57]

It is possible to see the guiding hand of the Press Bureau spin doctors in a dramatic first-person *Ashbourne Telegraph* report of the Battle of the Aisne from a Private T. Smithson.

There was no indication Private Smithson was from Ashbourne, and this lack of personal detail would suggest this report had been officially sanctioned to be 'wired' to the waiting media.

The story created a graphic picture of life on the front line, portraying Germans as evil scum and would have been intended to bolster patriotic support for the conflict. The opening sentence reads: "The first taste we got of the enemy in that action was the dirty use of the white flag."[58]

Private Smithson and his comrades took 80 Germans prisoner on the top of a ridge, it was reported, but it was all a ploy to bring them into open ground for other concealed enemy to attack.

In what the BBC may now describe as an 'unverified report' he continued with his dramatic tale: "There was a man lying near me and he was badly hurt. He asked for some water and I threw him my bottle, but before he could pick it up another shrapnel finished him."[59]

Reports were rife of German atrocities in Belgium, including the rape and killing of women and children and these were widely reported.

---

[56] *Ibid.* Page 82.
[57] *Ibid.* Page 82.
[58] *Ashbourne Telegraph*, October 2, 1914, page 6.
[59] *Ashbourne Telegraph*, October 2, 1914, page 6.

In December 1914 the government set up a committee, under the chairmanship of James Bryce, a respected academic and member of the House of Lords[60] to investigate allegations of brutality by German forces in Belgium. The Publication of the Report of the Committee on Alleged German Outrages (London 1915) - better known as the Bryce report - was widely reported and was seen as a major propaganda victory for the allies.[61]

Costing 1d, the price of a newspaper, this 360-page pamphlet contained a, 'summary of evidence' and an appendix - of some 300 pages - of selected case histories. The report described the execution of civilians, the torture and mutilation of Belgian women, the bayoneting of small children and just about every atrocity that could be committed by German soldiers.[62]

The *Daily Mail* carried some of these sensational stories but Corrigan states there was not a shred of evidence to support the claims.[63] And Knightley (1978) concludes:

> A Belgian commission of enquiry in 1922, when passions had cooled, failed markedly to corroborate a single major allegation in the Bryce Report. By then, of course, the report had served its purpose. Its success in arousing hatred and condemnation of Germany makes it one of the most successful propaganda pieces of the war.[64]

This development of propaganda proved to be successful; "By the time the First World War had ended in 1918, a great historical divide had been passed in the development of opinion manipulation."[65]

Part of the propaganda effort was to tell the public the Germans were misleading newspaper readers in Europe. The *Daily Mail* said: "Throughout eastern Europe dozens of newspapers are in German pay,[66]

---

[60] Messinger, G. (1992). *British Propaganda and the State in the First World War*. Manchester: Manchester University Press, page 72.
[61] *Ibid*. Page 75.
[62] *Ibid*. Page 143.
[63] Corrigan, G. (2003 (reissued 2012). *Mud, Muck, and Poppycock: Britain and the First World War*. London: Cassell, page 181.
[64] *Op. cit.* Knightley (1978), page 84.
[65] *Op. cit* Messinger, (1992), page 2.
[66] *Daily Mail*, 'Bribed Newspapers', November 3, 1914, page 4.

The task is easier because Italy and the countries of Eastern Europe are not, like England, countries of relatively few newspapers, widely distributed and of great circulations. In these countries there are scores upon scores of small newspapers, several in each town almost in each village. Although greedily read they have necessarily small circulations.[67]

This is evidence of a clear dismissal of the local newspaper's role in its community as if the *Daily Mail*, the biggest selling publication in the land, was unaware of the importance of the burgeoning newspaper market across England – including Derbyshire and Leicestershire. As stated above, both Ashbourne and Market Harborough had not one but two newspapers.

Hastings (2013) argues the relationship between the British government and the Press was poisoned by the manner in which censorship was enforced and the fact that news of events well known to the enemy was suppressed.[68] He argues that in this vacuum, wild rumours gained currency as 'news'.

The *Daily Mail* wrote an entirely fictional account of a naval victory[69] while other fantasy accounts were published elsewhere.

> The effect of this distortion was immense. The average Englishman had been accepting it all his life that if something was printed in the newspapers then it was true. Now, in the biggest event in his life, he was able to check what the press said against what he knew to be the truth. He felt he had found the press out, and as a result, he lost confidence in the newspapers, a confidence to this day never entirely recovered.[70]

This distrust of Press reports extended beyond British shores. Troops were said to be incredulous: "Soldiers at the front read the home press when they could and frequently laughed at its absurdities."[71]

---

[67] *Daily Mail*, 'Bribed Newspapers', November 3, 1914, page 4.
[68] Hastings, M. (2013). *Catastrophe: Europe Goes to War 1914.* London: William Collins, page 436.
[69] *Daily Mail*, 'Bribed Newspapers', November 3, 1914, page 438.
[70] *Op. cit.* Knightley, (1978), page 99.
[71] Winter, J. and Baggett, J. W., (1996). *The Great War.* London: Penguin, page 96.

And it was the regional press that was at least partly responsible for this change in attitude. Its real stories about real people undermined the propaganda and censorship that afflicted the national Press.

Even 100 years later the regional press is trusted more than its national counterparts. According to a Corporate Social Responsibility report in 2014, 64 percent of people trusted their local newspaper compared to just 27 percent trusting a national title.[72]

But there was no way the Press Bureau could check all the stories in the hundreds of local papers dotted around the country as the *Market Harborough Advertiser* and the *Ashbourne Telegraph* began painting a picture very different from the official line, largely basing their stories on comments by local soldiers writing home.

As Paxman (2014) observed, letters quickly found their way into the hands of editors and the regional press that published "remarkably accurate accounts of battlefield combat."[73]

And there was no shortage of opportunity for men at the front line to write home to their friends and family. There were three postal collections a day.[74]

The British Army Postal Service delivered around two billion letters during the war. By 1917 more than 19,000 mailbags crossed the English Channel each day, transporting letters and parcels to and from British troops on the Western Front.[75]

And it is clear from an article in November 1914 the editor of the *Ashbourne Telegraph* at least knew that by publishing these letters he was circumventing the censors, and the impact of doing so:

> During this Great War, when the powers that be have decided to exercise a strict censorship on the circulation of official information, a special interest attaches to the accounts sent by the soldiers themselves in their letters to their friends. Some of these show unmistakable signs of having been written under difficulties, which should make them all the more valuable to the recipients. It is in such letters that often the grim realities of war are impressed upon us. For the recipient is not reading the flowery and vivid description of an

---

[72] *Corporate Social Responsibility Marketing Report 2014.* (n.d.). Retrieved October 29, 2015, from The PRblog: theprblog.co.uk/corporate-social-responsibility-marketing-report-2014.
[73] Paxman, J. (2014). *Great Britain's Great War.* London: Penguin Viking, page 89.
[74] McKenzie, C. (2015, October 9). *Today.* BBC.
[75] Mason, A. and Parton, E. (n.d.). *Letters to Loved Ones.* Retrieved November 18, 2015, from Imperial War Museum: iwm.org.uk/history/letters-to-loved-ones.

engagement by a paid journalist, but the thoughts and impressions of one they know and for whom they have a deep affection.[76]

Of course, the papers were not totally reliant on hand-written correspondence for their supply of news. Soldiers, injured or on furlough, returned home and were able to vocalise their stories.

Ashbourne's first casualty of war, Bombardier William Simpson, was greeted back in town by a large crowd and he was carried on the shoulders of two townsmen to his parents' house. Not content with this genuine eyewitness account the paper interviewed the returning soldier. The report drove a coach and horses through DORA: "English guns, he said, were hopelessly outnumbered, but it was evident the Germans were surprised and angry at the stubbornness and pluck with which the English fought."[77]

There was no internet to upload stories from the battlefield and much of the news in the regional press was a week or more out of date, but readers would understand its limitations and still be interested as it would be 'news' to them.

For instance, *Market Harborough Advertiser* readers had to wait until three weeks after Christmas Day to hear about the extraordinary truce of 1914. The story originated from a Second Lieutenant attached to the Lancashire Fusiliers who said:

> On Christmas morning we received orders not to shoot unless it was absolutely necessary. This injunction seemed to 'wireless' itself across to the Germans as they stopped sniping altogether and an unearthly stillness reigned over the scene.[78]

Before long both sides were wandering into No Man's Land.

> I went out myself after a time with a copy of *Punch* which I presented to a dingy Saxon in exchange for a small packet of excellent cigars and cigarettes. As I walked back slowly to our own trenches I thought of Mr. Asquith's sentence about not sheathing the sword until the enemy be finally crushed. It is all very well for Englishmen living

---

[76] *Ashbourne Telegraph*, November 4, 1914, page 5.
[77] *Ashbourne Telegraph*, September 11, 1914, page 2.
[78] *Market Harborough Advertiser*, January 15, 1915, page 5.

comfortably at home to talk in flowing periods, but when you are out here you begin to realise that sustained hatred is impossible.[79]

These were extraordinary sentiments considering the censorship rules.

The letters written by soldiers, ordinary men in extraordinary circumstances, were often mundane in their content, enquiring how life was at home, and detailing everyday matters such as the weather and

Figure 7.5 2549 Pte. F.G. Luck Killed 29 October 1915, aged 19

what they had had to eat. But as the belligerents dug in on the Western Front, their letters increasingly began to reveal the terrible truth.

In December 1914 the *Market Harborough Advertiser* ran a story about Private Albert Swann, who was killed at Armentieres where 400 county men were lost in the space of just a few hours. The paper quoted a cousin, who saw a shell hit him: "It either knocked him right into the earth or blew him into fragments, as nothing was ever seen of him again."[80]

---

[79] *Ibid.* Page 5.
[80] *Market Harborough Advertiser*, December 11, 1914, page 6. Also see, Hudson. J. (2014). *Christmas 1914. The First Wold War at Home and Abroad.* Stroud: The History Press.

The horrors of life in the trenches was told even more graphically in an *Ashbourne Telegraph* story about Private A. S. Goodall, who wrote home in the typical matter-of-fact style of soldiers seeing active service.

> Most of my mates have been either killed or wounded, they keep falling right and left; my platoon officer got shot just as I was running past him and about all the officers got killed or wounded.[81]

He continued:

> I saw a shell kill six men and I don't know how many it wounded; another dropped on a section of Gordons and blew them to pieces. You could see legs and arms fly in the air as soon as it struck them.

It is difficult to imagine this gruesome account would have met with approval by the War Office as such brutish reality would do little to aid recruitment.

Although some letters published by national newspapers told tales of exploits that were later found to be exaggerated or imagined[82] those appearing in the *Ashbourne Telegraph* and *Market Harborough Advertiser* were more easily verified. Not only were they from men with family, friends and neighbours in the town, but also the contents of the letters were often corroborated by mail sent by other members of the same platoon.

Often the local paper would provide full identification of a soldier named in a story so the reader would know exactly who he was, or at least know of his family, street or place of work. For instance, in the *Market Harborough Advertiser* of November 1915, there was a story about Private Frederick Luck, 19, of 22 Queen Street, Desborough, who worked at CWS Corset Factory and was a member of the Congregational Church. He was shot in the head while fighting for the 1st/4th Northants Regiment.[83]

At a national level, the military and politicians did a deal with the publishers of the national press which saw much of the terrible reality of war suppressed.

They did this for altruistic reasons: "to enable the war to go on, the people had to be steeled for further sacrifices, and this could not be

---

[81] *Ashbourne Telegraph*, April 16, 1915, page 2.
[82] *Op. cit.* Hastings, (2013), page 101.
[83] *Market Harborough Advertiser*, November 2, 1915, page 5.

done if the full story of what was happening on the Western Front was known."[84]

But the "willingness of newspaper proprietors to accept this control and their cooperation in disseminating propaganda brought them rewards of social rank and political power."[85]

Local papers were providing the terrible truth through their unvarnished coverage and this in turn "undermined public faith in the [national] press."[86]

Language

The course of the First World War can be critically evaluated in a multiplicity of approaches.

It can be analysed through numbers - for instance, 956,703 British servicemen were killed and 2,272,998 wounded[87]; 65 million soldiers were mobilised from more than 20 countries[88] and it cost £2,300 for Germany to kill an Allied soldier but £7,300 for the British Army to kill a German soldier.[89]

It can be analysed through film on both small and large screen - for instance, *All Quiet On The Western Front* (1932) which "remains an essential piece of social history and a heart-wrenching film;"[90] *Oh What A Lovely War!* (1969), a film which "in retrospect [adds up] to a muddle of satire, protest and seaside-postcard fun that leaves you torn between laughter and tears, [and] it vividly reflects the muddle of war itself and is accordingly a masterpiece;"[91] *Gallipoli* (1981), "one of the most elegiac anti-war films ever made;"[92] and *Blackadder Goes Forth* (1989) "engages with the myths of the war in ways which move an audience."[93]

It can be analysed through literature - for instance, *Birdsong* (Sebastian Faulks 1997), "the experience of trench warfare is made so vivid that sometimes it is hard to go on reading;"[94] *War Horse* (Michael

---

[84] *Op. cit.* Knightley, (1978), page 80.
[85] *Ibid.* Page 81.
[86] *Op. cit.* Knightley, (1978), page 81.
[87] www.1914-18.net.
[88] Ferguson, N. (2015). *The Pity of War*. London: Penguin.
[89] *Ibid.*
[90] Chilton, M. (2015, 29 April). Telegraph.co.uk. *Daily Telegraph*. London.
[91] Wilson, C. (n.d.). movie-film-review.com. *Daily Mail*. (n.d.).
[92] Chilton, M. (2015, 29 April). Telegraph.co.uk. *Daily Telegraph*. London.
[93] Mason, E. (2014, 8 January). historyextra.com. *www.historyextra.com* and Connelly, M. (n.d.). historyextra.com/feature/blackadder-bad-first-world-war-history.*historyextra.com*.
[94] Campbell, A. (2000). acampbell.org.uk/bookreviews. *acampbell.org.uk/bookreviews/r/faulks-*

Morpurgo 1982), "although a first-person animal narrator asks a lot of the reader, Joey's voice - unsentimental and brave under fire - amplifies the emotional impact of the story;"[95] *A Farewell To Arms* (Ernest Hemingway 1929), "the impartiality of the presentation of war is as remarkable as the sincerity of the record of love passion."[96]

And it can be analysed through poetry - in particular, Wilfred Owen who is remembered for *Dulce et Decorum Est*, which is "harsh, effective in the extreme, yet maybe too negative to rank among [his] finest achievements"[97]; Rupert Brooke who wrote *The Soldier*, which was published in *The Times* "to great acclaim" shortly before his death in 1915[98]; and Siegfried Sassoon, who according to a contemporary said the "dynamic quality of his war poems was due to the intensity of feeling which underlay their cynicism."[99]

All of these media are consumed through the prism of the rear-view mirror of history and the words have, apart from the poets, come from the pens of those who did not actually live through that period in time. All of the examples above are also, quite rightly, celebrated as great examples of their genre - a simple truism that the cream always rises to top and it is the best of the authors, directors, poets and even statisticians, who are remembered and read.

But what of the contemporary chroniclers of the day, the journalists who wrote for the national and local newspapers that were read in real-time by both the men fighting the war and those on the Home Front? Inevitably, they detailed what was happening - the battles, the deaths, the feats of bravery; they reported the debating points - the need for more munitions or conscription; they recorded the mundane and everyday stories of people going about their ordinary lives - movements in the stock market, the success of the harvests or the outcomes of court justice.

Many of these articles used language that was simple, concise and devoid of literary device, constrained by the commerce of restricted pagination and the newspaper column width. This is not surprising. What is surprising is the difference between the pictures created by the

---

1.html .
[95] Marler, R. (2010, 8 September). nytimes.com. *New York Times*.
[96] *Op. cit.* Guardian. (2002, 31 August).
[97] Simcox, K. (2002). Wilfred Owen Association. *Wilfred Owen Association*.
[98] *Op. cit.* Guardian. (2008).
[99] Poetry, F. (2016). poetryfoundation.org/bio/siegfried-sassoon. *Poetry Foundation*.

national press and the local press, partly from the choice of sources and partly by the style of language used by those sources.

The national press and the press bureau

The national press already had correspondents in France before the war and although their access to information changed at various points throughout the four years they were essentially 'embedded'. This meant they were not allowed to go anywhere near the Front and were fed information via military attachés. Any articles they wrote, as noted above, were also subject to censorship.

Despite this shortcoming, the national press still had the advantage of being able to tell their stories quickly - for instance, the Battle of the Somme which began at 7.30am on July 1, 1916, was reported in the London newspapers the very next day. Being weekly publications, the *Market Harborough Advertiser* had to wait until July 4 and the *Ashbourne Telegraph* until July 7 before they could update the story.

We now know that day was one of the bloodiest in British military history. By nightfall, some 57,000 Commonwealth and 2,000 French soldiers had become casualties - more than 19,000 of whom had been killed.[100] The Battle of the Somme continued for another 140 days and when the offensive was halted in November 1916, more than 1,000,000 Commonwealth, French and German soldiers had been wounded, captured, or killed.[101]

This is not how the national - or local - newspapers reported the battle in those early days. The *Market Harborough Advertiser* was not alone in greeting "the long expected British Advance...with the greatest enthusiasm,"[102] the national newspapers were doing the same.

But as Knightley (1978) says in *The First Casualty*, the reporters "quickly realised the messages were untrue and the great part of the intelligence supplied to them had been utterly wrong and misleading."[103] Knightley quotes one reporter, Beach Thomas, as saying after the war:

---

[100] Somme2016. (n.d.). somme2016.org/en/history/#thiepval.
[101] *Ibid.*
[102] *Market Harborough Advertiser*, August 11, 1914, page 5.
[103] *Op. cit.* Knightley (1978), page 100.

I was thoroughly and deeply ashamed of what I had written for the good reason that it was untrue... the vulgarity of enormous headlines and the enormity of one's own name did not lessen the shame.[104]

This had been the approach from the beginning of the war and it continued. For instance, the *Daily Telegraph* of July 27, 1916, described the "storming of Pozières"[105] and failed to mention that there were 23,000 Allied causalities[106] during the few days of this battle and the Pozières ridge is "more densely sown with Australian sacrifice than any other place on earth."[107]

But the failure of the reporting was not just in the positive spin put on the story it was also in the reporter's choice of language. The story said: "After five days of furious fighting, described in Paris as equaling anything that has occurred even at Verdun, the British Army yesterday completed its capture of Pozières village, and according to the German admission, established itself there.

> The attack began on Sunday night and by midnight our soldiers had carried the outer works. On Sunday and Monday, despite the strength of the German defences, they made further progress. The place had been transformed by the enemy into a veritable fortress, with each house and cottage separately fortified and filled with machine guns, so that the task of the troops was extremely arduous.[108]

The reporter's language used many journalistic tricks to convey the message that this fighting was of some importance: it began with some effective alliteration, provided facts in a succinct and concise manner, and used the short, informative but descriptive phrases to give the paragraphs pace and rhythm.

Where it failed to convince, as did so many other national newspaper articles, was in its lack of human emotion. The article can be read as: "The attack began... they made further progress... the task was

---

[104] *Op. cit.* Knightley, (1978), page 100.
[105] *Daily Telegraph*, July 27, 1916, page 13.
[106] Bean, C. E. (1929). *Official History of Australia Volume III – The Australian Imperial Force in France: 1916. Available from,* awm.gov.au/collection/RCDIG1069752/.
[107] *Ibid.*
[108] *Daily Telegraph*, July 22, 1916, page 13.

extremely arduous. The Army completed its capture... and established itself there."

The readers were given plenty of information, in a tone of authority, but they were not involved. They were not told about the blood pumping through the veins of soldiers sick to their stomachs with fear as they struggled to come to terms with friends dying and their own imminent death.

The tone of this style of reporting had been set at the beginning of the war. For instance, the *Daily Telegraph* took just a day to report the beginning of the Battle of Mons in August 1914; "British troops in Belgium took an active and meritorious part in the great battle which began on Saturday and is still continuing."[109]

The action reported quickly – but again inaccurately – conveyed none of the despair and panic of Allied soldiers who fought a desperate rearguard action against a superior German force.

Local papers, like those in Market Harborough and Ashbourne, often included these Fleet Street reporter accounts and also, more frequently, those issued by the Press Bureau and Eyewitness. A typical report from the *Market Harborough Advertiser* in March 1915, is high on literary style but low on intimacy.

> The astonishing strength of medieval buildings, such as the Templars' Tower at Nieuport and the Church Tower of Messines, is evinced by the fact that they have resisted bombardment of modern artillery. The church belfry has been shot away, the interior is completely burnt out, but the framework though irregular in outline and full of gaping holes, still stands defiant amid the surrounding ruins.[110]

This approach is one-dimensional; it does not describe what munitions did to raw flesh, just what the bombs did to bricks and mortar.

Eyewitness was even heavily criticised by the national newspapers. In one report of *The Times*, a scathing and sarcastic attack was made.

> Descriptive accounts of the operations at the Front written by an 'Eyewitness' continue to be issued by the Press Bureau. Yesterday's

---

[109] *Ibid.* Page 13.
[110] *Market Harborough Advertiser*, March 12, 1915, page 5.

installment again illustrated the writer's optimism and eye for picturesque detail. A chauffeur in charge of a General Staff motorcar 'completing his morning toilet', a French cafe proprietor and his family eating artichokes 'dipped in melted butter and conveyed to the mouth with a flourish', a soldier servant 'frying something' for the dinner of the General Staff, provide the Eyewitness with the material for the exercise of his descriptive talent.[111]

Another Headquarters' report quoting a 'thrilling narrative' from General Ian Hamilton, which described the invasion of Gallipoli, read more like the daredevil antics from a *Boy's Own* comic.

The Munster Fusiliers, who with 'the great majority of their senior officers killed or wounded', gallantly followed two staff officers to success; the 'complete lack of the sense of danger and fear' displayed by the Lancashire Fusiliers, who 'literally hurled themselves ashore'; the heroic wire cutters 'who could be seen quietly snipping away under a hellish fire as if they were pruning a vineyard'; the Australians who 'like lightning, leapt ashore, and each man as he did so went straight as his bayonet at the enemy'.[112]

Local newspapers

The Vietnam War was described as being 'the first television war'.[113] Television journalists were able to get to the front and bring the sheer brutality of conflict into the homes of those families who were worried sick about their loved ones.

In fact, something very similar had already happened in the First World War, when those letters from 18-year-old soldiers who hadn't begun to shave, were used as sources by local newspaper editors to create simple, bite-sized pictures of the real fighting. Although often dated, it has been previously stated as to why the verification of the statements and news sense of the editors carried more authority than the statements from Sir Douglas Haig, the reports from Fleet Street's finest, or Press Bureau communiqués issued by Eyewitness.

---

[111] *The Times*, March 10, 1915, page 7.
[112] *Market Harborough Advertiser*, March 26, 1915, page 5.
[113] Pilger, J. (1986). Heroes. *Heroes*. London: Jonathan Cape, page 179.

The national newspapers did appeal for letters from readers and even offered payment. For instance, *The Times* ran a regular message: 'Give us your letters'.[114] However, national newspaper editors did not view the communications from soldiers as a primary source, after all, they had the advantage of filling their columns with quickly-filed reports from their own journalists and a graphics department that often used maps of the conflict areas to great effect.

But the Fleet Street editors were missing out because there was yet another untold story lurking in amongst these many millions of letters written by ordinary young men who had been thrust into extraordinary situations.

Many of those young men had a surprising grasp of the English language as evidenced by this simple soldier's description of life under shellfire in the *Market Harborough Advertiser* in February 1915.

> One night I witnessed what I can only describe as an awful battle. Imagine the worst thunderstorm you ever heard. It was as if some trapdoor in hell had opened and let loose ten thousand demons who traversed the air in roaring chariots of destruction.
>
> Canon belched flame, shells moaned like lost souls, and rifles spluttered death and destruction wholesale, while the sky was filled with a cold, flickering light which gave the whole an atmosphere as if the pit that is bottomless.
>
> You would have thought that nobody could have emerged alive from the inferno. It was too hot, however, to last and after an hour or two the disturbance subsided to the normal crack of musketry, which goes on night and day.[115]

Anyone reading these words, literary in style but full of emotion, could not feel other than moved by the horror.

This is not a one-off example. A week later the *Advertiser* published this thought-provoking eloquence from Trooper H. W. Breeze, who was in B Squadron of the Leicestershire Yeomanry.

---

[114] *The Times*, May 5, 1915, page 12.
[115] *Market Harborough Advertiser*, February 19, 1915, page 5.

> The shell-fire is appalling and unceasing, day and night. We pass, en route, many grim sights, which force home the cruel, murderous and inhumane aspects of this war.

He continued with almost poetic expression.

> It is beyond the greatest imagination - it must be seen - just one glance.[116]

And who could not be moved by the words of Quartermaster Sergeant J. Tetlow in the *Ashbourne Telegraph* in which you can almost hear the raw grief, written as if choking back emotion.

> Just a line. I don't know how to write. God help us. You must be prepared to hear some very bad news. When our company was in the trenches the Germans began to shell us, and a shell dropped right in the trench amongst the Ashbourne lads. I am sorry to say it killed four of them.[117]

The use of those four short sentences at the beginning of his story helped convey the grief in tone as well as content.

The examples of this emotive style are evident on a weekly basis. For instance, in a July 1915, edition of the *Market Harborough Advertiser* Sergt. G. Payne, a former employee at Messrs Eady and Dulley's Brewery, described the horror of trench warfare.

He wrote:

> As I sit in my dug-out now writing this there is an unceasing roar and rattle of big guns and rifle fire. What a pandemonium, or in simpler words, it is just hell let loose.

He described how his partly-built advance trench was earlier hit by German artillery.

> The shells seemed to burst all round us at once, they were ploughing up the ground in front of us, behind us, well all around us, burying us

---

[116] *Market Harborough Advertiser*, December 8, 1914, page 5.
[117] *Ashbourne Telegraph*, April 16, 1915, page 3.

with earth and I'm sure there was not one in the trench but what thought his last hour had come.[118]

The word and sentence structure was simple; there was even a colloquial grammar error in the last part of the quote that added poignancy and authenticity.

And in the *Ashbourne Telegraph* of April 1915, Private G. F. Taylor, serving with the Grenadier Guards wrote to his wife and children describing his experiences on the front line.

> We stay in the trenches four days and four nights: as long as I live I shall never forget the sights or the sensations. The Germans are only 150 yards away when we attacked, and what with the barbed wire and barricades it was a very difficult thing to get at them, but this we did although losing heavily. Shells fell about every ten yards; it was simply hell and nothing else. One shell I noticed in particular fell among a number of men, blowing them absolutely to pieces; you could see different parts of equipment up amongst the trees, hanging from branches.[119]

Later that year in an October edition of the *Ashbourne Telegraph* Jack Thompson's mother at Holme Farm, Mayfield, received a letter from Corporal Chas Wood that told of the explosion that killed her son in a single breathlessly long sentence.

> I was in the trench myself, and was about 50 yards or so from Jack when it occurred and I shall never forget it as I have not got over the shock myself yet, and when we came to look round we found that seven of our brave lads out of our platoon had been buried by earth that the mine had blown up, and I can assure you that Jack and the brave fellows could not have suffered any pain as death must have been instantaneous.[120]

The following sentence would have brought the family, little comfort.

---

[118] *Market Harborough Advertiser*, July 20, 1915, page 5.
[119] *Ashbourne Telegraph*, April 30, 1915, page 4.
[120] *Ashbourne Telegraph*, October 22, 1915, page 5.

> We tried to find poor Jack and the brave fellows, and kept on looking until the early hours of next morning, but could find no sign of them at all.

These words carried power and authenticity because of their simplicity and the images they created. They certainly rival the haunting writing of Sebastian Faulks' *Birdsong*.

> They feared shell wounds more than bullets... a direct hit would obliterate all physical evidence that a man had existed; a lesser one would rip pieces from him; even a contained wound brought greater damage to the tissues of the body than a bullet.[121]

It was not just powerful prose that the local papers published. In a February 1915 edition of the *Advertiser*, a poem written by one of the town's soldiers serving in Flanders takes pride of place on page 8. It will never be found among the celebrated War Poets on the A-Level curriculum, but in its way it is full of imagery that is worthy of analysis.

> A whistle, a whirr, a deafening crash,
> The crack of a shell-split tree,
> A cry, a shout, the stretcher's out –
> "Is it Blighty or R.I.P.?"
> Shrapnel, they send them now and then
> In the hope of catching a few –
> This is our way on Bank Holiday,
> Is it the same with you?[122]

In just 52 words the lot of a frontline soldier was captured: the incessant shellfire that sent many men mad; the indiscriminate roll of the dice that exploding bombs brought - life, death or a chance to go home with a 'minor' wound; and the sense of injustice that still at home there were many young men who had not volunteered. In fact, the poem is called *To The Slackers*.

Perhaps it didn't capture the despair of Wilfred Owen writing in *Dulce Et Decorum Est* but the message is the same.

---

[121] Faulks, S. (1993). *Birdsong*. London: Vintage Random House, page 147.
[122] *Market Harborough Advertiser, February* 15, 1915, page 5.

Bent double, like old beggars under sacks,
Knock-kneed, coughing like hags, we cursed through sludge,
Till on the haunting flares we turned our backs
And towards our distant rest began to trudge.
Men marched asleep. Many had lost their boots
But limped on, blood-shod. All went lame; all blind;
Drunk with fatigue; deaf even to the hoots
Of tired, outstripped Five-Nines that dropped behind.[123]

Back home

It wasn't just remarkable writing from the Front, there was equally eloquent oratory reported in the local papers, mainly from those charged with drumming up enthusiasm to enlist. Who could not be moved by reading the words of Colonel Earl of Denbigh at the Market Harborough Assembly Rooms when he implored the women of the town to do their bit too, in September 1914.

> The women had often been told love was a selfish thing, and the love would try and persuade any young man to stay at home... The real love, the unselfish love, was that which told the young man to go and do his duty, prayed for him while he was away, and if he came back, welcomed him with all the love possible.[124]

And at the outbreak of war in August 1914 the editor of the *Market Harborough Advertiser*, once again having to play catch-up with a first report seven days after the declaration, perfectly captured the feelings of the town.

> As the past week has been an eventful one in the history of the world, and of our beloved country, so it has been in the history of Market Harborough, and scenes have been enacted here which but a few days previously none of us would have dreamt of. Truly it has, as one Harborian put it, been 'the week of one's life'.[125]

---

[123] Owen, W. (n.d.). wilfredowen.org.uk/poetry/dulce-et-decorum-est, (1917) and Owen's 'Dulce Et Decorum Est' (1920). Available at, warpoetry.co.uk/owen1.html.
[124] *Market Harborough Advertiser*, September 8, 1914, page 5.
[125] *Market Harborough Advertiser*, August 7, 1914, page 5.

And the *Ashbourne Telegraph* editor demonstrated remarkable prescience in telling his readers:

> During this last week, Europe has been plunged into what may probably be the greatest war in the history of the world. It will certainly be the greatest from the point of view of the numbers of soldiers and sailors involved and the greatest as regards the modern equipment employed.[126]

They didn't always get it right though. The tactic of retailers in Market Harborough for three weeks around Christmas 1914 was, in hindsight, an appalling lack of judgement, as they used the crassest of language to sell their products.

> War Sales News - The enemy in retreat. As a result of the terrible onslaught of our customers, in every part of our stock, we can see how the goods have retreated. Reinforcements of bargains are still being brought in, and so the struggle continues. Their low prices, however, make them easy captures.[127]

And sensational news greeted readers of the *Market Harborough Advertiser* on December 22, 1914. Boldly screaming from the front of the eight-page paper was an advertisement declaring 'THE END OF THE WAR SALE'.

Sadly, it was not the end of the fighting. Using even more cringing language the advert went on to say:

> The last day of our War Sale is rapidly approaching, and all who have not yet bombarded our shop should do so without delay, before the chance is missed. The War Sale will conclude its very successful operation on Christmas Eve and Peace will reign once more.[128]

By the time the Christmas decorations had come down this kind of language had disappeared from adverts and was not to be repeated. A more fitting and sensitive approach was taken by retailers.

---

[126] *Ashbourne Telegraph*, August 11, 1914, page 3.
[127] *Market Harborough Advertiser*, December 15, 1914, page 1.
[128] *Market Harborough Advertiser*, December 22, 1914, page 1.

Conclusion

The First World War was a time of great innovation: the first time industrialised invention was used in the shape of monstrous shells, gas, tanks and aircraft; the first time such huge armies were gathered, mainly formed by inexperienced conscripts rather than professional volunteers; the first time thousands of young men could die in the space of a few bloody hours; and it was also the first time that propaganda on the grandest scale was used to conceal the true horror of all this innovation.

From August 4, 1914, right through to the Armistice on the 11th hour of the 11th day of the 11th month of 1918, the Government via the Press Bureau and Fleet Street's embedded reporters deliberately set about deceiving the national newspaper-reading public[129] even though the whole country was aware of the carnage being conducted across numerous battlefronts.

The ordinary Tommy in his rat-infested trench 'laughed' at the national papers[130] and the mothers, fathers, wives and sisters worrying about their loved ones in their small town homes in Britain turned a scathing, if not unpatriotic, eye towards the 'spin' of the Press Bureau and their daily national papers.[131]

It is understandable the Government took such an approach, less so the Fleet Street proprietors even though it seemed they had a vested interest in staying chummy with the politicians – many received honours for their pains – or the embedded reporters who allowed themselves to be used as puppets, "some of them had sufficient decency to feel shame at the way they were discrediting their craft...when the post-war revulsion set in."[132]

Analysis of more than 200 editions of the *Harborough Advertiser* and *Ashbourne News* has revealed that everyone knew what was 'really' happening because it came straight from the horse's mouth, straight from the men who suffered the torment of this butchery. The soldiers talked about the real story when they came home on leave, or as patients in military hospitals, but most importantly through the social media of 100 years ago: the handwritten letter home.

It appears many of these young men were sending several letters each day, the equivalent of a multitude of Facebook posts and tweets.

---

[129] *Op. cit.* Knightley, (1978), page 81.
[130] Baggett, J. W. (1996). *The Great War.* London: Penguin, page 96.
[131] *Ibid.* Page 96.
[132] *Op. cit.* Knightley, (1978), page 81.

The wealth of material was staggering - 12 million letters were sent every week.[133]

Ninety-nine percent of these letters were mundane and unremarkable. But that single percentage point equated to a significant proportion of messages telling the awful truth, in surprisingly unvarnished realism.

But most of these significant letters were not just treasured by the worried or grieving relatives, they were 'shared' with the rest of their 'friends' in the community and they did that on the Facebook equivalent of the early 1900s - the local paper.

This research project has established that the editors of these publications knew their news. The presentation of the stories looks old fashioned to a 21st century reader, however, the very best parts of those letters were spotted for angles that readers would want to talk about. That inevitably focused on the drama and the human interest and that meant the real story of what was happening, albeit weeks or even months after certain battles, was reinforced through the local papers. It provided a much-needed balance to the Press Bureau propaganda and it also outmanoeuvred the censorship rules, partly because it was impossible to check every one of the thousands of local papers around the country, and partly because they were obviously deemed unimportant.[134]

Small town readers believed their local papers because the stories were sourced from people they knew, their flesh and blood: Private Fred Jones, who used to work at the butcher's shop on the High Street of their small market town, was the perfect authenticated source if you wanted to know what was really happening under the hellfire shelling of German guns. This was, in direct contrast to the lack of trust in their national papers, destroyed by the misinformation and propaganda they willingly published.

The local press was more influential in its communities than any national newspaper owned by a grand and lofty peer. This is not a surprising conclusion; however, it is a conclusion that has rarely been acknowledged before. In fact Knightley, in the 426 pages of his seminal analysis of the war reporter, *The First Casualty*, does not mention the local newspaper, ever.

---

[133] Meyer, J. (2009). *Men of War, Masculinity and the First World War in Britain*. Basingstoke: Palgrave Macmillan: New York, T. (n.d.). nytimes.com/2010/09/12/books/review/Marler. *www.nytimes.com*, page 12.
[134] *Daily Mail*, 'Bribed Newspapers', November 3, 1914

The analysis of these First World War local papers reveals the power and glory of the language used by these ordinary people. The master craftsmen of every media over the past century have told the 'real' story of the First World War and there is no disputing the power of Sebastian Faulks, or Wilfred Owen, or even Rowan Atkinson. Often a single diary has been used as a source for a story, and the poignancy of the words brought to life with intimate clarity. But the diaries, by their very nature, were private and often only came to light many years after the Armistice. What this research has uncovered is the emotive and evocative vocabulary used by the common soldier to write his contemporary letters with such powerful imagery, stripped bare of the influence of propaganda or the pretence of literary loftiness.

The unique nature of the authors' research has shined a light on the role of the local media and its importance in a world in which national papers may be influenced by the ruling classes to act against the public interest. The analysis of the *Market Harborough Advertiser* and *Ashbourne Telegraph*, which has revealed previously unrecorded conclusions, has also presented opportunities for further research in the archives of other regional papers.

The title of Knightley's (1978) book echoes the words of Senator Hiram Johnson: "The first casualty when war comes is truth."[135] The 'truth' Knightley refers to is the 'truth' held back by politicians and national pressmen. However, perhaps another 'truth' has been a casualty of war – the truth that local newspapers managed to defeat the draconian First World War censorship laws of Kitchener and Churchill, outmanoeuvered the all-seeing eye of the Press Bureau propaganda machine, and gave a platform to the frontline Tommy in the trench who wrote as powerfully as the celebrity poets.

---

[135] *Op. cit.* Knightley, (1978). Frontispiece.

Chapter 8

Romance by Other Means: Scottish Popular Newspapers and the First World War

David Goldie
University of Strathclyde

Introduction

The history of popular journalism in U.K. from the abolition of the stamp duty in 1855 to the First World War offers an illustration of a truism, popular among newspapermen, that war is a very good thing for newspapers. The Crimean War famously made the reputation of William Howard Russell in *The Times*, and subsequent wars, from the American Civil War to the Boer War, served to increase the circulations of existing papers and to create the conditions for new papers to come into being.[1] One of the most significant newspapermen to exploit and benefit from this phenomenon was the founder of the *Daily Mail* and - by the time of the First World War - proprietor of *The Times*, Lord Northcliffe. When asked the question 'What sells a newspaper?', one of his editors is reputed to have replied:

> the first answer is 'war'. War not only creates a supply of news but a demand for it. So deep-rooted is the fascination in a war and all things appertaining to it that . . . a paper has only to be able to put up on its placard "A Great Battle" for its sales to go up.[2]

---

[1] See *The Tradition Established 1841-1884*. London: The Times, 1939, pages 166-92; Knightley, P. (1975). *The First Casualty: From the Crimea to Vietnam: The War correspondent as hero, propagandist, and myth make*. London: Andre Deutsch, pages 3-17; Royle, T. (1987). *War Report: The War correspondent's view of Battle from the Crimea to the Falklands*. London: Grafton, pages 19-33.
[2] Quoted in Ferguson, N. (1998). *The Pity of War*. London: Penguin, page 11.

That this was not merely a newspaperman's hunch, but an established fact has been shown by John M. McEwen, who plotted a direct correlation between newspaper circulation figures and the major engagements of the First World War, with, for example, events such as the German naval raid on the British East Coast in 1916 doubling the circulations of the *Star* and *Evening Standard*.[3]

Major battles and circulation figures of newspapers

McEwen's (1982) analysis of newspaper circulation figures and the major engagements shows that that while there were several failures of newspapers in the war, a pattern emerged, in which established quality newspapers and middle-market papers more or less held their readerships (rising in the early stages of the war, then settling back to pre-war levels) while 'the popular and tabloid newspapers increased their sales and circulation hugely during the war years'.[4]

To give examples: *The Times* suffered a decrease in readership from 183,000 to 130,000, while the increasingly respectable *Daily Mail*, which experienced large increases in readership in the early part of the war, gained overall only a small increase in its figures from 946,000 in 1914 to 973,000 in 1918. The relatively brash *Daily Express* (founded by Arthur Pearson in 1900 and taken over by Lord Beaverbrook in 1916) doubled its circulation between 1914 and 1918 to just under 600,000, while the least respectable of all papers, the jingoistic *John Bull*, also doubled its circulation in wartime from one million to almost two million copies.[5]

Scotland had been no exception to this general British rule - the Crimean War (coinciding with the abolition of Stamp Duty) had brought a number of new, if short-lived titles like Edinburgh's *War Telegraph* and *War Herald*, into being and had allowed regional papers like the *Aberdeen Free Press* to increase both sales and the number of weekly issues.[6] The Crimean War also brought about the first publication, in 1855, of the *Glasgow Daily Bulletin*, the first daily newspaper in Britain to be sold for a penny. Similar developments

---

[3] McEwen, J. M. (1982), 'The National Press During the First World War: Ownership and Circulation'. *Journal of Contemporary History*, 17, page 481.
[4] *Ibid.* Page 483.
[5] *Ibid.* Page 482.
[6] Donaldson, W. (1986). *Popular Literature in Victorian Scotland: Language, fiction and the press.* Aberdeen: Aberdeen University Press, page 108.

occurred during the American Civil War, which, for example, brought the pioneering *Glasgow Evening Citizen* into being - a paper that would last well over a century.[7] By the time of the First World War, Scotland had a thriving and diverse newspaper sector. Scottish exceptionalism meant that British national newspapers had only a limited purchase on Scottish readers. In a pattern that would persist for much of the twentieth-century, large British newspaper groups chose to publish distinct Scottish titles, or dedicated Scottish versions of their main titles, rather than simply distribute 'national' editions. One such example was Rothermere's, *Daily Record and Mail*, a popular illustrated daily created in 1901 by the amalgamation of the indigenous *Daily Record* and the *North British Daily Mail,* and which by 1914 was claiming on its masthead to have 'a larger sale than any other morning or evening journal in the country'.

For the most part, however, Scottish daily newspaper publishing tended to be regional, based on the nation's four main urban centres: the Edinburgh-based *Scotsman* offered the nearest thing to the Scottish paper of record; in Glasgow, the *Herald* was the pre-eminent paper; in Dundee, the *Courier* and *Advertiser* vied for dominance, as did the *Aberdeen Free Press* and *Aberdeen Daily Journal* in that city. For all their regional basis, each paper still had a considerable circulation. The *Glasgow Herald*, for example, consistently outsold in the years before the war not only *The Times* but its English provincial equivalents, the *Manchester Guardian*, *Yorkshire Post*, and *Birmingham Post*. The war saw the *Herald*'s sales rise from around 65,000 to 75,000 daily copies.[8]

Scotland, like Britain, also saw considerable growth in the sale of Sunday papers during the war. In the British context, the Boer War had prompted the creation of a *Sunday Daily Telegraph* and *Sunday Daily Mail*, while the First World War brought about the revival of the *Sunday Times* and saw the establishment of Rothermere's *Sunday Pictorial*, the Hulton *Illustrated Sunday Herald*, and, in 1919, Beaverbrook's *Sunday Express*.[9] By the end of the war, the *News of the World* - whose pre-war sales (1912) were around one and a half million was claiming the largest circulation

---

[7] See 'James Hedderwick 1814-1897', in Eyre-Todd, G. (1903). *The Glasgow Poets: Their lives and poems*. Glasgow & Edinburgh: William Hodge & Co., pages 313-15.

[8] Wadsworth, A. P. (1955). *Newspaper Circulations, 1800-1954.* Manchester: Manchester Statistical Society, page 34. The *Times* is estimated to have had a circulation of less than 50,000 until February 1914. When Northcliffe cut the price in that month, its circulation figures increased dramatically. See McEwan, 'The National Press During the First World War', pages 467-8.

[9] *A Newspaper History 1785-1935: Reprinted from the 150th Anniversary Number of The Times, January 1, 1935.* London: Times Publishing Company, 1935, pages 106-8.

in the world and selling around three million copies per week.[10] This was closely followed by the new *Sunday Pictorial* (launched March 1915), which was claiming a circulation of 2,600,000 at the end of 1917.[11]

This situation was even more pronounced in Scotland. Due to the power of Presbyterian Sabbatarianism, there were no indigenous Sunday newspapers in Scotland before the war. Papers such as the *News of the World*, *Observer*, and *Sunday Chronicle* circulated in the country but were considered beyond the pale to many respectable Scots. The accidental fact of the war breaking out on the August bank holiday in 1914 caused this state of affairs to change overnight. Such was the hunger for immediate news that the first issue of Glasgow's hastily-prepared *Sunday War Times* sold 'close on 200,000 copies' on the 2nd of August 1914.[12] A Presbyterian stronghold like Paisley found its customary Sabbath calm shattered, with, as one account put it, the town taking on a 'Saturday night-like appearance with every second man reading a war edition of the Glasgow papers'.[13] It was reported that in Aberdeen, too, 'the usual Sabbath calm had given place to stir and animation' on account of the news boys 'continually arriving with fresh editions' of the Sunday editions, with another Aberdeen paper describing the scenes on the streets as 'reminiscent of a Hogmanay evening'.[14] Several Sunday papers that began as special editions of daily and evening papers - papers such as Aberdeen's *Evening Express* - didn't last far past the initial excitement of the outbreak of the war. But others followed and would become staples of twentieth-century Scotland, papers such as the *Scottish Sunday Express* (1918), the *Sunday Mail* (1919), and most notoriously the *Sunday Post*. The *Sunday Post* grew during the war from an 8-page Sunday supplement (begun in October 1914) of the *Post* newspaper, into an 18-page newspaper in its own right shortly after the hostilities ceased.[15] It would become a twentieth-century Scottish institution - selling 1 million copies a week at its height - though not a particularly progressive one: it quickly became a byword for everything

---

[10] Engel, M. (1996). *Tickle the Public: One hundred years of the popular press*. London: Victor Gollancz, page 221.
[11] *Op. cit.* McEwen, (1982), page 483.
[12] *Glasgow Herald*, August 3, 1914, page 6.
[13] 'Town Talk', *Paisley and Renfrewshire Gazette*, 8 August 1918, page 5.
[14] 'Aberdeen and War News', *Aberdeen Daily Journal*, August 3, 1914, page 6; 'Aberdeen and the Crisis: Evening Street Scenes', *Aberdeen Free Press*, August 3 1914, page 4.
[15] The paper's first edition under the *Sunday Post* banner was on 19 January 1919. The *Sunday Mail* first came into being as a Sunday edition of the *Daily Record and Mail*, on September 6, 1914.

that was small-minded, sentimental, and regressive in Scottish culture, famously attracting the comment from Tom Nairn much later in the twentieth-century that, "as far as I'm concerned, Scotland will be reborn the day the last minister is strangled with the last copy of the *Sunday Post*."[16]

The popular press

The implication of these trends - the relative flatness of the circulation figures for quality papers, and the marked growth of popular dailies, weeklies and Sunday papers - suggests an emphatic continuation of the readership interests fostered by the New Journalism in the two decades before the war. Which is to say that the readerly interest in war was focused less on the immediate facts of the war - its strategy, politics, and economics - and more on the novel and heightened experiences that it brought about. It is perhaps worth noting here the relationship between the readership for down-market popular papers and the franchise - and in particular the likelihood that the majority of the readers of these papers did not have the vote. Sixty percent of adult men and zero percent of women were enfranchised citizens in the period between the Third Reform Act of 1884 and the Representation of the People Act of 1918, which meant that approximately only three adults in ten in the United Kingdom were parliamentary voters. The Elementary Education acts of 1870 and (in Scotland 1872) had helped ensure that this group had the basic literacy to read newspapers, but this group - the majority of the population - also often lacked access to higher levels of education and a direct say in the parliamentary decisions that affected their lives.

From the point of view of the popular press, then, while the business of informing its readers was important (especially at times of high drama or controversy such as the shell crisis, the introduction of conscription, or significant battles) its columns were speaking not to an electorate but to a form of public opinion that had only an indirect purchase on government. That press's influence, as such, was in helping define, and perhaps contain or harness, a popular mood as much as it was in holding a government to account on behalf of those who had put it in place. What political power popular newspapers had lay not in the

---

[16] Nairn, T. (1970). 'Three Dreams of Scottish Nationalism', in Miller, K. (ed.), *Memoirs of a Modern Scotland*. London: Faber, page 54.

arguments they made to their largely disenfranchised readers, but in their ability to mobilise popular feeling. Their aim, then, was not so much to understand the war analytically from a rational, economical or political viewpoint, but rather to promote an experiential apprehension of it - to sensationalise the war (in both senses of that word) and engender feelings of empathy towards its allied protagonists and of antipathy towards their antagonists.

Less cynically perhaps, the popular press also provided an important service to its readers in offering a perspective on war often lacking in the higher-browed 'quality' newspapers. The shifting of emphasis from objectivity and high politics toward human interest - the move from the general to the particular that characterised the New Journalism, pitched as it was to common readers rather than implicit electorates - enabled the war to be understood through individuals' common experiences as much as through their power to rationalise events at a distance. This would become crucial both to how the war was experienced and how it would be remembered.

Unofficial War reporting and human interest

The attitude of those officials responsible for prosecuting the war seemed, at it's beginning at least, to be particularly hostile to anything but the most centralised newsgathering and dissemination. The mistrust of the press shown by Lord Kitchener at the War Office and Winston Churchill at the Admiralty meant that there was an effective ban on unofficial reporting from the front - much to the frustration of the head of the War Press Bureau, F. E. Smith, who described the War Office as having a preference for running 'a nice private war of their own'.[17] The War Office might put out official communiques, but the sole official war correspondent until May 1915 was an old soldier, Lt Col. Sir Ernest Swinton, who wrote under the name 'Eye-Witness'. The way that most newspapers attempted to get around this prohibition, and the consequent shortage of genuine eye-witness news was to improvise what was effectively an early form of citizen journalism: collating and printing first-person testimonies from serving soldiers, either in the form of letters

---

[17] Quoted in Gibbs, P. (1946). *The Pageant of the Years: An autobiography.* London: William Heinemann, page 160. See also, Messinger, G. S. (1992). *British Propaganda and the State in the First World War.* Manchester & New York: Manchester University Press, page 151; and Towle, P. (1975). 'The Debate on Wartime Censorship in Britain 1902-14', in *War and Society: A Yearbook of Military History,* ed. by Bond, B. and Roy, I. London: Croom Helm, pages 103-16.

home - sometimes passed on by families to local newspapers - or by interviewing soldiers on leave.[18]

Several major English papers posted reporters at Victoria Station, to intercept and interview the wounded and leave-taking-soldiers arriving on trains from the Channel coast. These accounts found their way into Scottish newspapers, especially if the reports featured Scottish soldiers,

Figure 8.1 *Sunday Pictorial*, 14 March 1915

but more often the papers had to look elsewhere for snippets both of hard news and the softer human-interest material that their readers

---

[18] For an account of this phenomenon see, for example. MacCallum Scott, A. MP, 'T. Atkins, Correspondent: Soldiers Assume a New Role in Warfare: Traits Revealed in Letters', *People's Journal (National Edition)*, December 12, 1914, page 1.

appeared to value. This often took the form of letters home, and occasional diary entries passed on to the local press by families and friends. Several of these first-person accounts had a wider audience in mind and were published as books in their own right. Among these were Thomas M. Lyon's dispatches from the front to the *Kilmarnock Standard* that appeared as the collections *In Kilt and Khaki* (1915) and *More Adventures in Kilt and Khaki* (1917), and Captain Robert B. Ross's *The Fifty-First in France* (1918) that had appeared originally as articles, 'A Ross-shire Gordon Highlander's Diary of the War', in the *Ross-shire Journal*. The most well-known and best-selling Scottish book of the war, Ian Hay's *The First Hundred Thousand* (1915), began in a similar way as a series of bulletins for *Blackwood's Magazine* on the formation and exploits of a Scottish New Army battalion, the lightly fictionalised 'Wallace and Bruce Highlanders'.[19] Although arguably a more polished piece of propaganda, produced as it was by a successful pre-war popular novelist, Hay's book, and its successor volume *Carrying On - After the First Hundred Thousand* (1917), showed the power of the model of first-person reportage that had emerged in the relative vacuum of war news created by the War Office's early-war prohibitions on unofficial reporting. One of the most consistently salient of these groups of citizen journalists, sending back reports from the front, was the self-named 'Fighter Writers' of the Dundee newspapers. Dundee had established itself as one of the main centres of Scottish and British newspaper and magazine publication before the war, a process accelerated by the amalgamation of two notably entrepreneurial publishing groups, John Leng & Co and D. C. Thomson & Co in 1906. Their stable of popular titles (which later in the century would include the *Beano* and the *Dandy*, alongside Scottish staples such as *My Weekly Red Letter, and* the *Sunday Post*) employed many men who found themselves in the war areas, and who provided a valuable source of first-hand news to their erstwhile employer. Perhaps the most celebrated was Joseph Lee, news editor of the *People's Journal*, a popular poet and illustrator who had made his name with the poems published in local newspapers and collected as *Poems: Tales o' Our Town* (1910), who sent dispatches in prose and poetry to the *Dundee Advertiser* before being taken prisoner by the Germans. Another was Joseph Gray, a Northumbrian artist employed by D. C. Thomson, who sent regular

---

[19] See Urquhart, G. (1999). 'Confrontation and Withdrawal: Loos, Readership and 'The First Hundred Thousand', in Macdonald, C. M. M. and McFarland, E. W. (eds.). *Scotland and the Great War*, East Linton: Tuckwell, pages 125-44.

wartime dispatches back to the *Dundee Courier*. Following his discharge on medical grounds in 1916 Gray became a war artist for the *Graphic* illustrated newspaper, and drew on his experiences to write a wartime history of his battalion, the 4th Black Watch, which appeared in installments in the *Dundee Advertiser* between 3 December 1917 and 17 January 1918. Other notable Fighter Writers included Linton Andrews, a Yorkshireman and news editor of the *Dundee Advertiser*, and a young staff writer on the *People's* Journal, John Beveridge Nicholson who also enlisted in the Black Watch. Andrews and Nicholson combined to send joint reports to the *Dundee Advertiser* that were picked up by the *Daily Mail*, and which were reported to have particularly impressed its proprietor, Lord Northcliffe.[20]

The People's Journal

The papers to which the Fighter Writers contributed were mainly the Dundee daily newspapers. But the D. C. Thomson group was also responsible for a weekly paper, the *People's Journal*, that had a justifiable claim to be Scotland's most widely read publication, and which in its blend of news reporting, features, and serial fiction offers a particularly interesting case study of the ways in which Scotland's popular newspapers adapted themselves to the new conditions of war. The rest of this chapter will focus on this paper and its sister publication, the *People's Friend*, in order to explore in greater depth the various ways in which the war found its way into their weekly business of informing, educating, and entertaining.

The *People's Journal* had been founded in Dundee in 1858 by an enterprising 30-year old provincial newspaperman from Hull, John Leng. Leng went on to become an eminent public citizen and benefactor of Dundee as well as a Liberal member of parliament for the city. His paper established itself as a mainstay both of Scottish Liberalism and popular vernacular literature for much of the rest of the century, becoming widely-known (both fondly and derisively) as 'the ploughman's bible'. In 1898 John Leng & Co was advertising the *People's Journal* as the 'mouthpiece' of 'Scottish Radicalism' and was claiming for it a circulation of 250,000, which they believed translated into a weekly

---

[20] See Burrows, B. (2004). *Fighter Writer: The eventful life of Sergeant Joe Lee, Scotland's forgotten War poet.* Derby: Breedon Books, page 69.

readership of one million.[21] This meant that it was read by one in five of the Scottish population, which made it, according to William Donaldson, one of the United Kingdom's most widely-circulating weekly papers.[22]

Some of this early radicalism continued in the paper up to the First World War, but the commitment to the vernacular and high-mindedness had become somewhat attenuated. The geographical spread of the paper beyond Dundee - with, in 1914, editions tailored to audiences as far afield as Ulster and the North of England - tied to a policy of continuous technological and journalistic innovation typical of the New Journalism, meant that it had become in many aspects indistinguishable from other popular British papers occupying the lower end of the quality spectrum.

Sensation as much as information had by 1914 become a guiding principle of the paper - seen most clearly, perhaps, in the paper's news headlines, written in a characteristic triplet form, and dealing with the typical subjects of contemporary down-market newspapers:

'Don't Cry, Ellen, It was for You I did it': Infatuated Sailor Shoots Himself in Glasgow: Because his Love is Flouted

Fatal Slash after Singing Song: Young Wife's Head Severed from Body: Husband's Crime

White Slavers in Scotland: Extraordinary Affair on a Train: 'Come to London'[23]

Such sensationalism applied not only to current news reporting, but to the occasional features that dwelt on matters of Scottish history. The paper frequently featured historical accounts and serial stories about the heroes of Scottish culture, William Wallace, Robert the Bruce, and Robert Burns. But it did so in its own distinctive way. A feature, for example, on the Highland clearances of a century before ran in 1914 under the headline:

---

[21] *How a Newspaper is Printed: Being a Complete Description of the Offices and Equipments of the Dundee Advertiser, People's Journal, Evening Telegraph, and People's Friend.* Dundee: John Leng & Co, [1898], pages 18-19.
[22] Donaldson, W. (1986). *Popular Literature in Victorian Scotland: Language, fiction and the press.* Aberdeen: Aberdeen University Press, pages 24-6.
[23] *People's Journal,* January 24, 1914, page 9; July 25, 1914, page 10; August 1, 1914, page 9.

Houses Burned Before their Eyes: Centenary of Horrifying Highland Eviction Scenes: Men Go Insane; Deaths from Exposure[24]

When war came, the *People's Journal* met its challenge in ways that were consistent with many of its pre-war practices. Like many British weekly papers, it greeted the war with an odd mixture of sound editorial sense and somewhat overwrought and credulous reporting. While maintaining a detached, regretful tone in its editorials, its news stories led with misleadingly optimistic and rather fevered headlines, such as those of 1914 that dealt with the successful German siege of Liege ('Germans March to Death: Massed Troops Cut to Pieces at Liege: Brave Belgians' and 'Belgians Triumphant at Liege') and the near-disastrous allied retreat from Mons to the Marne ('Highlanders Battle Against Awful Odds: Germans a Good Mark and Fell like Ninepins: Dreaded Bayonets').[25] This tone was to continue throughout the war, from the revelations of German atrocities in Belgium ('Germans Shock Humanity: Appalling Atrocities Committed by Kaiser's Hordes: Men, Women, and Children Burned and Bayonetted') through to the war's end.[26] A story which appeared after two weeks of the relentless slaughter on the Somme in 1916, for example, ran under the headline, 'Victory in Sight: Great Events Impending on the West: German Army Exhausted: One Big Effort at Home will Clinch the Issue (by our Military Expert)'.[27]

Just as the all-purpose new journalistic style adopted by the *People's Journal* had proved able to shape Scottish experience to its particular template, so it was able to mould the new experience of Scots at war into immediately recognisable shapes. After the initial local excitements of the departure of reservists and territorials and the enlistment of New Army volunteers, the *People's Journal* settled behind its front page of war news into its usual habits. The knitting features of the page 'Where We Club Together' and cookery items on 'Our Special Cookery Page' continued, but were now often related to the special demands of war - the need to provide 'Comforts for the Troops' and the new realities of food shortages. The short stories and serials continued to deal with the romantic complications of working girls and the dilemmas of Dukes and

---

[24] *People's Journal, Aberdeen City Edition*, July 25, 1914, page 6.
[25] 'Germans March to Death', *People's Journal*, August 15, 1914, page 1; 'Highlanders Battle Against Awful Odds', *People's Journal*, September 5, 1914, page 1.
[26] 'Germans Shock Humanity', *People's Journal*, September 19, 1914, page 1.
[27] 'Victory in Sight', *People's Journal*, July 15, 1916, page 1.

the intrigues of industrialists, but now occasionally included the war as a complicating factor. A new short-story hero emerged, in the form of the Glasgow Irishman 'Private Dolan', whose humorous martial adventures were retailed week by week from September 1914.[28] Familiar features such as 'Granny's Gossip' continued to provide a reassuring homeliness, while occasionally allowing the latest war crazes to intrude, as when in September 1914, 'John is Taken for a Spy'.[29] Popular entertainment continued to be featured, too, with the printing of the latest war songs and humorous anecdotes. The paper also continued its pre-war affiliations with Robert Burns, running in January 1915 a 'Burns Telegrams to the Kaiser' competition in which readers were invited to compete for a cash prize by composing a short message from the dead Bard to the German emperor.

One of the more disconcerting elements of the wartime *People's Journal* was the manner in which it covered the actual fighting. In common with other British papers, it was starved of reliable news from the front, especially in the early stages of the war. It made up for this lack of hard content in innovative ways: for example, using drawings and artist's impressions where it could not get photographs, as in its coverage of the arrival of Scottish troops in France in August 1914. But it also took to reporting events, especially those dealing with fighting, with a latitude more characteristic of fictional rather than news writing. In late 1914, for example, it ran a story, which detailed the circumstances in which two members of the Royal Field Artillery had each won the Victoria Cross. The story was presented beneath an artist's impression of the heroic action and a variety of headlines that read, 'The Gunners' Last Stand: When Comrades Fall Two Men Defy Kaiser's Hordes. A Story of Marvellous Heroism: Daring Fighters Survive to Wear Victoria Crosses: Maintaining the Traditions of a Deathless Army.' An excerpt from the story gives an indication of the way in which this real-life event was dramatised:

---

[28] A close fictional relation, perhaps, of Spud Tamson, another Glasgow Irishman of dubious background who transforms into an exemplary, if incorrigible, soldier in R. W. Campbell's *Private Spud Tamson* (1915). Both, perhaps, might be said to be younger brothers of J. J. Bell's 'Wee MacGreegor', a fictional scamp made famous in the columns of the Glasgow *Evening Times* and then in *Wee MacGreegor* (1903) who was also pressed into service in *Wee MacGreegor Enlists* (1915).

[29] 'Granny's Gossip', *People's Journal*, September 19, 1914.

There was a momentary lull in the firing, and Nelson had a chance to get to the rear, which might not come again.

'I'm staying here,' gasped Nelson. 'I may be useful yet.'

As the words left his lips there came the scream of a shell. They felt the wind on their faces. It was the best-aimed shell that had come as yet, and as it struck the earth and burst, they were half-paralysed for a moment by the shock of the explosion. Brown whirling earth: green choking fumes blotting out everything next moment. The green fumes curled away, and revealed the shattered body of Lieutenant Campbell. 'Fight on Boys!' he gasped; then he crawled under a limber and died.'[30]

There is a marked blurring of the boundary between factual reporting and fictional romancing here, seen for example in the readiness to report, or more likely invent, direct speech ('"Fight on Boys!" he gasped') and to describe physical sensations ('they felt the wind on their faces'). The use of a formulaic thriller style ('the green fumes curled away, and revealed the shattered body') suggests, too, a greater concern for dramatic, sensational effect than for accurate observation. Here the expected commitment of a newspaper to truthful reporting is clearly being replaced by a fiction magazine's desire to thrill and to please, to entertain while telling us just a little bit about conditions at the front.

Another instance of this preference for the modes of sentimental fiction over hard reporting comes from an article, which appeared in 1915 under the title, 'The Corporal's Capture: Sing-Song, Shells, and a Sequel'. This story, of an ostensibly real action, told of the unusual ruse by which a handful of men from the West Kent Regiment, led by a Corporal 'Nobby' Rogers, had captured a trench holding 70 Germans:

Among the rubbish at the bottom of the trench was a broken gramophone. The trumpet was still intact. 'Nobby' picked it up, seized with a sudden idea.

'Boys,' he said, 'we're going to 'ave a little concert, just to keep our spirits merry. We ain't going to come crowdin' all to one end o' the trench and get firing lop-sidedly just because them Germans keeps on handin' out their Chinese crackers. So what I suggests is this: we considers as yonder end o' the trench is the stage o' the old Oxford

---

[30] 'The Gunners' Last Stand', *People's Journal, National Edition,* November 21, 1914, page 6.

music 'all, which, bein' brother Londoners, most of us knows. And, takin' our turns, we goes to that end o' the trench and does the 'Arry Lauder or George Robey stunt, singin' through this here 'orn to make our voices louder. And when the song's over, the chap as has been holdin' forth swings up his rifle and let's bang at any 'ead that comes poking up across the way to see what it's all about.

'As it's my idea I takes first go. What shall it be - a little thing o' Lauder's or a selection on the mouth organ?

They declared in favour of Lauder, and with a nod and a grin the ex-'bus driver splashed away to the other end of the trench, where the green reek of lyddite fumes still hung above the gurgling water. [...] The scream of a shell drowned the end of the second verse. With a speed that no quick-change artiste ever equalled, Corporal 'Nobby' left the stage. The shell burst horribly close, and his left arm dropped queerly to his side. But he did not fall. Pulling himself together with a supreme effort, he swung the rifle forward. A howl of rage from the German trenches followed the tingling crack, and a storm of bullets thudded on the breastworks of the British force or came tearing through the shell gaps.

'I got an officer that time, I reckon,' said 'Nobby,' as he reached his comrades. 'Here, tie my arm up, somebody,' he added; 'there's a shrapnel bullet through it... 'Ow did ye like my song?'[31]

Here we see, even more clearly than in the first example, the ways in which the coverage of factual stories has become governed and shaped by the tropes of fictional style. The characterisation and speech patterns of the generic chirpy cockney, Nobby Rogers, clearly owe as much to the representations of page and music-hall stage as to actuality. Nobby's direct speech - itself a device more familiar to fiction than journalism - is aimed, in the manner of fiction, at his readers rather than his comrades (why, for example, should he need to remind them of something they already know - that they are all 'brother Londoners'?). The Germans, too - stupidly popping their heads up to see what's going on as Nobby sings through his improvised megaphone - resemble the

---

[31] 'The Corporal's Capture: Sing-Song, Shells, and a Sequel', *People's Journal, Dundee Edition,* January 16, 1915, page 6.

sausage-eating ex-waiters of popular fiction and music hall more than the efficient and disciplined soldiers they were much more likely to be. The style of the narrative (does anyone in this kind of fiction ever pull themselves together with anything other than 'a supreme effort'?), the understated bravery, and the doggedly optimistic (and rather wearing) insistence that the war is little more than an extension of playground larks would be familiar to anyone who had grown up reading the *Boys' Own Paper* or attended a music hall.

By allowing its fictional house style to infect its coverage of real events, the *People's Journal* was able to reassure its readers. The war could not be so terrible; it seemed to suggest if its terrors and deprivations could be comprehended in the manner with which its readers were so familiar and comfortable. But if the war was, in fact, unprecedented in its scale and horror (as was quickly becoming clear) and if its new conditions were beyond the imagination of the pre-war mindset, then clearly this type of coverage was no longer wholly adequate. Reading it, one can perhaps get closer to understanding the rage of Siegfried Sassoon, C. E. Montague, and many other serving soldiers at the ways in which associated journalists, fiction-writers, and 'Yellow-Pressmen' were distorting and falsifying the experience of war.[32]

What was particularly strange was that a paper which had had no compunction in printing the gory details of assorted stranglings, stabbings, and decapitations in peacetime now had such difficulty in applying this style of sensational news reporting to the events of the war. The death of Lieutenant Campbell of the Royal Field Artillery was presumably as bloody and horrific as the murder and decapitation of the Preston woman of six months earlier ('Fatal Slash after Singing Song: Young Wife's Head Severed from Body: Husband's Crime'). But Campbell dies behind the curling green fumes of sentimental fiction rather than under the forensic glare of serious war, or sensational crime, reporting.

Having been able over many years to resolve everything into the sensational and sentimental goo of its adopted style, the *People's Journal* now found it difficult to talk about the war in ways that were adequate to the conflict's unprecedented enormity. The paper of the 1870s

---

[32] See, for example, Montague's *Disenchantment* (1922) and Sassoon's poem 'Fight to a Finish', for a flavour of the antipathy some soldiers felt towards popular journalists. Arthur Ponsonby's *Falsehood in Wartime* (1928) drew on such antipathies to expose, as he saw it, the extent to which the press had connived with wartime governments to foster popular ignorance and prejudice in order to suppress dissent.

described by William Donaldson would no doubt have made an attempt to confront these realities honestly and report them confidently in its vernacular voice. The new conditions of popular culture in Scotland appear to have made that far less possible.

The People's Friend

The People's Friend, founded by John Leng in 1869, had originally been an offshoot of *The People's Journal*. Edited between 1870 and 1884 by the popular novelist David Pae, the *People's Friend* had been used initially as an outlet for the surplus serial fiction and readers' fiction of its sister paper and though aimed more squarely at women it had, like the *Journal*, been established as a radical paper serving a distinct linguistic community. But it too had lost much of its early political and communitarian drive and its commitment to the vernacular by the outbreak of the war. It is difficult to gauge exact numbers, but it has been suggested that by 1914 the *People's Friend* had outstripped the *People's Journal* to become Scotland's most popular weekly title. When war broke out it was selling a little over 250,000 copies - a circulation that continued to rise steadily throughout the war and after.[33] It had achieved these sales by a characteristically shrewd application of New-Journalistic business principles to Scottish conditions, in combining large amounts of romantic fiction (of which the novelist and literary celebrity Annie S. Swan was the *Friend*'s doyenne) with practical pages of cookery and 'home hints'. The emphasis on readers' contributions and competitions was as strong as it had been in the nineteenth century, but took on forms closer to those of the typical women's penny weekly of New Journalism than of a community news sheet. Readers' correspondence now tended to be confined to the 'Your Health' column, and to the faux-domestic correspondence columns of 'Our Weekly Chat: Uncle Jack and his Nephews and Nieces' and 'The Home Circle: Where Eleanor and her Many Sisters Exchange Confidences Weekly' - themselves cognates of features such as the 'Mother's Chats', the 'Cheery Corner' and articles by 'Sister Rachel' to be found in a British-wide magazine like *Home Chat*. Competitions in the *People's Friend* were for 'Grand Scone Baking', 'Record Needle Work', or, as in 1914, a 'Love Gives Itself' competition in which readers vied with each other by

---

[33] McAleer, J. (1992). *Popular Reading and Publishing in Britain 1914-1950*. Oxford: Clarendon Press, page 163 and 73.

way of word and slogan games to win copies of Annie S. Swan's latest work.

As with many other publications of the New Journalism, the intimate manner and tone of good-neighbourly domesticity fostered in the *People's Friend* disguised the fact that the paper was by 1914 effectively an industrial product written, edited, and distributed according to a tried and tested business formula - a formula partially devised by the Leng and Thomson groups themselves but also based on successful models like the American *Ladies' Home Journal*.[34] Like many other commodities emerging into the marketplace of the period, the paper can also be seen to be employing the latest techniques of branding in constructing an identity and maintaining customer loyalty. This fact did not necessarily invalidate the paper's status as a component in a meaningful communal culture - many women still clearly identified with and willingly subscribed to its virtual community. But in rendering the complexities of that culture in reductive familial and domestic terms, the *People's Friend* arguably narrowed the conceptual world open to its female readers - maintaining their focus on the domestic rather than the public sphere. Its imaginative scope, too, was limited by the genre expectations of its fiction and its practical pages, with fictional plots that invariably resolved themselves in domestic felicity and financial stability, and practical advice that did little more than show readers how best to manage their limited means and express themselves in the domestic arts. There was, in short, very little in the paper that might ripple the calm expectation of housewife and mill girl that their one hope of happiness (and the proper end of Romance) was to be the capable supporter of a husband and the resourceful mainstay of a settled and well-run family home.

The possibilities of linguistic engagement with a vernacular culture had also become circumscribed by 1914. The paper had been founded with the aim that it 'should be the exponent and conserver of Scottish literature, and should contain Scotch stories, poetry, and other articles written by Scotchmen.'[35] But this had changed. Although it still

---

[34] The *Ladies' Home Journal* was, like the *People's Friend*, a sisterly guide to domestic and personal self-improvement that had devolved from a largely agricultural parent paper, in this case, Cyrus H. Curtis's *Tribune and Farmer*. See, Ohmann, R. (1996). *Selling Culture: Magazines, markets, and class at the turn of the Century*. London: Verso, pages 27-8.

[35] *How a Newspaper Is Printed: Being a Complete Description of the Offices and Equipments of the Dundee Advertiser, People's Journal, Evening Telegraph, and People's Friend*. Dundee: John Leng & Co, n.d. [1891], page 53.

published the work of many writers who were Scottish, including stalwarts such as Maude Crawford, Agnes C. Mitchell, May Morison, and Charles Procter, that work was often only incidentally Scottish in nature. Stories and serialisations might have Scottish settings, but their vocabulary and tone belonged, with the exception of the odd Scots dialect word, wholly to the world of British magazine romantic fiction. With characteristic titles such as 'Love Made Perfect', 'The Man Who Came Back', and 'Ashes of Vengeance', they were drawn to a standard pattern across the English-speaking world - parodied mordantly by James Joyce in the characterisation of Gertie MacDowell in *Ulysses* - in which love blossomed with mysterious strangers, romances and fortunes were broken and mended, and in which tender hearts ever found their just reward.[36]

The coming of war did not so much change this world view as intensify it, giving the paper's fiction writers a tragic world-historical backcloth before which they might play out their domestic dramas. The stock devices of magazine fiction, usually relating to the overcoming of impediments to love, financial security, and domestic bliss could take on a new dramatic charge and significance when set against the larger events of war.

Otherwise unremarkable stories, of, for example, virtue under trial, were able to gain a new frisson and immediacy from the events of war, as in the story 'Ian Stuart V.C.: A Hero of the War' by M. C. Ramsay, which appeared three months into the conflict.[37] The story offers a formulaic account of the triumph of self-sacrificing love, in which a young man, passed over by his fiancée for a rival, risks his life for her sake in saving the life of the rival. This bravery wins him the ultimate military accolade and also, predictably, the hand of his beloved as she quickly realises her error. What would have been a mildly diverting and partially implausible story in a peace-time setting gains a new credibility and glamour in war - the traditional romantic qualities of faithfulness and honour take on a new aspect when it is not merely pride or reputation that is at stake, but life itself and the winning of medals and military rank in a contemporary war.

In a similar manner, familiar generic stories of nurse-patient romance or holiday romance could take on new patinas of pathos and glamour under wartime conditions as in, for example, 'Wounded

---

[36] In the 'Nausicaa' episode of *Ulysses* (1922).
[37] 'Ian Stuart V.C.', *People's Friend*, November 23, 1914, pages 450-51.

Soldiers, Welcome!: The Romance of the Notice Board' by Gus Gordon, and 'The Zebra Girl: A Wounded Warrior's Seaside Romance' by Hilda F. Moore.[38] Conventional stories of the humble but virtuous love affairs of the working classes were also given a new edge, as in 'Susie the Flower Girl: A Romance of the War'. This is a story from 1915 that would appear to owe more to the values of 1815. In it, the eponymous heroine gains both the hand of her beloved, Joe, a packer in a post-card factory, and the patronage of Lady Denby after Joe receives a sabre wound while saving the life of his officer, Lady Denby's son, in the course of a cavalry charge.[39]

Another standard trope reinvigorated by war conditions was that of the redemptive power of the love and example of a good woman. J. B. Trenwith's 'A Man and a Briton: The Story of One whom the War Redeemed' offers an example.[40] In the story a worthless young ne'er-do-well tries and fails to rob a Colonel's daughter. Her spirited resistance and nobility of character prompts the young robber to mend his ways and enlist. In the manner of these fictions, he is redeemed by war and wins the Distinguished Conduct Medal. Wounded in the process, he sends the young lady the medal in gratitude, and dies fulfilled (singing on his deathbed 'Pack up your Troubles in your Old Kit Bag').

This appropriation of the general conditions of war to enhance well-worn stories could be given a further twist, and an even greater immediacy, by tying the stories more closely to specific actions and events. This is illustrated in an anonymous short story, 'On Her Wedding Day' which appeared in the *People's Friend* early in 1915.[41] Set in Scarborough in the previous month, December 1914, the story follows the fortunes of Elaine Weston. Like much women's-magazine fiction it draws on the stories of the Scottish ballad tradition - in this case, that of 'Auld Robin Gray', a ballad that was often revisited in the popular cinema and fiction of the war.[42] In this variant on the story, Elaine is a twin, and her brother Jack serves in France with the man who is both his best friend and Elaine's fiancé, Ted Wilton. When the story begins her father is under threat of bankruptcy at the hands of

---

[38] 'Wounded Soldiers, Welcome!', *People's Friend*, April 17, 1916, pages 370-71; 'The Zebra Girl', *People's Friend*, September 4, 1916.
[39] 'Susie the Flower Girl', *People's Friend*, January 25, 1915, pages 76-7.
[40] 'A Man and a Briton', *People's Friend*, May 15, 1916, pages 456-7.
[41] 'On Her Wedding Day. A Tragic Intervention. A Story of the Bombardment of Scarborough', *People's Friend*, January 11, 1915, pages 26-7.
[42] For example, Vitagraph's *Auld Robin Gray* (1910) directed by Laurence Trimble; Ideal's *Auld Robin Gray* (1917); and *The Master of Gray* (1918), directed by Tom Watts.

Richard Merton, a rich man long embittered by failure in youth to win the hand of Elaine's mother. Driven by Elaine's resemblance to her mother, Merton offers to cancel the debt owed by her father if Elaine will end her engagement and instead consent to marry him. She is agonising over this proposition when she reads of Ted's death in a newspaper. In her grief, and in the expectation of saving her father, she reluctantly agrees to sacrifice herself to a loveless marriage with Merton, choosing the 16th December, her birthday, for the date of the service.

Fate, cruelly, does not answer her nightly prayers that she might die before the allotted day. It does, however, arrange that she walks out on the promenade with Merton on the morning of her wedding. This date and time - as contemporary readers would no doubt have already realised - happens by a happy trick of cosmic irony to coincide with the notorious bombardment of the town by the German fleet.[43] Merton hands Elaine the promissory note that will release her father just before the shelling starts. Shortly afterward, he is hit by the shrapnel of an exploding shell and is killed instantly (and bloodlessly, in the accompanying illustration). Elaine's restoration to fortune and happiness is completed when she runs home to find a letter telling her that Ted is, in fact, still alive - he has been wounded in the right arm and so has been unable to write and tell her of the misunderstanding. As the story closes, Elaine, with material and amorous fortunes restored, sets off for London where she will be reconciled with Ted and her wounded brother.

There is plainly little sense here that the war is exerting a major effect on the ways in which people conduct their everyday lives, or promoting either deep or revisionary thought about their attitudes towards service and sacrifice. It would seem, rather, that for the fiction writers of the *People's Friend*, at least, War was little more than a continuation of Romance by other means - a slightly more plausible and immediate source of the reversals, misunderstandings, and sudden deaths and disappearances on which their business depended.

---

[43] An event that became the subject of a wide range of women's writing. Sylvia Pankhurst visited the town at Christmas 1914 and wrote movingly of the devastation. See, Pankhurst, E. Sylvia. (1987). *The Home Front: A mirror to life in England during the First World War*. London: The Cresset Library, pages 114-23. Winifred Holtby, who came under fire in the bombardment, would later write about it in her novel *The Crowded Street* (1924). Holtby's novel would, however, take a view on romance and marriage that was antipodal to that of the *People's Friend*. See, Wallace, D. (2000). *Sisters and Rivals in British Women's Fiction, 1914-39*. Basingstoke: Macmillan, pages 132-7.

This straightforward co-option of war to the domestic agenda was however complicated, especially as the war went on, with other and sometimes less frivolous considerations. The *People's Friend*, like other Thomson group publications, was understandably anxious to place in a positive light the contributions made by the women who were - especially in war - its main audience. Part of this effort lay in registering the importance of the traditional domestic role so that women were seen to be crucial to the war effort for the maintenance of the family unit in a time of crisis, for maintaining morale on the home front, and for husbanding crucial resources by careful domestic economy. This was a message that was coming through strongly, too, in popular books such as J. E. Buckrose's *War Time in Our Street: The Story of Some Companies Behind the Front Line* (1917) and Annie S. Swan's *An Englishwoman's Home* (1918) which hymned the significance of the vital, nation-preserving battles being fought by the household infantry on the Home Front.

The most visible way in which the contribution of the domestic women to the war effort could be marked was in the provision of comfort and assistance to the troops. Throughout the war, the Thomson papers prided themselves on their encouragement and practical advice to readers on the manufacture and distribution of 'comforts' for servicemen and the provision of foodstuffs, or so-called 'Tit-bits for Tommy'.[44] In November 1914 'Eleanor', convenor of the paper's Home Circle, exhorted readers to help the troops by knitting them 'the Dundee Helmet' - a balaclava, featuring ear holes, that had been 'specially designed for the *People's Friend*'.[45] The *People's Journal* ran a 'Comforts for the Soldiers' column which solicited contributions of clothes and tobacco, and which patted the backs of the other D. C. Thomson papers for their efforts in this direction.[46] In addition to this direct assistance, the *People's Friend* contributed in some useful, and some not so useful, ways to the sense of a unified war effort. The more useful interventions dealt with physical and moral wellbeing. The paper tailored its food and cookery pages to wartime conditions: with 'Kitty's Kitchen Club' advising its readers, for example, on economical recipes

---

[44] 'Tit-Bits for Tommy', *People's Friend*, February 8, 1915, page 119.
[45] 'Eleanor', *People's Friend*, November 16, 1914, page 426.
[46] See, for example, 'What women are doing in War Time: How the 'People's Journal' has helped the Tommies', *People's Journal, Dundee Edition*, 9 December 1914, page 9. The 'comforts' effort was largely co-ordinated by Elizabeth Craig, who would go on to become a well-known cookery writer. See Andrews, L. (1964). *The Autobiography of a Journalist*. London: Ernest Benn, page 87.

for the likes of 'Delightful Cheap Pickle', 'Economical Meat Pie' and 'War-time Pudding'; and on the acquisition of allotments and the cultivation of vegetables in articles such as 'Home Food Production: Why not get a Garden Allotment'.[47]

A series of articles on the contributions of Colonial and Dominion troops to the larger war effort in 1916 provided information on the sheer scale and diversity of that effort - though pieces such as 'The Gallant Anzacs: Tales of our Heroic Kinsmen from 'neath the Southern Cross', 'Canada's Contingent: How Sons of the Maple Leaf have Fought for the Empire', and 'Dusky Sons of the Empire: Battle Stories of Our Indian Fighting Men' are, as their titles suggest, rather longer on unreconstructed celebration than on military or political analysis.[48] That these were most likely state-sponsored articles, produced for the dissemination of a complaisant press, is perhaps best indicated by the article which began the series, 'Pat's Part in the War: Bravery of Irish Regiments on all Battle Fronts'. Appearing only months after the Easter Rising, and just as the Battle of the Somme was kicking off, the piece was a fairly unsophisticated attempt to allay British fears and discourage any incipient Scottish Sinn Feinism. It described not only the continuing patriotism of the Irish troops generally but also, more specifically, a purported incident involving the soldiers of the Royal Munster Fusiliers. These soldiers were taunted by placards raised above the facing German trenches, which referred to the troubles and alleged the abuse of Irish womenfolk by English soldiers. The unfased response of the doughty Fusiliers, according to the article, was to riddle the offending placards with bullets (while singing 'Rule Britannia') and later to capture the trench in order to destroy them altogether.[49]

While it tended to steer clear of covering war news directly (presumably the preserve of the more masculine *People's Journal*) the paper provided occasional, informative pieces on the ways in which the military effort was being organised. Articles such as 'The Battle Front: What it is Like', 'The Feeding of an Army: How Tommy Gets his Grub', 'Passed by Censor: How Letters are Dealt with at the Front', and

---

[47] 'Kitty's Kitchen Club), *People's Friend,* November 1, 1915; 'Home Food Production' *People's Friend,* January 22, 1917, page 77.
[48] 'The Gallant Anzacs', *People's Friend,* July 17, 1916, pages 56-7; 'Canada's Contingent', *People's Friend,* 10 July 1916, pages 29 and 38; 'Dusky Sons of the Empire', *People's Friend,* July 31, 1916, pages 93-4.
[49] 'Pat's Part in the War: Bravery of Irish Regiments on All Battle Fronts', *People's Friend,* July 3, 1916, pages 13-15.

even 'Fighting A-Wheel: How Army Cyclists Do their Bit', were typical of the kind of gossipy, informative articles that Alfred Harmsworth had made the mainstay of his popular newspapers.[50] They satisfied the curiosity of readers and were basically educative, but necessarily offered a rather limited sense of life in the war zones.

Humour had a part to play in this too. Articles, like 'Tommy's "French"', 'Fun in the Firing Line: Tommy the Irrepressible Joker', or 'Newspapers in the Trenches: How Tommy makes Fun', offered well-meaning attempts to humanise the war and maintain morale by offering glimpses of the persistent good spirits of its participants.[51] Though well-intentioned, pieces such as these effectively falsify the experience of war by concentrating only on the parts of it which the paper considers palatable and acceptable and which it can render within the bounds of its conventional style. The paper's overweening assumption that all experience is a form of sentimental grist for its human-interest mill denies expression to the full range of war experiences - both the heights of exhilaration and magnanimity and depths of boredom, degradation, and fear. This feeling is perhaps exacerbated when one sees a similar human-interest tone being applied to stories such as 'Mascots of War: Pets Beloved of Tommy and Jack' and 'Four-footed Fighters: Touching Stories of Our War Horses.'[52]

The paper's coverage was not always this reductive, it needs to be said. The *People's Friend*, like the other newspapers, noted above, published informative first-hand accounts of the conditions on the front. An example from a frequent contributor, Captain Horace Wyndham, is 'Encamped in France: How Men are Prepared for the Fighting Line' which does a similar job to Hay's *First Hundred Thousand* dispatches for *Blackwoods* in familiarising readers with the war preparations taking place across the sea.[53] Informative pieces with titles 'How Tommy Gets his Wages', 'How Tommy Gets his Grub,' 'How Tommy Makes his

---

[50] Harmsworth had encouraged snippety gossip pieces such as 'How Time-Tables Are Made' and 'About Smoking in Cemeteries' in the *Evening News* and would go on to use the device extensively in the feature pages of the *Daily Mail*. See, Taylor, S. J. (1998). *The Great Outsiders: Northcliffe, Rothermere and the Daily Mail*. London: Phoenix, page 29.
[51] 'Tommy's "French"', *People's Friend*, 4 October 1915, page 273; 'Fun in the Firing Line', *People's Friend*, November 1, 1915, pages 365 and 372; 'Newspapers in the Trenches', *People's Friend*, January 1, 1917, page 14.
[52] 'Mascots of War', *People's Friend*, November 13, 1916, pages 409 and 415; 'Four-Footed Fighters', *People's Friend*, November 20, 1916, pages 429 and 433.
[53] 'Encamped in France: How Men are Prepared for the Fighting Line', *People's Friend*, January 11, 1915.

Will', might have been light in tone and larded with humorous anecdotes but were likewise able to offer useful information for those curious on matters of military organisation. More helpfully, in the month after the Battle of Loos, at which many Scottish new army battalions received their first terrible blooding, the paper published a piece, 'Killed, Wounded, and Missing: How the Casualty Lists are Prepared', which offered practical information and a more straightforward acknowledgement of the grim nature of the war.[54] In the same year, 1915, the *People's Friend*'s 'Uncle Jack' sought to ameliorate the emotional difficulties of the enforced separations brought about by the war with his correspondence column, 'My Soldier Friends at the War', in which the mothers, sisters, and sweethearts of those away at the war were encouraged to share their thoughts and feelings with other readers.

Although the *People's Friend* made some effort to reach out and comprehend the realities of the war, its outlook and journalistic style most often proved ill-suited to the task. The paper did, very creditably, run a small number of articles throughout the war, which gave some indication of the conflict's horrors and potential for psychological damage. Articles such as 'Facing Death at the Front: How Soldiers Feel Under Fire' (27th March 1916) and 'Nerves in Battle: When the Brave are Tested' managed at times to break through the paper's relentlessly homely assumptions and provided honest, compassionate accounts of the degrading and unmanning effects of war-induced psychological breakdown. The overall message of 'Facing Death at the Front', for example, was one of the cheerful stoicism of the troops, but it did not wholly shy away from the paralysing fear felt by many servicemen, including, perhaps surprisingly, the admission of one soldier of his 'sobbing hysterically' in the face of danger.[55] But more often, good intentions were undone by the paper's inability to reconcile the realities of war with its dominant house-style of ameliorative domestication. For example, at a time when popular interest in all things relating to the tragic fate of 'little Belgium' was still high, the *Friend*'s readers were encouraged to show their solidarity by following some of the patterns in *The Belgian Crochet Book*, issued as a free supplement with the paper on 25th January 1915. Featuring on its cover a picture of a crocheted

---

[54] 'Killed, Wounded, and Missing', *People's Friend*, October 25, 1915, page 350; 'Nerves in Battle', *People's Friend*, February 5, 1917, pages 101 and 109.

[55] 'Facing Death at the Front: How Soldiers Feel under Fire', *People's Journal*, March 27, 1916, page 301; 'Nerves in Battle', *People's Friend*, February 5, 1917, pages 101 and 109.

Belgian Lion cushion cover, with lion rampant shield and motto 'L'Union Fait la Force', the supplement contained tips on making 'The Bruxelles Nightdress Top' and 'Louvain Insertion' (having lost its famed medieval library to German barbarism the Belgian town had, it seems, gained a commemorative crochet stitch). The *People's Friend* commended the crochet work to its readers in familiar terms, noting that a towel or tea cloth incorporating 'this pretty lace is one that will be welcomed by every girl who owns a bottom drawer. No matter though the boy is in khaki, his little sweetheart should not neglect preparing for that happy nest which is to be theirs when the cruel war is at an end.'

One wonders what the boy in khaki would have made of this. Or what he might have thought of the ladies' military-style velvet 'Tipperary Cap' promoted by the paper as a gesture of stylish support for his efforts, or of the many souvenirs given out free with the Thomson papers.[56] Among such gifts were the *People's Friend*'s 'Silky-Finish Pictures of the Royal Engineers', a 'silken souvenir' of the Battle of Mons, and a 'Charming War Song' (a 'four page song in praise of the Black Watch'), not to mention *My Weekly*'s 'The Battle of the Somme. A Charming Permanent Memento of the Big Push; Beautifully Reproduced on Silken Fabric.'

A Woman's Place…

One wartime development that the *People's Friend* had of necessity to deal with was the new relationship many women now enjoyed in the workplace. The pre-war *People's Friend* had often dealt with the experiences of mill girls and domestic servants, but usually as the subjects for romantic serial fiction. But the conditions of war meant that the paper was now producing articles as well as stories that reflected the wider range of occupations open to women. One such article from 1916 was 'Machinery and Humanity: A Sketch of "The Works Pal"' by Monica Cosens, billed as 'author of "Lloyd George's Munition Girls"'. Another, 'Queer Trades for Woman. Girls of all Nations in Odd Occupations' by WBC in the same year was ostensibly a celebration of the new possibilities open to women, but it betrayed in both its title and its tone a strong sense that such employment remained a series of interesting exceptions rather than the new normal.[57] The paper pushed,

---

[56] 'Eleanor' on 'The Tipperary Cap', *People's Friend,* January 4, 1915, page 10.
[57] 'Queer Trades for Women', *People's Friend,* August 7, 1916.

in a number of different ways, messages of empowerment through work as well as through domestic virtue - one such was the advertisement that featured in 1916 for Milkmaid Brand Milk Cocoa, which featured a statuesque Land Girl above the slogan 'The Lady with the Plough is doing a Man's Work and needs a Man's strength'.[58] Such empowering slogans were also present in the serial fiction published in the paper. The serialisation of Annie S. Swan's *Peggy Fordyce: A Story of Women's Work in War-time* (begun on 2nd October 1916), for example, featured above its title line a heading, which proclaimed that 'In this Great World Crisis the Country has been Saved by its Noble Women'.

Other serial fiction which explored the new working roles open to women, and which might be said to welcome such opportunities included Maude Crawford's *Marjorie M'Leod: Munition* Maker, begun on 8th January 1917, and Agnes C. Mitchell's novel *The Wartime Woman*, the first installment of which appeared in the *People's Friend* on 4th December 1916. The latter book followed the fortunes of three sisters who take up war work - one as a munitions worker, one as a gardener, and the other as a chauffeur.

Such combinations of fictional representation, factual reporting, and advertising imagery in the *People's Friend* undoubtedly bespoke a new confidence in women's abilities to take on the new roles of wartime. But there remained a strong sense, too, that this was simply romantic business as usual - only dressed up in working clothes. The ways in which exciting possibilities for employment and adventure could easily be reduced to a repeating and familiar formula is perhaps best illustrated by the titles under which much of the short fiction on these topics appeared. Titles such as 'Phyllis, the Mill Girl: A Romance of Woman's War Work', 'Lynettte Leigh, Land Girl: The Romance of an Autumn Dawn', and 'Her Country's Call: The Romance of a Girl Munition worker' perhaps speak less of marvelous opportunities for individuation and empowerment, than they do of the possibilities of finding reassuringly familiar forms of romantic fulfillment in the somewhat unfamiliar conditions of wartime occupations. [59]

The *Friend*'s view on female empowerment can perhaps best be summed up by a short article that appeared in July 1916. Developing an argument made by the Bishop of London, that the expectations of

---

[58] 'The Lady with the Plough', *People's Friend*, December 4, 1916.
[59] Hilda M. Shaw, 'Phyllis, the Mill Girl', *People's Friend*, November 8, 1915, pages 395-6; M. C. Ramsay, 'Her Country's Call', *People's Friend*, November 15, 1915, pages 418-9; Dora Fowler Martin, 'Lynettte Leigh, Land Girl', *People's Friend*, September 21, 1918, pages 136-7.

male and female workers will have changed by the end of the war, the article suggests that, men 'who have been taught to think for themselves', who 'have developed initiative and resource; and so have learned what great things they are capable of' will no longer be content to carry out menial jobs, like those of drapers' assistants, in which they had been employed before the war. Instead, however, of finding in this an encouragement for women to develop similar initiative, the article points only to the vacancies in relatively low-status jobs now open to women - roles they might fill which are beneath the dignity or initiative of ex-servicemen. As the article puts it, 'the man who has been trained to do a man's work, who has tasted life and adventure and faced danger in the trenches will not go back to work that can be perfectly well done by girls.'[60] This is progressive in that it acknowledges that women have indeed made a useful contribution - that there is work that they can do perfectly well - and that the workplace should now be open to them. Much less progressive, though, is the attendant assumption (one that seemed to be shared by most employers and trade unionists[61]) that their labours should remain ancillary to those of men - that their hands and minds are useful only insofar as they liberate the ambitions of men.

Conclusion

The *People's Friend* was, perhaps, a typical example of the way popular newspapers in Scotland as well as the rest of United Kingdom responded to the war. If it was a truism that war sold newspapers, it was also true that conflict brought out in them - in this war, at least - a strong streak of social and political conservatism. One of the most interesting features of the New Journalism was the kind of inverse relationship that it fostered between journalistic innovation and progressive social thinking. The more technically innovative a paper was, the less likely it was to be politically progressive - something that could be seen from Northcliffe's *Daily Mail* all the way to Thomson's *People's Journal* and *People's Friend*. It might be expected that war would exert a centrifugal effect on culture, its violence blasting apart the weak social bonds and inter-class structures that held it together. But as far as popular newspapers are concerned, the war appeared to exercise

---

[60] 'After the War. Things That Are Going to Happen', *People's Friend*, July 10, 1916, page 28.
[61] For examples of this see Braybon, G. and Summerfield, P. (1987). *Out of the Cage: Women's experiences in Two World Wars*. London & New York: Pandora, pages 47-56.

instead a centripetal effect, pushing readers back into the formulas and familiar certainties that had enchanted, consoled, and reassured them in the happier times before the conflict.

Scotland had, like the rest of the United Kingdom, to deal with a number of unprecedented threats to its economic and social stability in the war - much more than simply the existential threats and the dangers to families caused by warfare itself. The fundamental, though largely temporary, shift in gender roles and expectations was one such threat, domestic shortages and the rising cost of living were others, while rebellion in Ireland and revolution in Russia offered glimpses of wider instabilities massing on the horizon. In this context, popular newspapers played an important role in anchoring their readers in the stock certainties of their everyday worlds - amusing, diverting, gently advising, entertaining, and to a certain extent informing - and in so doing reinforced the resolve of their imagined communities. As such, they undoubtedly played a part in sustaining domestic morale, as well as assisting the continuous flow of matériel, that helped ensure an allied victory. But they did so at the cost of limiting the horizons of their readerships, of continuing to confine them in the narrow precincts of pre-war conventions and customary expectations. Their continuing popularity spoke directly to the need for consolation and comfort, and for solidarity and a sense of common purpose. But what was neglected in the process was an opportunity to open their readers' eyes fully to the actual, often discomfiting and disagreeable, facts of the war and to the potential for dynamic social change that their realisation might bring about. Instead of helping their readers understand fully the consequences of war and push confidently into the new world they had won, the popular press continued to insulate its readers in the comforting certainties to which they had long been accustomed, pushing them back gently but inexorably into the world they had lost.

Chapter 9

"And Yet They Tell Us Not to Hate the Hun" Atrocity Propaganda, and War Patriotism in Winsor McCay's *The Sinking of the 'Lusitania'*

Jesús Jiménez-Varea
Antonio Pineda
Universidad de Sevilla

Introduction

It is well-known that Allied propaganda during the First World War drew heavily on the depiction of atrocities in their effort to construct a demonised face for the so-called Hun. Accounts of German brutality against helpless civilians, such as the mutilation of children, belonged in the rich lore of heinous acts already attributed to enemies in previous military conflicts, but they were especially effective when combined with real-life events like the sinking of the Lusitania on May 7, 1915[1].

History shows that propagandists tend to use every single communication medium available, and World War I (WWI) propaganda was no exception to that principle. In the United States, every form of media and entertainment collaborated with the struggle to persuade American people to trust their leaders and adopt a radically jingoistic, anti-German stance. Illustrator, cartoonist, and one of the most versatile and accomplished popular artists of his time, Winsor McCay[2] was able to produce and direct almost single-handedly one of the most effective pieces of entertainment ever made to promote

---

[1] *RMS Lusitania* was a British ocean liner that was owned by The Cunard Line. Sailing from America to Great Britain the liner was sunk by a German submarine (*U-20*) on Friday 7 May, 1915, 11 miles (18 km) off the southern coast of Ireland and inside the war zone declared by Germany. The explosion of the torpedo was followed by a second internal explosion and the ship sank in 18 minutes, with the deaths of 1,198 passengers and crew, including 128 American citizens.

[2] Zenas Winsor McCay, September 26, 1869 - July 26, 1934.

American wish for revenge: the animated film *The Sinking of the 'Lusitania'*. (1918), a milestone in the history of animation because of its prolonged length (12 minutes), and the way it combined 'objective' newsreel-like images with a highly expressive style to recreate the eponymous tragedy. On the basis that McCay's motion picture is thematically in line with official WWI government messages, in this chapter, we attempt to analyse *The Sinking of the Lusitania* from animation as propaganda, focusing especially on the use of atrocity propaganda.

The First World War's Anglo-American propaganda

The propaganda of the so-called Great War was historically remarkable in many aspects. According to historian Alejandro Pizarroso (1993), the First World War is the event that marked the third qualitative jump in the history of propaganda-the first two being the invention of the printing press[3] and, the second the French Revolution. The Great War gave birth to scientific propaganda, that is, a kind of propaganda that relied on the conscious, systematic use of advertising's techniques and the mass media. Propaganda theoretician Lasswell (1938) points out that, before the conflict, the layman "lived in a world where there was no common name for the deliberate forming of attitudes by the manipulation of words (and word substitutes),"[4] unlike the scholar that "had a scientific inheritance which included the recognition of the place of propaganda in society." Lippmann (1965), looking back, follows Lasswell, when he wrote,

> this was the first great war in which all the deciding elements of mankind could be brought to think about the same ideas, or at least about the same names for ideas, simultaneously. Without cable, radio, telegraph, and daily press, the experiment of the Fourteen Points[5] would have been impossible. It was an attempt to exploit the

---

[3] The printing press was invented, around 1440, by Johannes Gutenberg. See, Pizarroso, A. (1993). *Historia de la propaganda*. Madrid: Eudema.

[4] Lasswell, H. D. (1938). 'Foreword', in Bruntz, G. G. (1938). *Allied Propaganda and the Collapse of the German Empire in 1918*. Stanford, CA: Stanford University Press, page v.

[5] The Fourteen Points was a speech delivered by President Wilson to Congress on January 8, 1918. His intention was to justify the American involvement in the war and to look at the terms of peace.

modern machinery of communication to start the return of a 'common consciousness' throughout the world.[6]

WWI propaganda also gave rise and use of the phrase *Psychological Warfare*[7] - the planned use of propaganda and other activities to achieve national aims - that would be developed in the Second World War, the Cold War, and other conflicts. In this regard, the impact of WWI propaganda was deep and lasting: besides causing a post-war general consciousness which was characterised, according to Sproule, (1989)[8], by a growing concern about the mass media and propaganda WWI communication efforts profiled modern propaganda techniques and had direct consequences on interwar and World War II propaganda. Regarding the media, it is worth pointing out that the First World War was the moment when the film medium was first used for propaganda aims in a general way.

Preceded by four decades of intensive, belligerent state propaganda Thomson, (1999)[9] argues WWI messages were aimed at combatants, enemies, neutral nations, and the home front. Using every medium available, a propagandistic intensity became possible due to the media infrastructure that nation-states had set up before 1914.[10] In this context, with an organised press and cinema, British propaganda was particularly pervasive. In contrast, German propaganda was poorly organised, and unimaginative. The British government focused in on and multiplied its propaganda efforts, utilising the newspapers, posters, and cinema from the beginning. Part of the reason for this was that public opinion was not in favour to entering the conflict. To sway opinion, the British government articulated a communication system that included a loyal press, censorship, information control, private organisations, and created institutions such as the War Propaganda Bureau and the Ministry of Information. Through these organisations,

---

[6] Lippmann, W. (1965). *Public Opinion*. New York: The Free Press, Collier Macmillan Publishers, page 133.
[7] Psychological warfare (PSYWAR), is a term used "to denote any action which is practiced mainly by psychological methods with the aim of evoking a planned psychological reaction in in other people." See, Szunyogh, B. (1955). *Psychological Warfare: An introduction to ideological propaganda and the techniques of psychological warfare*. Michigan: William Frederick Press, page 13.
[8] Sproule, J. M. (1989). 'Social Responses to Twentieth-Century Propaganda', in Smith, T. J. (Ed.), *Propaganda*. New York, NY: Praeger, pages 5-22.
[9] Thomson, O. (1999). *Easily Led. A history of Propaganda*. Gloucestershire: Sutton Publishing.
[10] See, Jowett, G. S. and O'Donnell, V. (1986). *Propaganda and Persuasion*. Newbury Park: Sage.

the message of the government was developed and propagated to the military and civilian population.

One of the main messages of British propaganda was atrocity stories about German behaviour. The War Propaganda Bureau[11] produced the first atrocity document, the Bryce Report[12]. The former British ambassador in Washington Lord Bryce chaired a governmental committee - created in December 1914 to study German atrocities in Belgium - that generated a report that was published on 12 May 1915, and translated into 30 languages. Containing exaggerations, inaccuracies, and falsities, the Bryce Report became the basis of WWI atrocity propaganda.[13] According to Cull (2003), "The suffering of 'gallant little Belgium' became a major issue in British war propaganda at home and abroad, especially in the United States."[14] By 1918, atrocity stories were part of the warfare lexicon of the Allied countries.

The British did not only propagate the virtue of the war to the home front. Convincing the U.S.A. government and people were important. President Woodrow Wilson had been elected on the back of anti-war ideas, a radical, quick turn from isolationism to pro-war jingoism had to be generated. "Elected apparently on the cry that he kept us out of war," wrote Lippmann in 1922 (1965), "Mr. Wilson within five months led the country into war."[15] Maybe this is why Lasswell (1971) described

---

[11] In August 1914, David Lloyd George appointed Charles Masterman MP, to head a Propaganda Agency, called War Propaganda Bureau, which had a distinguished body of literary talent such as Arthur Conan Doyle, Thomas Hardy, H. G. Wells, and Rudyard Kipling who wrote propaganda leaflets that were distributed to neutral countries. In 1917, the bureau was subsumed into the new Department of Information that employed all available technology in spreading propaganda advantageous to the British, including, radio telegraph, magazines, posters, cinema, handbills and newspapers. The British had several advantages over the German state when it came to international communications. The British controlled much of the undersea cable system then in operation, connecting Europe with America, Canada, India, Australia and many other countries. Many leading publishers worked for the Bureau such as Oxford University Press, Hodder & Stoughton, Macmillan, Methuen, Thomas Nelson, and John Murray.

[12] The Committee on Alleged German Outrages is most commonly known as the Bryce Committee after its chair, Viscount James Bryce (1838-1922). 'The Report of the Committee on Alleged German Outrages' (May 1915) is the most well known publication of the Committee for its 320-page Appendix A that includes sensationalist accounts of mutilations and rapes, for which there is no verifiable evidence.

[13] *Op. cit.* Pizarroso, (1993).

[14] Cull, N. J. (2003). 'Netherlands, Belgium, and Luxembourg', in Cull, N. J., Culbert, D. and Welch, D., *Propaganda and Mass Persuasion. A historical encyclopedia, 1500 to the Present*. Santa Barbara, CA: ABC-CLIO, pages 264-267, page 266.

[15] *Op. cit.* Lippmann, (1965), page 127.

Wilson as "the great generalissimo on the propaganda front."[16] This was more the remarkable given the British navy had, in 1914, cut the submarine cables[17] that linked Germany and the U.S.A. With a sizable population of German origin, this was not popular in America.[18]

Institutionally, the main arm of American propaganda was the Committee on Public Information (CPI), a bureau created by President Wilson in 1917 and chaired by journalist George Creel - hence the bureau was known as the Creel Committee. The CPI's propaganda campaign was astonishing: "Probably", wrote Lippmann (1965),[19] "this is the largest and the most intensive effort to carry quickly a fairly uniform set of ideas to all the people of a nation." The campaign paved the way for the belief propaganda could 'scientific'; an assumption that would continue throughout the Twentieth Century. The intensity of the campaign can be illustrated through the example of the Four Minute Men's[20] machinery, whereby 75,000 'Minute Men' gave at least 755,190 speeches (four-minute speeches, hence the name of the propagandists) to an audience of more than 300 million people (Lippmann, 1965).[21] The CPI's effort was particularly impressive regarding the range of media that were used. According to Creel (1920) himself:

> There was no part of the Great War machinery that we did not touch, no medium of appeal that we did not employ. The printed word, the spoken word, the motion picture, the telegraph, the cable, the wireless, the poster, the sign-board-all these were used in our campaign to make our own people and all other peoples understand the causes that compelled America to take arms.[22]

---

[16] Lasswell, H. D. (1971). *Propaganda Technique in World War I*. Cambridge, MA, and London: The M.I.T. Press, page 216.

[17] In 1914 Germany had five cables, which ran through the English Channel, then across the Atlantic linking them with the U.S.A., Spain, France and the Azores. In the first few hours of the war a British ship cut these cables meaning Germany could only use radio to communicate with their embassies in North and South America. Unknown to the Germans the British had acquired a copy of their codebook that was used to listen in to German communications.

[18] *Op. cit.* Pizarroso, (1993).

[19] *Op. cit.* Lippmann, (1965), page 31.

[20] The Four Minute Men were made up of approximately 75,000 volunteers who with authorisation of President Wilson gave four-minute speeches (hence the name of the propagandists) on topics given to them by the CPI. The speeches were given at cinemas, across the country, between newsreels. See Cornebise, A. E. (1984). *War as Advertised: the Four Minute Men and America's crusade, 1917-1918*. Philadelphia: American Philosophical Society.

[21] *Op. cit.* Lippmann, (1965).

[22] Creel, G. (1920). *How We Advertised America*. New York, NY, and London: Harper & Brothers

Pertaining to the 'parts of the great war machinery', the Committee used the by then new mass media, such as motion pictures. In Creel's (1920) words, the work of the Division of Films "played a vital part in

Figure 9.1 Winsor McCay 1906

the world-fight for public opinion."[23] America's "resources and determinations"[24] were driven home through films like *Pershing's Crusaders* (1918), *America's Answer* (Edwin F. Glenn, 1918), and *Under Four Flags* (S. L. Rothafel, 1918). From the viewpoint of discourse, the CPI tried to give direction and a vocabulary with which to frame the war and the enemy - which included loathsome images of the latter - soon to feed the patriotic fervor that swept the USA.[25] These loathsome images of the enemy that mirrored British atrocity stories probably helped to generate an anti-German hysteria - for instance, the CPI published in

---

Publishers, page 5.
[23] *Op. cit.* Creel, (1920), page 117.
[24] *Ibid.* Page 8.
[25] Jackall, R. and Hirota, J. M. (1995). 'America's First Propaganda Ministry: The Committee on Public Information During the Great War'. In Jackall, R. (Ed.), *Propaganda*. London: Palgrave, pages 137-173.

1916 a brochure on *German War Practices* that was one of the innumerable versions of the Bryce Report (Lasswell, 1971). As Lippmann (1965)[26] points out about Americans, "under the stress of war they created a compound object of hatred out of the enemy abroad and all their opponents at home."[27] Aside from the Creel Committee, other organisations and associations joined the war effort such as the 'patriotic societies',[28] the League to Enforce Peace[29], and the National Security League[30] Thus, the WWI propaganda effort did not only rely on wholly on governmental agencies. This leads us to the case of Winsor McCay and *The Sinking of the 'Lusitania'*.

Winsor McCay and *The Sinking of the 'Lusitania'*.

All consulted sources agree that Zenas Winsor McCay (Figure 9.1) was a genuine master of many trades within the field of popular graphic arts. Not only did he become one of the most brilliant practitioners of the already well established profession of newspaper editorial cartoonist, but he also made fundamental contributions to the then still emerging media of comics and - more pertinently to the subject of the present chapter - animation: "Winsor McCay was", according to Harvey (1994), "the first original genius of the comic strip medium. Ditto for the medium of animated cartoons. No question. He did things in both media that no one had done before."[31] For all his artistic proficiency, McCay was mostly a self-taught craftsman who did not complete grade school and had little formal training beyond a brief period of private art

---

[26] *Op. cit.* Lippmann, (1965), page 67.
[27] In any case, it must be noted that atrociousness narratives were not monopolised by Anglo-American forces. There was also German atrocity propaganda directed against Belgium (Lippmann, 1965), and, in Vienna, "an enterprising firm supplied atrocity photographs with blanks for the headings so that they might be used for propaganda purposes by either side" (Ponsonby, 1936, page 21).
[28] *Op. cit.* Lippmann, (1965), page 31.
[29] The League to Enforce Peace was established in 1915, in America to promote the formation of an international body for world peace based on the belief British Empire and American democracy were the ideal models for the peace. See, Herman, S. R. (1969). *Eleven Against War: Studies in American internationalist thought, 1898-1921*. Stanford, CA: Hoover Institution Press.
[30] The National Security League was founded in December 1914 to promote an American patriotism. Their aims included, universal military service, Americanisation of immigrants, government regulation of economic affairs, English as the national language, an interstate highway system and, among many others, national preparedness for conflicts.
[31] Harvey, R. C. (1994). *The Art of the Funnies: An aesthetic history*. Mississippi: University Press of Mississippi, page 21.

instruction in 1888 that influenced on McCay's mastery of perspective, as well as his distinctive Art Nouveau aesthetics.[32]

He debuted professionally in Chicago while still a teenager, painting posters for theatres and circuses that reveal the fantastic imagination that would characterise his posterior comics and animations. At the same time, McCay exhibited his ability to create highly detailed drawings in a matter of seconds while talking to a live audience in the so-called chalk talk acts. In 1891 he moved to Cincinnati, where he performed these routines in dime museums, and since 1898 he produced cartoons and illustrations for the local newspapers *Cincinnati Commercial Tribune* and *The Cincinnati Enquirer*, as well as the national magazine *Life*. During this period McCay made his first attempt at a visual narrative with the series of illustrated poems *A Tale of the Jungle Imps by Felix Fiddle* (1903). Though not strictly a comic strip, it gave him a chance to exercise his inventiveness in portraying the fluid transformations of figures, which would prove useful in his later animating endeavors.

McCay joined the staff of *The New York Herald* as an illustrator and editorial cartoonist in 1903. After several short-lived efforts, he finally succeeded in creating a couple of popular comic strips with *Little Sammy Sneeze* and *Dream of the Rarebit Fiend*. The latter depicted the nightmares suffered by a changing arrangement of characters in episodes aimed at adult readers. However, McCay considered that it might be a good idea to develop a series for a younger audience that would also explore the dreams of a recurring protagonist. The resulting strip was his most famous work in the field of comics, *Little Nemo in Slumberland*, which ran in *The New York Herald* from October 15, 1905, until July 23, 1911. It is celebrated as one of the most accomplished examples of the possibilities of this medium. Harvey, (1994) claims, "In this creation, McCay's genius, his originality, is revealed at its peak. From the very first of the Sunday pages, he was a master of the comic strip form."[33] He gained both nationwide popularity and enthusiastic critical appraisal for this strip and the rest of his works for newspapers. Also, he continued a parallel career in the vaudeville circuit that benefited greatly from his new fame. In this regard, chalk talks like *The Seven Ages of Man* (1906) which he performed in front of a live audience, along with a stage

---

[32] Canemaker, J. (2005). *Winsor McCay: His life and art*. New York, NY: Harry N. Abrams, page 26.
[33] *Op. cit.* Harvey, (1994), page 21.

adaptation of *Little Nemo* (1907), denoted McCay's interest in developing a spectacular dimension of his artistic skills that would culminate in his animated productions.

According to biographer Canemaker (2005),[34] McCay first got in contact with the cinematic medium around 1896 when he attended a demonstration of Charles Francis Jenkins and Thomas Armat's primitive film projector, the Vitascope, in one of the dime-museums for which he worked in Chicago. Later, some flipbooks gave him the idea to create the impression of fluid movement through a quick succession of pictures: "animated cartoons could be produced and thrown on a screen in the same manner as a photographic film was projected... From this germ I evolved the modern cartoon movies."[35] For that reason, McCay would proclaim that he was the inventor of animated cartoons, but strictly speaking, there were earlier pioneers, like Émile Cohl and J. Stuart Blackton. At this point, it is worth remarking that Blackton had already pioneered the propagandistic recreation of war-related events on 'documentary' film with his fake newsreel *The Battle of Manila Bay* (1898) - shot in his bathroom, substituting cigar smoke for that of the naval guns - during the Spanish-American conflict.[36]

Notwithstanding the existence of those precursors, it is true that the quality of McCay's productions at such an early stage in the evolution of the medium situated him in a league of his own for decades. McCay has deserved such a high consideration on the strength of the extraordinary brilliance of only a few animated films, starting with an adaptation of his great comic strip, *Little Nemo* (1911), a one-reel which he incorporated into his vaudeville routine. However, the delighted viewers annoyed the artist because they came to the erroneous belief that he had used photographs of real children to make the film, instead of 4,000 separate drawings on rice paper. Because of that, McCay made a deliberate effort to drift further away from realism in his next two films.[37] *The Story of a Mosquito* (1912) has been considered one of the earliest instances, of the horror genre since McCay demonstrates a talent to manipulate the viewers' fears that he would put to good use in his dramatic depiction of the Lusitania tragedy a few years later. However, before that, he would

---

[34] *Op. cit.* Canemaker, (2005), page 40.
[35] McCay, W. (1983). 'In His Own Words: Winsor McCay on Life, Art, Animation', *Nemo: The Classic Comics Library* 3 (October 1983), pages 34-39, page 36.
[36] Dewey, D. (2016). *Buccaneer: James Stuart Blackton and the Birth of American Movies*. London: Rowman & Littlefield, page 47.
[37] *Op. cit.* McCay, (1983), page 36.

strive for a more comical effect in his third animated cartoon, *Gertie the Dinosaur* (1914), where he apparently revived a prehistoric animal. Upon its release, this film proved itself a phenomenal success with audiences "awed by the dinosaur's lifelike movements, unaware that what they had seen would change the course of animation's young history for the better."[38] Nevertheless, in spite of such an encouraging reception, it would be four years before McCay's next and most ambitious animated project, *The Sinking of the 'Lusitania'* (1918), could be seen on screens.

Most probably, this interruption in his career as an animator was because he had left *The New York Herald* for William Randolph Hearst's *New York American* in June 1911. His new employer did not look favorably on the artist diverting his creative energies to whatever other interests he may have aside from drawing for his newspaper. To start with, Hearst forced McCay to cut down on his vaudeville activity brandishing "the exclusivity clause of his contract."[39] Thus, by 1914, McCay had abandoned his theatrical activity completely, but that was not enough for the temperamental press employer. Hearst wanted McCay to concentrate all his efforts on the production of editorial cartoons, even if that meant neglecting his cherished 'Little Nemo', whose adventures, published in the *New York American*, starting on September 3, 1911, under the name In the Land of Wonderful Dreams - that was interrupted on July 26, 1914[40]. Harvey, (1994) claims for the next few years, it looked as if McCay had given up being anything but an instrument in the hands of Hearst, whose,

> mission was to exercise power over public opinion. Seeking to employ the popularity of the cartoonist in ways that would advance the Hearst causes, the publisher wanted McCay to do his best work on the editorial page, producing cartoons that illustrated the moralising pontifications of his chief editorial lieutenant, Arthur Brisbane.[41]

---

[38] Lenburg, J. (2009). *The Encyclopedia of Animated Cartoons*. New York, NY: Facts on File, page 1.
[39] Crafton, D. (1993). *Before Mickey: The animated film 1898-1928*. Chicago, IL: University of Chicago Press, page 111.
[40] McCay would not retake this comic strip until 1924, when, instead of renewing his contract with Hearst, he preferred to return to *The New York Herald*, where it ran under the original denomination, *Little Nemo in Slumberland*, from August 3, 1924, until its final demise on December 26, 1926.
[41] *Op. cit.* Harvey, (1994), page 32.

Almost invariably, McCay's editorial cartoons of this period consisted of single-panel displays of his mastery of pen-and-ink technique and perspectives that encapsulated - usually in the form of solemn visual allegories - the commentaries on society and politics dictated by Brisbane in accordance with his publisher's dominant worldview. By that time, one of Hearst's foremost preoccupations was to prevent the United States from entering the European war in alliance with Great Britain. In consequence, McCay's cartoons regularly conveyed Hearst's isolationist and deceptively pacifist messages: the American Eagle would use her wings to protect the country against the violence that devastated Europe; marching troops would be depicted as cattle walking into a slaughterhouse; Uncle Sam would calm down American citizens in the face of the catastrophic events taking place on the other side of the Atlantic. Although the cartoonist did not share his boss's ideas in this regard, he submitted himself to his demands until Hearst's already controversial stance eventually won him nationwide antipathy in the wake of the sinking of the British-owned passenger liner Lusitania, torpedoed by a German submarine. Swanberg, (1961) observes,

> When the Lusitania was sunk in 1915, sending to the bottom sixty-three infants and children among the 1198 victims, the Hearst press called it 'a deed of wholesale murder' by the Germans. Later, when public horror had subsided a trifle, it pronounced the sinking justified 'under the accepted, principles of civilized warfare', saying, 'The Lusitania incident is, of course, no cause for a declaration of war'.[42]

Contextually, it must be taken into account that American attitudes towards World War I went from neutrality to "peace without victory" to armed neutrality to entering the war.[43] In this context, German submarine warfare was the element that led the US entering the war. Americans advocated Atlantic navigation freedom, and President Wilson strongly opposed the submarine warfare Germany was conducting against commercial shipping. The turning point took place on March 19, 1917, when merchant ship *Vigilancia* was torpedoed, thus leading to declaration of war by President Wilson.

---

[42] Swanberg, W. A. (1961). *Citizen Hearst: A biography of William Randolph Hearst.* New York, NY: Scribner, pages 298-299.
[43] Renouvin, P. (1994). *La Primera Guerra Mundial.* (J. García Jacas, trans.). Madrid: Globus Comunicación, pages 85-90.

Referring to the sinking of the Lusitania, Ponsonby (1936) writes that the crucial "political significance of the catastrophe... gave it special propaganda value in inflaming popular indignation, especially in America. Here obviously was the necessary lever at last to bring America into the war."[44] At the same time, the US entering the war changed the course of the conflict[45]; consequently, it could be concluded that the sinking of the Lusitania was a major factor in the outcome of WWI.

McCay felt outraged by this apparently unjustified attack that provoked the deaths of American citizens, so he decided to channel all that indignation into a new animated film that would recreate the disaster, of which no photographic record existed. As the finished project attests, his purpose was openly propagandistic, since he intended to encourage a hostile reaction against the German aggressors employing the specificities of animated pictures. It was to be a groundbreaking employment of the medium. Ehrlich, (2013) claims the film industry had already been confined to anecdotic amusement despite its potential to,

> increase the animator's agency by easily eliminating or adding visual elements to enhance a message. This characteristic elucidates animation's informative potential and explains animation's frequent use in educational contexts and historical propaganda.[46]

From the start, the European conflict was present in the plots of many fictional films, most often in ways that reflected the pacifist and neutral positions that predominated in the public opinion of the country. But the tragedy of the British liner became an immediate object of horrified fascination that coincided with - and probably contributed to - a turning point in regard to how Americans perceived the ongoing war through popular culture. According to Bottomore (2000),[47] it was the "most notorious shipping disaster to follow the Titanic," and there was little reticence to the circulation of films related to the sinking of the Lusitania. Thus, there were numerous newsreels that showed images of the survivors returning to their homes and

---

[44] Ponsonby, A. (1936). *Falsehood in War-Time*. London: George Allen & Unwin, page 121.
[45] *Op. cit.* Renouvin, (1994).
[46] Ehrlich, N. (2013). 'Animated Documentaries: Aesthetics, Politics and Viewer Engagement', in Buchan, S. (Ed.), *Pervasive Animation*. New York, NY: Routledge, pages 250-251.
[47] Bottomore, S. (2000). *The Titanic and Silent Cinema*. East Sussex: The Projection Box.

claiming for justice; the funerals of the hundreds of victims, along with photos of the most illustrious amongst them; the incensed reactions of either common people or famous figures such as former President Theodore Roosevelt; and commemorations of the event[48]. Of course, as McCay himself realised, there remained the lack of actual images of the event, but it was not long before visual culture started to fill in the gap with its interpretations of those fatal minutes. One of the earliest and most influential amongst such depictions were Fred Spear's poster for the Boston Committee of Public Safety, first published in June 1915. Accompanied only by the caption 'Enlist', the picture represents a beautiful woman lifelessly descending into the deep darkness of the ocean, still holding the body of her baby child between her arms. In his detailed study of the transcendence of this poster, Lubin (2016)[49] suggests that McCay borrowed its central motif for the final sequence of his animated interpretation of the tragedy.

The famed cartoonist started working on the film shortly after he got news of the event. Like in his other animated cartoons, McCay had the assistance of a young neighbour of his, John Fitzsimmons, plus, on this occasion, a fellow artist from the Cincinnati press, William Apthorp 'Ap' Adams.[50] Instead of using sheets of rice paper as he had done in his previous films, McCay, who financed the project all by himself, decided to try a new method, recently patented by Earl Hurd, which would become the standard of the future industry. Dobson, (2009) describes this as,

> a process called celluloid, or cel animation. This involved a stationary background painted onto a paper with characters painted onto various layers of celluloid, a transparent substrate, that would be laid on top. The process saved time as previous methods had involved all of the elements drawn onto translucent paper that was laid over others.[51]

---

[48] 'Lusitania Tragedy' (*Warwick Bioscope Chronicle*, May 1915); 'Anti-German Riots in Liverpool Following the Loss of Lusitania' (*Pathé's Animated Gazette*, May 1915); 'The Tragedy of the Lusitania' (*Pathé's Animated Gazette*, May 1915); 'Lusitania Survivor's Appeal' (*Topical Budget*, September 1915); 'Strong Man of U.S.A.' (*Topical Budget*, November 1915); and 'Lusitania Day' (*Topical Budget*, May 1916) (Bottomore, 2000, page 162).
[49] Lubin, D. M. (2016). *Grand Illusions: American art and the First World War*. New York, NY: Oxford University Press, page 26.
[50] *Op. Cit.* Canemaker, (2005), page 188.
[51] Dobson, N. (2009). *The A to Z of Animation and Cartoons*. Plymouth: Scarecrow Press.

In spite of all these technical improvements, the inevitably time-consuming nature of the animation work postponed the release of the film until near the end of the war. Even more so because McCay wanted to invest his pictures with an almost photographic realism to document as believably as he could those tragic moments that had never been recorded in actuality. To that end, he applied all the skills he had fine-tuned during his many years as an illustrator and cartoonist, plus the principles of the still-nascent grammar of film storytelling. Crafton, (1993) explains,

> Its documentary style called for a more realistic graphic style, so the detailed crosshatching, the washes, and the spatter techniques of the Hearst editorial illustrations were used... The animated sequences were conceived as alternating shots to simulate the editing of the newsreel.[52]

In effect, McCay succeeded in giving his animated cartoon an appearance close to that of the newsreels that preceded the feature-length films in the cinema theatre programs of the time. According to Dobson, (2009) "A very early example of an animated documentary... which depicts what happened as factually as any newsreel but injects emotion through the visuals."[53] In this regard, although *The Sinking of the 'Lusitania'* has been considered a singular departure from McCay's otherwise customary creed "that animation was best suited to the depiction of imaginary states and mythic creatures"[54], this film is no less a demonstration of the artist's imagination, in so far, as he managed to endow those historical happenings with a powerful emotional overtone. It has been suggested by Telotte, (2010), that underlying the iconicity of the surface, there is a symbolical plane of apprehensions:

> It is a work that achieves its propagandistic shock effect by interweaving two very different spatial conceptions: a literal concern with actual space and a stylised treatment of space... a further unsettling dimension, as if the submarine lurking in those depths

---

[52] *Op. cit.* Crafton, (1993), page 116.
[53] *Op. cit.* Dobson, (2009), page 60.
[54] Wells, P. (2009). *The Animated Bestiary. Animals, cartoons, and culture.* New Brunswick, NJ, and London: Rutgers University Press, page 86.

were metaphoric of some anxiety or threat that was more difficult to articulate or visualize.[55]

On top of that, the general atmosphere of *The Sinking of the 'Lusitania'* is similar to the humorless - even severe - solemnity of many of his editorial cartoons; and like his colossal portrayals of Uncle Sam or the American Eagle towering over North America, the ill-fated liner resembles a gigantic, peaceful cetacean, unaware of the zigzagging shark of metal that follows her. The passengers appear only when the vessel is fatally hit by the torpedoes, and they are just minuscule, horrified figures desperately trying to save their lives. The exceptions to the anonymity of the victims are the photographic inserts accompanied by captions that identify the more eminent personalities among the hundreds of dead. The catastrophe culminates with the above-mentioned elegiac motif of the drowned woman and her baby vanishing together, followed by the incensed declaration of hate that closes the film.

After twenty-two months during which McCay literally moonlighted, drawing cartoons for Hearst's newspaper by day and working on his film by night, the small team, he led produced a total of 25,000 drawings for a running time of 12 minutes.[56] Like with his previous animations, the cells were photographed in J. Stuart Blackton's Vitagraph studios. Finally, *The Sinking of the 'Lusitania'; An Amazing Moving Pen Picture by Winsor McCay* was released in July 1918 in the midst of a nation that differed greatly from the one where the initiative had started. Originally, it had been conceived to encourage American intervention in Europe, but the country had already entered the war in April 1917, despite President Wilson's electoral promises of neutrality. In this regard, for all its artistic merit, McCay's independent effort got naturally assimilated within the voluminous body of films that exploited the war theme and, more specifically, the shipwreck of the Lusitania. Among the various feature-length films that were more or less explicitly inspired by this tragedy, one of the earliest was the Italian *Il Siluramento dell'Oceania* (Augusto Genina, 1917). It had already been dealt with in the comical *A Submarine Pirate* (Charles Avery and Syd Chaplin, 1915). Also, it appears in a couple of films starring actual Lusitania survivor

---

[55] Telotte, J. P. (2009). *Animating Space: From Mickey to Wall-E*. Kentucky, KY: The University Press of Kentucky, page 49.
[56] *Op. cit.* Canemaker, (2005), page 195.

Rita Jolivet: *La Mano di Fatma* (Gino Zaccaria, 1916), and, more centrally, the failed super production *Lest We Forget* (Léonce Perret, 1918). Other films that present fabled accounts of the disaster are *Over the Top* (Wilfred North, 1918) and the 20-episode serial *The Eagle's Eye* (George Lessey and Wellington A. Playter, 1918). As a final point, it is interesting to mention that the documentary *Crashing Through to Berlin* (1918) "used animation to depict the sinking of the *Aztec* and the *Lusitania*" (Bottomore, 2000:161). At the opposite extreme, there were those films that, according to Mock and Larson, (1939), under "a deceptively patriotic title would contain material believed to have been inspired by the enemy."[57] Most remarkable among these is the 15-episode serial *Patria* (Leopold Wharton, 1917), produced by Hearst, which deviated hostility toward Mexico and Japan, instead of Germany. Mock and Larson, (1939) observe, "gradually through 1917 and 1918 evidence was pieced together indicating that Mr. Hearst's well-known dislike for the Japanese might not be the only thing behind Patria. German propaganda agents entered the picture".[58]

The Sinking of the 'Lusitania' was distributed by Jewel Productions in coincidence with one of the most infamous 'hate films' ever, *The Kaiser, the Beast of Berlin* (Rupert Julian, 1918), whose plot includes a fictionalised portrayal of the submarine commander responsible for the *Lusitania* atrocity, who goes mad after being decorated by the Kaiser. McCay's feature was advertised as "The World's Only Record of the Crime That Shocked Humanity" and "The biggest box-office attraction ever put in an open-market programme."[59] Upon its release, this ambitiously animated cartoon received favorable - sometimes enthusiastic - reviews in contemporary specialised magazines, like *The Cinema*, for its dramatism: "The best scene shows the explosion of the first torpedo. It is more real than reality."[60] However, the film did not succeed in revolutionising the animation medium - because it would be over a decade before other animators were able to catch up with its quality[61] - nor was it a commercial success since it only brought McCay 80,000 dollars after a few years in theatres[62].

---

[57] Mock, J. R. and Larson, C. (1939). *Words That Won the War*. Princeton, NJ: Princeton University Press, page 143.
[58] *Ibid.* Page 144.
[59] *Op. cit.* Bottomore, (2000), page 150.
[60] *Op. cit.* Canemaker, (2005), page 193.
[61] *Op. cit.* Harvey, (1994), page 241.
[62] In fact, from a strictly economic perspective, the incomes seem to be within - maybe above the common margins of benefits provided by films of that length during that period: "The

In the end, *The Sinking of the 'Lusitania'* remains as a beautiful rarity, technically ahead of its time and worthy of being studied today as a fascinating piece of war propaganda. In this regard, the case of McCay's film illustrates the fact that, aside from institutionally controlled propaganda films - the British Ministry of Information, for instance, had a section dedicated to propaganda in the movies and other media - private, independent artists can line up with the interests of state power.

Analytical Construct: Ponsonby's Principles and Atrocity Propaganda

The basic analytical tools with which we study the film consist of a set of war propaganda principles derived from British author and politician Lord Arthur Ponsonby. In his book *Falsehood in Wartime*, originally published in 1928, Ponsonby analyses and denounces the enormous amount of lies that characterised WWI - "There must", says Ponsonby, (1936) "have been more deliberate lying in the world from 1914 to 1918 than in any other period of the world's history"[63] - and gives samples taken from Great Britain and other countries. Interestingly, one chapter of Ponsonby's book focuses on the sinking of the Lusitania.

Ponsonby's (1936) description of propaganda mechanisms has been summed up and systematised by Belgian historian Anne Morelli in *Principes élémentaires de propagande de guerre* (2001).[64] The result is a set of 10 fundamental principles of war propaganda that conforms our analytical construct, and whose historical persistence is verified by Morelli - who, by the way, also cites in his book the sinking of the Lusitania. Morelli's account of the principles underlying war propaganda is as follows:

1 *We do not want war*. The idea behind this first principle is that given that war brings countless horrors, no government openly advocates conflict; on the contrary, governments tend to claim peaceful intentions. According to Ponsonby (1936),

---

motion picture industry generally did well during the war years. Moviemakers dutifully cranked out hundreds of one- and two-reel features with war plots, most of which brought an average return of a few thousand dollars." Isenberg, M. T. (2008). 'The Great War Viewed from the 1920s: The Big Parade', in Rollins P. C. and O'Connor, J. E. (Eds.), *Why We Fought: America's War in Film History* Kentucky, KY: The University Press of Kentucky, pages 138-155.
Probably, Canemaker's (2005) negative estimation of McCay's earnings from *The Sinking of the 'Lusitania'* is based on the outstanding amount of time and work the artist invested in the production.
[63] *Op. cit.* Ponsonby, (1936), page 19.
[64] Morelli, A. (2001). *Principes élémentaires de propagande de guerre*. Brussels: Éditions Labor.

the solemn asseverations of monarchs and leading statements in each nation that they did not want war must be placed on a par with the declarations of men who pour paraffin about a house knowing they are continually striking matches and yet assert they do not want a conflagration.[65]

2 *The enemy is the sole responsible for war.* Ponsonby (1936) regards this notion as universal, as well as quite relevant:

The accusation against the enemy of *sole* responsibility for the war is common form in every nation and in every war… It is a necessary falsehood based on a momentary biased opinion of one side in a dispute, and it becomes the indispensable basis of all subsequent propaganda.[66]

This tenet can be understood as a logical consequence of the former principle: if one side of the conflict is innocent, the other side must have triggered war. Thus, warring sides do not claim to perform acts of aggression, but acts of defense.

3 *The enemy has the face of the devil.* Demonisation is a classical, long-standing propaganda technique; war contexts just provide a fertile environment for the radicalisation of the procedure, and political rivals are thus turned into monsters from hell. Particularly, Ponsonby (1936) points out that "up to 1919 the Kaiser, as the villain of the piece, was set up in the Allied countries as the incarnation of all iniquity."[67]

4 *To conceal the real aims of war, and present them as noble causes.* This principle relates to the "We do not want war" one. In this respect, the task of propaganda is to cloud the real intentions of the powerful in an

---

[65] *Op. cit.* Ponsonby, (1936), page 15.
[66] *Op. cit.* Ponsonby, (1936), page 57. The relevance of this principle can also be supported by the following statement by Lasswell (1971, page 47): "So great are the psychological resistances to war in modern nations that every war must appear to be a war of defence against a menacing, murderous aggressor. There must be no ambiguity about whom the public is to hate. The war must not be due to a world system of conducting international affairs, nor to the stupidity or malevolence of all governing classes, but to the rapacity of the enemy. Guilt and guilelessness must be assessed geographically, and all the guilt must be on the other side of the frontier. If the propagandist is to mobilise the hate of the people, he must see to it that everything is circulated which establishes the sole responsibility of the enemy. Variations from this theme may be permitted under certain contingencies… but it must continue to be the leading *motif*."
[67] *Op. cit.* Ponsonby, (1936), page 76.

aura of respectability, using noble motifs like defending small countries or preparing the world for democracy.[68]

5 *The enemy's atrocities are intentional; if we make mistakes, it is unintended.* This principle is directly related to atrocity propaganda: given that horrid acts are all-pervading in war contexts, propaganda will try to show that the enemy's atrocities are business as usual, while painting at the same time a rosy image of 'our' actions. According to Ponsonby (1936), "the exaggeration and invention of atrocities soon becomes the main staple of propaganda."[69]

6 *The enemy uses 'dishonest' weapons.* This principle is a corollary to the former one, as well as another propaganda procedure that deepens in the negative depiction of the enemy as an immoral entity.

7 *We have very few losses; the enemy's are enormous.* This tenet pertains to the results of the conflict, appealing to the human desire to adhere to the winning cause.

8 *Artists and intellectuals support our cause.* By enrolling the men of the intellect, propaganda obtains a way of conveying lies in an emotive and aesthetic form.

9 *Our cause is sacred.* By interpreting the conflict's causes in religious terms, the war effort turns into an unavoidable crusade.

10 *Those who question war propaganda are traitors.* To a certain extent, this idea can be understood as a consequence of some of the former principles: if our cause is sacred and peaceful, and the enemy is an immoral, hideous devil, any intent of questioning our propaganda can be interpreted as unpatriotic or treachery.

The inclusion of atrocious acts in the Ponsonby-Morelli list, as well as the historical relevance of atrocity propaganda, leads us to consider this technique with more detail. The central idea is that atrocity stories enable propagandists to mobilise the hate of the people against a rapacious, menacing aggressor. Reflecting on the appeals to be

---

[68] *Op. cit.* Morelli, (2001).
[69] *Op. cit.* Ponsonby, (1936), page 128.

employed to mobilise hatred against the enemy, Lasswell (1971) writes that it is necessary to,

> represent the opposing nation as a menacing, murderous aggressor. Represent the enemy as an obstacle to the realization of the cherished ideals and dreams of the nation as a whole, and of each constituent unit. It is through the elaboration of war aims that the obstructive role of the enemy becomes particularly evident. Represent opposing nation as satanic; it violates all the moral standards (*mores*) of the group and insults its self-esteem. The maintenance of hatred depends upon supplementing the direct representations of the menacing, obstructive, satanic enemy by assurances of ultimate victory.[70]

Atrocity propaganda existed well before 1914; what is more, it seems to be a universal phenomenon. According to Lasswell (1971), atrocity "has been employed with unvarying success in every conflict known to man."[71] From stories of people tortured for the amusement of Turkish generals to Crusade-boosting tales about atrocities in the East[72] to the Gulf War's atrocity propaganda, terrifying the public has been an enduring technique. Regarding WWI, atrocity propaganda is the best-known and most-cited propaganda device, as well as an early output of the conflict. As Ponsonby (1936) points out in *Falsehood in War-Time*, "Atrocity lies were the most popular of all, especially in this country and America; no war can be without them."[73] As a technique, the depiction of awful acts was a must in WWI, as far as the American people, for instance, had to be persuaded to trust their leaders and quickly adopt a radically anti-German stance. Thus, through newspaper pieces and hundreds of books and pamphlets aimed at demonising the Germans, propaganda spread stories of massacre, mutilation, or torture. As Rudyard Kipling said in *The Morning Post* (London) of 22 June 1915, "however the world pretends to divide itself, there are only two divisions in the world to-day - human beings and Germans."[74] Such a dehumanisation of the enemy was achieved through stories like the one

---

[70] *Op. cit.* Lasswell, (1971), page 195.
[71] *Op. cit.* Lasswell, (1971), page 81.
[72] *Op. cit.* Lasswell, (1971) and Lumley, F.E. (1933). *The Propaganda Menace*. New York: D. Appleton-Century.
[73] *Op. cit.* Ponsonby (1936), page 22.
[74] *Op. cit.* Lasswell, (1971), page 91.

about a Belgian baby whose hands had been cut off by the Germans, which became one of the most popular narratives. Unsurprisingly, the levels of psychological pressure, excess, and overuse reached by atrocity stories led to the post-war Anglo-American questioning of propaganda.

Analysis of *The Sinking of the 'Lusitania'*

To begin with, McCay's film represents the first Ponsonby principle (We do not want war) through the depiction of war as retaliation, not as an

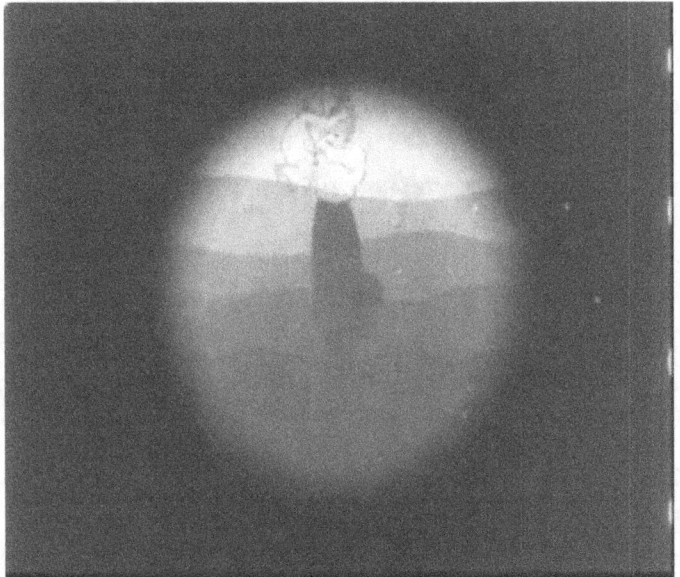

Figure 9.2 Women and children as victims of atrocities

aim of the American government. The first principle is logically followed by the second, which states that the enemy is responsible for war; in *The Sinking of the 'Lusitania'*, the need for retaliation is a result of Germany's blood-thirsty actions, thus representing Germany as responsible for war. Blaming the menacing aggressor in a one-dimensional way is essential to war propaganda; "Having declared the enemy the sole culprit and originator of the war," Ponsonby writes (1936), "the next step is to personify the enemy."[75] As Lasswell (1971) points out:

---

[75] *Op. cit.* Ponsonby (1936), page 71.

It is always difficult for many simple minds inside a nation to attach personal traits to so dispersed an entity as a whole nation. They need to have some individual on whom to pin their hate. It is, therefore, important to single out a handful of enemy leaders and load them down with the whole catalogue of sins.[76]

No personality drew more abuse of this sort in the last war than the Kaiser.

This personalisation of evil is a characteristic of McCay's film as well, with the Kaiser - who was christened by the London *Evening News* as the 'Mad Dog of Europe' and the 'War Lord', and was identified with the Beast of the Apocalypse by the *Libertè* of Paris - represented as a mass-murderer in the motion picture, which outrageously exclaims: "The man who fired the shot was decorated for it by the Kaiser! - AND YET

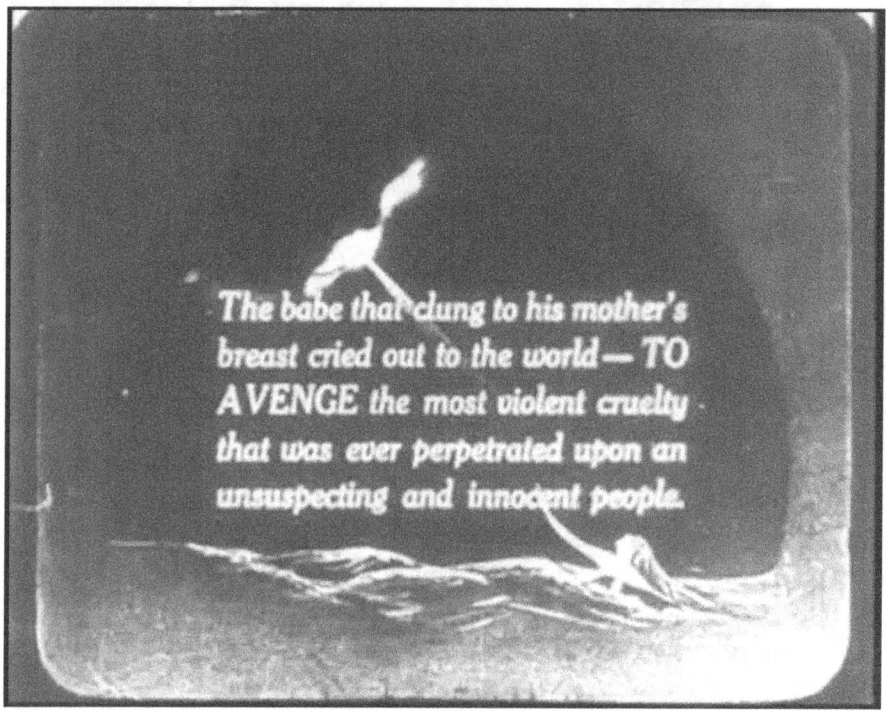

Figure 9.3 Divine vengeance against the forces of evil?

---

[76] *Op. cit.* Lasswell, (1971), page 89.

THEY TELL US NOT TO HATE THE HUN."[77] Aside from the fact that, in reality, the crew of the German submarine was not decorated it can be pointed out that the use of the term *Hun* in the quotation is an example of *lexicalisation*. As Van Dijk (1995) indicates, "probably the major dimensions of discourse meaning controlled by ideologies is the selection of word meaning through *lexicalisation.*"[78] This implies that the ideological meaning of nouns, clauses, adjectives, etc. usually takes the form of evaluative concepts, and it needs to be analysed in context. In the case of McCay's film, the use of the word *Hun* - a derogatory nickname used by Britons and Americans to refer to the German Army - must be understood in the context of the British stereotype of the 'spike-helmeted German Hun'.[79] Thus, WWI propaganda lexis is reflected in the film. Germany's blood thirst links the representation of the second and third principles. As the film states, "Germany, which had already benumbed the world with its wholesale killing, then sent its instrument of crime to perform a more treacherous and cowardly offense." Consequently, the depiction of Germany as evil itself matches the third principle, 'The enemy has the face of the devil'. The film also materialises the principle about presenting the real aims of war as noble causes. In this case, such concealment is performed through the need for avenging the mass-murder of the innocents, including babies. Entering the war, then, relies on moral, disinterested grounds in McCay's propagandistic reading.

The heinous actions that cause such a moral outrage lead us to the fifth principle: 'The enemy's atrocities are intentional; if we make mistakes, it is unintended'. So, the film focuses less on the Allies' mistakes than on the enemy's atrocities, which are central to the movie. In fact, atrocity propaganda takes place right from the beginning of the film, when it refers to "the crime that shocked humanity." The emotional side of the German attack is addressed by the words, "After the first torpedo struck there were scenes of pitiful partings", and feelings of horridness are pumped up by images of people falling to water, bodies floating, or the ship disappearing beneath the waves. Particularly, this atrocity propaganda is in line with the image of the 'gallant little Belgium': as the film states, "The babe that clung to his mother's breast cried out to the world - TO AVENGE the most violent

---

[77] *Op. cit.* Lasswell, (1971), page 90.
[78] Van Dijk, T. A. (1995). 'Discourse semantics and ideology'. *Discourse & Society*, 6(2), pages 243-289, page 259.
[79] *Op. cit.* Welch, (2003), page 25.

cruelty that was ever perpetrated upon an unsuspecting and innocent people." Pertaining to atrocity stories, Lasswell (1971) points out that stress "can always be laid upon the wounding of women, children, old people, priests and nuns, and upon sexual enormities, mutilated prisoners and mutilated non-combatants."[80] McCay's motion picture highlights horror by depicting a woman and a baby drowning and disappearing towards the end, surrounded by darkness (Figure 9.3). In doing so, the film somehow echoes "news reports about the German invasion of Belgium, which all too often used tales of violence against women and children to create a set of seemingly incontrovertible morals with which to silence opposition to the war and cajole recruits."[81]

The positioning of the film in the 'little Belgium' tradition is relevant since the concept of 'cruelty' can be understood as the semantic core of the film. Semiotically, *The Sinking of the 'Lusitania'* adopts an isotopic disposition, that is, a conceptual structure consisting in the repetition of the same semantic base throughout discourse. These are used to convey the concept of 'cruelty' in different forms, such as "While the life boats were being lowered a second torpedo crashed into the engine rooms," "No warning was given no mercy was shown," or the hyperbolic "the most violent cruelty that was ever perpetrated upon an unsuspecting and innocent people." By using 'cruelty' as a semantic backbone, McCay's film mirrors the extreme heartlessness of other WWI atrocity stories, like the one about a woman whose breasts were cut off.

Ponsonby's sixth principle focuses on the use of 'dishonest' weapons by the enemy. Interestingly, Morelli (2001) writes about the sinking of the Lusitania about this sixth principle, and Ponsonby's (1936) own interpretation of the sinking may be related to the depiction of Germans as rogue buccaneers:

> From the point of view of propaganda, it was necessary to show that the Germans had blown up a defenceless passenger ship flying the American flag and bearing only civilian passengers and an ordinary cargo. This was represented as a breach of international law and an act of piracy.[82]

---

[80] *Op. cit.* Lasswell (1971), page 82.
[81] Green, L. (2014). 'Advertising war: Picturing Belgium in First World War publicity'. *Media, War & Conflict*, 7(3), pages 309-325, page 316.

[82] *Op. cit.* Ponsonby (1936), page 121.

McCay's motion picture links the sinking and the principle through sentences like "Germany, once a great and powerful nation, had done a dastardly deed in a dastardly way." In this context, Germany's submarine warfare can be understood as an example of 'dishonest' weapons.

Figure 9.4 The Lusitania and the Statue of Liberty

There is no evidence of the seventh principle, but it can be concluded that the eighth ('Artists and intellectuals support our cause') is somehow contained in the very premise of the film, given Winsor McCay's job - that is, a graphic artist that privately supported the cause of war. The ninth principle, refers to the sacredness of the cause, is not conveyed by the film. However, we could cite an image (see Figure 2) which depicts what seems to be light from Heaven; since the light is juxtaposed with a copy stating the need for retaliation, the image may be interpreted as a call for divine intervention against satanic evil.

Regarding the tenth principle, "Those who question war propaganda are traitors," McCay's film indirectly calls not to believe anti-hate messages through the abovementioned sentence "AND YET THEY TELL US NOT TO HATE THE HUN." Ponsonby (1936) writes that, during war, "criticism of the country to which you belong cannot be publicly expressed"[83]; messages like the one conveyed by *The Sinking of the 'Lusitania'* may be understood as a way of deactivating potential anti-war criticism at home.

Our analysis exemplifies how individual principles are put into practice by the film. Additionally, McCay's work presents the co-existence of different principles in one textual fragment as well, as the following words illustrate: "Germany, which had already benumbed the world with its wholesale killing [Principle 3: devilish enemy], then sent its instrument of crime [Principle 5: deliberate atrocity] to perform a more treacherous and cowardly offense [Principle 6: dishonest weapons]."

Besides illustrating different propaganda devices, it can be said that McCay's film is in accordance with WWI propaganda techniques in general, and with Anglo-American atrocity propaganda in particular. However, and while the Bryce report conveyed unsubstantiated stories with no consideration of accuracy (Green, 2014)[84], *The Sinking of the 'Lusitania'* tries to be accurate. Through phrases like "the first record of the sinking of the Lusitania" or "a historical record of the crime that shocked Humanity," McCay tries to convey the idea that the film is based on fact. And, in reality, there is factual information, such as dates, names, and the sinking's time lapse, as well as details about Americans that were killed. In any case, it must be pointed out that the detailed account of the sinking and the massacre lacks context: while the horrible deed is foregrounded in detail, there is no information about the Germans, the Lusitania, or the role of the U.S. government. At the same time, the factual elements of the movie co-exist with a less rational component: American patriotism and nationalism, which also play a role in the film. Thus, the Statue of Liberty is shown (Figure 9.4), and the copy makes clear that the ship carried "more than 2000 passengers of whom 200 were Americans" - it even specifies that 114 victims were Americans. "Among these were men of world wide prominence," including philosopher Elbert Hubbard, playwright Charles Klein, multi-millionaire and sportsman Alfred G. Vanderbilt, and theatrical manager Charles Frohman. Consequently, it could be inferred that the atrocious act against the ship is even worse because it has killed distinguished Americans. Propaganda scholar David Welch (2003) points out that atrocity propaganda "played a major role in the wave of patriotism that

---

[83] *Ibid.* Page 114.
[84] *Op. cit.* Green, (2014).

enveloped Europe in the early stages of World War I."[85] *The Sinking of the 'Lusitania'* channels American patriotic fervour by representing horrendous actions, and depicts atrocities in a way that may lead to the boosting of nationalistic passion.

Conclusions

From mid-1915 to mid-1917, WWI information and propaganda were characterised, amongst other features, by a British campaign aimed to break American neutrality. This campaign was later strengthened by an American governmental campaign that became a milestone in the history of propaganda. Such an importance relied on the intense, all-encompassing communication effort of George Creel's Committee on Public Information, which channeled and directed American patriotic fervour during the war. The CPI's official propaganda was accompanied by an array of independent, unofficial contributions to the war of ideas; Winsor McCay's film *The Sinking of the 'Lusitania'* belongs to the latter category. The film's propagandistic content must be understood in the context of the Creel Committee's effort to advertise the war in a massive fashion; in this regard, it is interesting that McCay's mirroring of official propaganda themes is in accordance with what Leanne Green (2014), studying British WWI publicity, calls the "synergy between the rhetorical frameworks employed in the war publicity of government departments and independent charities."[86]

Aside from the institutional context, it must be taken into account that German submarine warfare was one of the factors that led the United States to abandon its position of neutralism. Since *The Sinking of the 'Lusitania'* focuses precisely on such warfare, it can be concluded that McCay's film utilises a relevant historical factor to convey an anti-German message. In this regard, the motion picture can be understood as a remarkable example of propaganda film - and, more specifically, as an outstanding example of atrocity propaganda, which is conveyed through words and images. On the other hand, the American patriotism that is displayed in the film must be understood in the context of First World War communication, where national sentiment was stimulated

---

[85] Welch, D. (2003). 'Atrocity Propaganda', in Cull, N., Culbert, J. D. and Welch, D. *Propaganda and Mass Persuasion. A historical Encyclopedia, 1500 to the present.* Santa Barbara, CA: ABC-CLIO, pages 23-26, page 25.
[86] *Op. cit.* Green (2014), page 322.

by propaganda.[87] In this respect, McCay's film illustrates the way independent, non-official propaganda may be perfectly in line with official psychological warfare. Wilsonian propaganda stated that American intervention was necessary in order to defend the right of neutral countries, against war methods that challenge their freedom, and, therefore, Germany's disregard for nation and individual rights is just cause for joining the Allies against Germany.[88] German methods, and their essential inhumanity, are dramatically highlighted by *The Sinking of the 'Lusitania'* and its portrayal of the slaughtering of the innocents. By conveying a discourse that is consistent with both atrocity propaganda and the idea of dirty war, it could be said that the film fits into one of the major propaganda objectives: in Lasswell's words (1971) to "mobilise hatred against the enemy."[89] In this regard, McCay's motion picture is also in line with the anti-German rhetoric that was used in media like pictorial publicity (by both public and private concerns) (Green, 2014).

Regarding the use of propaganda techniques, McCay's film evidences a remarkable propagandistic density, since 9 out of 10 of the Ponsonby (1936) principles, systematised by Morelli (2001), appear on the film. As far as propaganda theory is concerned, such a density indicates that a single propaganda message can employ different techniques simultaneously. In the context of this cornucopia of propaganda devices, the film can be particularly understood as a contribution to WWI propaganda's discursive core - atrocity stories about German deeds - in entertainment form. In so doing, *The Sinking of the 'Lusitania'* also exemplifies, through moving images, the central propaganda device of World War I.

---

[87] *Op. cit.* Welch, (2013).
[88] *Op. cit.* Renouvin, (1994).
[89] *Op. cit.* Lasswell (1971), page 195.

Chapter 10

The Murdochs and Gallipoli: Entertainments in Service of Myth

Chapter 10

The Murdochs and Gallipoli: Entertainments in Service of Myth

Tom D. C. Roberts
Macquarie University, Sydney

'Gallipoli is a defining event in the national character; in the Murdoch saga, it is *the* defining event.' Les Carlyon[1]
'It's going to be great. It's murder, history, war ... We can't lose.' Rupert Murdoch is describing the film *Gallipoli* [2]

Introduction

Sydney, August 1981. Flashguns strobed as Rupert Murdoch led his mother up the red and purple carpet for the black-tie premiere of his first feature film as producer: *Gallipoli*. The date had been timed for the sharpest possible significance: Rupert's *Weekend Australian* stressed in its front page coverage that it was "exactly 66 years after the bloody struggle", the 'Battle of the Nek', recreated as the final scene.[3] Although Rupert's father did not feature in the film, the newspaper photograph showed Keith Murdoch staring out, serious but dashing in officer's uniform as a war correspondent, above the beaming smiles of a young Mel Gibson and his co-star. The legend next to the photograph pointed to the 'Gallipoli letter that stunned Australia', reprinted in its entirety in the magazine section.[4] Following this, lavishly illustrated spread came two glowing film reviews.[5] This was the first, and - as it transpired - the only production from Associated R & R Films (see Figure 10.1).

---

[1] Carlyon, L. (1995). 'The Great Seducer', *The Sunday Age*, May 21 (emphasis added).
[2] 'Go go Gallipoli', *The Sydney Morning Herald*, July 11, 1981.
[3] 'Cheering crowd shares glitter of Gallipoli's world premiere', *The Weekend Australian*, August 8-9, 1981.
[4] 'War message that stunned a nation', *The Weekend Australian*, April 8-9, 1981.
[5] Williams, E. (1981). 'Gallipoli's grandeur'; Max Harris, 'Our sacred mystery', *The Weekend Australian*, 8-9 April.

R & R Films 'Gallipoli'

The film's plot delivered a three-act tragedy. In outback Australia, two young athletes answer the recruitment call drilled into them by the press and Kipling's tales. Training in Egypt, they bond over larrikin anti-

Figure 10.1 Poster for 'Gallipoli' (DVD)

English japes and the sowing of their wild oats. Finally, at the hellish war zone, they are sacrificed by incompetent colonial commanders in a diversionary action while the British are 'just sitting on the beach drinking cups of tea'.[6]

One otherwise glowing review, from outside the Murdoch stable, conceded that those "who resent emotional manipulation would be affronted by this film."[7] The charge of propaganda[8] was not only

---

[6] Radio Operator to General Gardner during the final scene of *Gallipoli*. See David Williamson's screenplay in *The Story of Gallipoli: the film about the men who made a legend*, Penguin: Ringwood, Vic, 1981, page 144.

[7] 'Gallipoli keeps all its promises', *Sydney Morning Herald*, 8 August 1981. "[T]he simplest possible narrative line' from within the Gallipoli history, indeed 'every aspect' of the film was brilliantly 'contrived to produce an emotional effect."

[8] One film historian has suggested *Gallipoli* "has the rhetorical tone and lack of moral ambiguity of a propaganda film"; see Freebury, J. (1987). 'Screening Australia: Gallipoli - a study of nationalism on film', *Media Information Australia*, Number 43, February, page 8.

levelled at the film; it has been levelled against Keith's famous 'Gallipoli letter' of a generation before. It is the letter that made his career and has been woven into an untouchable myth. It's a myth that Rupert has deployed to deflect criticism of the sharper edges of his career[9] - a myth that overshadows Keith's darker legacy: his actions beyond that 'sacred shore' in pursuit of an empowering Australianism through the elevation of an idealised race of men to feed the war machine of the Western Front. Keith's letter was an act of covert power and control. Properly understood, it undermines his reputation as fearless purveyor of truth to the masses and protector of lives. Far from remaining a thorn in the side of the existing order, the 'Gallipoli letter' would mark Keith's triumphant entry into the very heart of the new Establishment, where press and politics met.

> They were the angels that made that movie and then off they went.
> *Gallipoli's* director describing his backer's[10]

In commentary, both at the time and since, Rupert's decision to bankroll the film seemed to have been a typically opportune, largely financial consideration, with the sentimentality of the link to his father a happy coincidence. In the late 1970s and early 1980s, Australia was in the grip of a film-making fever, stoked by a government tax incentive for investors were so attractive that screens could not keep up with the output.[11] Despite this, the already successful young Australian director Peter Weir and playwright David Williamson had been turned down by all the big Hollywood studios; the project was deemed commercially unviable. What the Americans perhaps did not realise was that Australia was also under the grip of another building fever: the rise in First World War memory recovery and nationalistic commemoration centred on the

---

[9] For instance, facing a critical backlash on journalistic standards when mounting his takeover for *The Wall Street Journal* in 2007, Rupert wrote a personal letter in an attempt to persuade the Bancroft family to acceptance of the deal. He emphasised that 'the credit for building' their respective media giants 'goes to the members of the family', invoking one particular figure and episode: 'My father, Sir Keith Murdoch, was himself a celebrated journalist, best known for uncovering the British debacle at Gallipoli in 1915.' 'Rupert Murdoch's letter to the Bancroft family - May 11, 2007', *The Financial Times*, May 14, 2007.
[10] Interview with Peter Weir, *Gallipoli: 2-Disc Anniversary Edition*, 20th Century Fox Home Entertainment, 2005.
[11] See for example 'Cinema', *The Times*, July 16, 1981.

Anzac forces at Gallipoli. The Anzac 'tradition' was well on the way to becoming a 'civil religion'.[12]

Weir had been inspired by Bill Gammage's *The Broken Years* (1974), an 'emotional history of the AIF',[13] which focussed on the soldiers' stories and experiences and had kick-started a reappraisal of the war, and older Australians might recall the foundational myth - 'the Gallipoli legend' - of a doomed but heroic struggle against the odds. But Weir believed it had 'faded' so much that it meant 'little or nothing' for the young. His intention was clear: 'I hope the movie will reactivate it, and reinterpret it.'[14] In Rupert, Weir found a keen backer for a film that reimagined Gallipoli as an anti-Establishment - specifically, anti-English - romance.

On hearing the news that Robert Stigwood and Rupert Murdoch had come together to form R & R Films, Weir delivered the script by hand to the unlikely pair's hotel. Next morning Stigwood told Weir: 'Rupert, and I feel this should be our first picture. How quickly can you start?'[15] It would be the most expensive Australian production yet; after the 'epic battle for funding', Williamson was worried the film would now be labelled 'Murdoch's baby'. At the beginning of a preview screening at the Australian Film Institute, his fears seemed well founded: 'everyone hissed when the Murdoch credit came on the screen' - but the patriotic tale, skillfully crafted, worked its magic. 'By the end, of course, they were all cheering.'[16]

Rupert had not only tapped into a wave of national memorialising: through his newspapers, he would now help reframe it. In 1981, the year of the film's release, *The Australian* advocated that Anzac Day is made 'our true national day'.[17] For many, Australia Day was bound up with the baggage of White Australia. However, aided by the media, a new patriotic discourse was taking its place: about mateship and an

---

[12] Inglis, K. (2008). *Sacred Places: War memorials in the Australian landscape* (3rd edition), Melbourne University Press: Carlton, Vic. page 573; see also Amanda Lohrey, 'Voting for Jesus: Christianity and Politics in Australia', *Quarterly Essay*, June 22, 2006.

[13] Gammage. B. (1974). *The Broken Years: Australian soldiers in the Great War.* Canberra: Australian National University Press, page 34.

[14] 'Small bottle as big film charm', *Sydney Morning Herald*, January 25, 1981.

[15] 'Cinema', *The Times*, 15 September 1981. Rupert's co-producer, providing the other 'R', was the Australian Showbiz impresario and promoter who had proved his mettle with *Saturday Night Fever* and the Bee Gees

[16] Interview feature: 'Williamson: "I don't want to end in Barry Humphries land"', *Sydney Morning Herald*, August 1, 1981.

[17] 'One day for us all', [Vernon Wilcox], *The Weekend Australian*, April 25-26 ,1981; and 'Anzac Day - our true national day', *The Australian*, April 27, 1981.

idealised conception of the Anzac soldier fused with victimhood.[18] Gallipoli was still the blood sacrifice for the nation's creation. As '[w]riters, filmmakers and journalists performed narrative surgery on the Imperial history' it became a tale of Australian innocence exploited by the incompetency of colonial masters.[19] Keith's part, apparently at the heart of this, would be rediscovered and promoted.

The film, designed to reframe this legend for a new generation, was boosted by a publicity campaign orchestrated by Murdoch's press and TV interests.[20] Education packs drawing on it as a means to teach the history of Australia's involvement in the First World War were circulated to schools[21] and reproduced as lift-outs in *The Australian*.[22] There would even be an attempt at novelising the script[23] before an illustrated tie-in book was produced.[24] Although Keith was absent from the film, a book published during its production and serialised by *The Australian*[25] positioned him as the anchor to the new Gallipoli legend.

A decade earlier, in the year that Patsy Adam-Smith's bestseller, *The Anzacs*,[26] started a publishing phenomenon. Rupert commissioned Desmond Zwar to write a new life of his father.[27] The blurb to Zwar's slim volume declared: 'In September 1915 Keith Murdoch made a decision which was to change the course of war in the Middle East' through the 'Gallipoli letter'; this before any other information regarding his life was given. A quarter of the book was taken up with the Gallipoli letter (wrongly claimed to have been 'published here for the

---

[18] See Mark McKenna's 2012 NSW History Council Lecture, 'Australia: A Foundational Past?' delivered August 8, 2012, for an expansion of this thesis.
[19] McKenna, M. (2010), in Marilyn Lake and Henry Reynolds (with Mark McKenna and Joy Damousi), *What's Wrong with Anzac: The Militarisation of Australian History*. Sydney: University of New South Wales Press, page 116.
[20] During the week of its release, the Murdoch owned Channel 10 featured Michael Parkinson interviewing David Williamson and devoted a special edition of *Movie Scene* to the film.
[21] 'Peter Weir's Film of Gallipoli: Film Study Guide', Applied Media Resources, Special Services Division, Education Department of Victoria, 1981. See also Jenny Macleod. (2002). 'The Fall and Rise of Anzac Day: 1965 and 1990 Compared', *War & Society*, 20:1, page 165.
[22] 'The Australian presents a study guide: Gallipoli', 20 September 1981.
[23] 'Book Cases', *Sydney Morning Herald*, 28 February 1981.
[24] *The Story of Gallipoli: the film about the men who made a legend*, Penguin: Ringwood, Vic, 1981, included a preface by Weir, two chapters reproduced from *The Broken Years* (1974) by the film's historical consultant Bill Gammage and the entire screenplay by David Williamson.
[25] 'In Search of Keith Murdoch', *Weekend Australian*, November 15-16, 1980; *Australian*, November 17; and *Australian*, November 18.
[26] Adam-Smith, P. (1978). *The Anzacs*, Thomas Nelson: Melbourne.
[27] Rupert had personally vetted Zwar, taking the trouble to fly to the journalist's remote home. 'The day Rupert rode my Moke', Desmond Zwar, *Sydney Morning Herald*, 26 April 2012.

first time'), and Keith's brief visit to the Dardanelles.[28] Even so, the letter had been 'edited so heavily as to be misleading' - with facts 'easily falsified by reference to public records' and 'fallacious descriptive material' missing.[29] Its rear cover reproduced a photograph of Keith on the peninsula, eyes cloaked by the glare of the Mediterranean sun, a pith helmet clasped to his chest (See Figure 10.2). The legend printed with it was unequivocal: 'I have a clear conscience as to what I did...'.[30]

Letters of influence

Sydney, 1915. The war may have been raging in Europe, but Keith Murdoch was stuck in Australia. He had stood for election among his fellow journalists as the official war correspondent to be sent with the Australian forces, but had lost to C.E.W. Bean.[31] However, he was already putting his particular brand of war service into action. The blurring between reporter and government operative that was to become entrenched over the length of the war, and flourish in Murdoch's role as a propagandist, had begun.

Although disappointed at not being appointed to the official task, Keith was soon offered the plum position of managing editor of the United Cable Service in London, the news feed run by the Sydney *Sun* and Melbourne *Herald* for much of Australia's press. He moved to Sydney to learn the ropes before his departure while continuing as a parliamentary reporter. Sayers concedes that Keith was already in the habit of carrying out a little 'gentle espionage' for the Labour Prime

---

[28] The full text was first published by the *Sydney Morning Herald* under the headline 'The Murdoch Letter' following its release by the British Records Office over three daily instalments from 18 November 1968. Reviewers of Zwar's book pointed both to his mistaken claim of an exclusive on this point, and the unbalanced account of Murdoch's activities during the First World War that a focus on Gallipoli had produced. See Geoffrey Serle, 'A Patriot and a Blunderer', *Australian Book Review*, April 1981 and Angus McLachlan, 'The Search for Keith Murdoch Continues', *Sydney Morning Herald*, November 21,1980.

[29] Avieson, J. *The Reporter Who Stopped a War*, unpublished manuscript, copy held by Bunty Avieson. page 27. Avieson records Zwar explained "the editing was carried out to achieve editorial balance for his book, and there is no reason to reject that explanation" but stresses "the unfortunate results of that editing are another matter."

[30] "...It compelled the wavering and hesitant Coalition Cabinet to make up its mind...." The image and text were a direct lift from the 1952 HWT publication *Keith Murdoch, Journalist*, page16.

[31] Though only one vote behind Bean in the first round of the AJA's vote, the second preferential ballot saw Keith lose seven to three, though he was nominated as substitute should anything happen to Bean. See Clem Lloyd. (1985). *Profession - Journalist: A history of the Australian Journalists' Association*, Sydney: Hale & Iremonger, page 114.

Minister Andrew Fisher.[32] It is in this light perhaps that Keith's letter seeking Fisher's blessing for his new job, written toward the end of June 1915, is best viewed. Keith recognised the power that went with having "sole control and responsibility for the cable service... the mainstay of hundreds of thousands of Australian readers" but he wanted reassurance that he was making the right decision. Conceding that "all the cabling and writing in the world is not going to win this war." Keith reassured his 'friend' that he was open to the idea of serving in the military: "I could joyfully perform any task you set me in the service of my country."[33] Fisher's pithy reply on where Keith's skills would be most useful was clear: 'Advise London'.[34]

Keith's service to the government, and to his prospects, had started soon after his return to Australia in 1909. His family's Scots heritage had given him an instant link and tribal affinity with many of the movers and shakers of the increasingly powerful Scottish Diaspora in Australia.[35] The connection not only opened doors but also emboldened Keith to barge through them.[36] His prowess on the golf course proved handy in cultivating relationships, too, most particularly with the Scots Prime Minister.[37]

From 1910 Keith had 'boosted George Pearce', the increasing militarist Minister for Defence. In the corridors of power Keith became

---

[32] Fisher had in 1910 become the first Prime Minister to wield a majority in both Houses of the fledging Commonwealth Parliament.
[33] Murdoch to Fisher, 2 June 1915 From Sydney, Fisher Papers, MS 2919 /1/109-10, NLA.
[34] Pencilled instruction from Fisher to his secretary written on KM's letter of June 2, 1915, Fisher Papers, MS 2919 /1/109-10, NLA.
[35] Tracking the fortunes and membership of the Royal Caledonian Society of Melbourne serves to reveal this increasing influence. In its official history, alongside the Rev. P. J. Murdoch, Andrew Fisher, a Presbyterian Scots emigrant, receives multiple mentions for his support and involvement during the society's growth. In the period immediately following Federation, it is claimed that 'Scotticism' was so 'in the air ... that many other nationals began to subject themselves to mental blood-tests in the hope of discovering traces of Scottish ancestry!' Alec Chisholm. (1950). *Scots Wha Hae: History of the Royal Caledonian Society of Melbourne*, Angus and Robertson: Sydney, page 53.
[36] Esther Paterson, from a family of artists, recalled how Keith had once come to their studio home. Where Fisher used to drop in for a rest away from his busy household: 'he was waiting outside the place' before 'he pushed his way into the hall and ...said "I want to see Mr Fisher." Esther told him Fisher wasn't there and so Keith left to sit on the wall outside and wait. "He wanted some information for the press, so father came in and woke Andrew, and he said: "Keith Murdoch's out there." "I don't want to see him" came Fisher's reply. But Paterson said "Oh come on, Keith's a Scot like ourselves," and Andrew said "Oh, all right."' Esther Paterson interviewed 26 June 1971, transcript, nla.oh-vn265402, NLA.
[37] Retained alongside coronation invitations and official certificates in the Labour Prime Minister's papers is a 'Riversdale Golf Club, Scoring Card', dated 16 March 1912 and signed by the two players - 'A Fisher' and 'K. A. Murdoch.' Fisher Papers, MS 2919/11/168a, NLA.

known as 'Pearce's publicity agent', it was claimed, 'no doubt getting much in return'.[38] Since the outbreak of war he had cranked up the production line of puff pieces, and glowing profiles[39] while contributing publicity strategies for the Department of Defence, in the drive to secure the recruits, Australia had promised to contribute to the Imperial Forces.[40] In an 'unofficial' letter, Pearce thanked Keith for rallying the public to the cause and cited one particular scheme the reporter had 'initiated' to support soldiers.[41] As Pearce stressed, writing in the aftermath of the 'Recruitment Week' push, not all of the press had been so helpful in helping stir enlistment.[42] The editorials in *The Sun*, to which it is likely that Keith contributed, were unequivocal in their support for conscription both back in the mother country and in Australia if the call came.[43]

Despite his best efforts to stir Sydneysiders to enlist, Keith complained to Fisher that they were simply 'pluming themselves in the newest military fashions' while crowding the cinemas and theatres.[44] Nevertheless, it was in the new cinemas that the *Sun* worked with the Department of Defence to promote a new type of Australian film. In April, an article detailed how 'a stimulus should be given to recruiting' by the new 'patriotic drama *Will They Never Come?*. The *Sun's* readers were informed of the film's upcoming premiere and presented with a stirring advertisement for it. Pearce had 'officially sanctioned' the production. He "readily perceived that the appeal for men could be put

---

[38] Frederick Eggleston, 'Confidential Notes', ANUA 107/3/16 page 16.
[39] See for example Murdoch's article titled 'Federal Headquarters – War Machine At Work – The Men Who Command', which was widely syndicated in regional newspapers such as the *Gippsland Gazette*, April 27, 1915.
[40] Keith was disappointed, though understanding, when credit for the *Sun's* 'Australia Day' scheme for fundraising for the wounded was taken by NSW politicians, KM to Fisher June 2, 1915 From Sydney, Fisher Papers, MS 2919 /1/109-10, NLA.
[41] Pearce was likely referring to the 'The Sun (Sydney) Gift Scheme' to send parcels to soldiers in the Dardanelles. See the June 1, 1915 edition. A century later, Rebekah Brooks would tell the Commons CMS Committee Hearing how 'throughout my editorship of *The Sun* [UK] ... one of the main campaigns that we have had is for 'Help for Heroes'. I think *The Sun* is the paper for the military ....' Q563, July 19, 2011.
[42] Pearce to KM, June 23, 1915, Murdoch Papers, NLA MS 2823/2/12. The newspaper was most likely the Melbourne *Argus*; 'Defence Administration: Senator Pearce Resents Comments – "The Argus" Campaign', *The Argus*, June 18, 1915; and '100,00 Men: Enlistment Declines – "Scare" Stories Blamed – Senator Pearce's Opinion', *The Argus*, June 2, 1915.
[43] See 'Conscription In England', 1 June, and 'Preparing For More War' July 12, 1915. Signed implorations of service and duty from the Premier were also printed daily during these months, given centre spot on *The Sun's* front page.
[44] KM to Fisher, June 2, 1915 From Sydney, Fisher Papers, MS 2919 /1/109-10, NLA.

no more forcibly, more powerfully, and more entertainingly than in the films."[45]

As Keith prepared to leave, in early July 1915, the finishing edit was being applied to a sequel: *A Hero of the Dardanelles*. Billed as 'The Official Recruiting Film' it told 'The Story of the man that *did* come' and would prove sensationally popular. Again, Pearce had supported it.[46] As with Weir's production,[47] the Department of Defence provided soldiers for the re-enactment of the landing.[48] Gallipoli had come to life on the big screen for the first time. *The Sun's* pre-release tie-in article described how the scenes had been 'recorded by the camera with realism that is stirring and inspiring ... exactly as reported by Ashmead-Bartlett',[49] the British war correspondent who had seeded the Anzac myth[50] with his description of 'this race of athletes'.[51] (His account of the landing was remarkable for its evocative detail - given that he had been over a mile away offshore, in the black of night, when he 'witnessed' the action). The same edition reported 'exclusively' that Pearce was 'exceedingly pleased' with the way recruiting had progressed.[52] A week later, the day after the premiere, *The Sun* would trumpet a 'Great Recruiting Week' – the intake included 'three actors' - with the highest figures since records

---

[45] 'Will They Never Come? An Appeal to Australians', *The Sun*, April 4, 1915. Films indeed were the coming attraction: a couple of months before in America, the scramble to invest had resulted in the birth of a new company. Solomon, A. (2011). *The Fox Film Corporation, 1915-1935: A History and Filmography.* Jefferson, NC: MacFarland & Company, page 19. Seventy years later, and just four years after his first movie venture, Rupert Murdoch would seize ownership of Twentieth Century-Fox, renouncing his Australian citizenship to smooth the deal.

[46] Curator's notes, Australian Screen, see, aso.gov.au/titles/features/hero-of-the-dardanelles/notes/.

[47] Weir employed a beach near Port Lincoln in South Australia as his stand-in for filming, while also receiving support and extras from the Australian Department of Defence, credits to *Gallipoli*, 1981.

[48] The film was subsequently advertised as 'the one in the production of which the Minister for Defence sanctioned the co-operation of the military forces of N.S. Wales, and in which more than a thousand participated.' 'A Hero of the Dardanelles' (advertisement), *The Sun*, July 18, 1915.

[49] 'A Hero of the Dardanelles: Recruiting Film', *The Sun*, July 11, 1915. (In fact, the shooting script even went as far as instructing "All scenes at Dardanelles to be produced according to Ashmead-Bartlett's report." Australian Archives Victoria, Accession No. B539, Dept. of Defence, Correspondence Files 1914-1917 File No. 144-1-274A, page 2.)

[50] Eric Andrews concludes his assessment with a call to look 'with clear eyes, at the myths surrounding the Anzac legend. For in fact, 'Anzac' was a myth in every sense of the word.' Eric Andrews. (1993). *The Anzac Illusion: Anglo-Australian relations during World War I*. New York: Cambridge University Press. Page 215.

[51] Ellis Ashmead-Bartlett's vivid report was the first to be published in Australian newspapers, 8 May 1915.

[52] 'Brisk Recruiting', *The Sun*, July 11, 1915.

began the previous September.[53] *The Sun's* extended, laudatory review gave a behind-the-scenes insight into the production.[54] The even more lavish and text-heavy advertisement for the film revealed the extent of the cooperation between the parties and emphasised Pearce's loaded line: "I'll give you all the soldiers you want."

Due to the colonial lines of communication and control, centred in London, Fisher and Pearce had been kept in the dark on many aspects of the campaign; they had not even been informed of the plan to land at Gallipoli until after the event. However, they feared the worst, given the blunt facts of the casualty tolls for no gains. Fisher and Pearce wanted an inside account of the campaign's management and a realistic assessment of its prospects. Keith saw his chance to oblige but under the cloak of investigating mail arrangements and provisions for the wounded in Egypt.[55]

Keith's *official* letter to the Minister for Defence, supposedly proposing the idea to Pearce for the first time, addressed the friend whom he usually greeted with the salutation. 'My dear George'[56] as 'Dear Sir'.[57] Appearances were being maintained.[58] Following the announcement of the unusual commission Pearce told questioning Senators that, despite the rumours, Murdoch had not accepted a role in London 'with the Defence Department'. He was undertaking his inquiries in Egypt while remaining a civilian. After all, a reporter was 'just about the best man' that could be assigned such a task. Senators joshed in response: "Sometimes they ferret out things you do not want them to know" and "frequently they ferret out things which never happened at all!" Pearce good-humouredly agreed before making a

---

[53] The perhaps rather helpfully woolly principal officer was however only 'speaking from memory' on the figures. 'Great Recruiting Week - 2240 Volunteers - Actors and Policemen', *The Sun*, July 18, 1915.

[54] 'Hero of Dardanelles – Gallipoli Landing – Reproduced in Films', *The Sun*, July 18, 1915.

[55] Keith's letter to Fisher would state 'Your fears have been justified.' His cover note to the copy sent to Asquith explained the letter had been written 'in conformance with' Fisher's 'request that I should write him fully on the subject.' Copy of letter from Murdoch to Asquith, September 25, 1915, Northcliffe Papers, M1641, ACJP. See also Robert Donald to Winston Churchill: '[Murdoch]' promised to send Mr Fisher a report for his private information.' 1 October 1915, Churchill Archives, CHAR 21/43.

[56] See, for example, KM to Pearce, September 13, 1915, Murdoch Papers, MS 2823/2/1, NLA, and April 6,1916, Pearce Papers AWM 3DRL/2222/ 5/3.

[57] KM to 'The Minister for Defence', July 1, 1915, Defence AIF Papers, 279/1/262, NAA.

[58] The layout of one particular page of *The Sun* a week before Keith's departure is itself illuminating. An account of the 'Return of the Wounded' from the Dardanelles is followed by a piece headlined 'Australia's Losses - Gallipoli Campaign.' The article 'Soldiers' Letters - Complaints of Non-Delivery' is relegated to the bottom. *The Sun*, July 4, 1915.

further, prescient observation: reporters also 'sometimes exercise a very lively imagination'.⁵⁹

The letters of introduction Keith took with him were acknowledgements of his position and indicators of the possibilities their authors saw for his ability to act for them. Most crucially, Pearce gave Keith a letter, which introduced him to the British Commander of the Dardanelles campaign, Sir Ian Hamilton. Hamilton was informed how 'It might just happen that circumstances will favour' Keith 'to the extent

Figure 10.2 Photograph of Keith on the peninsula

of meeting yourself'.⁶⁰ Fisher wrote to the Liberal Minister for Munitions, David Lloyd George, stressing how Keith was now the representative of "a very influential cable service for several important

---

⁵⁹ *Commonwealth Parliamentary Debates*, Senate, Wednesday, July 7, 1915.
⁶⁰ Pearce to Hamilton, July 13, 1915, Murdoch Papers, MS 2823/2/1, NLA.

newspapers in Australia."[61] The ambitious Lloyd George was vocal in his support for a greater push to war organisation in Britain. Although he had originally supported the Dardanelles second front strategy, he was now one of the coteries already plotting its abandonment. Keith's eventual report, the 'Gallipoli letter', ostensibly directed back to Fisher but circulated in London, would prove expedient grease to cogs already in motion.

Arriving in Cairo in mid-August, Keith investigated the mail arrangements, and hospital conditions for the Australian wounded recuperating there. A copy of the *Sunday Sun*, which contained the launch publicity for *A Hero of the Dardanelles*, was put to good use as the centerpiece of an inspiring photograph sent back to Sydney on the next ship south.[62] However, Keith soon wrote to Hamilton, enclosing Pearce's letter and requesting permission to visit the Anzac force on the Peninsula. He stressed he would be going across "in only a semi-official capacity so that [he] may record censored impressions in the London and Australian newspapers" he represented. To allay concerns, Keith emphasised (in a line that would become infamous given his subsequent actions) that "any conditions you impose I should of course, faithfully observe." To this, he added a few more obsequious lines of praise together with the passionate plea: "may I say that my anxiety as an Australian to visit the sacred shores of Gallipoli while our army is there is intense."[63] Hamilton 'hesitated' on receipt of Keith's letter but was persuaded by "the emphasis laid... upon his acceptance of censorship."[64] In his diary a month after their meeting, when the first rumblings of Murdoch's actions reached him, Hamilton wrote: "All I remember of his visit to me here is a sensible, well-spoken man with dark eyes, who said his mind was blank about soldiers and soldiering." He had entered into 'an elaborate explanation of why his duty to Australia could be better done with a pen than a rifle'.[65]

Keith landed at Anzac Cove on 3rd September 1915. He claimed to have spent the next three and a half days walking 'many miles through

---

[61] Andrew Fisher to Lloyd George, July 14, 1915, Lloyd George Papers, M1124 D/20/2/27, ACJP.
[62] 'Wounded Australians at No.2 General Hospital, Ghezireh Palace Hotel, Cairo', *The Sun*, 11, October 1915.
[63] KM to Hamilton, AIF Intermediate Base, Cairo, August 17, 1915, Murdoch Papers, MS 2823/2/1, NLA.
[64] Ian Hamilton. (1920). *Gallipoli Diary*, Vol.II, George H. Doran, New York, page 269.
[65] Ian Hamilton diary entry for 5 October 1915, *Gallipoli Diary*, Vol.II, George H. Doran Company, New York, 1920, page 241.

the trenches', speaking with soldiers and "what senior and junior officers [he] could reach."[66] Hamilton would later snipe "He was one week at the Press Correspondents' camp' on the island of Imbros 'and spent, so they tell me, a few hours only at Anzac and Suvla."[67] Regardless of the actual days or hours spent with the soldiers, it was Keith's meeting with Ashmead-Bartlett at the press camp on Imbros that informed (in Sayers' phrase 'infected')[68] the terms in which he was to write his letter. The British correspondent was a flamboyant and volatile personality, recently 'hauled over the coals' by the War Office[69] for spreading disillusion and boasting of his machinations to remove Hamilton from command. (Ashmead-Bartlett, as a perennial bankrupt always in need of a moneymaking opportunity, had a £5 bet riding on this happening before the end of September.)[70] In the version of events agreed by the pair, Keith encouraged Ashmead-Bartlett to write a letter to the British Prime Minister, Herbert Asquith.[71] Keith would carry this back to London, so evading the censorship restrictions. In Sayers' view, what followed had the whiff of a "serio-comic cloak and dagger happening."[72] Hamilton, having got wind of the plot, managed to cable ahead so that at Marseilles the sealed envelope was seized from Keith by military police.[73] Even if Ashmead-Bartlett's letter did not make it to Downing Street, Keith had absorbed the complaints and criticisms, and as the

---

[66] KM to Fisher, September 23, 1915 - 'The Gallipoli Letter' - Murdoch Papers, MS 2823/2/1, NLA.
[67] Ian Hamilton diary entry for 5 October 1915, *Gallipoli Diary*, Vol.II, George H. Doran Company, New York, 1920, page 241.
[68] Sayers manuscript page 89, NLA, Murdoch Papers, MS 2823/2/1.
[69] Hamilton to Churchill, June 30, 1915, Hamilton Papers, 7/1/1, Liddell Hart Centre for Military Archives (LHCMA).
[70] [Henry] Nevinson to Hamilton, October 12, 1916, Hamilton Papers, 8/1/50. A fellow correspondent at Gallipoli, Sydney Moseley, wrote that Ashmead-Bartlett's "campaign against you was from first to last inspired by personal spite… a wager … that you should be recalled … was a culmination of his vendetta." Moseley to Hamilton, May 4, 1917, Hamilton Papers, 8/1/48, LHCMA
[71] See the emphatic re-detailing of their meeting in Ashmead-Bartlett's letter to KM of May 27, 1920, Ashmead-Bartlett Papers, M 2582, AJCP.
[72] Sayers manuscript page 98, NLA, Murdoch Papers, MS 2823/2/1.
[73] A disgruntled fellow journalist, Henry Nevinson of the *Manchester Guardian*, it is commonly accepted informed Hamilton. However, another, plausible account did the rounds: "One night at dinner in Sheppard's Hotel [sic – the Cairo institution], Murdoch tapped his pocket very confidentially and said to his companion, "I have Ian Hamilton's recall in my pocket." This remark was overheard by an intelligence officer at the next table" (Frederick Eggleston, 'Confidential Notes', ANUA 107/3/16 page17). Keith himself wrote to Ashmead-Bartlett of his 'higher regard for the British Secret Service', following the discovery of the letter's existence. KM to Ashmead-Bartlett, October 1, 1916, Ashmead-Bartlett Papers, M 2582, NLA.

boat continued towards England, he began to compose his letter, to his own Prime Minister.

Having arrived in London from Gallipoli, with information, Keith was in demand. With barely a chance to settle in at the United Cable Service office, housed in *The Times* building, he was whisked off for lunch with the newspaper's powerful editor Geoffrey Dawson. Northcliffe, it was later claimed, declared 'He may prove to be the lever we want', on hearing that an Australian journalist was on the way to London from the Dardanelles.[74] In line with the views of its proprietor, *The Times* had wanted to expose the true course of the campaign.[75] Dawson was "moved by the sincerity and vividness" of the "word pictures"[76] Keith painted of organisational debacles and dire conditions. In a flurry of letters and meetings, the cogs started to bite. Keith retold his story to Sir Edward Carson, Chairman of the British Cabinet's Dardanelles Committee. Recording the details of a secret meeting of the following day, Baron Murray of Elibank tried to disguise the names of those who had been there. The report's recipient 'Mr H', it has been speculated, was the Conservative leader Andrew Bonar Law.[77]

> Today, Lord ---, Mr A, and Mr B lunched with me. Mr B is an Australian of high standing and influence, which has been despatched by the Australian Government to report to them on the condition of affairs in the Dardanelles. ...Mr B who is rather inarticulate owing to a stammer in his speech apparently did not convey to Sir --- the gravity of the situation, and therefore Lord --- was very anxious that Mr A, whom he regards as a man of action, should hear the full story. Mr B is making a confidential report to his government, but we persuaded him to see Lord Kitchener and likewise to give a copy of his report in advance to the Prime Minister and Mr A so that it might be communicated to the Cabinet.[78]

---

[74] Northcliffe, A. (1923). *My Journey Round the World 1921-22*. John Lane: London, page 289.
[75] "I believe the hushing up of the Dardanelles difficulty to be a fatal blunder." Northcliffe to Lloyd George, June 1915. Quoted by John Robertson. (1990). *Anzac and Empire: the tragedy and glory of Gallipoli*. London: Leo Cooper, page 110.
[76] Campbell Jones' recollection of the meeting, *The Sun* (Sydney), May 23, 1920.
[77] John Avieson, *The Reporter Who Stopped a War*, unpublished manuscript, copy held by Bunty Avieson. Page 19.
[78] Report to Mr. H, September 24, 1915, Elibank Papers, National Library of Scotland. An alternative reading has 'Lord ---' as being most likely Viscount Haldane, Lord High Chancellor - see John Avieson 'The correspondent who stopped the war', *Australian Journalism Review*, Vol 8, January-December 1-2, 1986, page 67. However, Haldane had been forced to resign in May, so this appears unlikely.

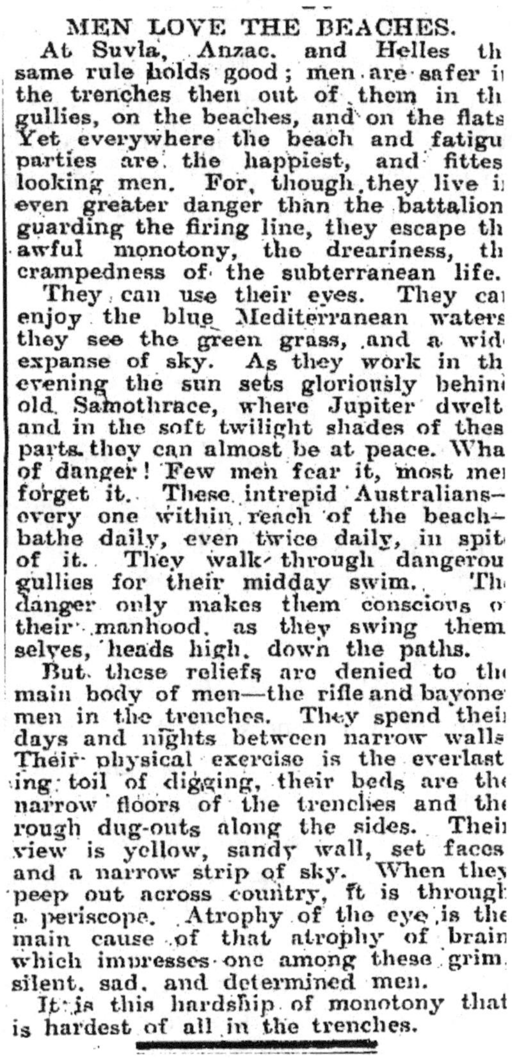

MEN LOVE THE BEACHES.

At Suvla, Anzac, and Helles the same rule holds good; men are safer in the trenches then out of them in the gullies, on the beaches, and on the flats. Yet everywhere the beach and fatigue parties are the happiest, and fittest looking men. For, though they live in even greater danger than the battalion guarding the firing line, they escape the awful monotony, the dreariness, the crampedness of the subterranean life.

They can use their eyes. They can enjoy the blue Mediterranean waters, they see the green grass, and a wide expanse of sky. As they work in the evening the sun sets gloriously behind old Samothrace, where Jupiter dwelt, and in the soft twilight shades of these parts they can almost be at peace. What of danger! Few men fear it, most men forget it. These intrepid Australians—every one within reach of the beach—bathe daily, even twice daily, in spite of it. They walk through dangerous gullies for their midday swim. The danger only makes them conscious of their manhood, as they swing themselves, heads high, down the paths.

But these reliefs are denied to the main body of men—the rifle and bayonet men in the trenches. They spend their days and nights between narrow walls. Their physical exercise is the everlasting toil of digging, their beds are the narrow floors of the trenches and the rough dug-outs along the sides. Their view is yellow, sandy wall, set faces and a narrow strip of sky. When they peep out across country, it is through a periscope. Atrophy of the eye is the main cause of that atrophy of brain which impresses one among these grim, silent, sad, and determined men.

It is this hardship of monotony that is hardest of all in the trenches.

Figure 10.4 'Men love the beaches' article

Substituting Northcliffe for 'Lord ---',[79] Carson for 'Sir' --- and Lloyd George for 'Mr A' offers the most likely reading. Lloyd George was certainly keen to bring Law onboard, writing to him the following day.[80] Keith would describe how the 'most pregnant interviews' he had at this time 'were with Mr Lloyd George and Mr Bonar Law'.[81] So, as he dictated his letter to Fisher, Keith was able to incorporate the reactions and confidential views of ambitious Cabinet Ministers.[82]

The letter

'Oh sure, it may not have been fair ... But it changed history, that letter.'
Rupert Murdoch[83]

Keith began telling Fisher: "I shall talk as if you were by my side" and over the twenty-five typed pages that followed, his language would grow increasingly emotive. Complicated issues were dramatically over-simplified by the "very lively imagination" Pearce had feared. "Australians now loathe and detest any Englishman wearing red" he wrote; the "countless high officers and conceited young cubs" were "plainly only playing at War", and sedition was "talked round every tin of bully beef on the peninsular". Although Keith disclaimed any "military knowledge", General Hamilton was described as having 'failed' as a strategist. The prescription, devised by Ashmead-Bartlett, was straightforward: "Undoubtedly, the essential and first step to restore the morale of the shaken forces is to recall" the General and his Chief of Staff. Keith recommended that Hamilton is replaced with a "young leader... around whom the officers can rally." However, contrary to myth, Keith did not want to abandon the campaign and evacuate the

---

[79] Northcliffe and Murray were certainly corresponding on government and press strategy during this period. See Stephen Koss. (1990). *The Rise and Fall of The Political Press In Britain*. London: Fontana Press, page 724.
[80] Lloyd George to Bonar Law; and to Carson, September 25, 1915, Lloyd George Papers, M 1124, AJCP.
[81] 'Dardanelles Failure ... Mr Keith Murdoch's Reply', *The Press* (New Zealand), May 17, 1920.
[82] See the statement: 'Cabinet ministers here impress me with the fact that a failure in the Dardanelles would have most serious results in India.' KM to Fisher, 23 September 1915, Murdoch Papers, MS 2823/2/1, NLA.
[83] Rupert Murdoch in conversation, Gerard Henderson, *Australian Answers*, Random House: Milson's Point, NSW, 1990, page 252. Rupert conceded that his father had 'depicted a very idealised sense of the Australian soldier being sent to slaughter by the gin-and-tonic-swilling Brits three miles off the shore.' But it was a 'Very powerful letter.'

peninsula.[84] Since "the Australian divisions would strongly resent the confession of failure that a withdrawal would entail", he hoped "the Cabinet [would] decide to hang on through the winter for another offensive, or for peace... The new offensive must be made with a huge army of new troops. Can we get them?"[85]

Keith's overriding priority, he insisted, was the protection of the Australian forces' both in strength and reputation. He assured the Prime Minister that although they were 'dispirited', having "been through such warfare as no army has seen in any part of the world", they were 'game to the end.' Keith was placing the Australians on the highest of pedestals. Bean would later write of how during the war 'Murdoch's admiration of the Australian soldiery rose almost to worship.'[86] By contrast, the lowly Tommies were 'toy soldiers' showing "an atrophy of mind and body that is appalling... childlike youths without strength to endure or brains to improve their conditions." Their cowardice, anathema to the Australian troops, had led to an order "to shoot without mercy any soldiers who lagged behind or loitered in advance." A sentence Keith 'did not like to dictate' - and would regret even more when asked to prove 'the fact' at the Dardanelles Commission the following year.[87] The Australian stock was eulogised as 'all of the good parentage':[88]

> But I could pour into your ears so much truth about the grandeur of our Australian army, and the wonderful affection of these fine young soldiers for each other and their homeland, that your Australianism would become a more powerful sentiment than before. It is stirring

---

[84] Writing to Bean eighteen years later, hoping 'to appear well' in the latest volume of Bean's official History of the War, Keith declared: "I maintain that all my actions at that time were entirely regular and necessary. I did not urge the removal of the troops. All I urged was a change of Commander so that a new mind could get the position summed up." KM to Bean, November 20, 1933, Murdoch Papers, MS 2823 3/14, NLA.

[85] Keith continued "Already the complaint in France is that we cannot fill the gaps, which after an advance our thinned ranks cannot be replenished. But I am not a pessimist, and if there is military necessity for this awful ordeal, then I am sure the Australian troops will face it." KM to Fisher, September 23, 1915, Murdoch Papers, MS 2823/2/1, NLA.

[86] C. E. W. Bean. (1941). *Official History of Australia in the War of 1914–1918, Volume V – The Australian Imperial Force in France during the Main German Offensive, 1918.* (8th edition). Sydney: Angus & Robertson, page 8.

[87] Avieson, J. (1989). 'Sir Keith Murdoch: The Unwilling Witness', *Australian Journalism Review*, 11, pages 43-49.

[88] Keith, as others have since, fell in into the same myth perpetuating distortion that these were mostly 'fine country lads, magnificent men' and not his fellow city and town dwellers in the main.

to see them, magnificent manhood, swinging their fine limbs as they walk about Anzac. They have the noble faces of men who have endured. Oh, if you could picture Anzac as I have seen it, you would find that to be an Australian is the greatest privilege the world has to offer.[89]

To protect reputations and morale, Fisher was advised "to take up the case of Sir John Maxwell", the English commander overseeing Australian recruits in Egypt, and to 'fight out' his 'lecturing orders'.[90] Keith had been incensed at Maxwell's expression of regret at the 'wilful murder' by Australians who had been rioting in the Whasa brothel district of Cairo. Only "a very few of our men", he insisted, "burnt some houses in which they had been drugged and diseased." Against Maxwell, he attacked this blasting of "the good name of our clean and vigorous army." The men's reputation was "too sacred to leave in the hands of" those who would undermine it with unpalatable truths. [91]

For a man who had had been brought up in a city and until now had mainly socialised with middle-aged men, the "special capacity of the Australian physique" was particularly impressive. To convey immediacy and paint the scene for his readers back home he not only eulogised the men's bodies in evocative, articles about his time at Gallipoli;[92] but also experimented with writing in the first person, present tense. Praise was wrapped in self-deprecatory rhetoric. Though he did not "wish to

---

[89] KM to Fisher, September 23, 1915 (page18), Murdoch Papers, MS2823/2/1, NLA.
[90] Maxwell would half a year later gain infamy through his heavy-handed actions in the wake of the Easter Rising in Ireland.
[91] Keith would stand firm to this view over the years despite the civilian deaths and atrocities committed by the soldiers. Ernest Morrison records in his diary entry of March 23, 1919 Murdoch's continuing defence of the soldiers' actions. Morrison Papers, MLMSS 312/26. Pearce was informed by the Official Secretary of the Australian High Commission in London that the report on the conduct of some Australians in Egypt made for 'really dreadful reading': 'The Egyptians must think they would be just as well off to have Germans there as to have Australians.' Muirhead Collins to Pearce, August 18, 1915, Pearce Papers AWM 3DRL/2222/7/2. The Australian forces would record the highest level of VD among any of the armies. See Frank Bongiorno's chapter 'Bringing the war back home', in Crotty, M. and Larsson, M. (eds.). (2010). *Anzac Legacies*. North Melbourne, Vic.: Australian Scholarly Publishing, pages 85-7. Bean had been compelled to deliver a veiled, though still controversial, despatch on the soldiers' conduct in Egypt earlier in 1915 (see John Williams. (1999). *Anzacs, the Media and the Great War*. Sydney: University of New South Wales Press, pages 58-60.). He conceded privately in his diary that 'our force contains more bad hats than the others'; Kevin Fewster (ed.). (2009). *Bean's Gallipoli: The Diaries of Australia's Official War Correspondent*. Allen & Unwin: Crows Nest, NSW, page 45, a diary entry for January 30, 1915.
[92] See for example the articles headlined 'The New Australians ... Type of the Anzacs', *The Sun*, [n.d.] 1915, cuttings album, Murdoch Papers, MS 2823/2/13, NLA.

idealise the Australian soldier", the contrast "between him and other fighters" was so great "that the tendency everywhere in the Eastern Mediterranean" was "to worship him as a super-type".[93] For those enlisting, "Tales of hardship from Anzac act more like a magnet than as a repeller."[94]

Two days after sending his 'private letter' to Fisher, at the suggestion of Lloyd George, Keith sent a copy to Asquith. If it adds "one iota to your information, or presents the Australian point of view", he observed, it will be of service at this most critical moment." Although he acted out of 'affectionate regard for our soldiers' interests,'[95] Keith's interests also stood to benefit.

Copying the whole letter revealed to Asquith the close relationship[96] between the newly arrived cable manager and the Australian Prime Minister. Through the letter's references and tone, Keith demonstrated his position of trust at the heart of the Australian government. It proved his ability to be candid in discussing issues about which others may have been more reticent.

Asquith circulated the letter to the War Cabinet. Indeed he did so on 'the famous duck's egg foolscap of the Committee of Imperial Defence', as an incredulous Hamilton cried, "the stamp of the ministerial Holy of Holies."[97] Keith's letter was being read by those at the highest level in the world of the press as well as politics. The seed of another intergenerational relationship is revealed by a handwritten note at the top of one remaining copy: 'Please return to Lord Northcliffe, The Times'.[98] However, within a week, the British Prime Minister was backing away from a letter 'largely composed of gossip and second-hand statements' and doubting the 'antecedents' of its writer.[99] Winston Churchill, then First Lord of the Admiralty and the originator of the

---

[93] See 'Never Driven Back – Australian's Proud Claim' *The Sun*, [undated] 1915, cuttings album, Murdoch Papers, MS 2823/2/13, NLA.
[94] 'Life in Burrows – Daily Round at Anzac', *The Sun*, [undated] 1915, cuttings album, Murdoch Papers, MS 2823/2/13, NLA.
[95] Copy of letter from KM to Asquith, September 25, 1915, Murdoch Papers, MS 2823/2/1, NLA.
[96] Day, D. (2008). *Andrew Fisher: Prime Minister of Australia*. Sydney Fourth Estate, page 270.
[97] Ian Hamilton. (1920). *Gallipoli Diary*, Vol.II, New York: George H. Doran Company, pages 259 and 262.
[98] Northcliffe Papers, M1641, AJCP. Sayers received a copy of this version while access was otherwise still restricted to the official state records after Rupert Murdoch made an 'urgent request' to Sir Geoffrey Harmsworth, Northcliffe's nephew. Handwritten note (n.d.) by Sayers in Murdoch Papers, MS 2823/2/1.
[99] Asquith to Dawnay, October 2, 1915, quoted in *Op. cit.* Andrews, (1993), page 58.

Dardanelles strategy, believed Hamilton should not be troubled with "defending himself from the malicious charges of an irresponsible newspaper man."[100] He had forwarded Asquith a note from the editor of *The Daily Chronicle* who had met with Keith and "was not much impressed":

> When I questioned him on details of his report, he gave me rather evasive replies. It is quite obvious that he had not seen the things, which he described, nor has any personal knowledge of the men he condemned. His information was largely second-hand. I do not say that much of it is not correct, or that some of his criticisms are not justified, but my personal feeling about him is that his statements must be accepted with caution. [101]

Writing a few days later to Lord Murray with a copy of his report to Fisher, Keith was almost apologetic – not for dissembling but for putting "the case with perhaps excessive frankness". However, he had "lived long enough in the world to know that reforms are secured only after heavy jottings."[102]

Welcome everywhere

> 'Anzac has soaked into the minds of this country… London is now a great place for an Australian to be in, for his identity with his country makes him welcome everywhere.'[103]
> Keith Murdoch, December 1915

In contrast to his first sojourn in London, Keith hit the ground running. He wasted no time in exploiting a climate that had blurred the usual demarcation of power as Britain struggled to wage and manage its first large-scale industrialised military conflict.[104] Keith joined with the

---

[100] Winston Churchill to Lord Curzon, October 2, 1915, Churchill Archives, CHAR 21/43.
[101] [Robert] Donald to Churchill, 1 October 1915, Churchill Archives, CHAR 21/43.
[102] Murdoch to Murray, 4 October 1915, Elibank Papers, National Library of Scotland.
[103] 'Diary of the War – Dardanelles Withdrawal – Anzacs Imperishable Spirit – Feat That Amazed the World', written 30 December 1915, *The Sun*, [n.d.] 1916, cuttings album, Murdoch Papers, MS 2823/2/13, NLA.
[104] Northcliffe, giving Lloyd George a leg-up in the process, had sought to undermine Asquith and Kitchener through exposure of the 'Shell Scandal.' Though on this occasion at least the popular will would not bend to his, with the *Daily Mail* 'burnt on the floor of the Stock

Australian business and political elite in the city: in Bean's view, he would come to be "much the most influential figure"[105] among them. Thanks to the letter, Keith was becoming a central player Empire-wide. The Canadian Prime Minister cabled the powerful press and political operative, Sir Maxwell Aitken, to obtain a copy of it.[106] Keith's goal now was to influence political and military strategy more generally.[107] The heat of intrigue over the Dardanelles debacles would forge a lasting relationship between Keith, Law and Lloyd George - and an even closer, life-changing bond was being struck with another figure, the supreme moulder and destroyer of reputations, Lord Northcliffe.

Keith initially expressed concern at how widely the owner of *The Times* was circulating his letter.[108] The letter "was of so intimate a character" that its circulation would expose a friendship with Fisher which he held 'sacred'.[109] Nonetheless, Keith placed himself in Northcliffe's hands: "Any information I ever collect is at your disposal and that of the "Times" Staff". The young cable manager was soon signing his notes 'Yours very truly'.[110] Northcliffe, in turn, started addressing notes to 'My Dear Murdoch', displaying a paternal interest in both Keith's professional advancement and his wellbeing. He advised him to join the Automobile Club - most useful for interacting with Cabinet Ministers[111] provided him with stopgap funds, and invited him to his palatial Tudor home, Sutton Place.[112] Being based in the same

---

Exchange, thus paying the penalty for its lapse into truth.' A.J.P. Taylor. (1963). *The First World War: An illustrated history*. London: George Rainbird, page 65.

[105] Bean, C. (1937). *The Official History of Australia in the War of 1914-18*. Sydney: Angus and Robertson, page 5.

[106] Borden to Aitken, 30 November 1915, Beaverbrook Papers, M1126. The later Lord Beaverbrook would become a key figure in Keith's career and ultimately a defining influence for the Murdoch dynasty.

[107] Keith did not want the political capital, and goodwill towards Australia gained through the contribution of its forces now weakened by a public protest in London about the true situation in the Dardanelles. He hoped that nothing would be "done to give an idea that Australasians are whining because they are hurt." KM to Northcliffe, October 19, 1915, Northcliffe Papers, M1641, AJCP.

[108] KM to Northcliffe, September 27, 1915, Northcliffe Papers, M1641, AJCP.

[109] KM to Northcliffe, October 1, 1915, Northcliffe Papers, M1641, AJCP.

[110] Keith deployed flattery while testing how strings could be pulled through the press baron. One typical line summing up his influence over strategy, politicians and press read: 'I am confidant Fisher would come [to London] if 'The Times' suggested it.' KM to Northcliffe, 19 October 1915, Northcliffe Papers, M1641, AJCP.

[111] The Automobile Club proved the pick of the recommendations for the interaction with Cabinet Ministers ('of both parties'), 'excellent food' and 'swimming baths', Northcliffe to KM, 29 October 1915, Northcliffe Papers, M1641, AJCP.

[112] *Ibid.*

building as *The Times*' - 'the greatest newspaper in the world'[113] - gave him a workaday proximity to Northcliffe. Keith had failed utterly in 1909. Now he was secure at the very heart of Fleet Street - and crucially, he was his own boss. Keith told his readers he had been "privileged these days to get far behind the scenes - to meet and talk frankly with the men in London who decisions mean life and death to thousands"; Cabinet Ministers were asking him "anxiously what Australia would think of this or that projected move."[114]

In his letter to Fisher, Keith described how 'You would have wept' as had he, going "over the ground where two of our finest Light Horse regiments were wiped out." That was the action, which marks the emotional climax of Weir's film. Keith, in one of his first newspapers, despatches back to the 'saddened Australian homes'[115] rescued a sense of achievement from this tragedy. The "heroism and sacrifice have not been in vain" as "the reputation of our nation has been placed as high as any national reputation can be." His narrative to the public moved on to invoke another emotional image, the scene conveying Keith's new standing as well as the high regard in which the Anzacs were held:

Yesterday I was with a London newspaper proprietor, who is sometimes called Emperor, so powerful is his influence. We discussed a picture of the men of an Australian field battery feeding the guns. Stripped to the waist, straining at their work, with faces like classical statues of ancient gladiators, these magnificent Australians gave an impression of noble young manhood. The Londoner turned away his head. "I cannot look at it," he said, "or I shall weep at the sight of such splendid life".[116]

Now it was not the loss of life, but a superman vitality that was stirring. Keith waxed lyrical about the fame that the Anzacs had achieved. As they rested and 'holidayed' in England, the "splendour of

---

[113] 'Unrestful Russia Ruled By Iron Hand', *The Sun*, [undated] 1915, cuttings album, Murdoch Papers, MS 2823/2/13, NLA.
[114] 'Diary of the War – Behind the Scenes', *The Sun*, November 17, 1915.
[115] Written on the day that as Keith detailed "great prominence [had been] given in the principal London and provincial newspapers to Captain Bean's stirring account of the Light Horse charge in August - that painful and yet heroic affair in which Australians went face forward to certain death."
[116] 'Australian as a Fighter: Englishman's Appreciation: 'The Kind of Chap He Is', *The Sun*, written October 1, 1915, [date of publication not stated] cuttings album, Murdoch Papers, MS 2823/2/13, NLA.

their manhood is a constant appeal to all observers." On the copy of the photograph Northcliffe gave Keith as a personal memento,[117] the 'Emperor' wrote 'Splendid Men' (see Figure 10.4).[118] The image would soon gain a massive public circulation when printed as an illustration in the next volume of *The Times History and Encyclopaedia of the War.* Writing up the chapter on Gallipoli provided Keith with an early chance to fix the history and mythology of the tale.

In a promotional despatch for the volume, [119] Keith told his Australian readers how it would be 'devoted to the spirit of Anzac.'[120] Sandwiched between the other chapters of propaganda to be printed, bound and distributed around the world,[121] Keith held a new religion aloft: 'Australianism' - "Anzac was sacred soil; the Australian army was a sacred institution."[122] Though beset by problems of communication and - he implied - command strategy, the Dardanelles campaign had 'stiffened' the backs of the Australians, leading to a "renewed determination to see the war through" as its leaders "moved Londonward ... to take a greater part in Empire control." Australia had

---

[117] KM to Mr Price (Northcliffe's private secretary, H.G. Price) October 28, 1915, Northcliffe Papers, M1641, AJCP. Keith asked that his thanks be passed on for the "pictures [Northcliffe] sent me last week from the Daily Mail, stressing that he was "deeply sensible of his many kindnesses."

[118] Australian War Memorial photograph A00879.

[119] Begun during the early part of the war, twenty-two volumes would eventually be produced by *The Times* up until 1921. The photograph is presented with the legend: "Stripped to the Waist" Anzacs working their guns on Gallipoli Peninsula', *The Times History of The War, Vol. VI.* The Times: London, 1916, page 109. Keith wrote in his chapter how the Australian soldier was "built on generous lines in every way. Not just open-handed and kind, 'His physique was the wonder of the Mediterranean." The sight of the men swinging "themselves down the steep sides of Anzac or working, stripped to the skin, besides the guns in their emplacements, brought emotion to the observer at the sight of so much fine life." Page 139.

[120] 'Spirit of Anzac: A New Australianism: Our Place in the Orbit of Nations', [n.d.] *Sun*, cuttings album, Murdoch Papers, MS 2823/2/13, NLA. Volume VI was first trailed in *The Times* on December 13 under the headline 'The Spirit of Anzac.' On the day of its publication, the newspaper stated how '[t]he writer gives a brilliant description of the work done' impressing that the 'main product of the Dardanelles adventure was "renewed determination".' 'Anzac in Gallipoli – New Part of 'The Times" History', December 14, 1915.

[121] Another chapter 'The Execution of Miss Cavell', narrated the tale of the British nurse who faced a German firing squad and became the subject of multiple propaganda initiatives, including the film *Nurse and Martyr.* See Nicholas O'Shaughnessy. (2004). *Politics and Propaganda: Weapons of Mass Seduction.* Manchester Manchester University Press, page 127; and Anthony Aldgate and James C Robinson. (2005). *Censorship in Cinema and Theatre.* Edinburgh: Edinburgh University Press, page 42.

[122] Keith cabled how "The article describes the joy and eagerness, amounting almost to a sacred desire, with which each draft lands at Anzac… every conception fitted in with the sublime conception that this work for their race and their country was God's work… the highest thing possible."

received a boost, but the commission to write this new history would be used by Keith to help his own cause, too.

In his recent bestselling book on *Gallipoli*, Les Carlyon suggests that Keith at the time "might just have been walking around with "pawn" written on his back."[123] Keith was cannier than that: he may not have been the 'official' war correspondent, but he could access the Western Front another way. Keith's 'keenest ambitions', as Bean noted, were "[t]o wield great power", his diplomacy to this end "heavy and obvious, but masterful and usually successful."[124] Keith's letter to Pearce, the Defence Minister, seems a perfect example:

> I have been asked today to write the Anzac number of the Times History of the War, and you can bet that I mean to do justice to my country, its leaders, and my countrymen. But I am wondering, the purpose of this letter is to beg you to send me to the front here.

Invoking his actions and the Gallipoli letter - "all the time I was burning with a sense of the splendour of our men and the chance I had of impressing men here with a good idea of that splendour" - Keith put forward that the British government "would have no objections. Indeed, many Ministers I have seen at their own request have told me the Ministry is under an obligation to me for what I was able to tell them about the Dardanelles." The request was successful.[125]

On the day that *The Times* proudly advertised the special volume of its *History*, 'A Story Without Parallel in the Annals of the Empire', it emphasised how the work was revealing of 'Australian psychology'. In particular "the unfairness of the accusation of "recklessness" so often brought against the Anzacs." There was a motive for this emphasis. As the editorial noted, the *History* should be read 'in conjunction' with another 'important article' published that day from 'an Australian Correspondent, who defines the Australian attitude very carefully'. The Australian people and government were united in supporting "the home authorities without cavilling and without seeking "special soothings or consideration."[126] The anonymous correspondent - possibly Keith himself - asserted how "we in Australia disown the complainers and

---

[123] Carlyon, L. (2001). *Gallipoli*. Sydney: Pan Macmillan, page 599.
[124] *Op. cit.* Bean. (1937), page 8.
[125] KM to Pearce, November 4, 1915, Pearce Papers, AWM 3DRL 2222/5/8.
[126] *The Times* welcomed the 'manliness of these assurances.' 'The Spirit of Anzac' editorial, *The Times*, December 15, 1915.

deny the unrest." The 'real attitude of real Australians' was typified, the correspondent continued, in a recent speech by the new Prime Minister W.M. Hughes. (The ailing Fisher had resigned to become High Commissioner for London). Hughes had declared that it was the Australian Government's duty to 'mind its own business' and "provide the quota of men which the Imperial Government" deemed necessary.

The correspondent was anxious to stress that his were "not the opinions of an individual assuming to speak for a continent." Rather, he had "been asked to put them before *The Times* as the mouthpiece of a great many men representing many interests and practically all classes."[127] A small cable item on the same page reported how the result of the by-election to fill Fisher's once-safe seat was in the balance. The swing away from Labour[128] was "ascribed to antagonism of the Labour Party to the referendum compact, to the conscription recruiting scheme, and to the popularity of the Liberal candidate."[129] In the 'Late War News' section of the same edition, other developments were detailed. Over a million circulars had been sent to men of military age throughout Australia asking them whether they were "willing to enlist now or at a later date, and, if not, to state the reason." The *Age* (Keith's former newspaper) had called on the Trades Council "to retract its "lawless and senseless resolution" urging unionists to ignore the circular."[130] The nation was not speaking with one voice.

Moving pictures

There is a parallel story of Murdoch's contact with Ashmead-Bartlett, one also missed by the previous accounts. It, too, centres on emotion and public engagement, image, film and profit. When Keith arrived at the correspondents' camp on Imbros, Ashmead-Bartlett had just

---

[127] 'Australia and War Criticism – The Real Attitude (From A Correspondent in Australia)', *The Times*, 15 December 1915.

[128] Labor plunged from having won 64% of the votes cast the year before to a loss of the seat. 'Wide Bay Election – The Result of the Re-count', *Brisbane Courier*, December 21, 1915.

[129] 'Mr Fisher's Seat', *The Times*, December 15, 1915. Hughes was set on a collision course with his party and the unions over both his referendum push for greater Commonwealth powers over commerce, monopolies and industrial relations as well as the issue of conscription. See Judith Smart in C. Wilcox (ed.) (1995). *The Great War: Gains and Losses – Anzac and Empire*. Canberra: Australian War Memorial and Australian National University, pages 52-8.

[130] 'The Call for 50,000 More Australians - A Local Labour Boycott', *The Times*, December 15, 1915.

returned from filming a staged charge from the trenches at Gallipoli.[131] The conspiratorial chat a few days later between Keith and the English correspondent, which led to the writing of their respective letters, almost did not take place. Ashmead-Bartlett's plan to film more action that day

Figure 10.3 'Splendid Men' photograph (Australian War Memorial)

had been stymied "as the weather was so bad."[132] As they plotted in the tent, the hand-held 'Aeroscope' cinematograph camera sat idle.[133] It had been supplied to Ashmead-Bartlett by his commercial agent, with a promise of significant profits. Alongside the dramatic footage of artillery bursts, Ashmead-Bartlett was excited by the sensational appeal that images of the 'magnificent' soldiers bathing would create: "a few hundred of them naked under fire ought to draw all the ladies of London who are not shell making." Although unsure if one "can exhibit

---

[131] He thought it 'ought to make an excellent picture.' Diary entry, September 2, 1915, Ashmead-Bartlett Papers, M 2581, AJCP. The Australians and New Zealanders had been particularly happy to be filmed, it was claimed, when they realised the 'tremendous stimulus to recruiting' it would provide back home; Ashmead-Bartlett to Mr Butt July 26, 1915, Bartlett Papers B/3/116.
[132] Diary entry, September 7, 1915, Ashmead-Bartlett Papers, M 2581, AJCP.
[133] Driven by compressed air and with a gyroscope for stability - 'by modern standards heavy and bulky but in 1915 the last thing in portable modernity.' Philip Dutton, 'More Vivid than the Written Word': Ellis Ashmead-Bartlett's film, *With the Dardanelles Expedition* (1915)', *Historical Journal of Film, Radio and Television*, Vol. 24, No. 2, 2004, page 208. See also FN13, page 220.

such things in a theatre", he suggested to his backer that perhaps "your expert will be able to shove in a few faked fig leaves."[134]

Keith, too, realised the stirring power of the bathing imagery, invoking comparisons with antiquity and classic epics under the headline 'Men love the beaches'.[135] (The artist George Lambert, who would become a firm friend of Keith's, was inspired to paint a romantic imagining of the scene (see Figure 10.5). Another of his reports described how the Australian soldiers' "magnificent limbs ... gave them the appearance of giants." Their 'big chests' had "that sinewy look that one associates with professional athletes." Keith was just one among many at this time who saw the war as a regenerative process for the Anglo Saxon race.[136] Significantly, Bean would go further in describing Keith's admiration for the Diggers as 'almost idolatrous'.[137] Keith's fascination with development towards physical perfection, at times verging on the homoerotic, would last for the rest of his life. A passion finding outlet in his shearing sheds,[138] at sports grounds,[139] and into the pages of his newspapers.[140] Back in 1915, he described in inspirational terms how each recruit was 'a changed man': whether originally a city office boy or outback farmhand, all had risen to the new 'Type of the Anzacs'.[141] In his Gallipoli letter, Keith had told Fisher that "the stench in many of our trenches is sickening" from "the good human stuff that

---

[134] Ashmead-Bartlett to Mr Butt, July 26, 1915, Ashmead-Bartlett Papers, M 2581 B/3/116, AJCP. An evocative, dreamlike scene by Weir 75 years later would place his naked protagonists underwater as shrapnel plunged in around them.
[135] 'Fierce Dangers and Hardships - Type of the Anzacs', an article reproduced widely throughout Australia and New Zealand, as in the *Poverty Bay Herald* of November 26, 1915.
[136] For a survey, overview see Bradley W. Hart (Cambridge University), 'Public and Private Memory of the First World War and the British Eugenics Movement', paper delivered at the 29th Conference of the APHES, November 14, 2009, accessible at web.letras.up.pt/aphes29/data/5th/BradleyHart_Texto.pdf.
[137] 'Sir Keith Murdoch: He Was for Empire and Australianism', *The Sun*, October 6, 1952.
[138] Ralph Simmonds stressed to Sayers, at the end of a letter otherwise dealing with business and political involvement, that in later life Keith would eulogise on watching the stripped and muscled shearers at his sheep stud. Murdoch Papers, MS 2823/11/2, NLA.
[139] Daughter Helen recalled: "One thing that embarrassed me was when Dad took us to the football and he'd have binoculars and would be in the outer and say things like: 'Magnificent, look at those wonderful young Australians. If he did it today, it would be very suspect." Helen Handbury, appendix, *Elisabeth Murdoch: Two Lives*, Pan Macmillan: Sydney, 1994, page 308.
[140] *The Sun Pictorials'* 'Perfect Man' physique competition in October 1936 was typical.
[141] "Fierce Dangers and Hardships - Type of the Anzacs', *Poverty Bay Herald*, November 26, 1915.

their lies buried."[142] By contrast, to his readers, he encouraged: "Anzac makes great men out of this good Australian human stuff."[143]

Anzac could also make lots of 'folding stuff'.[144] Soon after Keith departed Ashmead-Bartlett wrote to a theatrical promoter back in England; he would now 'only lecture in big centres' for 'big money'. His head had been turned by the prospect of a more lucrative market for his slides and talks; "I could make a very great deal in Australia."[145] Wasting no time after leaving Imbros, in Cairo Keith cabled a Melbourne promoter to line up a deal.[146] Writing when safely back in London, Keith insisted Ashmead-Bartlett, who had now been dismissed by Hamilton, should see him 'as soon as' he landed.[147] Ashmead-Bartlett managed to 'smuggle in' his 'precious cinematograph films' and met with his agent. They "sat discussing matters for a great [money-making] campaign" until the early hours.[148] Two days later Ashmead-Bartlett had secured a deal for 25 lectures in England at £100 apiece. Having toasted his success, he headed for his first meeting with Northcliffe at *The Times* office. This had been arranged by Keith who "has apparently become a great friend of the Napoleon of the Press", Ashmead-Bartlett wrote in his diary.[149] The next edition of *The Sunday Times* had a damning account of the Gallipoli situation by Ashmead-Bartlett; presented as an interview, it side-stepped the censor.[150]

---

[142] KM to Fisher, September 23, 1915, page13, Murdoch Papers, MS 2823/2/1, NLA.

[143] 'Life in Burrows', *The Sun*, [n.d.] 1915, cuttings album, Murdoch Papers, MS 2823/2/13, NLA.

[144] In these same weeks, Bean recorded in his private diary the fear that if he wrote the complete truth on the character and physique of the soldiers, "the tender Australian public, which only tolerates flattery, and that in its cheapest form, would howl me out of existence.' Although he had 'some satisfaction in sticking to the truth in spite of the prejudice against it' he suspected he had spoilt his 'chances forever of being some day tolerably well off." September 26, 1915, Bean Papers AWM 38/3DRL606/17/1.

[145] Ashmead-Bartlett to Christy, September 16, 1915, Ashmead-Bartlett Papers, M 2581 B/3/155-6, AJCP.

[146] Tait to Ashmead-Bartlett, 30 September 1915, and Murdoch to Ashmead-Bartlett October 1, 1915, Ashmead-Bartlett Papers, M 2581 B/3/170,173, AJCP.

[147] Murdoch to Ashmead-Bartlett, October 1, 1915, Ashmead-Bartlett Papers, M 2581 B/3/173-4, AJCP.

[148] Diary entry, October 10, 1915, Ashmead-Bartlett Papers, M 2581, AJCP. While the 'lecturing business' in England would be 'fixed up' within the next few days – the more hushed, and potentially lucrative film deal would have to wait. The War Office had become anxious over the possible effect of the footage. Diary entry, October 12, 1915, Ashmead-Bartlett Papers, M 2581, AJCP.

[149] Diary entry, October 14, 1915, Ashmead-Bartlett Papers, M 2581, AJCP.

[150] 'The Near East Situation – Mr Ashmead Bartlett's views… 'Sunday Times' Interview', *The Sunday Times*, October 17, 1915.

Northcliffe asked to reproduce it in *The Times* and *Daily Mail* while Keith rang to confirm he had cabled the account to his Australian newspapers.[151]

As Keith relayed to his readers back in Australia, the first lecture of the English tour was delivered to an audience of 6000 at the Queen's Hall on 27th October 1915. Advertisements had highlighted the fact it would be 'Illustrated by special Lantern Views'.[152] Sitting among the "the immense crowd of sheltered men and women" Keith expressed disgust that "never during the two hours in which that brilliant talker told of the splendid heroism and endurance of this ill-fated venture did the audience rise from its own temperate level." The only time they cheered was "when on the screen were thrown pictures they had learnt to admire ... of the Australians preparing for the landing ...and of the heroes of Anzac in their daily life." Keith claimed that the English correspondent's dispatches had been "more valuable to Australia than probably any other writings of any other man since Australia was discovered." Ashmead-Bartlett's actions following his return to London had "dragged out into the open, past the censorship, facts about the bungling at the Dardanelles expedition." Keith gave a heavy hint of his involvement in this tale, alluding to "circumstances which have not yet been published connected with Mr Ashmead Bartlett's return" and an important letter "entrusted to a man who was making direct for London, but it was intercepted at Marseilles."[153]

Keith, mindful of the Australian tour he was encouraging, was putting the best spin he could on the lecture's muted reception. Ashmead-Bartlett's diary reveals how, already ill, he had sought fortification in getting drunk before being "pushed on to the stage, really not knowing exactly what was happening", finding everything "to be in a kind of haze."[154] Little wonder perhaps that the audience only stirred at the sight of the Anzacs – the projected slides were the only thing in

---

[151] Diary entry, October 16-21, 1915, Ashmead-Bartlett Papers, M 2581, AJCP. *The Sunday Times* was then owned by the Berry brothers, William and Gomer, with whom Ashmead-Bartlett's agent appears to have already signed a deal.

[152] Sponsored by *The Sunday Times*, and first advertised on the day of its interview exclusive, it was also trailed by Northcliffe's press – see 'Lecture by Mr Ashmead Bartlett', *The Times*, October 26, 1915.

[153] 'Gallipoli Strategy – Mr Ashmead Bartlett's Story – Series of Blunders Imputed – from the Sydney 'Sun's' Special Correspondent, Mr Keith Murdoch, London October, 28,' widely published, for example in the *Ashburton Guardian*, December 30, 1915.

[154] Diary entry, October 27, 1915, Ashmead-Bartlett Papers, M 2581, AJCP.

focus that evening.[155] Still, he managed to revive for the celebrations that followed, mixing with high society and heading off "to see the wonderful film 'The Birth of a Nation' at the Scala Theatre."[156] A charity performance had been organised with the proceeds going to a special Dardanelles fund.[157] W. G. Griffith's epic of the American Civil War was billed as the cinema event of the year in Britain.[158] It was destined to remain the highest grossing film in the world for a quarter of a century. As the historian of Fox Films noted, it was that film which showed bankers and investors "the potential of the movie industry."[159] It also sparked discussion in London on the "great progress of the art of the cinematograph" with the success of this 'ambitious attempt' in presenting a 'historical drama'.[160] According to *The Times* the pre-war "anxiety in some quarters about the effect upon public morals and taste wrought by" the new medium, where the "clergy foresaw the corruption of youth and the hardening of mature wickedness." And "school teachers had good cause to complain that their pupils" faculty of keeping awake and attending was being impaired", had been blasted away by such an instructive and rousing tale.[161] Another article, circulated back in Australia, described how the battle scenes were so 'beautiful' the author could "believe hundreds of young men, have been stirred to enlist by them… willing to endure all the miseries of trench warfare for the one culminating rapture of a glorious old-fashioned charge."[162]

---

[155] One friendly correspondent urged Ashmead-Bartlett to face his audience more; pointed out that the 'films were often confused in order' with some of them referring to subjects not even touched upon; and described how when speaking he was 'inclined to slur over some of the best things for want of the art of definition.' A post-script added how it was perhaps not politic to 'directly disparage the English troops by suggesting that the Australians & c, might have done more or better if they had been in the Western trenches.' Burdett-Coutts to Ashmead-Bartlett, 24 November 1915, Ashmead-Bartlett Papers, M 2581 B/5/2/3, AJCP.
[156] Ashmead-Bartlett Diary, November 1, 1915, ML M2581. Advertised as 'D.W. Griffith's Mighty Spectacle', it was 'The Last Word in Motion Pictures – In Conception, Production and Presentation', 'The Birth Of A Nation.' *The Times*, September 27, 1915.
[157] 'Death Of An Australian Cricketer', *The Times*, November 2, 1915.
[158] Film Distributors Association, 'The origins of UK film distribution', launchingfilms.com/origins-of-uk-film-distribution.
[159] Solomon, A. (2011). *The Fox Film Corporation, 1915-1935: A History and Filmography*. Jefferson, NC: McFarland & Company, pages 5-6.
[160] 'Progress Of The Cinema', *The Times* (London, England), September 28, 1915. It was of particular 'interest to the film industry to note the degree of popularity which may be obtained by a serious work' rather than a Charlie Chaplin film.
[161] 'The English Film', *The Times*, November 26, 1915.
[162] 'A Moving Story - D.W. Griffith As Super-Film-Man' (By Harold Begbie, in the *London Daily Chronicle*.) *The West Australian*, December 27, 1915. Immersed in the wonder, the viewer felt "a

Keith believed that not using this new cheap form of 'amusements' in the Dardanelles had been a wasted opportunity. He had criticised the War Office in his Gallipoli letter for not providing 'cinemas, or entertainments' to raise the spirits of those diggers in the trenches. He expanded the point in his *Times* History, stressing how communication was valued above all by the men:

> There were three great days in Gallipoli – the first when the troops first got news through the issue at General Headquarters of a daily broadsheet, *Peninsular* [sic] *Press*; the second, when they got meat; the third when they got bread.[163]

Keith continued to smooth the way for the international leg of the lecture tour. The Australian government raised its fears with the Colonial Secretary that 'a great deal of harm' could be done to morale if the criticism of the Dardanelles campaign was too severe. When summoned to meet Bonar Law, Ashmead-Bartlett promised he would do his "best to put the best construction on a bad case."[164] Concerns allayed, official approval for the tour was granted.[165] A couple of days later Keith organised a final meeting, bringing together Ashmead-Bartlett, along with his agent, the Australian theatrical promoter and the London correspondent of *The New York Times*.[166] America would be a crucial first stop in the itinerary, providing a chance to spread the fame of the Anzacs and inspire public support for the war in a country still then neutral.[167]

---

boy again': 'Fancy clapping a picture-a picture thrown on a sheet! It makes you wish to be a hero. It makes you wish to be honest, down right masculine valorous, and splendid. It makes you willing to do noble things at whatever cost."

[163] *The Times History of the War, Vo. VI*. London: The Times, 1916, page 134. ('The Peninsula Press was the daily news sheet printed at General Headquarters, Mediterranean Expeditionary Force, and distributed to British troops on the Gallipoli Peninsula.' See, cas.awm.gov.au/item/C01933.

[164] Diary entry, November 3, 1915, Ashmead-Bartlett Papers, M 2582, ACJP. For an account of the censorship applied during the tour see Kevin Fewster 'Expression and Suppression: Aspects of Military Censorship in Australia during the Great War.' PhD Thesis, University of New South Wales, 1980, pages119-24. (Fewster stresses that despite left-wing hopes the lectures would tell "something truthful about the war", they were "more akin to a recruitment rally", pages 123-4.)

[165] Diary entry, December 18, 1915, Ashmead-Bartlett Papers, M 2582, ACJP.

[166] Diary entry, December 20, 1915, Ashmead-Bartlett Papers, M 2582, ACJP.

[167] Things did not go well. *The New York Times* put Ashmead-Bartlett in a diplomatic hole by trailing how he would make 'sensational claims' and 'revelations.' His maps and lantern slides were seized by customs forcing a change in the lecture topic to the 'whole war situation' as it was

The day before setting off, Ashmead-Bartlett joined Keith and Northcliffe for a farewell round of golf.[168] The trio finessed the publicity strategy to come. Northcliffe had arranged an introduction to 'the

Figure 10.5 British officers drinking tea

sinister Mr William Randolph Hearst' (as Ashmead-Bartlett would later describe him) in New York.[169] Keith handed over a bundle of tailored letters of introduction for use in Australia. Key figures in politics and the press were told Ashmead-Bartlett 'should get the best of treatment': "He and I have stood under fire together." Whether this fire was the heat of criticism or battle, or perhaps both, was left for the recipient to ponder.[170]

A surviving text of the lecture shows the emphasis placed upon the 'Colonials' achievement, with Ashmead-Bartlett rolling out his favourite adjective - 'magnificent'. His opening lines called for an end to the 'carping criticism' of errors, which now belonged 'to the past'. Instead, the audience was told if they put 'the same energy and the same fighting men into the future' they could be 'absolutely confident of success.'[171]

---

too difficult for him to present without them. Diary entry, January 1-6, 1916, Ashmead-Bartlett Papers, M 2582, ACJP.
[168] Diary entry, December 22, 1915, Ashmead-Bartlett Papers, M 2582, ACJP.
[169] Diary entry, 5 January 1916. Ashmead-Bartlett would find the Hearst press ended up highlighting only the 'pro-German' parts of his lecture. Diary entry, January 8, 1916, Ashmead-Bartlett Papers, M 2582, ACJP.
[170] Northcliffe and Murdoch to various, December 21, 1915, Ashmead-Bartlett Papers, M 2582 C/1/3/47-67, ACJP. In the letter addressed simply to 'Dear Tom', Thomas Trumble, acting secretary at the Department of Defence, Keith acknowledged 'you are good to us.'
[171] 'Mr Ashmead Bartlett's Lecture 12.2.16', Ashmead-Bartlett Papers, M 2582 C1/3/18, ACJP. Writing to Ashmead-Bartlett at the conclusion of the tour. A representative of the New

Ashmead-Bartlett cabled a press notice for *The Times* during the tour and certainly trumpeted this view: "The spirit of the Australians is magnificent; they are very keen on the war, and will easily raise 300,000 men."[172]

Intriguingly, filed with the text are extensive and detailed notes on the specific soldiers and actions to mention, accompanied by directions

Figure 10.6 Cut from British officers drinking tea to men charging

for the tone and pace that Ashmead-Bartlett should follow: "Dwell on the sacrifice of these boys in leaving their horses and their dreams of cavalry work … get a lantern slide made of the Southland – it's [sic] an undying tale." A clue to the author of these instructions is given by the paper on which they are typed: the shadow of The United Cable Service letterhead presses through from the reverse.[173]

With Ashmead-Bartlett despatched and 1915 drawing to an end, Keith could reflect on his own extraordinary, rapid elevation. He had secured the scoop of an interview with Bonar Law, whose own power was in the ascendant, following the order to evacuate Gallipoli given on

---

Zealand Department of Defence described how he was 'greatly struck with the value' of the lectures 'from a recruiting point of view.' [Major James] Sleeman to Ashmead-Bartlett, 12 May 1916, Ashmead-Bartlett Papers, M 2582 C1/3/69-70, AJCP.

[172] Sent via his uncle 'Mr Robinson' for publication, [n.d.], Ashmead-Bartlett Papers, M 2582, AJCP.

[173] Ashmead-Bartlett Papers, M 2582 C1/3/38-9, AJCP. The Southland was a transport ship torpedoed by a German submarine on September 2, 1915 on its way from Egypt to Gallipoli with Australian forces.

23rd November.[174] Even in withdrawal, triumph was spun. On the day *The Times* announced the successful evacuation of the peninsula, 'A Special Correspondent' (described as having visited *after* August, so fitting Keith's timings) detailed how "The Anzac Corps fought like lions and accomplished a feat of arms in climbing these heights almost without parallel." They had been close to 'a great success' were they not handicapped by others failing to secure positions. "It was a combat of giants in a giant country" which had proved "the Marvellous hardihood, tenacity, and reckless courage" of the Anzacs.[175]

For the 'special army and navy supplements' to the Christmas and New Year newspapers in Australia, Keith had solicited messages from a raft of leading imperial figures.[176] An impassioned Rudyard Kipling, the figure used as shorthand in Weir's film for the Boys' Own-style fervour to enlist, told Keith the appeal was redundant: "You ask me for a message to Australia. Is there any need for a message to a nation whose sons … have joined valour to endurance and a high heart beyond praise and almost beyond belief."[177]

With the imminent visit of the new Prime Minister Hughes to be planned and press managed and the building issue of conscription on the horizon, Keith's war service was about to be elevated to another level. He would seize new roles as publicist, unofficial press secretary to the Prime Minister, and propagandist for the cause. Far from railing against the futility and the waste of life in the war, he would soon be actively campaigning for more Australians to be compelled to take part in the far deadlier Western Front action.[178]

---

[174] Writing to the Governor General of Australia, Law relayed how 'The other day I gave an interview to Mr Murdoch. I have hitherto made it a rule never to do anything of the kind, but at the time he asked me to do so the evacuation of the Dardanelles was just on the point of being carried out, and I thought it would not harm to have an interview with me telegraphed to Australia.' Law to Ferguson, December 23, 1915, Bonar Law Papers, M 1123, AJCP.

[175] 'The Anzacs at Gallipoli - A Gallant History - Eight Months Hard Fighting", *The Times*, December 21, 1915.

[176] Lord Grey relayed to Keith the view that the Anzacs "were of such fighting stuff as the world had never previously seen, not men of flesh and blood like ourselves, but supermen, demigod, demons." Secretary to the Commander-in-Chief to Murdoch, December 17, 1915, Murdoch Papers, MS 2823/2/10, NLA; Grey to Murdoch, December 19, 1916, Murdoch Papers, MS 2823/2/12, NLA.

[177] Kipling to KM, December 20, 1915, Murdoch Papers, MS 2823/2/10, NLA.

[178] The mortal toll of Gallipoli would number 8,141 Australians and 2,721 New Zealanders; the Western Front would see five and a half times that figure, over 46,000 Anzacs, die, at, ww1westernfront.gov.au/journey.html [accessed December 2017].

Due to an exclusivity clause in his contract, Ashmead-Bartlett was barred from releasing the film of his Gallipoli footage during the tour.[179] He could only observe ruefully how the people in Sydney were "mad about the Cinema and will take in any rubbish thrown them."[180] Australians would have to wait until May 1916 to see the first and only live-action scenes from the Dardanelles.[181] Ashmead-Bartlett did not have to wait that long for profits to roll in, however. His film *With the Dardanelles Expedition: Heroes of Gallipoli* was released in Britain during January - though not with a hoped-for charity matinee at the Palace before the King.[182] *The Times* was impressed by how the film illustrated conditions "more vividly than is possible with the written word."[183] Iconic imagery of the campaign had entered the popular imagination, ready to be twisted into 'received history' over the decades. In one light-hearted sequence, British officers (and possibly Ashmead-Bartlett) sit safely behind walls of sandbags at Suvla Bay 'drinking tea' (Figures 10.5 and 10.6) - before a dramatic cut to Australian troops charging.[184]

Conclusion

Seventy-five years later, Weir's film received a Royal premiere in London.[185] This nod from the establishment had followed Rupert Murdoch's own successful recent battle in taking over *The Times*. *Gallipoli's* artistic and commercial success internationally would sharpen 'Murdoch's appetite for more of the same'.[186] One commentator

---

[179] Memorandum of Agreement between Messrs. J. and N. Tate [sic – Tait] and EAB, December 4, 1915, Ashmead-Bartlett Papers, M 2582 C 1/3/40-46, ACJP.
[180] 'Some comments on Sydney and Australians', Ashmead-Bartlett Papers, M 2582 C1/3/5-6, ACJP.
[181] Advertised as 'A Thrilling Realisation of the Mighty Deeds of the Anzacs', *The Mercury* (Hobart), May 18, 1916.
[182] Ashmead-Bartlett to Mr Butt July 26, 1915, Ashmead-Bartlett Papers, M 2582 B/3/116, ACJP.
[183] 'Films of the War', *The Times*, January 18, 1916.
[184] The juxtaposition of 'these enduring images of inaction immediately next to purposeful shots of Australians' may have appeared in the original edit by Ashmead-Bartlett. "Or, more contentiously, it may have been rearranged later, as an editorial amendment by Bean' who recut the film following its donation to the Australian War Memorial in July 1919, Philip Dutton, 'More Vivid Than the Written Word…'", *Historical Journal of Film, Radio and Television*, Vol. 24, No. 2, 2004 pages 216-7.
[185] It was one of the first public appearances for the new Princess of Wales and Prince Charles following their globally broadcast wedding. 'Film Festival', *The Times*, October 28, 1981.
[186] Tuccille, J. (1989). *Rupert Murdoch: creator of a worldwide media empire*. New York D.I. Fine, page 90.

claimed that following *Gallipoli's* triumph at the box office, Rupert was preparing to take the plunge straightaway and buy a Hollywood studio, quipping that MGM could soon become 'Metro Goldwyn Murdoch'.[187] Still, the film ran into 'a certain amount of critical machinegun fire'[188] in Britain, both for its historical inaccuracy and emotive treatment. The *Sydney Morning Herald* pointed out that *The Times'* film critic 'was one of the few to give an unrelievedly rhapsodic review'. There were concerns too in Australian academia. Lamenting how the film 'refused to interrogate the myth', instead 'consenting only to re-illustrate it', Sylvia Lawson drew a direct comparison with imagery used in *The Hero of the Dardanelles*. The two productions were separated by two-thirds of a century, but there was 'almost no ideological space between them at all.' Both films 'do not invent; they emphasise and sermonise'. The makers of the latest version simply stood 'devoutly before the story' of mateship and set out to serve it.[189] The film had almost been used to portray a very different story, however.

In a 1984 interview, Weir revealed the genesis of the project: he had wanted to make a First World War film set on the Western Front. It would "have been more fictional because so little was known about it, it would have been an entirely different sort of film" - but an emotional first visit to Gallipoli 'changed all that'. For Weir, Gallipoli marked 'the birth of a nation'. Crucially, however, this was not just because of "the battle and our part in it, but most importantly the referendums on conscription" that followed. Key for Weir was what happened when the public back in Australia 'absorbed' the truth of Gallipoli:

> It became part of the 'no' vote from the people in the face of the establishment calling for a 'yes' vote to conscription in this hour of Empire's need. And they were so obviously staggered at the 'no' that they called for the second referendum and got another 'no'. It was the beginning of a turning away from the Empire.

An early script "dealt with wide aspects of the battle from Churchill and the meetings of key figures in London through to the conscription

---

[187] 'The Sunday Carlton Report: Cecil B de Murdoch?', *Sydney Morning Herald*, October 11, 1981.
[188] 'Now Gallipoli's accuracy under fire from historians', *Sydney Morning Herald*, December 24, 1981.
[189] Lawson, S. (1981). 'Gallipoli: Picnic at the Pyramids - you are being told what to remember', *Filmnews*, November/December, page 11.

issue" but the drafts became "successively less complex as we stripped one element after another out." The detail of politics was dropped, and the focus on 'mateship' rose to the fore.[190] Fortuitously, the risk of a producer/director conflict down the line had been avoided. After all, depicting the actions of one of those 'key figures', campaigning for a 'yes' vote for conscription, may have proved unacceptable to some.

---

[190] Interview with Weir in Sue Mathews. (1984). *35 mm Dreams: Conversations with Five Directors About the Australian Film Revival*, Melbourne: Penguin, pages 101-2.

Chapter 11

All Quiet on the Musical Front? German Music Production as Source for a History of Attitudes of the First World War

Dietrich Helms
Universität Osnabrück

Introduction

This chapter is about changes in the attitude of the German public towards certain aspects of the war as reflected in the music production of the years 1914 to 1918. The approach is based on the idea that the music business as an industry that sells emotions closely responds to changes in the attitude of their customers. I searched the titles and first lines of newly published scores as listed in *Hofmeisters musikalisch-literarischer Monatsbericht* from 1914 to 1918 for keywords related to the war: names of battlefields, new technologies of warfare and words from semantic fields of mourning, peace and victory. My research shows that in the summer of 1916, at the end of the battle of Verdun and the beginning of the battle at the Somme, the attitude of the German public or at least of German customers of printed music changed rapidly and radically.

It is a commonplace that the music market has a highly developed sense for changes in the general feelings and the mentalities of its customers.[1] As an industry that sells emotions producers of music adapt their products to the topics of their times to address issues that they hope may concern and move their customers. Consumers of music in

---

[1] See, Helms, D. (2000). 'Was die Wellen dir zärtlich erzählen. Anmerkungen zum Schlager als Quelle historischer Forschung', in Rösing, H. und Phleps, T. (ed.). *Populäre Musik im kulturwissenschaftlichen Diskurs.* (Beiträge zur Popularmusikforschung 24/25) 308. Karben, pages143-167.

turn buy those products, which they feel come up best to their needs - and this includes music that touches them most in the context of their current social and psychological situations. The most emotional incidents in recent history, be it wars, the first landing on the moon or the terrorist attacks of 9/11[2] have always been accompanied by music. Popular songs in particular string together metaphors, which at that time everybody may associate a meaning with according to his or her experiences and knowledge. They use catchwords that are on everybody's lips and have a power to inspire associations. This makes music an interesting source to look at changes in the feelings and the mentality of its consumers. Metaphors repeatedly used in the titles, lyrics and sounds of some songs, may be interpreted as of importance for their audience.

Music, however, is no easy source for historical information. Not every event in history makes a good topic for a song or an operetta, and the fact that a certain historical phenomenon is *not* mentioned in a song does not prove that it was unimportant in public discourse. Abstract ideas and events that need complicated explanations and rational considerations hardly ever make it into music, if they have no emotional aspects.[3] An ideal topic for a song is one that moves and concerns a large part of society. Moreover, it is important that it may be adapted easily to the traditions and customs of the respective musical genre. The topic of battle, e.g. can be easier adopted to the form of a march than to a string quartet; the topic of war only makes a successful operetta if it is associated with the war of the sexes.[4]

Sources

Although most musicologists seem to agree that history leaves its traces on the lyrics and the sound of music, few have undertaken empirical studies to prove their point. The largest study of German music production analysed the lyrics of all top-40 hits from the German charts between 1945 and 1989.[5] An application of the methods of this study

---

[2] Helms, D. and Phleps, T. (eds.) (2004). *9/11 - The worlds all out of tune. Populäre Musik nach dem 11. September 2001*, (Beiträge zur Popularmusikforschung 32). Bielefeld: transcript.

[3] *Op. cit.* Helms, (2000), page 155.

[4] D. Helms, (2017). 'Der Soldate, der Soldate ist der schönste Mann im ganzen Staate. Deutsche Mannsbilder in der Operette der ersten Kriegssaison 1914/15', in, Rode-Breymann, S. (ed.). *1914: Krieg. Mann. Musik.* Hildesheim: Olms, pages 71-94.

[5] Brandhorst, J. and Gerke, H. Joachim, (1992). 'Politischer Wertewandel und Populäre Musik. Ein Forschungsprojekt an der Westfälischen Weilhelms-Universität Münster', in von

for the time of the First World War, however, is impossible for a number of reasons. In Germany music charts only exist from the 1950s onwards; there is no reliable material for sales figures of records or printed music before that time. Therefore, scholars working on the ties between history and music usually base their work on single pieces of music. As a matter, of course, this approach may give us information about the thoughts and ideas of a single composer in his time, but not of larger groups or even a majority of people of a particular culture. Since an analysis of all pieces of music that came out in Germany during a period as long as the four years of the First World War must remain a task for future research when all music is digitised and available on the internet. A search was made for an alternative source of information that would provide reliable data about the sentiments of the music scene during the war; the source located was *Hofmeisters musikalisch-literarischer Monatsbericht*.

Since 1829 the publishing house of Friedrich Hofmeister in Leipzig had edited a catalogue of newly published printed music on a monthly basis. The editors of the catalogues sought to give a complete survey of the production of music publishers available in the German-speaking market, including publishers from Switzerland, the Austrian Empire and German language publications from other European countries. They even included self-published material as long as it was printed. By 1900 the annual total of entries amounted to about 13,000 titles from small prints of a single opening to large opera scores.[6] The outbreak of the war reduced the production considerably.

The Hofmeister catalogues usually reproduce a title and in the case of songs the first line of the lyrics. In most cases, the title is more representative of the content of the lyrics than the first line. To give an example: in January 1918 the catalogue specifies a song for the male choir by Emil Kraemer with the first line 'Ich weiss einen Lindenbaum

---

Schoenebeck, M., Brandhorst, J. and Gerke, H. Joachim (eds). *Politik und gesellschaftlicher Wertewandel im Spiegel populärer Musik*, Essen: Verlag Die Blaue Eule, pages 38-57; Meier, A. (2000). *Politischer Wertewandel und populäre Musik* (= Studien zur Politikwissenschaft, Ser. B, 92). Münster: Lit.

[6] *Op. cit.* Hofmeister XIX, hofmeister.rhul.ac.uk/2008/content/about/project.html. In 1829 the Leipzig music publisher Friedrich Hofmeister began publishing a series of monthly or bi-monthly catalogues of printed music, largely but not exclusively based on the products of publishers in the German-speaking world. These *Monatsberichte* at first comprised about 2,000 records per year, but by 1900 the annual total had risen to 13,000, yielding a total of over 330,000 records for the period 1829-1900. Hofmeister XIX makes this key resource available on the web.

stehen' (I know where a lime tree grows). This rather innocent line is specified by the title 'O schöner Soldatentod' (O happy soldier's death).[7] I am conscious of the fact that empirical research based on titles and first lines misses out information hidden further down in the lyrics. Song titles, however, sum up the ideas of the lyrics and may, therefore, be taken as representative of the contents as a whole. They are significant enough to give an idea of the general tendencies and ideas of a piece of music.

Other than charts or comparable sources for sales figures publishers' catalogues are no sources for the popularity of certain topics with their audience. They rather show, which topics their producers - composers, librettists, lyricists and publishers - thought to be promising on the market. Nonetheless, they can be used as a source of the mentality of their time. Most of the items listed in the *Monatsberichte* were written for commercial purposes. We can presume that their producers thought carefully about which topics might be a success with their audience.

Times of war are times of censorship. One might presume that the government tried to control all publications including the printing of pieces of music. At the beginning of the war, censorship was administrated by a great number of local military authorities with hardly any central control and very diverging ideas of their job. Their task was to prevent the leakage of military secrets. Prints of music were hardly in the focus of their attention. Only in the second half of the war German authorities recognised the need for a centralisation of censorship and propaganda to influence the mood of the population. The administration, however, lacked experience in propaganda and never gained full control of all media. The more than 1,000 publishers of music in Germany were hard to control by a state that was still lacking experience in an effective propaganda.[8] Moreover, a glance at the catalogues of the years before the war shows that already they contained a considerable amount of national and nationalistic songs, of music glorifying the war and the heroism of death on the battlefield. There was no great need to control music production. The catalogues of

---

[7] *Hofmeisters Musikalisch-literarischer Monatsbericht*, 90. 1918. No. 1, page 10.
[8] For censorship in Germany see, Deist, W. (1991). 'Zensur und Propaganda in Deutschland während des Ersten Weltkrieges', in, Deist, W. *Militär, Staat und Gesellschaft. Studien zur preußisch-deutschen Militärgeschichte*. München: Oldenbourg Verlag, pages 163-163. For music production and censorship see Helms, D. (2013). 'Das war der Herr von Hindenburg. Mythenbildung und informelle Propaganda in der deutschen Musikproduktion des Ersten Weltkriegs', in Glunz, C., Hanheide, S. and Helms, D. *Musik bezieht Stellung. Funktionalisierungen der Musik im Ersten Weltkrieg*, Göttingen: V&R Unipress, pages 65-67.

music printers show no traces of any direct and far-reaching influence of military or civil authorities; they represent the social consensus of the German public.

Battlefields

When looking for traces of history in the music of the time, it makes sense to start with occurrences that had a strong effect on a large number of people. My first approach to the data in the Hofmeister catalogues, therefore, was to search for titles of musical compositions that mention the battles of Verdun and the Somme. Today in Germany Verdun has gained the status of a symbol for the horrors of the First World War and its attrition warfare. The battle of the Somme that is of such great importance to the English-speaking world never really made it into German collective memory. Thus, I was not surprised to find only one single piece of music with the name of the Somme in its title: a march called Die Garde an der Somme (Guards at the Somme), written by Fritz Brase and published in June/July 1917, exactly one year after the beginning of the allied offensive in July 1916.[9] The great importance of Verdun for the memory of the war, however, is also not reflected in German music production during the war. We can find a march for a military band called 'Vor Verdun' (In front of Verdun)[10] Published already in March 1915, a year before the offensive, but some weeks after German troops had reached the fortifications of the city at the Meuse river. A second march of the same title, composed by Carl Hubert and dedicated to a unit of the 58th infantry division was published in August and September 1916.[11] Besides these two marches, I found a single song mentioning Verdun in its title. The piece quotes the old traditional song 'Als ich an einem Sommertag' (When I on a summer's day) that was known in many versions already in the early 19th century.[12] The song deals with a man who meets a shy girl in the woods and convinces her to become his lover. At the beginning of the First World War, soldiers rewrote the song and changed its refrain to a

---

[9] *Hofmeisters Musikalisch-literarischer Monatsbericht*, 89. 1917, No. 4, page 70.
[10] *Hofmeisters Musikalisch-literarischer Monatsbericht*, 87. 1915, no. 3, pages 41 and 44. The entry reads, 'l.ehnert, R. Vor Verdun. Marsch f. Militärmusik. qu. 16°. Leipzig, Schuberth jun'.
[11] *Hofmeisters Musikalisch-literarischer Monatsbericht*, 88, 1916, No. 8, page 105 and 88, 1916, No. 9, page 135: Hubert, C. Vor Verdun. Marsch der Kolonne F. K. 3 f. Pfte. Leipzig, Germann & Co.
[12] Published in von Zuccalmaglio, W. A. (ed.). (1840). *Deutsche Volkslieder mit ihren Originalweisen*. Vol. 2, Berlin, no. 76, page 158.

rather optimistic 'Hinter Metz, bei Paris, in Chalons' (After Metz, close to Paris, in Chalons). The contrafactum tells the story of a French girl that falls in love with a German soldier. In July 1916 the *Monatsberichte* listed a song that quotes this particular phrase in its title - adopting it to a more realistic idea of the front line: 'Hinter Metz, auf Paris, vor Verdun' (After Metz, approaching Paris, in front of Verdun).[13] The song, composed 'im Felde', i.e. on the battlefield, by a lieutenant Georg Graesse and published privately, is about happily marching soldiers that beat the French thinking of their beloved ones and some dying as heroes on the way. It has all the standard lore of soldiers' songs, but it contains no traces of what Verdun stands for today.[14] The search results show that during the war neither Verdun nor the Somme gained a strong symbolic function - at least not in music.

Indeed, only a few battles of the First World War were commemorated by more than a handful of military marches and songs. Besides the three marches on the battles of Verdun and the Somme, we have, e.g. two marches and three songs on Ypres[15] from 1915 and 1918 and two marches and three songs published between 1916 and 1918 with the Isonzo[16] in their titles. Tannenberg, the place associated in

---

[13] *Hofmeisters Musikalisch-literarischer Monatsbericht*, 88. 1916, No. 7, page 95: Graesse, G. Metz, H. auf vor Verdun, C. 'Holla he, Herr Franzos! " Kriegslied"' f. 1 Singst. m. Pfte. Coblenz, (Falkenberg).

[14] Grasse, G., Metz, H. auf vor Verdun, P. 'Kriegslied für eine Singstimme mit Klavierbegleitung'. Published by the author 1916. [N.P.]

[15] *Hofmeisters Musikalisch-literarischer Monatsbericht*, 87. 1915, No. 7, page 102: Sauter, H. Vor Ypern. Marsch f. Pfte. Würzburg, Banger Nachf; No. 11, page 165: Bax, A. Vor Ypern. Marsch des 2. Bat. R.-I.-R. 244 f. Pfte. Leipzig, C.A. Klemm; No. 12, page 176: Bax, A. Vor Ypern. Marsch des 2. Bat. R.-I._R. 244 Ausg. f. Militärmusik. Leipzig, C.A. Klemm; No. 12, page 185: Burg, Bernhard. Op. 6. Zwei Kriegslieder f. 1 Singst. m. Pfte. (No. 1. Der Tod von Ypern: Wir schreiten vorwärts Schritt um Schritt...). Leipzig: Hug & Co. *Hofmeisters Musikalisch-literarischer Monatsbericht* 90. 1918, No. 2/3, page 27: "Friedenthal, Albert: Das flämische Volkslied. (Der Stimmen der Völker 2. Sammlung.) Berlin, Simrock, Abteilung III. Altflämische Zwiegesänge m. Pfte. [... incl. as no. 10:] Das Lied von Ypern: ‚Ypern, o Ypern, page 38: Kelterborn, Otto. Das deutsche Lautenlied. Neue Lieder zur Laute u. Zupfgeige. Leipzig, Rainer Wunderlich. [... incl. as no. 3:] Auf den Tod der jungen Kriegsfreiwilligen vor Ypern: Wir haben ein Grab gegraben.

[16] *Hofmeisters Musikalisch-literarischer Monatsbericht* 88, 1916, No. 10, page 142: 'Kraus, Leo. Huldigungsmarsch f. die Isonzo-Armee. Konzertmarsch f. Pfte. Wien: Karczag.' *Hofmeisters Musikalisch-literarischer Monatsbericht*, 89, 1917, no. 5 [August], page 92: Schreiber, D. An die Isonzofront. Marsch f. Pfte. Moarburg a. d. Drau (Höfer), no. 6 [September, October], page 117: 'Zitta, Franz. Die Wacht am Isonzo: Am Grenzwall ringt' f. 1 Singst. m. Pfte. Wien, Mozarthaus; *Hofmeisters Musikalisch-literarischer Monatsbericht* 90, 1918, no. 2/3, page 18: 'Schmal, René Richard. Lieder f. Salonorch. bearb. Wien, Rosé [... incl.:] Braunes Isonzo-Mädel'; page 21: 'Schmal, René Richard. Lieder f. V., V. obl., Vcello u. Pfte bearb. Wien, Rosé [... incl.:] Braunes Isonzo-Mädel; no. 5, page 50: Frankowski, Hans v. Lieder f. Salonorch. Wien, Karl

German propaganda with the first victory of the German troops at the eastern front in August 1914 is commemorated in four marches and three songs.[17] The commander of the victorious 8th army, General Paul von Hindenburg, appears in two more songs as the winner of the battle of Tannenberg.[18] The relatively high number of compositions on Tannenberg can be explained by the fact that it was one of the very few battles during the First World War that ended with a clear victory for the German troops. Later battles ended with the winning of a few square metres of the ground rather than the surrender of the beaten army. Tannenberg was a huge boost for the patriotism and enthusiasm of the first months of the war and became a metaphor for the strength of the German troops and the cunning of its leader von Hindenburg.

Nonetheless, the battlefield mentioned most frequently in German compositions is a place that today has entirely lost its symbolic function: the forest of Argonne not far from Verdun. Between March 1915 and May 1917, we can find ten publications of nine different compositions

---

Mück. Op. 68. Da drunten am Isonzo! and Frankowski, Hans v. Wienerlieder f. 2 V. Gitarre u. Akkordeon arr. v. Anton Ernst. Wien, Karl Mück. [...incl.:] Op. 68. Da drunten am Isonzo!

[17] *Hofmeisters Musikalisch-literarischer Monatsbericht* 86. 1914, no. 10, page 194: Lubbé, Curt. Op. 13. Tannenberger Marsch f. Orch. gr. 80. Berlin-Schoeneberg, Neuer Berliner Musik-Verlag; no. 12, page 235 reissue.; no. 11, page 221: Frey, Martin. Aus Deutschlands grosser Zeit. [...] Leipzig, Steingräber [... incl. as no. 2:] Tannenberger Marschlied: Von Polen zog der Russ daher. *Hofmeisters Musikalisch-literarischer Monatsbericht*, 87. 1915, no. 7, page 106: Bülow v. Dennewitz, Gertrud Gräfin. Deutsche Lieder f. 1 Singst. m. Pfte. gr. 80. Leipzig, C.A. Klemm [...incl.:] Zwischen See u. Sumpf. Bei Tannenberg und Hohenstein; no. 11, page 171: Selden, G. Op. 32. Vier deutsche Kriegslieder f. 1 Singst. m. Pfte. [...incl. as no. 3:] Tannenberg: Landbreite ward zum Krieger; no. 12, page 181: Quarder, H. Der Tannenberger. Ostpreuss. Siegesmarsch (1914) f. Pfte. Stralsund (Bergholz Nachf.). *Hofmeisters Musikalisch-literarischer Monatsbericht*, 88. 1916, no. 4/5, page 48: Henning, Max. Op. 34. Drei Kriegsmärsche [... incl. as no. 2:] Zur Erinnerung an die Schlacht bei Tannenberg [...]. Ausg. f. Orch. Berlin-Westend, Westend-Verlag; no. 9, page 125: Görlitz, Rudolf. Op. 45. Tannenberger Marsch f. Pfte. Quedlinburg, Görlitz' Selbstverl.

[18] Hunderds of songs published between 1914 and 1935 celebrate Paul von Hindenburg. Christin Bultmann, see Helms, D. and Vaupel, S. 'Und dich grüßt so manches Lied'. Verzeichnis von Liedern über Paul von Hindenburg. In Stefan Hanheide et al. (2013). *Musik bezieht Stellung. Funktionalisierungen der Musik im Ersten Weltkrieg*, Osnabrück: V&R Unipress, pages 101-120. The following songs mention Hindenburg as winner of the battle of Tannenberg, *Hofmeisters Musikalisch-literarischer Monatsbericht*, 87. 1915, no. 8, page 106: Blanck, Theodor. [...] Drei Lieder v. Ludwig Thoma f. 1 Stingst. m. Pfte. (No. 1. Der Sieger von Tannenbert u. Lyck: 'Wie klingt ein Name hell und laut'. [...] Berlin, Drei Masken-Verlag; the same song arranged for Salonorchester: page 126; *Hofmeisters Musikalisch-literarischer Monatsbericht*, 89. 1917, no. 4, page 78: Frommel, E. u. C. Der Feldmarschall von Tannenberg: 'Der Hindenburg, der Hindenburg, was der nicht alles macht'. Nach einer älteren Melodie f. 1 Singst. m. Pfte. Leipzig. Ernst Wiegandt.

with Argonne in their title.[19] Again, the most popular of these compositions, the so-called 'Argonnerwald Lied' was inspired by an older song: 'In Kiautschau um Mitternacht' (At Midnight in Kiautschou) had been sung in the German Navy already before the First World War.[20] This song about the colonial troops in China, in turn, has some parallels to Wilhelm Hauff's 'Steh' ich in finst'rer Mitternacht' (When I stand in dark midnight) from the beginning of the 19th century.[21] In 1914/15 Hermann Albert von Gordon adapted the lyrics of the Kiautschau song to the fate of the engineer troops at the Western front. His version was printed in January 1915 and entitled 'Argonnerwald, um Mitternacht' (The forest of Argonne around midnight). The song is about an engineer digging trenches, thinking of his love and fighting the French with mines and hand grenades. 'Argonnerwald, um Mitternacht' mentions the horrors of the warfare in the trenches and foresees that the forest of Argonne will soon become a graveyard.[22]

The titles of the seven songs and two marches on the 'Argonnerwald' listed in the Hofmeister catalogues reveal why the forest of Argonne obviously was more attractive to composers and lyricists than e.g. Verdun or the Somme: Popular media tend to be based on well-known

---

[19] *Hofmeisters Musikalisch-literarischer Monatsbericht*, 87. 1915, no. 3, page 52: Richardy, Johs. Op. 101. Das Mägdelein aus den Argonnen: 'Der Feind ist im Lande' f. 1 Singst. m. Pfte. Pelizig: Vetter'; no. 5, page 93: 'Hirblinger, M. Argonnenwald: 'Der Wald. Wie traut klingt'. Ein Kriegsgesang f. 1 Mittelst. m. Pfte. Regensburg, Gleichauf; no. 8, page 117, Cassimir, Lorenz. Argonnenritt: 'Es stieg ein Reiter früh am Tag' f. Männerchor. Würzburg, Banger Nachv, no. 9, page 127: 'Mertens, Fr. Wilhelm. Im Argonnenwald. Jägermarsch 1914-15 f. Militärmusik. Berlin: Parrhysius' [also no. 11/12, page 158 in an arrangement for 'Infanteriemusik'; *Hofmeisters Musikalisch-literarischer Monatsbericht*, 88. 1916, no. 2, page 27: Krause, Otto. Op. 24. Zwei Kriegslieder f. 1 Singst. m. Pfte. Breslau, Hainauer. [...incl. as no. 2:] Die alte Mühle: 'Tief drinnen im Argonnenwald' no. 4/5, page 67: 'Hirsch, Fritz. Neue lustige Kriegslieder f. Laute (Gitarre) od. Pft. Königsberg: Harpf. Heft 1, [...incl. as no. 5:] 'Soldatenlied aus den Argonnen: Denkt ja nicht, dass mir's schlecht ergeh' *Hofmeisters Musikalisch-literarischer Monatsbericht*, 89. 1917, no. 2 [February and March], page 29: "Skiebe, R. Die alte Mühle im Argonnenwald: 'Tief drinnen im Argonnenwald' f. 1 Singst. m. Pfte. Dresden-Weinböhla, Verlag Aurora; no. 3 [April and May], page 35: Solle, W. Kriegsverlobt. Musik-Zeitbild. Berlin: Mars-Musikverlag. [... incl.:] Unser Kronprinz. Argonnen-Marsch; page 55: 'Pesold, Gustav. Das Grab in Flandern u. andere Kriegslieder f. 1 Singst. m. Pfte. [... incl. as no. 3:] Die Argonnenmühle: 'Mitten im Argonnenwalde'.

[20] Steinitz, W. (1979). *Deutsche Volkslieder demokratischen Charakters aus sechs Jahrhunderten. Berlin: verlag das europäische buch/Zweitausendeins*. Berlin: Verlag das eurpaische Buch fur Zweitaunsendeins. vol. 2, pages 480-489. [I wish to thank Dr. Eckhard John for his help with the identification of this source.]

[21] Wilhelm Hauff: Wilhelm Hauff's sämmtliche Schriften. W. Hauff's Leben von Gustav Schwab. Gedichte. Stuttgart: Fr. Brodhag 1830, page 88.

[22] *Op. cit* Steinitz, (1997), page 481.

clichés and traditions. Three of the nine pieces make use of the same text, entitled 'Die Argonnenmühle' or 'Die alte Mühle im Argonnenwald' (The old mill in the forest of Argonne); another song begins with the line 'Der Wald. Wie traut klingt' (The forest: How familiar sounds…). The forest is one of the most important locales of German romantic poetry. For a German of the 19th and early 20th century (and even of today), it was a place heavily loaded with associations and symbolic traditions - as well as the mill in the wood and the beautiful maid living in the forest.[23]

The preference for the battlefield in the forest of Argonne can also be seen in another popular media: the picture postcard (see figure 11.1).

Figure 11.1 Lyrics of 'Argonnerwald Lied'

The picture postcard archive at the University of Osnabrück, collected by Sabine Giesbrecht, has two cards with the full text of 'Argonnerwald, um Mitternacht', both illustrated by a picture showing a solitary soldier in a forest at night.[24] The romantic association of the forest as a place of love is proved by a series of cards published by the bookshop of the fifth German army around 1917 with the title 'Ein Argonnentraum' (A dream of Argonne). The cards show young girls in a wood, two dressed

---

[23] For the importance of the forest as topos of German poetry and music see, Jung-Kaiser, U. (ed.). (2008). 'Der Wald als romantischer Topos'. 5. Interdisziplinäres Symposium der Hochschule für Musik und Darstellende Kunst Frankfurt am Main 2007. Bern: Peter Lang.
[24] See images of the postcards at bildpostkarten.uni-osnabrueck.de/displayimage.php?album=search&cat=0&pos=1 and bildpostkarten.uni-osnabrueck.de/displayimage.php?album=search&cat=0&pos=2.

in rustic dresses, one in a rather erotic gown, holding flowers in their hands.[25]

Modern warfare and music

The development of weapons of mass destruction as machine guns and - later in the war - gas changed the strategies of warfare deeply and lastingly. Music production reveals that the idea of war in the public consciousness remained 'traditional', particularly in the first years of the war. Songs, published between 1914 and 1918 retain the idea of a heroic fight man against man on the battlefield, fighting with swords and on horseback.[26] To find out about the influence of the reality at the front on music production I searched the Hofmeister catalogues for the second group of keywords.

The search for the keyword 'Schützengraben' (i.e. trench) resulted in 22 entries having the word in their title or containing a piece with the word in its title. Five of these prints are collections with titles like 'Zwölf heitere Lieder zur Laute aus dem Schützengraben' (Twelve funny songs from the trenches).[27] 16 of these 24 publications appeared in 1915. In 1916 I found only three music prints - including one collection of three instrumental marches dedicated to the heroes of the trenches.[28] In 1917 and 1918 only two publications appeared each year - two of these were reprints of music published already in 1915.[29] Hence, in 1915 fighting in trenches was a novelty and producers of music could suppose that it was attractive to German citizens. The trench could be stylized to a place of the funny and the sentimental aspects of a soldier's life. Songs are about soldiers' hair growing ever so long, or about the grey wool they wear on their feet. They are about writing letters and sentimental moods.[30] However, it is obvious that the more the horrors of the war in

---

[25] bildpostkarten.uni-osnabrueck.de/displayimage.php?album=search&cat=0&pos=5, bildpostkarten.uni-osnabrueck.de/displayimage.php?album=search&cat=0&pos=6 and bildpostkarten.uni-osnabrueck.de/displayimage.php?album=search&cat=0&pos=8.
[26] Eckhard J. (2017). Über alles. Zur Kriegstauglichkeit von Liedern, in Frick, W. and Schnitzler, G. (eds.). *Der Erste Weltkrieg im Spiegel der Künste*. Freiburg: Rombach, pages 299-334, see page 308.
[27] *Hofmeisters Musikalisch-literarischer Monatsbericht*, 87. 1915, no. 8, page 123.
[28] *Hofmeisters Musikalisch-literarischer Monatsbericht*, 88. 1916, no. 4/5, page 48, page 63; no. 8, page 114.
[29] *Hofmeisters Musikalisch-literarischer Monatsbericht*, 1917, no. 4, page 77; no. 6, page 117; 1918, no. 2/3, page 33; no., 6, page 65.
[30] *Hofmeisters Musikalisch-literarischer Monatsbericht*, 87. 1915, no. 3, page 51, 53; no. 2, page 21.

the trenches became known, the less it was a topic a publisher could hope to sell.

Newly invented weapons turned the fights into a form of industrialised slaughter. The most effective and cruel weapons, however, never made it into music: no piece listed in the Hofmeister catalogues mentions toxic gas in its title. No wonder, the use of toxic gas is impossible to be romanticised as heroic warfare or as a glorious achievement of German engineering. The machine gun is mentioned only once in the title of a scene for a solo singer by Julius Jehring 'Knallmaxe von der Maschinengewehr-Abteilung' (Max the banger

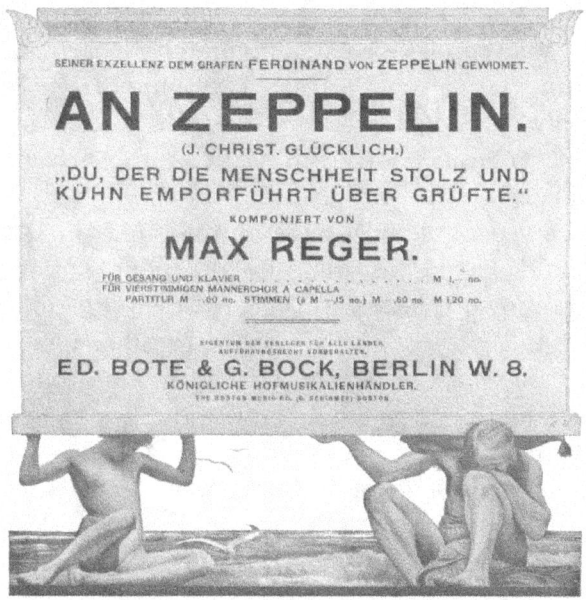

Figure 11.2 Cover page of 'An Zeppelin'

from the machine gun detachment) in 1916.[31] Composers rather celebrated superlative weapons like e.g. the largest gun of the German artillery, the calibre 42cm cannon produced by Krupp in Essen and affectionately called 'Dicke Bertha' (fat Bertha) or 'Brummer' (buzzer) by soldiers and the German public. For some time at the beginning of the war, propaganda used the Dicke Bertha as a symbol for the strength and the technological superiority of the German forces. In music, the peak was in 1915. I found four entries of titles celebrating the Dicke

---

[31] *Hofmeisters Musikalisch-literarischer Monatsbericht*, 88. 1916, no. 2, page 26.

Bertha in 1914, three in 1916, none in 1917 and 1918 but 29 in 1915.[32] The same is true for another high-tech weapon that was rather a success of the propaganda war than an effective weapon: The Zeppelin is mentioned in four entries in 1914, five in 1915 and one in 1917, but in 24 in 1915. Even Max Reger contributed a song to honour the famous engineer Count Ferdinand von Zeppelin: 'An Zeppelin: 'Du, der die Menschheit stolz und kühn' (To Zeppelin: You, who mankind proud and brave).[33]

Other high-tech weapons grew in importance for music production as the war went on. Submarines are the topic of one entry in 1914, four in 1915, two in 1917 and three in 1918, but 13 in 1916. These 13 entries comprise four different songs; eight are arrangements and reissues of W. Vahrenhold's song and march 'Unsere U-Bootsleute. 'Schwer geht und donnernd die See" that must have been quite a success from July to September that year.[34] It came out only a few months after the intensification of the submarine war by the German admiralty from late February onwards.

Airplanes[35] gained a role as a topic in music only in 1915 when the Hofmeister catalogue has 13 entries mentioning this symbol of technological progress. The figures decrease in the following years (1916: 8; 1917: 4; 1918: 5), but compared to other types of weapons airplanes, and their pilots remain present in music production. In the German army tanks never gained the importance they had for the British and French troops. This may explain the fact that the Hofmeister catalogues list no piece of music with the words 'Tank' or 'Panzer' in its title.

Emotions

Popular media does not only sell positive feelings. Emotions like sadness and mourning and the feelings of loneliness and homesickness are all part of the repertoire of music. One might presume that the battles of 1916 by Verdun and at the Somme with many hundreds of thousands

---

[32] For German picture postcards illustrating songs about the Dicke Bertha, see Giesbrecht, S. (2014). *Musik und Propaganda. Der Erste Weltkrieg im Spiegel deutscher Bildpostkarten*. Osnabrück: epOs, pages 137-141.
[33] *Hofmeisters Musikalisch-literarischer Monatsbericht*, 87. 1915, no. 2, page 27.
[34] *Hofmeisters Musikalisch-literarischer Monatsbericht*, 88. 1916, no. 7, page 63; no. 8, page 106; no. 9, pages 116, 120, 122, 123, 130.
[35] I searched for the following terms: 'Flug-', 'Flugzeug', 'Flieger', 'Taube' (i.e. 'Rumpler Taube', a type of planes that was used during the first years of the war).

of soldiers killed, wounded or missing led to a significant change in music production. To prove my hypothesis, I searched the Hofmeister catalogues, not for single terms but larger semantic fields. My first

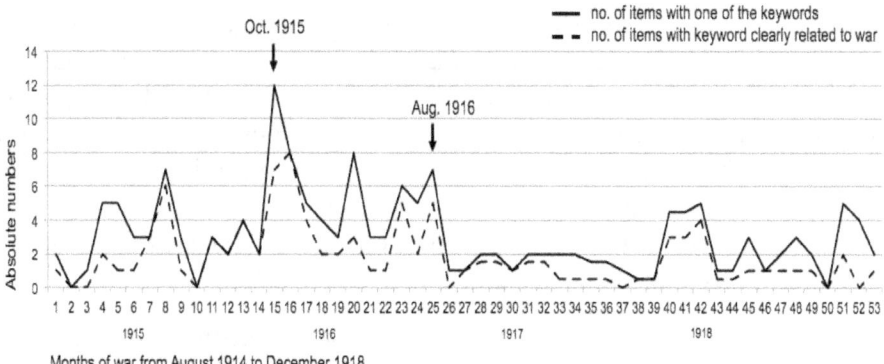

Figure 11.3 Number of entries touching the topic of grave (absolute numbers)

semantic field comprises words from the context of graves and graveyards: 'Grab', 'Gräber', 'Friedhof', (Grab-) 'Hügel', 'Erde' (= Grab), 'Grund' (= Grab), 'Leichenfeld' (graves, church yard, hill, earth, ground and burial field). Like in all statistics in this chapter I counted entries in the catalogues and not compositions, i.e. different re-arrangements and reissues of the same piece are reckoned as separate items. It was assumed that reprints and re-arrangements are indicators of its success on the marked. This success, however, is of the same significance for the importance of a certain topic to the public as the occurrence of this topic in different pieces of music printed only once. During the wartime, the editors of the Hofmeister catalogues sometimes deviated from their regular, i.e. monthly frequency of publication in summing up the data of two months in one issue. In my statistics and the graphs shown below, I reckoned double issues by splitting the numbers of hits into halves and allotting them to two months.[36]

My search through the months of the war from August 1914 to December 1918 resulted in the figures of entries with one of these words from the semantic field of grave in their title (see figures 11.3. to 11.7). The continuous line shows the number of all entries having one of my

---

[36] Double issues appeared in April/May and November/December 1916, in February/March, April/May, June/July, September/October and November/December 1917 and in February/March 1918.

keywords in their title; the broken line registers those songs among them that are clearly and recognisably related to the war.

The 'grave' has always been a locale for sentimental songs and to write music for burials has always been a business for composers. The topic, therefore, was not new, but it changed its emphasis during the war. We can see that the continuous and the broken lines have nearly identical trends in most months. Most songs are about soldiers' graves. In figure 11.3 we can make out a distinct block of songs between October 1915 (month no. 15) and August 1916 (month no. 25). From September 1916 onwards, the grave loses its importance as an emotional symbol in the titles of published music - except for a smaller peak from November 1917 to January 1918 (40-43).

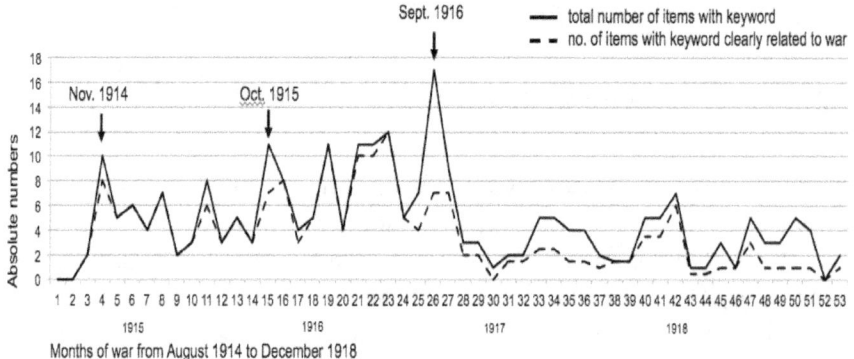

Figure 11.4 Number of entries touching the topic of death (total and related to war)

To support the results, a second semantic field search was conducted. This time the search looked for words in the context of death: 'Tod', 'tot', 'Schnitter', 'sterben', 'starb', 'gestorben', (ge-) 'fallen', 'fiel' (death, dead, reaper, to die, died, has died, fallen, fell). In figure 11.4 the count includes the most popular song about a dead soldier until today: 'Ich hatt' einen Kameraden'. The following diagram shows the numbers of pieces of music with one of these words in their titles for every month of the war. I differentiated total numbers and numbers of items clearly related to war (broken line).

The general tendency in figure 11.4 is pretty much the same as in figure 11.3 The topic of death is well represented in the music production of the first half of the war. It had a first peak already early in November 1914 (no. 4), a second one in October 1915 (no. 15) and its absolute peak with 17 items in September 1916. After this, the graph falls and remains at a low level until the end of the war. The peaks in the autumns of each year might be explained by the protestant feast of Totensonntag (Sunday in commemoration of the dead), which traditionally is celebrated late in November, and with the Catholic feast of Allerseelen (All soul's Day) celebrated on the 2nd of November. Obviously, music production anticipated the needs of their customers for the celebration of these feasts. Indeed, many compositions in September 1916 are explicitly dedicated to these feasts in their title with the phrase 'Zum Totenfest' (for the feast of the dead). We can see the fourth peak, although much smaller late in 1917. In November 1918,

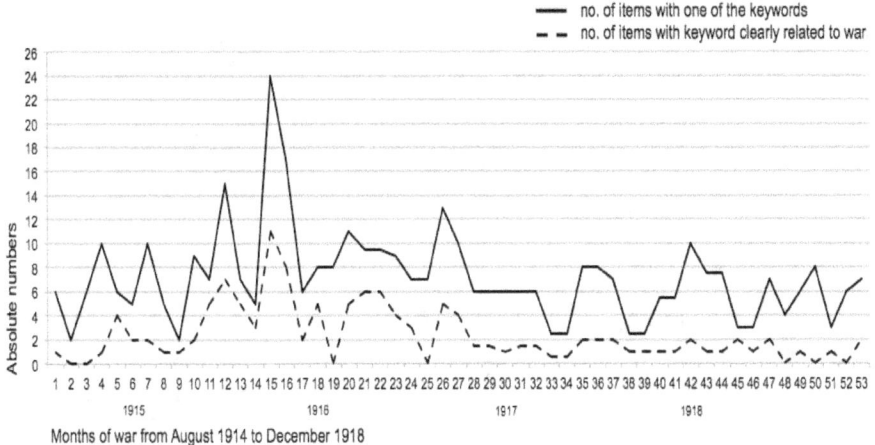

Figure 11.5 Number of entries touching the topic of mourning (absolute numbers)

however, there is no song on death at all in the Hofmeister catalogue. During the first two years, the lines for total numbers and war-related items have an almost identical course. Figure 11.5 shows that from August 1916 onwards the number of pieces related to the war is considerably smaller than the total for most months.

On a closer look at the word field of death, we notice that one fifth, i.e. 53 out of 262 pieces are based on the same five texts, all are arrangements or settings of older lyrics. They demonstrate how much the idea of war and a soldier's fate was based on much older traditions. The best known of these 'hits' until today is 'Der gute Kamerad' (The good comrade), written in 1809 by Ludwig Uhland and composed by Friedrich Silcher. Hofmeister lists 13 arrangements of this song between

January 1915 and January 1918. Two more songs of these five were made popular through Achim von Arnim's collection 'Des Knaben Wunderhorn', first published between 1805 and 1808: 'Kein selger Tod ist in der Welt, / Als wer vorm Feind erschlagen' (There is no happier death than being killed by the enemy) was used in 13 publications that appeared during the war. Besides Friedrich Silchers well-known setting we find nine other versions in the Hofmeister catalogues.

The second text from the Wunderhorn-Lieder is 'Es ist ein Schnitter, heißt der Tod' (There is a reaper, called death), also composed by Silcher and published in nine versions between 1914 and 18. The last two songs are from the mid 19th century: Friedrich von Bodenstedt's

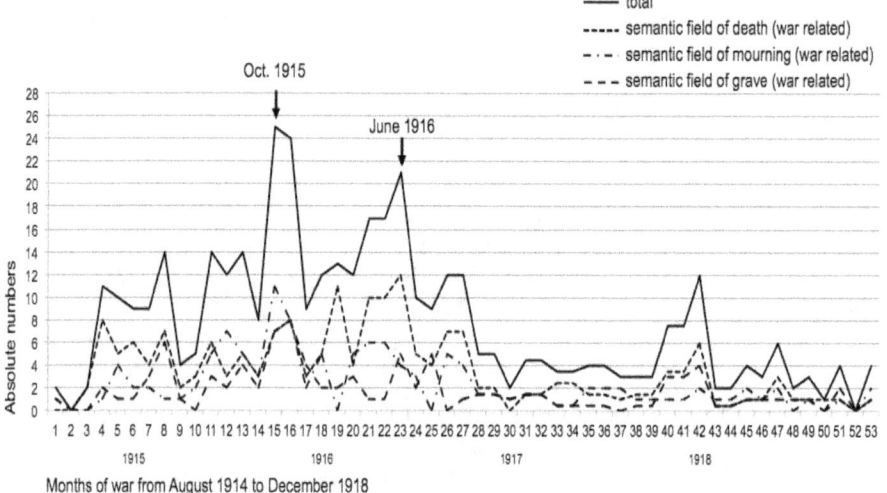

Figure 11.6 Total of entries on death, mourning (war related) and grave (war related)

'Des Kriegers Sterbelied' (Warrior's death song), first published with music by Heinrich Marschner in 1855[37] and listed in 10 versions during the First World War and Detlev von Liliencron's 'Tod in Aehren' (Death in a cornfield), published as a poem in 1883[38] and set to music in eight versions between November 1914 and October 1916 (see figure 11.6). 'Tod in Aehren' tells of a wounded soldier who lies in a cornfield. His comrades do not find him, and it takes him two days to die. It is

---

[37] *Hofmeisters Musikalisch-literarischer Monatsbericht*, 1855, no. 6, page 782.
[38] von Liliencron, D. (1883). *Adjutantenritte*. Leipzig, page 14.

very obvious why these lyrics were no longer set to music in the second half of the war.

A third search I undertook was on the semantic field of mourning: 'Trauer(n)', 'Leid(en)', 'Schmerz', 'Pein', 'Gram', 'Träne(n)', 'Klage', 'Weine(n)' (mourning, suffering, pain, torment, grief, tears, lamenting, crying).

The pain of lovers, their tears and their sadness are a standard fare of music. In figure 11.7 the continuous line of my graph that represents the total figures of songs of mourning develops rather horizontal. There are no significant changes in numbers, except one significant peak with a doubling of numbers from October to November 1915 (months no. 15 and 16). The broken line represents all those titles that make clear that the song is about mourning as a result of the war. The amplitude of this graph is even flatter and more linear. Particularly at the end of the war, the songs on war-related mourning are greatly outnumbered by those on other kinds of sadness.

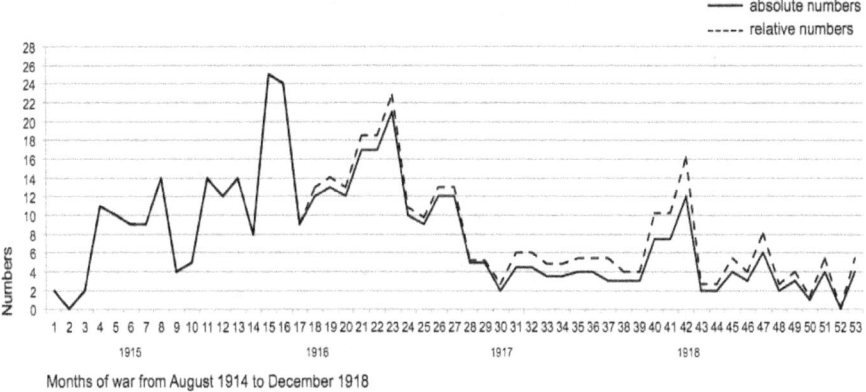

Figure 11.7 Relative and absolute numbers of entries on mourning, death and graves

The three semantic fields of grave, death and mourning may well be merged into one large category of death and suffering. In figure 11.7 I added up all three statistics: the war related numbers of published music on death (broken line) on mourning (dotted broken line) and on graves (broken line).

Figures 11.3 to 11.7 show the absolute numbers of entries. The numbers of titles produced and listed in the Hofmeister catalogues, however, decrease significantly during the war. To make sure that my interpretation is not misleading, I tested my statistics in setting my results in relation to the decrease in length of the Hofmeister lists. With the outbreak of the war, the volume of the catalogues fell from 284 pages in 1913 to 243 pages in 1914, a decline of nearly 17 % percent that was greatly caused by the last five months of the year when only 32,5% percent of the annual production was published. Figures remained stable from August 1914 to December 1915. In 1916 the catalogues documented a decrease of 8% percent and in 1917 of 26.5% percent. The numbers of 1918 remain on this low level. To set my numbers in relation to this decrease, I took the numbers of 1914 and 1915 as 100% percent and added 8% percent to the numbers of 1916 and 26.5% percent to the numbers of 1917 and 1918.

We can see in figure 11.7 that two-thirds of all items of my three semantic fields of mourning, death and grave were produced in the first half of the war up to July 1916 (i.e. 274 titles out of 410). We find clear peaks in October and November 1915 (nos. 15, 16), in June 1916 (no. 23) and in September and October 1916 (no. 26, 27). The peaks frame the months of the battle of Verdun and mark the beginning of the battle

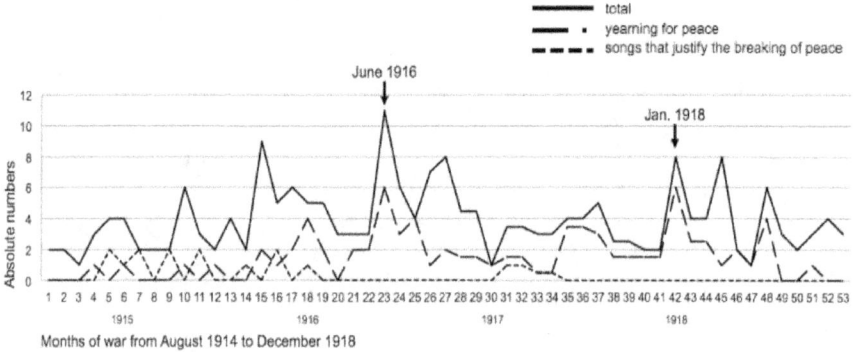

Figure 11.8 Entries with the keyword Frieden (peace)

at the Somme in July 1916. It seems that in autumn 1915 it became clear that the war would cost high casualties. The music industry prepared to sell commemorative music for the celebration of All Soul's Day and the protestant Totensonntag. When the battle of Verdun started in February 1916, the music market was well prepared, and it reacted to the news from the front until the middle of the year, when death came so close to most Germany families that music ceased to express the war. The peak from November 1917 to January 1918 is hard to explain. It might be a seasonal effect caused by the feasts of All Souls and 'Totensonntag'.

Music works well as an emotional comment on reality, making fun of its hardships or turning them into a sentimental or melancholic mood. However, it should not come up too close to reality - particularly if it wants to sell on the market. In the face of the hundred of thousands of deaths in the second half of the war, death, graves and mourning became so real for nearly everyone in Germany that music was in danger to lose its function as the key to another world, to a world that is needed as relief from and not as a reminder of the grim truths of everyday life. When the battle of the Somme was at its height, music production made its peace with war and withdrew to more neutral topics.

Figure 11.8 shows the absolute numbers of pieces with the word 'Frieden' (peace) in their title. The continuous line documents the total of these entries in the Hofmeister catalogues. For a more differentiated picture of the situation, I specify titles, which try to justify Germany and Austria as peace-loving nations that were forced into the war by their enemies (dotted line). Except for a little peak from February to May 1917 we can see, that there are no songs trying to justify the breaking of peace from January 1916 onwards. The small peak in 1917 is a reaction to the death of the Austrian emperor Franz Josef I in November 1916, who was commemorated in three songs as 'Friedenskaiser' (emperor of peace).

The broken line counts all titles that clearly express a desire for peace. We can see that the numbers of these songs grow from January 1916 (no. 18) onwards. When the battle of Verdun started in February this year, the German public, we can presume, was already yearning for peace, a feeling that was expressed even stronger in June 1916 - shortly before the outbreak of the battle of the Somme. In January 1918 we can see another peak of the broken line that represents the number of songs that express a yearning for peace parallel to various initiatives to reach peace in the second half of 1917 beginning with the peace resolution of the German Reichstag on 19th July and the Popes initiative a month later.[39] Peaks are reached in January and April 1918 parallel to the massive strikes of up to a million workers and the peace negotiations of the new Bolshevik government of Russia and the Central Powers that

---

[39] Hoff, H. (2014). 'Friedensinitiativen', in Hirschfeld, G., Krumeich, G. and Renz, I. (eds). *Enzyklopädie Erster Weltkrieg*. Paderborn: Ferdinand Schöningh, page 511.

ended with the peace treaty of Brest-Litovsk on 3rd March 1918.[40] The chart shows only the absolute figures. If we consider that the production of music was reduced by a fourth in 1917 and 1918 compared to the first months of the war, we can claim that the desire for peace made itself increasingly felt from the beginning of 1916 onwards. How this peace was supposed to be reached my sources do not tell. What we can see is that a victorious end of the war lost its importance as a topic in music production. My search for entries with the word 'Sieg' (victory)

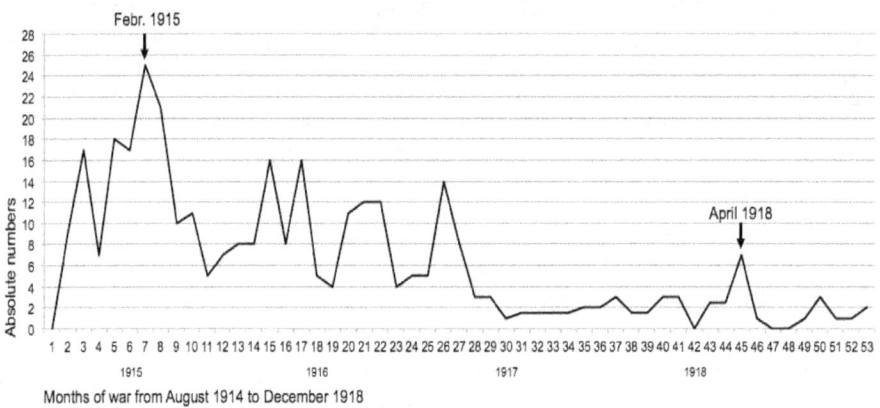

Figure 11.9 Entries with the keyword 'Sieg' (victory)

shows an early peak of 25 items in February 2015, a gradual decline until September 1916 and a massive fall after this date. The euphoria about the outbreak of war in August 1914, the so-called 'Augusterlebnis' (August experience) that had swept the media during the first months of the war,[41] led to a production of many compositions on the topic of victory (see figure 11.9). This euphoria, however, was only short-lived. During the last two years of the war, the term hardly plays a role in the titles of newly published songs - except a little peak of seven entries in April 1918, a month after the peace treaty of Brest-Litovsk and the beginning of the last great offensive at the Western front on 21st March 1918. My sources seem to support the impression historians have won

---

[40] Bruendel, S. (2014).'Ideologien: Mobilmachungen und Desillusionierungen', in, Werber, N., Kaufmann, S. and Koch, L. (eds). *Kulturwissenschaftliches Handbuch*. Stuttgart: Metzler'sche Verlagsbuchhandlung, pages 280-310, page 308.

[41] Verhey, J. (2000). *Der Geist von 1914 und die Erfindung der Volksgemeinschaft*. Hamburg: Verlag; Kruse, W. (1991). 'Die Kriegsbegeisterung im Deutschen Reich zu Beginn des Ersten Weltkrieges. Entstehungszusammenhänge, Grenzen und ideologische Strukturen', in van der Linden, M. and Gottfried Mergne (eds.). *Kriegsbegeisterung und mentale Kriegsvorbereitung*. Berlin: Duncker & Hamblot, pages 73-88.

from the analysis of ego-documents that the end of the fighting in the east meant a boost to a renewed but short-lived hope for a victorious end of the war.[42]

Conclusion

Music production is no easy source for history. Its reactions to events are selective and indirect. We should, therefore, be cautious to interpret the above statistics in too much detail: An incident in history must not necessarily affect the publication of songs and instrumental music. The success of a composition is not dependent on its title and lyrics alone but also on the music. Moreover, the number of items in some cases is so small that it cannot be ruled out that chance has had its hand in some less distinctive trends of my graphs. One result of my study, however, is very clear: The summer of 1916 was a decisive moment for the feelings and the attitudes of the German population towards the war. Sometime around the end of the battle of Verdun and the beginning of the battle at the Somme it must have dawned upon the producer's und publishers of music in Germany and Austria that compositions relating to the war neither in a positive nor in a sentimental way were in demand any longer. The machinery of war ceased to be a novelty and disappeared from the titles of pieces of music. The realities of war, death, suffering and mourning had reached every family and every household. Who wants to sing songs of heroic death and heroes' graves on the battlefield, if he or she is mourning a father, a brother or a husband? Who wants to buy songs on the funny side of soldiers' life, if he or she knows, how wretched the situation in the trenches is? Moreover, what is heroic about death if death becomes normality? The musical theatre had turned its productions from propaganda back to diversion already in 1915.[43] In summer 1916 the rest of the music business followed.

---

[42] Bruendel, S. (2014). *Zeitenwende 1914: Künstler, Dichter und Denker im Ersten Weltkrieg*. München: Herbig, page 308.
[43] *Op. cit.* Helms, (2017). 'Der Soldate, der Soldate', pages 76-78.

Chapter 12

Englishness and the 'Other'. Mata Hari and Edith Cavell[1] On Celluloid

Rosie White
Northumbria University

Introduction

There is a longstanding connection between Englishness and the figure of the (good) spy. Britain formally established the first national intelligence agency in 1909, and their activities have inspired (and been influenced by) a number of iconic fictional spies, from John Buchan's 'Richard Hannay' to Ian Fleming's 'Bond'.[2] While these male fictions usefully foreground the link between Britishness and the secret service, they tend to overshadow the position of actual women spies. Women have played a central role in espionage from the establishment of spying as a profession. Proctor (2003), in her account of the founding of British intelligence during WWI, cites the central role of women in MI5,

[a]s clerks, supervisors, report writers, translators, printers, searchers, messengers, and historians, women made it possible for a tiny spy-tracking office created in 1909 to become a massive information clearinghouse by the end of the war.[3]

---

[1] A version of this chapter was originally published in Hart, C. (2008). *Heroines and Heroes. Symbolism, Embodiment, Narratives & Identities*. Kingswinford: Midrash. Pages 1-14.
[2] Knightly, P. (2003). *The Second Oldest Profession: spies and spying in the Twentieth Century*. London: Pimlico.
[3] Proctor, T. M. (2003). *Female Intelligence: women and espionage in the First World War*. New York: New York University Press, page 53.

More recently Dame Stella Rimington became the first woman Director General of MI5 in 1992, having worked her way through all areas of the secret service. This is not to say that espionage is an equal opportunities profession; while most of MI5's staff is female, few women occupy senior positions.[4]

Although the fictional spy is more often characterised as male the illicit nature of espionage has strong links with pejorative Western ideologies of femininity - it is deceptive and seductive. Spying as an

Figure 12.1 Margaretha Zelle MacLeod, as Mata Hari. n.d

activity involves employing 'feminine' skills such as disguise and dissimulation, while spies are 'masculinised' as observers and agents. The spy is thus a hermaphrodite figure within popular culture, an unstable signifier, exposing contradictions inherent in dominant ideologies of gender, race and sexuality. Spies in fiction, if not in fact, inevitably operate between legal and illegal spheres, between public and private spaces. The right female spy presents a complex problematic as she moves between public and private realms; this may be why women

---

[4] See, White, R. (2007). *Violent Femmes: Women as Spies in Popular Culture*, New York: Routledge for an extended treatment of this subject.

are more often depicted as honey-traps and *femmes fatales* in mythologies and fictions about espionage.

My discussion, therefore, begins with the consummate image of the (bad) female spy, Mata Hari, whose name has entered the language as an allegory of seduction and betrayal. As an alleged spy shot by the French during the First World War, Mata Hari represents not only the apogee of feminine espionage but also the epitome of an Orientalised other (Said, 1978).[5] Edith Cavell has come to represent all that Mata Hari is not. Cavell's Englishness is to the fore in most accounts of her life; her identity as an English woman specifically cast regarding appropriate femininity, 'pure' whiteness and middle-class respectability. This representation of the good woman spy continued to resonate during and after the Second World War in cinematic accounts of Cavell and the women of the SOE (Special Operations Executive).

Mata Hari

Mata Hari was the fictional persona created by a middle-class Dutch woman, Margaretha Zelle MacLeod (1876-1917)[6]. Margaretha reinvented herself as an exotic dancer of misty Javanese origins, loosely based on her colonial experience in the Dutch East Indies. Through her reincarnation as Mata Hari, Margaretha Zelle MacLeod crossed boundaries of race, class and sexuality, leaving behind her white femininity and her middle-class respectability. At the height of her fame, Mata Hari was the toast of Europe, but as the First World War began she was trapped in Berlin and struggled to return to the city of her success, Paris. It was almost inevitable that she would be suspected of espionage. Mata Hari's persona made her culpable in terms of a hysterical response to fears of invasion and the corruption of French national identity. She was suspect as a foreigner, as a stage performer and as a woman whose sexuality was neither proper nor respectable. Mata Hari's affairs and friendships with a variety of men in the forces of various armies, with bankers and with politicians - in fact, her liaisons with men of any description in wartime, together with her public image, all constituted evidence of her 'guilt'. At worst, Margaretha Zelle

---

[5] Said, E.W. (1978). *Orientalism*. London: Routledge & Kegan Paul.
[6] The idea of Mata Hari has throughout the 20th and into the 21st century continued to attract attention in non-fiction as well as fiction. See, for example, Craig, M. W. (2017). *A Tangled Web: Mata Hari: Dancer, Courtesan, Spy*. The History Press, and Arbuckle, A. (May 2016). 'The Dramatic Tale of Mata Hari Dancer, courtesan, scapegoat, spy?' *Retronaught*.

MacLeod was an opportunist, but under the fearful scrutiny of her prosecuting council, she came to represent all that France was fighting against. Her *femme fatale* image was not the least of this. Unwittingly, Margaretha Zelle MacLeod had come to represent the most feared and desired aspects of the modern world in the person of the modern woman, and for this reason, she was executed.

Arrested in her hotel room on 13th February 1917, Mata Hari was prosecuted by Captain Pierre Bouchardon, acting on information provided by Georges Ladoux, whom she knew as her contact in the *Deuxième Bureau*, French military intelligence. Ladoux had recruited Mata Hari as an agent on first meeting her in August 1916. She had sought Ladoux's help in getting a travel pass to visit her lover and in the course of the meeting he suggested that she could work for French interests, despite his alleged suspicion that she was a German agent.[7] The assignments Mata Hari conducted between this meeting and her arrest were unsuccessful and indiscreet. Margaretha had little idea of how to go about being a spy, beyond perhaps some dramatic images rendered in popular fiction and theatre of the time.[8] As with Margarethe's performances onstage as Mata Hari, it was the image of the spy that she attempted to reproduce, not a professional identity that was secure or authentically grounded in training. Ladoux was complicit in this, as from the outset of their relationship he insisted on seeing her as a seductive *femme fatale* with the morals of a cat. Julie Wheelwright (1992) argues that Laudoux used the Mata Hari case to justify his position as head of French counter-intelligence during the war, and Bouchardon was a willing aide in this, regarding Mata Hari as a 'savage' and a 'negress'. In her abject state as an alleged traitor and imprisoned woman, Bouchardon projected onto Mata Hari 'the underside of the racist 'Oriental fantasy'.[9] In this manner, the 'evil' female spy in the first half of the twentieth century stood for all the fears modernity inspires. The female spy, as *femme fatale*, is thus according to Doane (1991) "not the subject of feminism, but a symptom of male fears about feminism."[10] This exotic and deadly figure is reproduced in European and North American media and has come to represent the

---

[7] Wheelwright, J. (1992). *The Fatal Lover: Mata Hari and the myth of women in espionage*. London: Collins and Brown, pages 51-52.
[8] *Ibid.* Wheelwright, (1992), pages 50-64.
[9] *Ibid.* Page 77.
[10] Doane, M. A. (1991). *Femmes Fatales: feminism, film theory, psychoanalysis*. London: Routledge, pages 2-3.

consummate 'other', in the form of atavistic femininity, deviant sexuality and decadent orientalism.

Margaretha Geertruida 'Margreet' MacLeod was executed by firing squad on the 15th October, 1917.

Mata Hari is complemented by a number of representations following her death that has continued to the present day. The film, fiction, biographical and photographic representations of Margaretha execution built upon the fairy extensive newspaper reporting of her behaviour while she was alive.

Mata Hari is complemented by a number of representations during and after the Second World War, where women spies working for the Allies are depicted as pure, white and feminine, particularly in films such as *Nurse Edith Cavell* (dir. Herbert Wilcox, 1939, UK). In the early twentieth century, the female spy thus came to represent modern femininity that was either eroticised (and demonised) as exotic or fetishised (and exalted) as the epitome of 'pure' English womanhood, often for a potential American audience.[11]

Edith Cavell

While Mata Hari embodied the female spy as *femme fatale*, she was complemented by the figure of Edith Cavell. The mythologies around Cavell established the role of the 'good' female spy, primarily because she worked for the right side, but also because she was understood as a secular saint and martyr through her role as a nurse rather than as a spy. Despite their distinct differences within the popular imagination, both Mata Hari and Edith Cavell were inevitably mired in the contradictory discourses surrounding women and war work during World War One.

Sharon Ouditt (1994) describes the British Voluntary Aid Detachment as providing a place in which middle-class English women could take an active role in war work; work which was entirely understood as being a natural extension of the feminine predilection for nurture: "[t]his form of public recognition was dependent on a feminine piety that implied deference to masculinity, militarism and the

---

[11] See, Bade, P. (1997). *Femme Fatale: Images of Evil and Fascinating Women*, New York: Mayflower Books and White, R. (2007). *Violent Femmes: Women as spies in popular culture*, New York: Routledge.

patriarchal nation-state."[12] Women who took on caring roles during the war were thus understood within the terms of conventional bourgeois femininity. Women who stepped outside such roles were regarded with some horror. The Women's Army Auxiliary Corps of the British Army, for example, was greeted upon establishment in 1917, by letters to the papers decrying the unnaturally militaristic tendencies of its officers. Such evident discomfort was riddled with overt or implicit concerns about the connections between any change in women's roles and the issue of the franchise - a debate that had been efficiently halted in many quarters at the outbreak of war - and by the not unconnected question of deviant sexuality. The connection, according to Gould (1987) made before the war between feminism and lesbianism continued to have its effect on any discussion of women's role in the forces:

> [w]omen who displayed 'symptoms' of lesbianism (an inclination to dress up in masculine clothes, to drill, and to shoot) were considered not only distasteful but abnormal and in need of medical help. Any attacks on them were thus fully justified. Women in military organisations were a target for those who held such views, and it was not uncommon during the First World War for women who joined the military services to be regarded as peculiar at least, if not downright immoral.[13]

Yet women had been playing an active role in intelligence long before the war began and became vital during the First World War – indeed, their diligent and poorly paid work kept the British intelligence services going.[14] In roles ranging from the Girl Guides employed as messengers in MI5, to the employment of more than 3,500 women by MI9, the Postal Censorship Branch, women rapidly became central to the daily functioning of British intelligence services.[15] Even here, however, there was ambivalence about women's role in the services. While women offered a plentiful, cheap and obedient workforce, according to Proctor, (2003)[16] the organisations which employed them

---

[12] Ouditt, S. (1994). *Fighting forces, Writing Women: Identity and ideology in the First World War.* London: Routledge, page 7.
[13] Gould, J. (1987). 'Women's Military Services in First World War Britain'. In Higonnet, M. R., Jenson, J., Michel, S. and Weitz, M. C. (eds.), *Behind The Lines: gender and the two world wars.* New Haven and London: Yale University Press, page 121.
[14] *Op. cit.* Proctor, (2003), page 27.
[15] *Ibid.* Pages 53-73.
[16] *Ibid.* Page 30.

began to develop a gendered understanding of agents in the field as opposed to intelligence gathering: "[e]spionage was referred to as domestic, hidden, and sneaky - in other words, it was feminine. Intelligence, on the other hand, was professional, bureaucratic, and officially secret - or masculine in its endeavours." This was also an attempt to draw a moral distinction between the imagined enemy agents who threatened Britain from within before and during World War One, and the developing secret services employed by the British government. The artificial distinction between feminine and masculine roles bears no relation to the numbers of women employed within the bureaucracy of intelligence gathering.

The imaginary distinction between the bad, feminine spy and the good, masculine intelligence officer is visible in the opposing figures of Mata Hari and Edith Cavell. Like Margaretha Zelle MacLeod, Edith Cavell's public image owed much to popular mythology. In their examination of women spies in the fiction of the First World War Craig and Cadogan (1981) note that, like Mata Hari, Edith Cavell "seems to be as much the end result of late Victorian and Edwardian fictional projections as an influence on the espionage stories that came after her."[17] Both women are thus framed by discourses of femininity that preceded and succeeded them. During the First World War, women played key roles not only in the British intelligence services but also in the intelligence networks in occupied countries such as Belgium. The *La Dame Blanche* network in Belgium was a militarised espionage group for both men and women - albeit dropping the term 'spy' in favour of 'agent' or 'soldier'.[18] This was one instance where the organisation was remarkably egalitarian, basing its rankings on service to *La Dame Blanche* rather than an individual's age, class or gender, and often including whole families within its ranks. As Proctor (2003) notes, "*La Dame Blanche* was a chance to join men on an equal footing in wartime service."[19] After the war, however, the women of *La Dame Blanche* were largely forgotten, in part because of the fluctuating definitions of wartime activities, 'soldiers' and the home front. Proctor (2003) asserts that for the women of *La Dame Blanche* their homes were in occupied territory, so that the distinction between the battlefield and the domestic arena was not absolute: "[t]he women of *La Dame Blanche* had no

---

[17] Craig, P. and Cadogan, M. (1981). *The Lady Investigates: Women detectives and spies in fiction*. London: Victor Gollancz, page 54.
[18] *Op. cit.* Proctor, (2003), pages 78-79.
[19] *Ibid.* Pages 80-98.

concept of a home front because their own homes became fronts when their nations were occupied." Once the war was over such women were rapidly erased from public memory in favour of more sensational images of female spies - namely Mata Hari and Edith Cavell. In this manner, the contradictions made visible in wartime femininity were effaced, as was the lack of distinction between the battlefield and the domestic arena.

Cavell was a middle-class Englishwoman who grew up in East Anglia and trained as a nurse. In 1907 she moved to Brussels to establish a training school for nurses, having already worked as an instructor in Britain. She was forty-eight when war broke out in August 1914 - ten years older than Margaretha Zelle Macleod, and far more successful as an agent for the Allied resistance in occupied Belgium. As Proctor (2003)[20] notes she was not really a spy as such; Cavell's resistance work consisted in organising an escape network for Allied soldiers trapped in Belgium, rather than gathering information or passing on secrets. The humanitarian aspect of her work fits well with public perceptions of the nursing profession, so that when she was caught, arrested and imprisoned in August 1915, she was a martyr-in-waiting. Unlike Mata Hari, Edith Cavell freely admitted her role in hiding and transporting Allied soldiers out of Belgium. She was tried with thirty-five other prisoners, found guilty and executed on 12th October 1915. Philippe Baucq, a Belgian architect who also helped to plan and organise the escape routes, was executed with her. Comtesse Jean de Belleville, Louise Thuliez and Louis Severin had their death sentences commuted following appeals on their behalf.

The narrative and image of Cavell's life and death were immediately caught up in a propaganda war between Germany and the Allies. While the Germans sought to use Cavell's fate as a warning to other activists in occupied territories, the public outcry in several countries, particularly the United States and Canada, quickly produced a backlash from the Allies, which began the reconstruction of Cavell as a passive victim rather than an active agent.[21] Cavell's death inspired a range of patriotic images on postcards distributed as propaganda by the Allies; they present a marked contrast to the postcards that promoted the exotic image of Mata Hari.[22]

---

[20] *Ibid.* Pages 100-102.
[21] *Ibid.* Pages 102-103.
[22] See Hageman, P. and Kosanovich, J. (1999-2004b). 'Miss Edith Cavell'. ww1-propaganda-cards.com/miss_edith_cavell.html.

Cavell is almost exclusively depicted clothed in white and either nursing soldiers or lying supine as a monstrous German shoot her. A series of six cards published in Brussels in 1915 depicts her 'story' from 'Miss Cavell as a nurse' through to the memorial in Brussels, while the Italian artist Tito Corbella designed a more allegorical series which pits Cavell against 'Kultur' and the 'Kaiser'.[23] Cavell is described as a 'martyr' or 'victim' in the captions for such images, which merely serves to reiterate the visual message of her as passive, feminised and saintly. Set against the image of Mata Hari, Cavell was represented as Madonna in opposition to Margaretha's performance of the archetypal whore and *femme fatale*. One of Cavell's resistance colleagues endorsed such a binary understanding of the two women. Louise Thuliez (1992),[24] who escaped execution for life imprisonment, commented in her 1934 autobiography:

> [i]n trying to defend themselves the Germans have pushed their insolence so far as to compare Edith Cavell to Mata Hari. Edith Cavell had worked for her country, consecrating to this noble task all her career of faith and sacrifice. Mata Hari, thinking only of her personal charms, had sold herself to the highest bidder. While Edith Cavell, wept over the sufferings of her fellow-countrymen, at the bedside of the wounded men she was tending, Mata Hari in the luxury of palaces betrayed indiscriminately all who approached her. Which of these two women deserves to be called a 'spy'?

If nothing else this statement, written nearly two decades after the deaths of Cavell and Mata Hari, denotes the extent to which both women have entered the realm of mythology. They have exceeded the limits of memory and have been rewritten as types rather than individuals. While Mata Hari is the villainous traitor, *femme fatale* and spy, Cavell is the innocent patriot, feminine and pure.

Cavell Re-created on Celluloid

The implicit purity and innocence of Cavell's white garb in images contemporary with her death were also to the fore when her life was recreated on celluloid. Whereas Mata Hari was derogated by her

---

[23] *Ibid.*
[24] Louise Thuliez, cited in *Op. cit.* Wheelwright, (1992), page 120.

prosecutors as 'primitive' and 'savage', Cavell becomes whiter than white - representing femininity, which is symbolic of England's civilisation. The discourses, which surround both women, are written across stereotypes of gender and race. Regarding race, the figures of Cavell and Mata Hari are complicit with debates about racial purity and difference during the first half of the twentieth century. Rather than examining the work of women in the intelligence agencies on both sides, post-war accounts of women and espionage on the Allied front tended to ignore their activities as spies or to forget them altogether. As Proctor (2003) notes, "descriptions of spy-martyrs usually emphasised the moral character, generosity, patriotism, and naïve spirit of the women who died for their nations. Why are these women celebrated more than the female agents who survived the war without declaration or capture?"[25] The silent dead are more malleable fodder for mythologised understandings of femininity and race that do not readily challenge hierarchical binaries of gender and difference.

Such a clear understanding of Cavell is evident in *Nurse Edith Cavell* (Herbert Wilcox, 1939). Wilcox had already produced a silent version of the Cavell story; *Dawn* (1928), starring Sybil Thorndike, which was censored by Austen Chamberlain, then Foreign Minister of the Conservative Government, as likely to damage British relations with Germany, but exhibited with the approval of the London County Council.[26] The talking version of Cavell's story was no less controversial. Released as World War Two began, the patriotic iconography of Cavell's life was replayed for British and American audiences in this film; a reminder to the former of what was being fought for, and to the latter of what was at stake in the battle. The director/producer Herbert Wilcox (1967)[27] claimed in his autobiography that it was 'the first British-Hollywood co-production' but also that the film led to accusations of propaganda: "[t]here was a broadside of criticism alleging breach of the Neutrality Code, but *Nurse Cavell* weathered the storm and was accepted as a film of first-class entertainment." Indeed, its star (who became Wilcox's wife in 1943), Anna Neagle, was nominated for the best actress Oscar for her performance. While Wilcox and Neagle were not official propagandists, it is hard to miss the ideological thrust of their work. Herbert Wilcox

---

[25] *Op. cit.* Proctor, (2003), page 100.
[26] Wilcox, H. (1967). *Twenty-five Thousand Sunsets: The autobiography of Herbert Wilcox*. London: The Bodley Head, pages 73-74, and pages 79-83.
[27] *Ibid.* Page 124.

directed Neagle in 32 films, often presenting her in roles, which played upon her star persona as an emblem of English femininity, and frequently casting her in historical parts with national resonance, such as Queen Victoria, Florence Nightingale and Amy Johnson.[28] Contemporary critics such as Street (1997)[29] saw Neagle's Englishness "as much a part of Britain as Dover's white cliffs" and that appeal was to the fore in *Nurse Edith Cavell*:

> her screen roles [...] celebrated individual stoicism in the face of adversity as a means of communicating the overall liberal-conservative political ideology of the Wilcox-Neagle films. Neagle epitomised middle-class values of thrift, hard work, stoicism and feminine modesty. Just as the White Cliffs of Dover are associated with Britain's self-consciousness as an island, vulnerable to foreign invasion, Neagle also represented a resolutely British, non-European and white identity.

Questions of class and conflict are repressed in these films in favour of a mythologised English stoicism. This elision is evident in *Nurse Edith Cavell* where Neagle/Cavell mixes happily with the soldiers she rescues, most notably a chirpy cockney, and reminisces with one of the soldiers she is treating about cricket and Norwich. There are no apparent divisions between Neagle/Cavell as a middle-class woman and the working-class men she tends and commands.

In this biopic, Neagle as Cavell takes on a saintly aura, inspired to set up the escape route while reading the bible in her bed. Even captured, imprisoned and informed of her fate, Neagle/Cavell is a model of otherworldly calm, saying "I thank God for these few quiet weeks [...]. This time of rest has been the great mercy." At times Cavell's stoical calm appears almost trance-like as she floats through her scenes, dressed throughout in her nurse's uniform. Anna Neagle's performance in *Nurse Edith Cavell* reiterates her cinematic persona through costume, physical posture and acting style. Landy (1991), examining her performance in *Victoria the Great* (Herbert Wilcox, 1937), describes Neagle as a powerful figure contained by a style of acting which now appears dated:

---

[28] Dolan, J. (2000). "'They Flew Alone' and 'The Angel of the Air': crossings between respectability, nation and empire'. *Visual Culture in Britain*, 1(2), pages 25-41.
[29] Street, S. (1997). *British National Cinema*. London: Routledge, pages 124-126.

[t]he actress looks and behaves according to preconceptions and myths of 1930s female gentility. Her demeanour [sic], not unlike that of the other British female stars of the era, such as Deborah Kerr and Phyllis Calvert, is restrained. Her status is defined by rather stiff body movements, a walk that is measured, giving her the impression of gliding, and gestures and looks that are imperious. Her expensive costumes are fashionable but decorous, unlike the sexually provocative costumes of the 1940s Gainsborough melodramas. Her image is matronly. [...] The men in the film are dwarfed by her presence. As an actress and as a character, she monopolises the screen.[30]

While Edith Cavell is a different role to that of the monarch, Neagle's performance in *Nurse Edith Cavell* draws upon a similar range of reference. Both films, released 1937 and 1939, are good examples of the roles, which made Neagle a transatlantic star during the thirties, forties and fifties. The film foregrounds her role as a nurse, prefacing the narrative with a eulogy to Cavell's fortitude and that of her profession:

[t]his is a tale, based on fact, of heroic life and a conflict of loyalties, told in reverence and without bitterness. [...] Nursing is a dedication to mercy and healing. War is a dedication to brutal force. Neither admits the distinction of race or person. Each is the uncompromising foe of the other.

Thus, even in the opening titles, Cavell's role as an active agent of resistance in occupied territory is obscured in favour of a more passive representation of divine femininity. Rather than an individual, Cavell is made to represent an archetypal nurse-mother-virgin, and the narrative focuses almost entirely on her heroic actions. While *Nurse Edith Cavell* does show the escape route through Belgium as a group effort, the other women are merely supporting characters, often given comedic or pathetic roles. In this way, the film offers a depiction of strong women but curtails their radical potential by fitting each figure into stereotypes that are always already available. Their main function is to be displayed as victims of oppressive German military and thus to remind audiences of the moral distinction between the Allies and the Enemy. Dyer writes

---

[30] Lant, A. (1991). *Blackout: Reinventing women for wartime British cinema*. Princeton, New Jersey: Princeton University Press, page 69.

how such whiter-than-white women were lit in photographs and films; the use of lighting effects and filters combine to make such figures appear saintly, often giving them, argues Dyer (1997)[31] a literal 'halo' of light: "[i]dealised white women are bathed in and permeated by light. It streams through them and falls from above. In short, they glow." In the sequence following the announcement of her death sentence, Cavell is

Figure 12.2 Poster for 1938 *Nurse Edith Cavell*

shown kneeling in her cell before a crucifix; a beam of light shines down on her face so brightly that it erases her features. While Neagle's heroic performance often shows Cavell as the 'glowing' white woman Dyer describes, this image takes that trope to its logical political limit in virtually erasing Cavell's face.

---

[31] Dyer, R. (1997). *White. Essays on race and culture.* London: Routledge, page 122.

Spy films between the two world wars, says Landy (1991), were inevitably "attuned to the possibility of another war"[32] (and women playing spies were often depicted as ambiguous figures, drawing on the complete contrast presented by the mythologies of Mata Hari and Edith Cavell. Landy (1991:124) writes of Vivien Leigh's role as a World War One double agent for the British in *Dark Journey* (Victor Saville, 1937): "[c]haracteristic of the espionage film; the female is treated as a mysterious, exotic object of desire whose motives are ambiguous. [...] Before her identity is known, she is presented as a *femme fatale*, a mysterious Mata Hari." Towards the end of the 1930s, there was a flurry of spy films,[33] several of which placed their female leads at the centre of a nexus of public and sexual politics regarding identity and power. Anna Neagle's role in *The Yellow Canary* (Herbert Wilcox, 1943), where she played a double agent in Nazi Germany - a fact not revealed to the audience until the closing scenes - played upon public expectations and her star persona; even trailers promoting the film implied that she was playing against type.[34]

Another British actress who often took on the role of the female spy was Valerie Hobson. As a teenager she had been under contract to Universal, starring in Hollywood shockers such as James Whale's *The Bride of Frankenstein* (1935). In the late thirties, she returned to England and developed a successful career in roles that depicted her as variations on the quintessential Englishwoman, although she was born in Northern Ireland. She took the female lead in three spy dramas at the end of the thirties: *Q Planes* (Tim Whelan, 1939), *The Spy in Black* (Michael Powell, 1939) and *Contraband* (Michael Powell, 1940). In *Q Planes*, directed by the American Tim Whelan, Hobson plays Kay Lawrence - not a spy but an investigative journalist who at one point is called 'a newspaper spy'. Lawrence/Hobson is working undercover in the cafeteria of a factory developing experimental aircraft that are being stolen by enemy forces, who shoot them with a ray-gun over the sea and then 'rescue' the plane and its crew once they have crash-landed on water. The main protagonist is Kay Lawrence's brother; an intelligence

---

[32] Landy, M. (1991). *British Genres: Cinema and society, 1930-1960*. Oxford: Princeton University Press, page 123.
[33] See Aldgate, A. and Richards, J. (1986). *Britain Can Take It: The British cinema in the Second World War*. Oxford: Basil Blackwell, page 79; Chapman, J. (1998). 'Celluloid Shockers', in Richards, J. (ed.), *The Unknown 1930s: An alternative history of the British cinema 1929-1939*. London: I B Tauris. pages 93-4; *Op. cit.* Landy, (1991), page 126.
[34] *Op. cit.* Street, (1997), page 127.

officer called Major Hammond, played by Ralph Richardson. Richardson's role was one of the early inspirations for Patrick McNee's performance as John Steed in sixties spy series *The Avengers*.[35] Hobson's role appears influenced by the style of the Hollywood screwball comedies of the 1930s, but is also a forerunner of Cathy Gale and Emma Peel in *The Avengers*; a woman who argues her corner as a professional. In this film's odd mixture of witty romantic comedy, spy thriller and science fiction there is a foretaste of sixties spy films and television series, which dealt lightly with changes in gendered power relations while offering a nostalgic account of Englishness. Richardson's intelligence officer is an endearing eccentric who sniffs out the truth, while Hobson's 'newspaper spy' is confident and right-headed; despite early intimations that she might be an enemy agent. The film ends with Hobson marrying Laurence Olivier's test pilot, while Hammond is comically astonished that 'Daphne', whom he has repeatedly stood up throughout the film in a running joke phone call sequence, has married someone else. In this way threats to national borders and gender roles are neatly curtailed, and espionage is represented as the great game fostered by an English public school ethos.[36]

In Michael Powell's *The Spy in Black*, also released in 1939, Hobson plays a more ambivalent character; in her early scenes, it is not clear what side she is working for. This film, set during the First World War, begins with an innocent schoolmistress on her way to a job in the Orkneys being killed en route by two female German spies. Hobson takes her place, working as a double agent for the British, and assuming a role as the local schoolmistress on the Old Man of Hoy, a strategic naval outpost. Conrad Veidt, as a German U-boat commander is put ashore and hidden in Hobson's schoolhouse. The relationship between them is ambiguous throughout. While Veidt plays a naval captain, Hobson's undercover schoolmistress is in command. Gender roles are topsy-turvy, and this is carried through into the dialogue, as they debate the ethics of war – literally discussing the ethics of murder. This is followed by a scene in which Hobson is disturbed by the knowledge that her actions have led to the death of the U-boat crews. The simple moralities of a propaganda war are questioned in *The Spy in Black*. Sue

---

[35] *Op. cit.* Richards, (1998), page 247.
[36] See, Denning, M. (1987). *Cover Stories: Narrative and ideology in the British spy thriller*. London: Routledge and Kegan Paul, page 33.

Harper (1998) notes an exchange between Hobson and Veidt at one point:

'You are English! I am German! We are enemies!'
'I like that better!'
'So do I! It simplifies everything!'

She reads this as evidence of a moment in Veidt's career when Britain mobilised for war: "[t]he balance between the good and bad Germans which had informed Veidt's earlier 1930s films was no longer welcome."[37] It is possible, however, to read that melodramatic exchange as exactly the opposite - as an ironic comment on the oversimplification of national identities during wartime. Veidt's U-boat captain becomes increasingly hysterical, Hobson's spy frequently confused: the absolute binaries of good and evil mobilised in wartime propaganda are challenged as the film draws to a close. In the final minutes, Veidt follows Hobson onto the steamer taking her back to the mainland, takes over the boat by freeing the German prisoners of war on board. Hobson voices her feelings against the war shortly before the steamer, commanded by Veidt, is shelled by his craft. The film ends with Veidt's U-boat sunk by a British destroyer while he remains on board the sinking steamer. Hobson weeps on a life raft as she sees him go down with the boat. Hobson's ambivalent role in *The Spy in Black* is carried through into the narrative itself; nothing is secure in this film, and the conflict of war is exposed as traumatic and complicated, rather than straightforwardly patriotic. By *Contraband* (1940), another Hobson and Veidt /Powell and Pressburger production, such ambiguities had been closed off: even Powell noted that Pressburger's script was "all pure corn, but corn served up by professionals, and it works."[38]

Nevertheless, such films featuring Hobson, and Neagle's momentary ambivalence in *The Yellow Canary*, reveal a potential for ambiguity. The English female spy is a figure ripe for multiple readings, readings that may be made available by the script, the production or an actor's performance. Some of the films cited explore that multiplicity – *Dark Journey, Q Planes, The Spy in Black* – while others attempt to contain it – *Contraband* – or to shut it down entirely in favour of a more

---

[37] Harper, S. (1998). ' 'Thinking Forward and Up': the British films of Conrad Veid', in Richards, J. (ed.), *The Unknown 1930s: an alternative history of the British cinema 1929-193.* London: I B Tauris, pages 121-137.
[38] *Ibid.* Page 136.

straightforwardly patriotic narrative - *Nurse Edith Cavell*. All these films are more or less successful in their resistance to the unsaid other of the white femininity of the good and pure Englishwoman-spy, for they are always shadowed by the figure of Mata Hari. The slur of aberrant feminine sexuality tracks such narratives and each film attempts, in its way, to 'purify' its heroine; most obviously in *Nurse Edith Cavell* by creating a mythical figure who lacks sexuality and is almost inhuman in her stoical martyrdom. These dichotomous stereotypes even impinge on autobiographical accounts of the real women involved in secret service work during the first and second World Wars, as Van Seters (1992) notes in her examination of such writings:

> Consciously and unconsciously, these women indicate the extent to which, as individuals, they both conformed to, and departed from, contemporary stereotypes. Thus, not only do these accounts illustrate certain traits that have previously been noted as being common to female autobiographies in general, but they also offer reflections specifically concerning the realm of the secret services that are more complex and less predictable than those characterising their fictional sisters.[39]

Conclusion

It is important to note, again, the distance between real women's experiences of wartime in everyday life, as in the secret services at home or abroad, and the representations of women available in popular fiction and film. Lant (1991)[40] in her examination of how women were depicted in popular culture and film during the Second World War, notes how such representations attempted to close down or efface the contradictions inherent in wartime reformulations of femininity even as they bore witness to the anxieties such contradictions aroused, citing Christine Gledhill's argument that stereotypes "potentially open up a challenge to patriarchal assumptions, making visible a whole regime of practices, modes of feeling and thought which generally go unrecognised even by women themselves." This is particularly pertinent for fictional representations of women as secret agents where the

---

[39] Van Seters, D. (1992). 'Hardly Hollywood's Ideal: female autobiographies of secret service work, 1914-45'. *Intelligence and National Security*, 7(4), pages 403-424, page 412.
[40] *Op. cit.* Lant, (1991), page 89.

ambiguities surrounding femininity and espionage are often omitted in preference for the Mata Hari/Edith Cavell dichotomy, in an attempt to hide the contradictions inherent in that role. It would seem, from Van Seter's (1992) account, that even women who understood the gap between their real secret service work and fictionalised versions of it were unable to ignore the cultural weight of Mata Hari/Edith Cavell, even to the extent of measuring their experience about such popular stereotypes. Despite attempts to contain her through mythologies of the *femme fatale* or the angelic heroine, the woman as a spy, an agent, or as resistance activist, throws into question the West's ideological investment in passive femininity. She embodies the contradictions between the foreign 'other' and the purity of the English woman central to how English identity is imagined.

Chapter 13

Defining Musical 'Germanness': The Reciprocal Influences of Music and National Identity Formation

Lucy Claire Church
Independent Scholar

Introduction

This chapter is about music and the ways in which it both flows from and contributes to the formation of national identity. There can hardly be a better era to examine issues of national musical identity than in the years surrounding World War I, where the broadly European canon of Western art music collided with a wartime mentality, and issues of nationalism, morality, and musical expression became inseparable. Germany was at the time a relatively new country with a nevertheless long and distinct cultural history, and its art music was nearly unanimously thought to be the finest in the world, both aesthetically and morally. It is for this reason that we take up German national identity formation as our primary topic of study.

During World War I, the increasingly vitriolic rhetoric between military enemies heightened both the perceived and the intended moral significance of music. At the start of the twentieth century, German music claimed nearly all the great composers, including Bach, Beethoven, Brahms, and Wagner. The repertoire of these composers dominated concert programs as much as it dominated the hearts and ears of concert-goers. Furthermore, German music had come to be seen as morally superior to other national musics. In his widely popular *Music and Morals*, first published in 1871, the Reverend H.W. Haweis, a British minister and amateur musician, declared:

It is because German music takes emotion fairly in hand, disciplines it, expresses its depressions in order to remove them, renders with terrible accuracy even its insanity and incoherence in order to give relief through such expression, and restores calm, flinches not from the tender and the passionate, stoops to pity, and becomes a very angel in sorrow; it is because German music has probed the humanities and sounded the depths of our nature - taught us how to bring the emotional region not only into the highest activity, but also under the highest control - that we place German music in the first rank, and allow no names to stand before Gluck, Bach, Handel, Haydn, Mozart, Beethoven, Schubert, Spohr, Mendelssohn, and Schumann.[1]

With the advent of war, however, music that once transcended national lines was now questioned - could 'enemy music' still be performed? In France, Nadia and Lili Boulanger sent a gazette to French music students on the front lines, asking for responses to the question 'Les musiciens allemands doivent-ils garder leur place?' (Should German musicians keep their place?). In America, lootings, bomb threats, riots, restraining orders, internments, and deportations plagued German-American and German musicians, as well as those who dared to perform German repertoire. Music had come to be seen as a conduit through which morality was communicated.

How did it come to this? How did certain musics come to be associated with national identities - how did notes on a page become symbols of a country? How did German musical style come to be known as 'German'? And how did this type of music come to be favored above all others, not to mention seen as morally superior? This chapter will examine how music cooperates in and sometimes transforms national identity formation by looking at the ways that critics and writers in the nineteenth century perceived musical national identity and by looking at the ways in which Germany itself used the great composers as a resource to consolidate and promote allegiance to 'Germanness'.

---

[1] Haweis, H. R. (1872). *Music and Morals*. New York: Harper, pages 60-61.

National musics

> ...the war, if it be prolonged, will mean the drawing of a line across the ledger and the commencement of a new account. It is impossible for the Continent to pass through so great a strain as this without a setting free of great funds of dormant emotion, and a turning of old emotions into new channels... But there is one danger of which we must not lose sight, - the danger that a bad political settlement may keep the old national animosities alive till they once more find their inevitable outlet in war... It is just possible that each of the great nations, swollen with vanity or blindly nursing a grievance, may build round itself a wall more impassable than exists at present; and if that happens music will have to wait another twenty years for the new flight that we have all lately felt to be imminent. The day has gone by when one country can build up a school in ignorance or contempt of what is going on in other countries; it will reject a foreign culture at its peril. We can only hope that the result of the war will not be a perpetuation of old racial hatreds and distrusts, but a new sense of the emotional solidarity of mankind. From that sense alone can the real music of the future be born.[2]

British music critic Ernest Newman offered this account of the tension between nationalism and international relations in music at the start of World War I. In an article written for *The Musical Times* less than one month after declarations of war resounded around Europe, Newman pointed to a pre-war musical culture in which national animosities impeded the overall success and development of music. He lamented the recent lack of vitality in the world of music, saying,

> Were we writing about the situation as if it were five hundred years behind us, and so a subject merely for unimpassioned scrutiny of forces and correlation of causes and effects, instead of something blindingly and terrifyingly near to us, we might perhaps say that some such war was necessary for the re-birth of music.[3]

According to Newman, each nation's art seemed to be struggling:

---

[2] Newman, E. (1914). 'The War and the Future of Music', *The Musical Times* 55, no. 859 (September 1, 1914), pages 571-72.
[3] *Ibid.* Page 571.

German music... has settled into a complacent tilling of an almost exhausted field... The French are... indubitably small... Italian music is strangling in the grip of a commercial octopus... [and] Russia is divided between men who see the wisdom of building upon the classical tradition but are not quite big enough to give the tradition an unmistakably new life, and men who reject the past before they are sure of the future, or even of the present.[4]

Indeed, according to Newman, England had only the 'impressive' figure of Edward Elgar, but no others were fulfilling or even showing their promise. Part of the answer to this dilemma, Newman posited, would be 'cross-fertilisation,' from which both French and German music would benefit:

French music is still suffering in all sorts of ways from 1870. It is so small because it is so bent on being exclusively French. By its refusal to fertilise itself with the great German tradition it deliberately cuts itself off from permanent spiritual elements in that tradition that would give it a wider range and deeper humanity. The German tradition in its turn would be all the better for some cross-fertilisation from modern France, but again Chauvinism intervenes, and new harmonic possibilities are not developed as they might be because they are associated primarily with French music.[5]

According to Newman, it was the dissolution of fervent nationalism that would revitalise the music of the twentieth century. What was more, the war had the potential to be the impetus that could accomplish this re-birth of music.

In contrast to Ernest Newman's account of highly nationalised and consequently dying musics, French author Romain Rolland, most famous for his novel *Jean-Christophe*, told a story of utterly cross-pollinated European musics: German composers were too Italianised, Italian composers were too Gallicised, and so on. His contemporary musical history, 'A Musical Tour across Europe in the Eighteenth Century', originally published in the *Revue de Paris* and then reprinted in the book *Voyage musical au pays du passé* (*A Musical Tour Through the Land of*

---

[4] *Ibid.* Page 571.
[5] *Ibid.* Page 572.

the Past), tells the history of music as a distinctly cosmopolitan phenomenon. Of German and Italian interaction, Roland asserted:

> ...the leaders of German music, those who were afterwards to be its foremost liberators, were all without exception profoundly Italianised.[6]

and

> ...it is a remarkable fact that Italian opera and Italian music were represented in Europe, about the middle of the eighteenth century, not by Italians, but by Germans; by Gluck in Vienna, Johann Christian Bach in London, Graun in Berlin and Hasse in Italy itself.[7]

Furthermore, Rolland analysed what he saw as a thoroughly 'Italianised' German musical identity as a hindrance to be overcome:

> How could it be otherwise than that a new spirit should find its way into this Germanised Italianism? In these German masters, *conscious of their superiority* [emphasis added], there gradually developed a desire, avowed or unconfessed, to conquer Italy with her weapons. We are struck by the German pride which we perceive increasing in Gluck and Mozart. And these brilliant Italianisers are the first to try their powers in the German Lied.[8]

According to Rolland, the development of Lieder and the flowering of instrumental music (particularly the symphony) served as the 'salvation of German music'. Germany "had the good fortune to find, in the sudden outgrowth of instrumental music, the equivalent, and more, of what she had lost."[9] Nevertheless, Rolland lamented, "magnificent as was the development of German music in Haydn, Mozart, Beethoven and their successors, it is permissible to believe that this was not the normal development of German music as it would have been had the

---

[6] Rolland, R. (1967). *A Musical Tour through the Land of the Past*, translated by Bernard Miall. Freeport, N.Y.: Books for Libraries Press, page 235.
[7] *Ibid.* Pages 225-26.
[8] *Ibid.* Pages 225-26.
[9] *Ibid.* Page 227.

latter, in taking shape, relied only upon its resources, drawing only upon its own capital."[10]

Here, we find Rolland bemoaning the cosmopolitan mixing of musical styles, wishing that German music had, from its beginnings, been purely German. Likewise, in speaking of French and Italian interaction, Rolland postulated,

> Italian influence... was brought to bear no less upon Parisian society and Parisian artists; and Italianism, which found a vigorous support among the 'philosophers' of the Encyclopaedia - Diderot, Grimm, and above all Rousseau - gave rise to a positive warfare in the musical world, and in the end it was partly victorious; for in the second half of the century we may say that French music was a prey which was divided up like a conquered territory, between three great foreign artists: an Italian, Piccinni; an Italianate German, Gluck; and an Italianate Belgian, Grétry.[11]

Furthermore, once German music had fulfilled its potential in the person of Wagner, it too became a significant - and even dominant - influence on French music. In his 1903 publication *Enquête sur l'influence allemande*, French author Jacques Morland dedicated a chapter to the discussion of the German influence on French music, citing Wagner as the key figure. He wrote,

> The influence that Germany has had during the last quarter of a century, predominantly in France, seems to me to be undeniable... In terms of music, this influence can be summarised in only one name, a name that has filled the world: Richard Wagner... Indeed, we are not ignorant that his work carries, in some part, the imprint of a Germanic spirit which is contradictory to our French genius... All or nearly all, even those who proclaim themselves strangers to Wagnerian art, have legitimately borrowed from him.[12]

---

[10] *Ibid.* Page 235.
[11] *Ibid.* Page 164.
[12] Morland, J. (1903). *Enquête sur l'influence allemande.* Paris: Société du Mercure de France, pages 201-2.

Although, according to Rolland, this flourishing of foreign-influenced music, both Italian and German, represented France's fall to the 'most miserable depths', he nevertheless saw hope in the developments of recent years. In 1870, he argued, the hardships suffered during the

Figure 13.1 *Jean Christophe*, a novel in 10 volumes

Franco-Prussian War brought about the regeneration of the French spirit - undoubtedly through a combination of wartime nationalist fervor and a new distaste for 'enemy' culture. In cooperation with a renewed appreciation for the history and potential of French music (most clearly demonstrated by the organisation of a Berlioz Festival in March of 1870 to celebrate the recently deceased composer, claimed by Rolland as France's 'greatest musical genius'), this significant time marked the beginning of the renewal of the French musical style. Although French music, like German music, had a history that began with syncretism, Rolland saw in that same history the potential for independence:

The mind of Paris has made a journey - a hasty journey, it is true - through the music of other countries and other times, and is now becoming introspective. After a mad enthusiasm over discoveries in strange lands, music and musical criticism have regained their self-possession and their jealous love of independence. A very decided reaction against foreign music has been shown since the time of the Universal Exhibition of 1900. This movement is not unconnected, consciously or unconsciously, with the nationalist train of thought, which was stirred up in France, and especially in Paris, somewhere about the same time. But it is also a natural development in the evolution of music.[13]

Furthermore, "…this revolt against foreign influences was directed - one had expected it - against the strongest of the influences - the influence of German music as personified by Wagner."[14] In fact, Romain Rolland described Morland's *allemande: musique* as "a shout of deliverance",[15] and cited another article, Paul Landormy's "L'état actuel de la musique française" in the *Revue bleue* (1904) as the new French school's declaration of independence.

Despite his hopefulness, however, Rolland had concerns about the ability of the two greatest representatives of the new French music movement - the Schola Cantorum de Paris and the 'independent party' represented by Claude Debussy - to fulfill their potential as ambassadors of the new French art. He wrote, "the artists, instead of working steadily at their own tasks and uniting in a common aim, are given up to sterile disputes."[16] Rolland then turned to military language to impress upon French musicians the importance of working together to develop a particularly 'French' style:

> It is the historian's duty to point out the dangers of the present hour, and to remind the French musicians who have been satisfied with their first victory that the future is anything but sure, and that we

---

[13] Rolland, R. (1919). *Musicians of To-Day*, 4th edn., trans. Mary Blaiklock. London: Kegan Paul, Trench, Trubner and Co., Ltd., page 316.
[14] *Ibid*. Page 316.
[15] *Ibid*. Page 316.
[16] *Ibid*. Page 320.

must never disarm while we have a common enemy before us, an enemy especially dangerous in a democracy - mediocrity.[17]

The unwritten implication of this statement seems to be that German music, especially once it fully developed its 'Germanness' through the work of Beethoven and Wagner, no longer succumbed to mediocrity. In order for France to recover from its near-fatal syncretism, it would need to produce works of such greatness - and particularly *national* greatness - that they could compete with the abundance of German nationalist masterpieces.

Rolland, writing at the very beginning of the twentieth century, constantly discussed music in national terms. In his inaugural lecture at the Sorbonne, published in 1915 as 'De la place de la musique dans l'histoire générale', Rolland defined music as "an architecture of sound in certain centuries of architecture and with certain architectural people, *such as the Franco-Flemings* [emphasis added] of the fifteenth and sixteenth centuries"; "drawing, line, melody, and plastic beauty, with people who have an appreciation and admiration for form, with painter and sculptor people *like the Italians*"; and "inner poetry, lyrical outpouring, and philosophic meditation with poets and philosophers *like the Germans.*"[18] For Rolland, it seems, the ideal musical world would be one in which each nation develops its own particular and true nationalistic sound, but rather than fighting against each other, each fights against mediocrity.

Rolland was thinking well ahead of his time, for here is pluralistic thought: that all national styles are valid and to be encouraged, as long as they produce art of high quality. This is a far cry from Ernest Newman's call for 'cross-fertilisation' of national styles. Rolland's viewpoint was not particularly popular, and in fact, it seems to be appropriate only for someone who stood firmly on the outside of the war. What made this stance possible - this idea that music, though a powerful national tool, stands above political conflict - was Rolland's deep commitment to pacifism. In *Au-dessus de la mêlée*, a series of articles that incited controversy when they first appeared in French journals in the fall of 1915, Rolland denounced the war from all sides. To be sure, he saw Prussian Military Imperialism as the worst of all the

---

[17] *Ibid.* Page 322.
[18] Rolland, R. (1948). *Essays on Music.* (trans. David Ewen). New York: Allen, Towne & Heath, page 10.

enemies of morality. But his even-handed criticism of the Allies and his humanising attitude toward Germany and German culture caused significant upset among French writers and publishers. To communicate his allegiance to Germany, he divided its cultural output into 'past' and 'present':

> You, my German friends - for those of you who were my friends in the past remain my friends in spite of fanatical demands from both sides that we should break off all relations - know how much I love the Germany of the past and all that I owe to it. Not less than you, yourselves, I am the son of Beethoven, of Leibnitz, and of Goethe. But what do I owe to the Germany of today, or what does Europe owe to it? What art have you produced since the monumental work of Wagner, which marks the end of an epoch and belongs to the past? ...What German writer can you set up against Tolstoi and Dostoievsky, those giants of poetic genius and moral grandeur? ...In music, Germany, so proud of its ancient glory, has only the successors of Wagner, neurotic jugglers with orchestral effects, like Richard Strauss, but not a single sober and virile work of the quality of Boris Godunov. No German musician has opened up new roads. A single page of Moussorgsy or Strawinsky shows more originality, more potential greatness than the complete scores of Mahler and Reger.[19]

Here, Russian art is pitted against German art in Rolland's declaration that PanSlavism (Czarism) is the lesser of the two evils. The difference between the horrors of pan-Germanism (Imperialism) and those of PanSlavism, according to Rolland, is that in Russia, artists and intellectuals stood firm against the moral corruption of their political leaders. In Germany, however, the best of the country's cultural representatives - intellectuals, theologians, writers, artists, and musicians - were slavishly devoted to their political leaders, without questioning their morality. Rolland pointed to the infamous document now known alternately as the 'Manifesto of the Ninety-three' and 'An Appeal [or Manifesto] to the Civilized World' as the primary and most repulsive example of this capitulation. In the document, written in late October 1914, ninety-three of Germany's "most distinguished scientists, thinkers,

---

[19] *Op. cit.* Rolland, (1916), pages 54-55.

and artists" repudiated any claims of German fault in the outbreak of the war. A series of denials reads like a list of soon-to-be-refuted claims:

> *It is not true* that we trespassed in neutral Belgium... *It is not true* that the life and property of a single Belgian citizen was injured by our soldiers without the bitterest self-defence having made it necessary... *It is not true* that our troops treated Louvain brutally... *It is not true* that our warfare pays no respect to international laws. It knows no undisciplined cruelty. *It is not true* that the combat against our so-called militarism is not a combat against our civil nation, as our enemies hypocritically pretend it is.[20]

Moreover, the 'Professors of Germany', who included only three musicians - Engelbert Humperdinck, Siegfried Wagner, and Felix Weingartner - appealed to the authority of Germany's greatest cultural figures as a means of supporting their argument:

> We cannot wrest the poisonous weapon - the lie - out of the hands of our enemies. All we can do is to proclaim to all the world that our enemies are giving false witness against us. You, who know us, who with us have protected the most holy possessions of man, we call to you: Have faith in us! Believe that we shall carry on this war to the end as a civilized nation, to whom the legacy of a Goethe, a Beethoven, and a Kant is just as sacred as its own hearths and homes.[21]

Rolland's naming of Goethe and Beethoven as his cultural fathers in *Au-dessus de la mêlée* seems to have been an attempt to reclaim them for humanity rather than solely for Germany. In fact, for most of his career, Rolland was preoccupied with Beethoven above all others. David Ewen, the publisher of a collection of Rolland's essays on music remembers the author, in his last days, saying,

> Now that I am old and there cannot be much time reserved for me, I find that such energy and strength that is left to me must be directed exclusively to Beethoven. Of all the composers of the past, he alone

---

[20] 'Professors of Germany, 'To the Civilized World'', *The North American Review*, 210, no. 765 (August 1919), pages 284-85.
[21] Professors of Germany, 'To the Civilized World', page 285.

remains unfathomable to me. The more deeply you penetrate into his music, the more you discover what you never suspected to be there. A lifetime is not sufficient to uncover all the secrets to be found in his score. I should like to learn a few more of these secrets before I die.[22]

Sadly, it appears that Rolland's steady devotion to Beethoven may have eventually been overcome by Imperialist Germany's politicisation of the great composer. Ewen remembers a visit with the composer in 1935:

> My second visit... was in 1935. Rolland had watched with no little apprehension the rise of Hitler's power in Germany... As we spoke of the terrible things that were happening in Germany, it became apparent that the momentous and terrible events of the time were drawing him away from music. I recall asking him what progress he was making on his Beethoven magnum opus. He replied with weariness that the task was going too slowly. He seemed reluctant to speak about it... 'Europe is in a state of decay, of which Hitler is only one of many symptoms,' he said. Once again eager to bring the conversation back to music, I asked him whether he felt that this decay would also be perceptible in the music of European composers. 'It is in everything,' he said...[23]

Rolland never fully completed his mammoth Beethoven study. Nevertheless, at the time of the First World War, he maintained overwhelming respect for the universality of Beethoven's work and a desire to use his memory as a super-national, peace-generating force. As a 'son' of Beethoven, Rolland acknowledged the dominance of Germany's cultural output, but he feared for its legacy as it turned into the Idol of Kultur. He proposed that "every ideal which ought to liberate is transformed into a clumsy idol. The history of humanity is the history of Idols and of their successive reigns; and as humanity grows older the power of the Idol seems to wax greater and more destructive."[24] According to Rolland, the idols of the past - religions,

---

[22] *Op. cit.* Rolland, (1948), page x.
[23] *Op. cit.* Rolland, (1948), pages x-xi.
[24] *Op. cit.* Rolland, (1916), page 101.

nationality, liberty - had given way to 'two new species' in the twentieth century: the Idol of Race and the Idol of Kultur. He expounded:

> The common feature of the cult of all Idols is the adaptation of an ideal to the evil instincts of mankind. Man cultivates the vices which are profitable to him, but feels the necessity of legitimising them; being unwilling to sacrifice them, he must idealise them. That is why the problem at which he has never ceased to labour throughout the centuries has been to harmonize his ideals with his own mediocrity.[25]

Here again, Rolland describes the enemy not as nationalism but as mediocrity. In fact, we might argue that the ideal that had been adapted into the Idol of Kultur through the evil instincts of mankind was true national cultural expression. Rolland did not wish for the cessation of all German cultural expression but only of all that was not thoughtfully standing against the Idol of Kultur. In Thomas Mann's article 'Gedanken im Kriege', Rolland finds a terrifying definition of Kultur that pushes the relatively calm and reserved Kultur of chemist-philosopher Wilhelm Ostwald (one of the '93') over the edge. The difference between Mann and Ostwald, Rolland asserted, was that:

> While an Ostwald endeavours to identify the cause of *Kultur* with that of civilisation, Mann proclaims: 'They have nothing in common. The present war is that of *Kultur* (i.e., of Germany) against civilisation'. And pushing this outrageous boast of pride to the point of madness, he defines civilisation as Reason (*Vernunft, Aufklärung*), Gentleness (*Sittigung, Sänftigung*), Spirit (*Geist, Auflösung*), and Kultur as 'a spiritual *organisation* of the world' which does not exclude 'bloody savagery'. Kultur is 'the sublimation of the demoniacal' (*die Sublimierung des Dämonischen*). It is "above morality, above reason, and above science." While Ostwald and Haeckel see in militarism merely an arm or instrument of which Kultur makes use to secure victory, Thomas Mann affirms that Kultur and Militarism are brothers - their ideal is the same, their aim the same, their principle the same. Their enemy is peace, is spirit (*Ja, der Geist ist zivil, ist bürgerlich*')... Ostwald preached the victory of Kultur, if necessary by Force; Mann proved that Kultur is Force.[26]

---

[25] *Ibid.* Page 102.
[26] *Ibid.* Pages 107-8.

Furthermore, Rolland followed this train of thought to its next logical step, a statement that essentially said: "Force alone. All else be silent." German journalist Maximilian Harden, in a discussion of the violation of Belgian neutrality, wrote: "Why on earth all this fuss? Might creates our Right. Did a powerful man ever submit himself to the crazy pretensions or to the judgment of a band of weaklings?"[27] Rolland called this statement a "testament... to the moral anarchy of this Empire."[28] If then, Kultur stood 'above morality' and as a sign of 'moral anarchy', in contrast, true national art of the kind that Rolland desired must be essentially moral, a testament to the moral stability of nations and of the world. Rolland seems to have been operating on the basic premise that music's unique strength lies in its ability to communicate and build morality, and that music fulfills its potential most radically insofar as it is morally good.

Building a German national identity

To understand how the German musical identity and its morality came to be, we must understand how its national lines were drawn, encouraged, and formed. In his seminal work *The Civilizing Process*, twentieth-century sociologist Norbert Elias (1998) examines the development of a European concept of 'civilization', particularly as it began to distinguish itself from 'barbarism' at the end of the Middle Ages. Furthermore, in *The Germans*,[29] Elias attempts to follow a historical thread of civilising and decivilising processes that allowed for and ultimately resulted in the atrocities of the Second World War. He outlines the changing social patterns that grew out of the process of state-formation, its concurrent centralisation of power, and the formation of monopolies of physical force, identifying some historical realities that contributed to the particularities of German state-formation (and national identity formation). These included Germany's geographic location between the Slavic and French nation-states and its vulnerability to invasion, the discontinuous and disjunctive nature of the development of the German state, and the superiority of the aristocracy to the middle class regarding political accomplishments. He recognises that Germany's long history of invasion by neighbouring peoples

---

[27] *Ibid.* Page 109.
[28] *Ibid.* Page 109.
[29] Elias, N. (1998). *The Germans*. Columbia: University of Columbia Press.

instilled in it an idealisation and valorisation of military action and that the fact that aristocratic military action proved successful in the unification of Germany set a precedent for war and violence as positive political tools. Because the development of the German state was so precarious and fragile, Elias posits, the collective became more important than the individual in an attempt to stabilise national worth. Furthermore, the tension between nationalism and democracy was appeased as national identity came to play a central role in the formation of individual identity. In his discussion of German identity development, Elias affirms what has come to be known as the *Sonderweg* concept: the idea that Germany had at some point diverged from the path Europe was taking to democracy, forging its own particular way. In her *History in Mighty Sounds*, Barbara Eichner identifies two uses of this term, one by Germans in the latter part of the nineteenth century to "express the superiority of their spiritual culture compared with materialist Western 'civilisations'" and one by historians in the second half of the twentieth century to identify where Germany history 'went wrong' on its way to the horrors of the Holocaust.[30] Elias fits into the second camp, understanding the barbarisation of Germany - or, otherwise stated, the failure of the civilising process in the Germanic lands - in terms of its deviation from the path of Western European history.

The three main concerns with the *Sonderweg* theory are best articulated by David Blackbourn and Geoff Eley in *The Peculiarities of German History*. First, the idea that Germany came 'late' to nationhood requires a 'normative' model (for Elias in *The Germans*, this is Great Britain, and, by way of extension, France as discussed in *The Civilising Process*). In the development of this normative model, a dichotomy between Western and Eastern nationalisms was encouraged, with moral judgment overlaid upon it. Barbara Eichner describes it this way:

> 'Western' nationalism was... assumed to have developed in France and England during the Enlightenment, steeped in positive values such as rationality, liberalism and civic responsibility. 'Eastern' nationalism, on the other hand, was constructed as an envious counter-reaction of the not-yet enlightened peoples of Eastern Europe, who, since most did not have nation states, defined their

---

[30] Eichner, B. (2012). *History in Mighty Sounds: Musical constructions of German national identity 1848-1914.* Rochester, NY: Boydell Press, page 11.

nationhood in terms of ethnicity, heritage and destiny without much regard for the institutions of modern states.[31]

This dichotomy not only idealises the 'early' developed Western nations but also places negative connotations on the use of cultural expression as a determinant of national identity. A second flaw in the *Sonderweg* theory is its location of the German middle class at the centre of the failure of timely national formation. According to the *Sonderweg* model, instead of achieving a proper bourgeois revolution in 1848, the educated middle class's idealisation of national community over individuality resulted in the revolution's failure. Blackbourn and Eley place Germany's revolutions within their broader continental context, asserting that the ideas of most European revolutionaries (whatever their class) were hardly ever ratified or practiced immediately and that national unity was never achieved through revolution alone. Thus, even if the German middle class was ineffectual in national identity formation, this fact does not in itself identify the German bourgeoisie as weak, useless or undeveloped. In fact, the German middle class was the cultural and social centre of German life in the nineteenth century. Finally, the *Sonderweg* theory is criticised for treating German history as if the atrocities of the Holocaust were anticipated in every event and action. According to Blackbourn and Eley, there is no 'normative' course of political development, especially not one that draws a teleological straight line through the nineteenth and twentieth centuries. In fact, one of the primary facts we will encounter as we pursue the history of German national identity formation is its distinctly wave-like character.

Barbara Eichner's *History in Mighty Sounds: Musical Constructions of German National Identity 1848-1914* is a thorough and impeccably researched examination of notions of 'Germanness' within the self-conception of German middle-class citizens and the ways in which these ideas were communicated in the under-studied German-composed music of the time. In her introduction Eichner summarises the complicated history of German national identity, first presenting a fundamental understanding of 'German' people as "everybody who made a point about considering himself or herself as part of the larger German linguistic, historical, cultural or ethnic community, whichever

---

[31] *Ibid.* Page 13.

state or region they belonged to."[32] This broad definition of Germanness, alongside the relatively late development of the unified German nation-state, gave rise to deep-seated insecurity concerning national identity. As Friedrich Nietzsche astutely observed in his *Beyond Good and Evil* (1886), "It is characteristic of the Germans that the question 'what is German?' never dies out among them."[33] This statement only proved itself to be more fully true in the remaining years of the long nineteenth century and continues to be applicable even into the twenty-first. In *History in Mighty Sounds*, Eichner notes several recent attempts at exploring German national identity, including a 2006 exhibition at the Germanisches Nationalmuseum in Nuremberg titled *Was ist deutsch? Fragen zum Selbstverständnis einer grübelnden Nation* (What is German? Questioning the self-conception of a ruminating nation) and a special issue of the magazine *Der Spiegel* from 2007 titled 'Die Erfindung der Deutschen: Wie wir wurden, was wir sind' (The invention of the Germans: how we became what we are).[34] This insecurity of identity finds a logical basis in the lack of German political unity in the years between the establishment of the German Confederation at the Congress of Vienna in 1815 and the official nation-state that only emerged in 1871 as a result of the Franco-Prussian War. To be sure, nationalist sentiment was not absent, but it suffered blow after devastating blow throughout the mid-nineteenth century.

Beginning with the strangulating Karlsbad Decrees that, in 1819, placed severe regulations and restrictions on nationalist political activity in German universities and in the press, a series of crushed revolutions left the liberal national movement weak. Despite the hopeful regeneration of these political ideas in the 1860s after the lifting of the ban on political organisations, it meant much for national identity that when statehood finally came, it was not as a result of a collective revolutionary effort 'from below', but rather it came 'from above', in the form of a military scheme devised by Prussian chancellor Otto von Bismarck.[35] Furthermore, the formation of the nation-state was not the final solution to Germany's decades-long problems; to begin with, it could not possibly live up to the utopian expectations that had been placed upon it. Wolfgang J. Mommsen identifies several fundamental

---

[32] *Ibid*. Page 6.
[33] Nietzsche, F. (2003). *Beyond Good and Evil: Prelude to a philosophy of the future*, (trans. R. J. Hollingdale, intro. Michael Tanner). London: Penguin, page 174.
[34] *Op. cit.* Eichner, (2012), page 2.
[35] *Ibid*. Page 8-9.

concerns with the new Empire, including a weak parliament, vague rules concerning division of power, and old elites retaining their former power.[36] Finally, the persistence of regional identities among the population made a unified German identity much more difficult to attain than political and geographical unity.

Noting the persistence of the national identity question well after political unification, Barbara Eichner sees three issues as particularly relevant in considering the German effort at identity formation. First is the competition for loyalty between specific regional, religious, or political identities and the broader *Vaterland*. This tension was exacerbated by the largely federal structure of the German Empire, which consisted of 26 constituent states each governed by its own king, duke, or prince; by the Catholic/Protestant conflict; and by the success of the Socialist Workers' Party of Germany (Sozialistische Arbeiterpartei Deutschlands, the SAPD). In each case measures were taken to ensure national loyalty over either transnational or local loyalty: the SAPD was banned between 1878 and 1890 under the provisions of the Anti-Socialist Laws (*Gesetz gegen die gemeingefährlichen Bestrebungen der Sozialdemokratie*); the Catholic church was heavily persecuted by Otto von Bismark's *Kulturkampf*, which lasted for most of the 1870s; and culture, science, and the arts were promoted and exploited for their unifying nationalist qualities. If this was not enough, intense animosity towards other European countries was encouraged as a means of fostering positive nationalist sentiment.

Of fundamental significance for the development of a German national identity was, paradoxically, the development of a strong French national identity. France served as both inspiration and enemy when it came to identity formation. Post-revolutionary France, the model of modern nationhood, had been able to replace its unifying dynastic bond with a shared sense of 'Frenchness', something that was not only encouraging but necessary for the Germanic peoples who themselves had had no singular dynasty in power. Furthermore, the long and complex history of Franco-Prussian military struggle following the dissolution of the Holy Roman Empire in 1806 made France a true enemy. Under Napoleon's rule, the previously undefined German culture seemed to be threatened, and the response was an impassioned search for a shared identity. Eichner notes, "From the start, therefore,

---

[36] Mommsen, Wolfgang, J. (1995). *Imperial Germany, 1867-1918: Politics, culture, and society in an authoritarian state*, (trans. Richard Deveson) London: Bloomsbury, pages 1-40.

the German nation was only thinkable vis-à-vis a hostile 'other', and for the most part of the nineteenth century France fulfilled that role."[37] This Franco-Prussian opposition was particularly easy to identify and encourage when it came to music, as we have seen in our examination of nationalised narrations of music history. It also became quickly infused with notions of morality; once a national dichotomy is created, it is only natural to superimpose that most ancient of dichotomies on top of it: good and evil. This dichotomised model was applied to other countries as well, most notably with Russia and England. Combined with the ever-increasing militarisation of German society and competing local or transnational identities, this antagonism against other countries left Germany poised to fight what could be promoted as a holy war. As Barbara Eichner asserts, "these fault lines meant that Germans tended to think of their national development as a series of narrowly averted failures rather than comfortable achievements, which allowed them to conceptualise their history from the perspective of the 'underdog', a nation constantly embattled and besieged by outside and inner enemies."[38]

Another dichotomy stands strangely alongside these national enemy oppositions: that of nationalism and cosmopolitanism. In the introduction to *Nationalism Versus Cosmopolitanism in German Thought and Culture, 1789-1914*, Mary Anne Perkins examines the development of the concepts of nationalism and cosmopolitanism throughout the long nineteenth century and the role of this dichotomy in the history of German political thought and culture. She traces German thought on the subject through early nineteenth-century Catholic Romantic thinkers and Idealist philosophers, past the defeat of Napoleon and the Congress of Vienna, to Nietzsche and the creation of the Pan-German League at the end of the century. Perkins argues that, though at times one or the other has been dominant, the two identities (universality/cosmopolitanism and identity/nationalism) played equal roles in the German idea of nationhood, the tension ultimately being resolved by the idea that the Germany identity was itself a representation of the universal European culture.[39] Thus, nationalism and cosmopolitanism in Germany were not necessarily opposing values. German national identity not only could be claimed to constitute a

---

[37] *Op. cit.* Eichner, (2012), page 7.
[38] *Ibid.* Page 11.
[39] Perkins, M. A. and Liebscher, M. (eds.), (2006). *Nationalism Versus Cosmopolitanism in German Thought and Culture, 1789-1914.* Lewiston, NY: Edwin Mellen Press, page 28.

representative of the values of universal humanism but was also seen as playing a crucial role in saving Europe from degeneration. Here is a cosmopolitanism that served to broaden and intensify nationalistic sentiment. Rather than welcoming diversity, much German thought in the nineteenth century called for a cosmopolitanism that involved German leadership and other countries' assimilation. Yes, Germans called for a unified Europe, but only if it were to be one that looked very much like Germany.

Music and German national identity

In his work on the theory, ideology, and history of nationalism, ethnographer Anthony D. Smith identifies the foundational elements and functions of national identity. For Smith, national identity is created by "a historic territory or homeland, common myths and historical memories, a public mass culture, common legal rights and duties and finally a common economy."[40] Moreover, national identity functions primarily as a means of creating social bonds through "repertoires of shared values, symbols and traditions" and by providing "a means of defining and locating individual selves in the world, through the prism of the collective personality and its distinctive culture."[41] To this list of defining characteristics and functions, Barbara Eichner adds one caveat: these symbols are only meaningful insofar as they are invested with '*Nationalgefühl*' (national feeling/emotion).[42] It is to these qualities, functions, and needs that music responds so effectively.

In Germany, making up for lack of long-established historical homeland is a strong sense of cultural history. Though a politically a unified nation for only a few decades before the First World War, Germany clung to a legacy of distinguished writers and composers to create its identity. Musically, it could be credited with the production of many of the composers who had begun to be singled out as geniuses in the telling of music history. Bach, Haydn, Mozart, and Beethoven were embraced by Europe and claimed by Germany. The character of Beethoven, already salient in our discussion of Romain Rolland, looms largest over German national character. In his *Beethoven in German Politics, 1870-1989* David Dennis argues that Beethoven's music was

---

[40] *Op. cit.* Eichner, (2012), page 14.
[41] Smith, Anthony D. (2001). *Nationalism: Theory, ideology, history*. Malden, MA: Polity Press, pages 15-16.
[42] *Op. cit.* Eichner, (2012), page 14.

used to support a vast swath of political ideas, including German patriotism (when associated with Wilhelm II and Otto von Bismarck), pessimistic and racist ideas, humanist and socialist-realist ideology, and a broader nationalism (as articulated by Wagner), as well as the French ideals of *liberté, fraternité* and *egalité*. Dennis notes that Beethoven himself, even when communicating political messages, was inconsistent with his political stance. Beethoven's music and persona contained the material for the support of every political faction represented in Germany in the years leading up to the war. This is largely to be explained by the fact that Beethoven's musical style can be seen as supporting the heroic biographical image which, Dennis argues, is at the heart of his significance and, as we have seen, speaks particularly to the German desire for heroism (the victory of the underdog). Beethoven was, like Germany, both transcendentally universal and ultimately national.

Secondly, the common myths and historical memories required by Anthony Smith in national identity formation are reflected in musical texts or programs. As Barbara Eichner argues primarily in *History in Mighty Sounds*, "composers relied on historical topics to make a (more or less obvious) statement about what being German meant,... openly advertised these histories in titles, texts or programmes, and... invited their audiences to identify with the national images and narratives their music brought to life."[43] Indeed, part of Wagner's outstanding national appeal lay in his use of mythical programs and his creation of historical memories. Furthermore, music is particularly capable of invoking historical memories through melody; folk songs passed down through generations carry with them a national identity that even transcends speech.

Smith's third component of national identity, public mass culture, is undoubtedly fulfilled by music's overwhelming cultural presence. Music communicates values, helps form traditions, is fundamentally symbolic, and is particularly well-suited to communicating a sense of collective personality. As Pamela Potter and Celia Applegate demonstrate in *Music and German National Identity*, German national identity in the nineteenth century had at its core the concept of *Bildung*: the continual spiritual, intellectual, and cultural self-improvement that results in the improvement of German culture overall.[44] Music was a fundamental,

---

[43] *Ibid.* Page 5.
[44] Applegate, C. and Potter, P. M. (2002). *Music and German National Identity.* Chicago: University of Chicago Press.

even primary, aspect of this self-improvement. If taken as part of the aforementioned discussion of nationalism and cosmopolitanism, the concept of *Bildung* might even be applied to the broader cultural improvement of Europe through the successful cultivation and spreading of German national culture. Furthermore, music is imbued with a distinct ability to create or encourage emotional attachment. It is clear, then, that music has a distinctive - and one might say indispensable - role to play in national identity formation. This is as true in Germany as it is anywhere else, and in the long nineteenth century perhaps even more so.

Musicology and German nationalism

A brief diversion towards the history of musicological thought surrounding German nationalism will help us to see how recent ideas have differed significantly from those of the past. In music, the nationalist inclination has often manifested itself in the use of traditional folk tunes, atypical rhythms or meters, and non-Western scales and harmonies, as well as folk topics and texts. Although nationalism has long been recognised as a predominant force in the composition of music (especially since the nineteenth century), it has also been seen as the sole territory of peripheral Eastern-European or non-European countries. In fact, Italy, France, and Germany seem to be the only countries that escaped the primary categorisation of 'nationalist' in the nineteenth century. Russian music has commonly been placed under the heading of 'Nationalism' (particularly with reference to the *Moguchaya kuchka*), as have Bohemian composers such as Bedřich Smetana and Antonin Dvořák, Edvard Grieg in Scandinavia, Spanish composers Isaac Albeniz and Enrique Granados, Edward Elgar in England, and the Americans of the Second New England School. Are Verdi's operas or Wagner's music dramas or, for that matter, Carl Maria von Weber's operas any less nationalist than these?[45] In fact, in some cases, German representatives are significantly more concerned with nationalist expression than their named 'nationalist' counterparts; for example, the musical style of American Romantic composers such

---

[45] Interestingly, French composers seem to have been much more interested in exoticism than in nationalism, if not in their intellectual pursuit of a French voice, then definitely in their compositions. Lalo's *Symphonie Espagnole*, Bizet's *Carmen*, Berlioz's *Harold en Italie*, Delibes's *Lakmé*, Saint-Saëns's so-called 'Egyptian' Piano Concerto (number 5), and Debussy's *Estampes*, featuring 'Pagodes' and 'La soirée dans Grenade', serve as only a few examples.

as Edward MacDowell and Amy Beach generally tends to fit quite comfortably into a European Romantic style, one that had in most cases been learned by study overseas. Why, then, have Germany and Italy so often been excluded from discussions of musical nationalism, especially given the fact that these two late-developing countries were so primarily concerned with their nationhood? An entry by Willi Apel in the 2nd edition of the *Harvard Dictionary of Music* (1969) articulates the long-held claim that "the nationalist movement is practically non-existent in Germany" and that nationalist musical inclinations in other countries had been "a reaction against the supremacy of German music."[46] Furthermore, Italy "had an old musical tradition to draw upon and did not need to resort to the somewhat extraneous resources of the nationalist movement." Given the overwhelmingly Germanic origins of the field of musicology (and the widespread influence of what Richard Taruskin calls the 'German scholarly diaspora'), it is not surprising that German conceptions of 'mainstream' repertoire shaped the canon as well as the way music's history was narrated. Nevertheless, recent currents in musicology have rejected this position, confirming the discord we feel given our explorations of both conscious German musical national identity formation and alternative narrations of music history like those of Romain Rolland, which recognise nationalist tensions in the 'mainstream' musics of Germany, Italy, and France.

Richard Taruskin's article on nationalism in the *New Grove Dictionary of Music and Musicians* devotes a large swath of space to German nationalism. Indeed, although Taruskin bucks the trend of German supremacy, he places his discussion of German nationalism at the very beginning of the article, recognising that German nationalism certainly had a singular effect on the development of other nations' musical nationalisms. Taruskin's first mention of a German nationalist attitude reaches all the way back to J. J. Quantz's famous 1752 flute treatise. Taruskin relays Quantz's assertion that "the virtue of German taste lay in knowing 'how to select with due discrimination from the musical tastes of various peoples what is best in each' and blend it all into a higher unity"[47] and reminds the reader that "later... this eclecticism

---

[46] Apel, W. (1969). *Harvard Dictionary of Music*, 2nd edn. Cambridge, MA: Harvard University Press, page 565.
[47] This sounds remarkably like Ernest Newman's ideal conception of music with its cross-fertilisation of national styles, yet while Newman seemingly had the whole of twentieth century music in mind, Quantz seems to be communicating the primary or universal

could (and would) be taken, under the rubric of 'universality', to be a mark of German superiority."[48] To bridge the gap between Quantz's treatise and this German universality, Taruskin explores the role of cultural nationalism during the rise of German Romanticism. Identifying the Romantic valuing of difference as nationalism's "natural ally and its most powerful stimulant," he introduces Johann Gottfried Herder's 1772 *Treatise on the Origin of Language* (*Abhandlung über den Ursprung der Sprache*) as a foundational document in the connection of Romanticism and nationalism. Taruskin summarises Herder, saying,

> It is language that makes humans human. But language can only be learnt socially, that is, in a community. Since there can be no thought without language, it follows that human thought, too, was a social or community product - neither wholly individual nor wholly universal. Herder insisted that each language manifested... unique values and ideas that constituted each language community's specific contribution to the treasury of world culture. Moreover... since there is no general or *a priori* scale against which particular languages can be measured, no language, hence no language community, can be held to be superior or inferior to any other. When the concept of language is extended to cover other aspects of learnt behaviour or expressive culture... Those aspects will be seen as essential constituents of a precious collective spirit or personality... It became an explicit goal of the arts, not just an inherent property, to express the specific truth of the 'imagined community' they served, and assist in its self-definition... What united all Germans was their linguistic heritage and the folklore that gave that heritage its most autochthonous (or, to use Herder's word, *urwüchsig*), hence authentic, expression.[49]

In the arts, this valuing of German language and folklore was given the name *Volkstümlichkeit*. An upsurge in published collections of folklore, poetry and song such as *Des Knaben Wunderhorn* reflected a new artistic respect for what had once been 'simple' or 'rustic'. It was not

---

nature of *German* style particularly Richard Taruskin, 'Nationalism', *Grove Music Online*, oxfordmusiconline.com.

[48] Taruskin, R. 'Nationalism: 2. Origins and earliest manifestations', *Grove Music Online*,.oxfordmusiconline.com.

[49] Taruskin, R. 'Nationalism: 4. Cultural nationalism and German Romanticism', *Grove Music Online*, oxfordmusiconline.com.

long before the 'folk' was valued over the civilized, in a movement Taruskin calls primitivism. The quintessential primitivist concept, according to Taruskin, is clearly communicated in Jean-Jacques Rousseau's *The Social Contract*: "man was born free and is everywhere in

Figure 13.2 Cover of *Des Knaben Wunderhorn; Alte deursche Lieder* – folk songs

chains."[50] Thus, when "the values celebrated in the German tales - the 'Prince Charming' values of honesty, seriousness, simplicity, fidelity, sincerity and so on - were projected onto the German language community, which in its political fragmentation, economic backwardness and military weakness (its primitiveness, in short)

---

[50] *Ibid.*

represented a sort of peasantry among peoples, with all that that had come to imply as to authenticity,"[51] German expression came to be seen (at least by its own people) as the best or most primitive cultural expression, not in spite of but because of its 'underdog' status. The

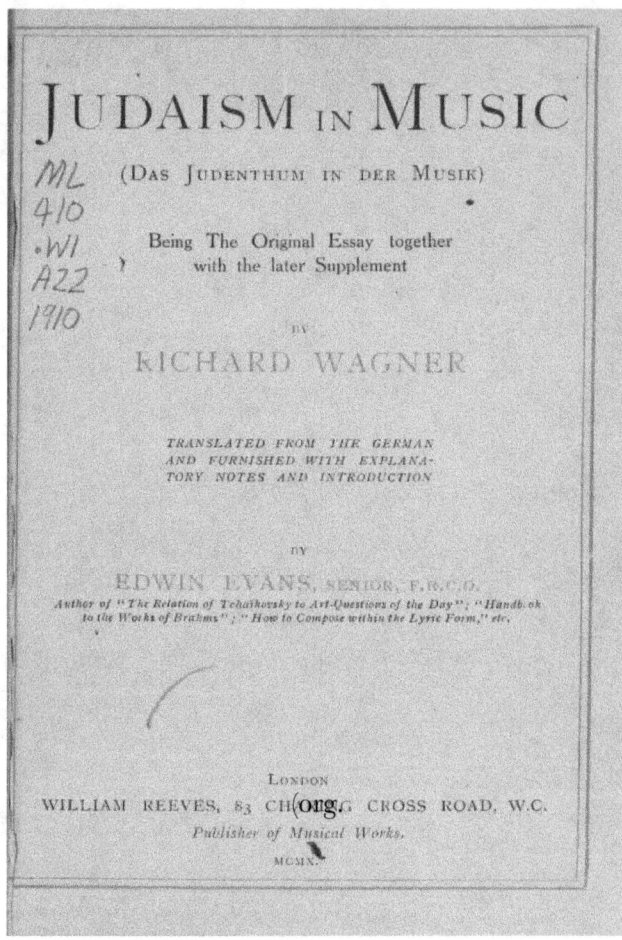

Figure 13.3 Wagner's *Judism in Music* Published in 1850)

German values of pure spirituality and inwardness (*das rein Geistige* and *das Innige*) were not only superimposed onto music (and particularly instrumental music) but were also seen to be in fundamental opposition to the values of French and Italian culture and music. At this time, many German writers and critics (Forkel, Hoffmann, A.B. Marx, and

---

[51] *Ibid.*

others) began making public knowledge of the lives and works of great German composers, with Bach and Beethoven looming large. As Taruskin suggests, "By the middle of the century, instrumental music was identified in the minds of many Europeans, not just Germans, as being (to quote the Russian pianist and composer Anton Rubinstein) 'a *German* art' [Taruskin's emphasis]. Thus what began as a philosophy of diversity became, in the case of music, one of hegemony."[52] Taruskin thus confirms what we had seen in our account of the confusingly unnationalistic telling of German music history: "In the history of no other modern art has nationalism been so pervasive - yet so covert - an issue."[53]

In the Vormärz period leading up to the revolutions of 1848, popular Romantic musical genres such as Lieder (settings of Romantic poetry of which Goethe's *Erlkönig* was an overwhelming favorite), the Romantic Singspiel or German opera (of which Carl Maria von Weber's *Der Freischütz* was the first), and the new Handelian-Bachian hybrid chorale oratorio (exemplified by Mendelssohn's *Paulus*) ventured an answer to the ever-echoing question, "What is German?" They pointed to, respectively, "nostalgic or neo-primitivist themes of hidden reality, invisible truth, the superiority of nature over culture (or, to put it Germanically, of *Kultur* over *Zivilisation*)... the imagery and diction of folkore"[54]; the representation of peasants as main characters rather than sidekicks, representatives of their country rather than their class; and traditions of *volkstümlich* singing (such as *Männerchöre*) and the grand choral festivals that unified the German population in the second quarter of the nineteenth century as well as stylistic connections to the increasingly popular J. S. Bach.

In the decades after the 1848 revolution, a new layer was added to the Germanic identification: ethnicity. This insistence on race as a German identifier seems to flow at least partly out of the fear that transnational identities, like Jewishness, would take precedence over a broader German loyalty. Nonetheless, these biological claims took on a new vibrancy in the second half of the nineteenth century. In music, the first victim of this exclusive nationalism was Felix Mendelssohn. Once the poster child for German Romanticism - conductor of the Leipzig Gewandhaus orchestra, director of the Leipzig Conservatory, director

---

[52] *Ibid.*
[53] *Ibid.*
[54] Taruskin, R. 'Nationalism: 6. Music and German nation-building: the Vormärz phase', *Grove Music Online,* oxfordmusiconline.com.

of the Berlin Cathedral Choir, and champion of German composers - Mendelssohn's cultural worth was now distilled down to only one thing: his race. An article in the *Neue Zeitschrift für Musik* titled 'Das Judenthum in der Musik' ('Judaism in Music') claimed that Jews, by virtue of their biological difference, could not contribute to fundamentally gentile German music. Since they were incapable of calling forth "that deep, heart-searching effect which we await from Music," that "expression of an unsayable content,"[55] they were, therefore, a 'corrupting' or 'diluting' influence on true German national music. Although published under a pseudonym, K. Freigedank (K. Freethought), the article was later claimed by Richard Wagner who, we will see, came to embody the rest of the qualities required of a German nationalist musician.

Wagner was a key figure in the subtle and finely-crafted shift from an attitude claiming the superiority of German music to a belief in the universality of German musical style characteristics. This shift was also aided greatly by a neo-Hegelian and teleological narration of music history in which the development of a distinctly European spirit (that 'world soul' of Italy, Germany, and France) was of greatest concern. Music critic Franz Brendel seems to stand at the center of this universalising of German values, both in his popular history of music *Geschichte der Musik in Italien, Deutschland und Frankreich von den ersten christlichen Zeiten an bis auf die Gegenwart* (History of Music in Italy, Germany and France from the Earliest Christian Times to the Present) and in his position as editor of the *Neue Zeitschrift für Musik*. According to Alexander Rehding, Brendel shaped music history into two strands: the German or nationalistic strand, led by Bach and Beethoven, and the universal or cosmopolitan strand, led by Handel, Gluck, and Mozart.[56] This sentiment finds its echo in Romain Rolland's narration of the Italianised history of German music. Like Rolland, and in opposition to Ernest Newman, Brendel saw the future of all music depending on the propagation of this German nationalistic style (the nationalist style becoming the universal). It was Brendel who coined the term *Neudeutsche Schule* (New German School) to identify the German music being created by living composers inspired by the old nationalistic style. The old school, led by Bach and Beethoven, had elevated German music to

---

[55] Taruskin, R. 'Nationalism: 7. After 1848', *Grove Music Online*, oxfordmusiconline.com.

[56] Rehding, A. (2006). 'Wagner, Liszt, Berlioz and the 'New German School'', in Perkins, M. A. and Liebscher, M. *Nationalism versus Cosmopolitanism in German Thought and Culture, 1789-1914*, (ed.). Lewiston, NY: Edwin Mellen Press, page 169.

its preeminent status through the encouragement of a Protestant Reformation-inspired sense of individualism.[57] Now Brendel positioned two non-Germans, Berlioz and Liszt, at the centre of the new German style. In his statement that "the birthplace cannot be considered decisive in matters of the spirit,"[58] Brendel introduced a type of Germanness that ironically transcended ethnicity (just as long as the subject was not Jewish), claiming the German spirit as a universal ideal. He posited that Berlioz and Liszt, though born elsewhere, "would never have become what they are today had they not from the first drawn nourishment from the German spirit and grown strong with it. Therefore, Germany must out of necessity be the true homeland of their works."[59] Moreover, Liszt, Berlioz and Wagner would lead the musical world to its logical peak:

> ...Wagner's art is currently a national one; the artwork of the future, however, for which the ground is paved by Wagner's art, is of a universality that predestines it, in my view, to gather all nations around it, and to become the basis of a world art.[60]

As Taruskin summarises:

> Germanness was no longer to be sought in folklore. One showed oneself a German not ethnically but spiritually, by putting oneself in humanity's vanguard. The new concept obviously made a far greater claim than the old. Germany was now viewed as the "world-historical" nation in Hegelian terms, the nation that served as the executor of history's grand design and whose actions led the world (or at least the world of music) to its inevitable destiny.[61]

Of course, there existed nationalism apart from the New German School, Johannes Brahms being one exemplar. Richard Taruskin identifies the *Triumphlied* of 1872 as "the most blatant example of sacralised nationalism in the whole literature of German music," citing

---

[57] *Ibid.* Page 169.
[58] Brendel, F. (1859). 'Zur Anbahnung einer Verständigung,' *Neue Zeitschrift für Musik*, 26, pages 265-73, as translated in Richard Taruskin, 'Nationalism: 7. After 1848', *Grove Music Online*, oxfordmusiconline.com.
[59] *Op. cit.* Taruskin (2014).
[60] *Op. cit.* Rehding, (2006), page 174.
[61] *Op. cit.* Taruskin, 'Nationalism: 7. After 1848', *Grove Music Online*, oxfordmusiconline.com.

Brahms's use of text from the Book of Revelation to compare Bismarck's Reich with God's reign and defeated France with the Whore of Babylon.[62] The *Triumphlied*, which was composed in celebration of Prussian victory and German unification, obeyed German ideals in other ways also. It was undeniably 'big', featuring the largest orchestra Brahms ever employed and two mixed choruses placed antiphonally; it communicated a German subject through its title, which references both military triumph and *volkstümlichkeit* through the use of the term *lied*; and it borrowed stylistically from Bach, in the lineage of Mendelssohn, particularly in the style given to its three trumpets.[63]

The *Triumphlied*, however, is rare among Brahms's works in terms of its obvious program. Brahms's alternate German style, of which Joseph Joachim also served as guardian, placed a high priority on absolute music as the most distinctively German. The symphony, in particular, was thought to communicate something essential about the German spirit. In *Symphonic Aspirations: German Music and Politics, 1900-1945*, Karen Painter discusses the symphony's role in conceptions of German musical identity, specifically in light of the early twentieth-century shift to shorter forms required by Schoenberg's new atonal vocabulary. She identifies within the symphony certain traits of Germanness: a concept of individualism within unity (multiple movements within a larger whole reflecting the political reality of German unity in difference), the notion of heroism or overcoming (Beethoven's *Eroica* legacy reflecting Germany's eventual military success after decades of underdog struggle), and an association with a certain social class (undoubtedly, the nineteenth century saw a blossoming of art music in middle-class culture, with amateur choirs, concert societies, journals, music education, and cultural participation being valued as never before). There was also a sense in which absolute music communicated with a power that could not be matched by words, placing it in line with Germany's reigning connection with emotion (that universal human experience). This association between absolute music and Germanness did even more to declare German music as the ideal universal musical style.

Franz Brendel, who did much to define Germanness in music, was only one of a thriving pool of writers and thinkers who shaped German musical nationalism through words rather than notes. The nineteenth

---

[62] *Ibid.*
[63] *Ibid.*

century saw the rise of both music criticism and music history, both of which were intimately tied to the steady formation of a German identity. Alexander Rehding posits a theory that such looming figures as Bach and Beethoven led would-be composers to be overly concerned with their position in history, saying, "... it is perhaps not surprising that many of the creative minds of the 1850s would rather turn to theoretical speculation than to composing works that might not pass the test of time."[64] Similarly, Pamela Potter and Celia Applegate argue in the introductory article of *Music and German National Identity* that the connection between music and German identity is more appropriately attributed to music critics, music educators, conductors, impresarios, audiences, and thinkers than to the composers themselves. Although it is important to remember that it was common in the nineteenth century for composers to take on multiple roles, including critic, educator, conductor, and impresario, the basic notion is well-received; Schumann and Mendelssohn shaped music at least as much through their writing and conducting as through their compositions. While the nascent field of music criticism sought to turn the question of 'What is German?' to the field of music, a growing interest in the musics of the past (best known through Mendelssohn's Bach revival) helped critics find their answers.

There was in the nineteenth century, as we have seen, a steadily developing repertory of concepts of 'Germanness' in music, one which encompassed a diversity of styles, political affiliations, and ethnicities (Mendelssohn, Brendel, Wagner, Berlioz, Liszt, Brahms, Joachim, and infinite others). As it turns out, though the question of what constituted Germanness had been asked and many answers attempted, it was still fraught with confusion.

In the end, intention and reception seem to be the final determinants of German national music identity. As Carl Dahlhaus writes in his discussion of nationalism and music in *Between Romanticism and Modernism: Four Studies in the Music of the Later Nineteenth Century*,

> [If] a composer intended a piece of music to be national in character and the hearer believes it to be so, this is something which the historian must accept as an aesthetic fact, even if stylistic analysis -

---

[64] *Op. cit.* Rehding, (2006), page 161.

the attempt to 'verify' the aesthetic premise by reference to musical features - fails to produce any evidence.[65]

Thus, as much as historical, cultural and stylistic analysis can help us to determine Germanness in music, there is also a broader sense in which Barbara Eichner's definition of a German as anyone and everyone who "made a point about considering himself or herself as part of the larger German linguistic, historical, cultural or ethnic community"[66] is applicable to Germanness in music: a 'German' piece of music is one which is either intended or perceived to be distinguishably German.

Conclusion

As we have seen, German national identity formation in the long nineteenth century was an arduous, lengthy, and undulating process, with nearly as many contributing factors as there were causes for the eventual War. Furthermore, we have come to agree with Philip V. Bohlman's argument, as summarised by Barbara Eichner, that music "not only symbolises and articulates nationalism but actively participates in its formation."[67] German nationalists, desperate to give their claims cultural ballast, eagerly grabbed onto German music as a signifier of German national identity. Similarly, German musicians and critics embraced nationalism as a means of defining their musical identity. Thus, we must conclude that German music, through both intention and perception, was undeniably intertwined with German national identity formation in the century leading up to the First World War.

---

[65] Dahlhaus, C. (1980). *Between Romanticism and Modernism: Four studies in the music of the later Nineteenth Century*, (trans. Mary Whittall). Berkeley: University of California Press, pages 86-7.
[66] *Op. cit.* Eichner, (2012), page 6.
[67] *Ibid.* Page 29.

Chapter 14

Dichotomies of Representation and Interpretation: A Pacifist's Story

Sonja Andrew
University of Huddersfield

Introduction

Oral histories passed down through generations provide a glimpse into past lives, often conveying the character of individuals, the hardships they faced, and the impact of their beliefs and values on their families and communities. These personal stories often remain with the family and may never reach another audience in an oral, written, or visual form. At the centenary of World War I the hidden stories from these years deserve acknowledgement, particularly the experiences of those who rejected war and were marginalised within the mainstream narratives of this period.

The life of John Edgar Bell, a Quaker and conscientious objector[1] in World War I, was pieced together from conversations with his daughter and other family members. Alongside this oral history, a small number of family photographs and extracts from his daughter's diary were assembled, forming an overview of the pacifist, his family, and the social exclusion they faced in the First World War, and in the post-war years.

---

[1] The Religious Society of Friends (Quakers) committed itself to peace and opposed all war including the First World War. See, *The Testimony,* August 24, 1916 at quaker.org.uk/about-quakers/our-history/quakers-and-wwi.

Conscription

As a committed pacifist John Edgar Bell refused to join the armed forces and fight in the war, he remained in Bradford, part of the West Riding of Yorkshire, working as a mechanic. The Military Service Act passed on 27th January 1916 established conscription and the Act came into effect on 2nd March 1916, with public information posters preceding the date stating "WILL YOU MARCH TOO OR WAIT UNTIL MARCH 2?"[2] The previous year Lord Kitchener's famous campaign 'Your Country Needs You' encouraged over 1 million men to volunteer by January 1915, but even this number was not enough. The reason for mandatory subscription was, therefore, that within a year of fighting it was clear there were insufficient volunteers to replace the men being killed and wounded. The Military Service Act was imposed on all single men aged between 18-41 years of age, and was in May 1916 extended to married men. The Act allowed for exemptions for men deemed to be medically unfit, or who were in protected occupations such as the clergy, teaching and some industrial occupations. Nonetheless, conscription was unpopular. In April 1916 over 200,000 men demonstrated in Trafalgar Square against it.[3] The Act also allowed for conscientious objections to be heard by local tribunals.

Local military service tribunals were established to consider exemptions from conscription. Applications could be made on the following grounds:[4]

> On the ground that it is expedient in the national interests that the man should, instead of being employed in military service, be engaged in other work in which he is habitually engaged.

---

[2] Goodall, F. (1997) *A Question of Conscience, Conscientious Objection in The Two World Wars*. Gloucestershire: Sutton Publishing, page 8.
[3] See the following from the National archives (UK) for more details, hnationalarchives.gov.uk/pathways/firstworldwar/spotlights/antiwar.htm
[4] See HC Deb 20 June 1918 vol 107 cc607-42 retrieved from api.parliament.uk/historic-hansard/commons/1918/jun/20/military-service-medical-grading; HC Deb 11 May 1916 vol 82 cc1016-59 retrieved from, api.parliament.uk/historic-Hansard/commons/1916/may/11/new-clause-exemption-on-the-ground-of; HC Deb 08 March 1917 vol 91 cc534-6 retrieved from, api.parliament.uk/historic-hansard/commons/1917/mar/08/conscientious-objectors

On the ground that it is expedient in the national interests that the man should, instead of being employed in military service, be engaged in other work which he wishes to be engaged.
If he is being educated or trained for any work, on the ground that it is expedient in the national interests that, instead of being employed in military service, he should continue to be so educated or trained.

On the ground that serious hardship would ensue if the man were called up for Army service, owing to his exceptional financial or business obligations or domestic position.

On the ground of ill-health or infirmity.

On the ground of a conscientious objection to the undertaking of combatant service.

On the ground that the principal and usual occupation of the man is one of those included in the list of occupations certified by Government Departments for exemption.

Reports in local press on tribunals

The front-page stories of Bradford newspapers, such as the *Bradford Weekly Telegraph*, *The Bradford Daily Argus*, and *The Shipley Times and Express*, focused on the military tribunals. However, in Shipley's first Recruiting Tribunal on 21st February 1916, it was capitalism, not pacifism, that dominated the proceedings, with exemption applications from employees at Salts Mill in Saltaire who were engaged in roles associated with woven textile manufacture. Many of these applications were rejected by the tribunal panel, leading the mill owner James Roberts to appeal the decisions, as the Board of Trade was calling on companies to maintain their export business and he felt it was impossible for them to continue trading if their office and shipping clerks were withdrawn.[5] The editorial writer for the newspaper expressed concern regarding the pressure on the tribunals from businesses in the area, noting:

---

[5] *Shipley Times and Express*, Friday March 3, 1916, page 7.

> People who honestly feel that they are entitled to exemption on personal or business grounds or because they are engaged on work of national importance, should confine themselves to evidence in support of their claims and not make comment which is calculated to discredit the bona-fides of the Tribunal.

With an estimated sixteen thousand British men registering as conscientious objectors,[6] newspaper reports on the local military tribunals in the following weeks of March 1916 had greater focus on the applications from pacifists, and demonstrate the general antipathy towards those applying for exemption on these grounds. Editorial in the *Shipley Times and Express*, for the 10th March states:[7]

> We agree with Mr Butterfield [the prospective Unionist candidate for Shipley] in the opinion that the men who are genuine in their objection to combatant service are very few in number. Many of the applicants for exemption under the conscientious objection clause of the Military Service Act have not stood the test of cross-examination before the Tribunals. What they call conscientious objections to fighting were wretched excuses for shirking their duty at a momentous crisis in their country's history.

On Friday 24th March the newspaper reported derisorily on the local Military Service Tribunal hearings against enlistment on the grounds of conscience. Of the 32 cases heard at that tribunal, 22 were conscientious objectors. The objectors were asked a series of questions, such as the length of time they had held their opinions, and if their conscientious objection was widely acknowledged in the community. This was usually followed with hypothetical questions that often resulted in ridicule. An example of this can be seen in the report of the tribunal questioning of Arthur Emmett, a boot machine operator, employed at Windhill Cooperative:

> Tribunal: Has it occurred to you what you would do for your breakfast to-morrow morning if everybody had taken your views?
> Objector: I am quite confident there would have been no war.

---

[6] *Op. cit.* Goodall, (1997).
[7] *Shipley Times and Express* March 10, 1916, page 7.

Tribunal: Yes, every man, but I am asking you under present circumstances, if we had no Navy how would you get your food?

Objector: I have never asked for the protection of the Navy. In early days people lived upon the land of this country. I am quite convinced that if we had no Navy we should be able to provide the food that was necessary.

Tribunal: My good man, we are not living in the Garden of Eden now, we are in 1916.[8]

The questions continued, with the tribunal reminding the objector to "Talk about 1916, never mind the early Christians."

Whilst greater press was given to public opinion against conscientious objectors in local newspapers, a few articles appeared to provide some balance of opinion. Ethel Snowden, a socialist, suffragette,[9] and wife of Phillip Snowden MP[10], spoke in support of conscientious objectors at a meeting of the Independent Labour Party, organised by the Bradford Council Against Conscription. She provided an argument against conscription, referring to a speech given by Winston Churchill. The *Shipley Times and Express* report of the event noted:

> She heard Mr Winston Churchill make a speech in parliament with regard to the use made of our troops, and she regarded that speech as one of the most practical arguments against conscription. He declared that not more than one in six of our men are being effectively used in this war. Five out of six are either behind the lines or in this country. That being the case, there is no need to introduce conscription.[11]

In The House of Commons debates on 11th May 1916, questions were also being raised regarding how best to deal with conscientious objectors, through the Non-Combatant Core or working in roles such as agriculture on home soil.[12] The lack of parity in the treatment of

---

[8] *Shipley Times and Express*, Friday March 24, 1916, page 9.
[9] Full title, Viscountess Snowden whom in 1917 became the organiser and principal speaker for the Women's Peace Crusade.
[10] Phillip Snowden was a Labour Member of Parliament for Blackburn, becoming the first Labour Chancellor of the Exchequer in 1924. His opposition to conscription and calls for a peace to be negotiated as early as 1916 meant he was unpopular and in 1918 he lost his Blackburn seat in Parliament.
[11] *Shipley Times and Express*, Friday June 9, 1916, page 3.
[12] See, menwhosaidno.org.

conscientious objectors by the tribunals appeared to be a source of concern to some members of parliament. Mr. Leifchild Jones MP joining in the debate noted:[13]

> I wish to join in the appeal to the Government to take some action in regard to the genuine conscientious objectors in different parts of the country. The number of conscientious objectors is not very large, but there are a certain number of people whom no amount of compulsion by Parliament will compel to take part in anything that savours of military action, and this House and the Government must provide in a measure of this kind for dealing with those cases. One of the main difficulties which have arisen under the working of the last compulsion Act has been the inequality of treatment dealt out to men of exactly similar opinions when they have come before the tribunals. I have in mind the case of three brothers who are all conscientious objectors on religious grounds. I have known the family for thirty years. They were brought up in a strict Nonconformist sect, hating all war; taught by their father to hate war. They are all conscientious objectors on account of their religion and past teaching. They are an extremely obstinate family. These three brothers - aged eighteen, twenty-two, and twenty-five, I think - have all been before tribunals, and declared against undertaking any sort of military service. What has been their fate? This is what I want to put to the Government with most emphasis. The brothers are in different parts of the country. One secured absolute exemption at the hands of his tribunal. The second was granted exemption from combatant service by the local tribunal. He appealed for absolute exemption, to which he thought himself entitled, and the Appeal Tribunal, not content with dismissing the appeal, actually said that he must go for combatant service. The third was sent to combatant service by the local tribunal. I defy anybody to distinguish between the religious opinions of these brothers. They hold exactly the same views, and put them in practically the same way.[14]

---

[13] Liberal MP for Nottinghamshire, Rushcliffe Division.
[14] HC Deb 11 May 1916 vol 82 cc1016-59.

The experiences of John Edgar Bell

The focus on conscientious objectors in the local newspapers of Bradford and its environs diminished for a time, as emphasis shifted to reports on casualties following the battle of the Somme on 1st July 1916, but this event only increased the open hostility towards conscientious objectors and their families in the Bradford area and neighbouring districts. John Edgar Bell's daughter Myrtle recounted that her father was imprisoned (she thought in Wakefield) for refusing to fight. It is likely, given his pacifist stance, that John made an application for a certificate of exemption from conscription that was rejected, but currently no records on this have been located. Myrtle noted that her father only spoke to his children of his experiences and the conditions of his imprisonment years later. He told of being treated harshly in prison as a conscientious objector and his health deteriorating rapidly. Myrtle said that due to this, in the final year of the war, he agreed to sign up for non-combatant service.

The oral history of John Edgar Bell recalled by his daughter provided a brief glimpse into John's experiences as a conscientious objector, and she was correct in stating that he was imprisoned. Although no records have yet been located to provide evidence of his imprisonment prior to 1918, recently recovered military service records show that John Edgar Bell, aged 23, was enlisted for military service on 26th April 1918, as a private in the 18th York Regiment.[15] In the military records he is listed as conscripted under category B1. Soldiers in this category were classed as,

> Free from serious organic diseases, able to stand service on lines of communication in France, or in garrisons in the tropics. Able to march 5 miles, see to shoot with glasses, and hear well.[16]

This category was not the front line, but included manual labour work for the war effort on military bases.

---

[15] Military Service Record miuk1914f_127322-00252 (ancestry.com).
[16] HC Deb 20 June 1918 vol 107 cc607-42.

In John's military service records an army memorandum dated 9th May 1918 reveals that he received a court martial. He was tried,

> at Halifax 9th May 1918 and convicted of disobeying a lawful command given by his superior officer and sentenced to imprisonment with hard labour for six calendar months.[17]

The memorandum states that he was awaiting "trial, promulgation and removal to prison 26/4/18 to 10/5/18",[18] so it would appear that he disobeyed the command given by his superior officer on the first day of his conscription in the army. The memorandum continues "H.M. Prison Wormwood Scrubs 11/5/18 to 6/11/18" showing that the six months imprisonment with hard labour was to be carried out at one of Britain's most notorious London prisons. Goodall (1997:) notes:

> At the end of their sentence, conscientious objectors were released, returned to barracks where they would disobey an order and be court martialled once again and returned to prison. It was a strategy used against the suffragettes - what was termed the 'Cat and Mouse' treatment.[19]

Aware of the cycle of non-compliance and imprisonment, some Members of Parliament, such as Arthur Beck, MP for Saffron Walden, questioned the treatment of conscientious objectors in prison, as the deteriorating health that many of the men suffered would not make them fit for military service in the army.[20]

Social exclusion and hostility

Military service records show that John Edgar Bell was discharged by the 3rd May 1919, some months after the end of World War I, but he returned to a local community that was openly hostile towards conscientious objectors and their families. Countless people had experienced personal loss and this fuelled resentment that John's family had not experienced the same. John's pacifist stance meant that his

---

[17] Military Service Record miuk1914f_127322-00252 Military Service Record miuk1914f_127322-00252 (ancestry.com).
[18] *Ibid.*
[19] *Op. cit.* Goodall (1997) pages 30-31.
[20] HC Deb 08 March 1917 vol 91 cc534-6.

family faced social exclusion, even when they moved to another area in the Bradford district of the West Riding of Yorkshire. Figure 14.1 shows an extract from Myrtle's diary (2004), she writes:

> We moved when I was 6 months old to Denholme, a little village midway between Halifax, Keighley and Bradford. My father John Edgar Bell had been a conscientious objector during World War I, because of this he could not get employment in his own trade, he was a skilled 'time served' man in mechanical engineering, so he took a job in the village as the lamp lighter to feed his family

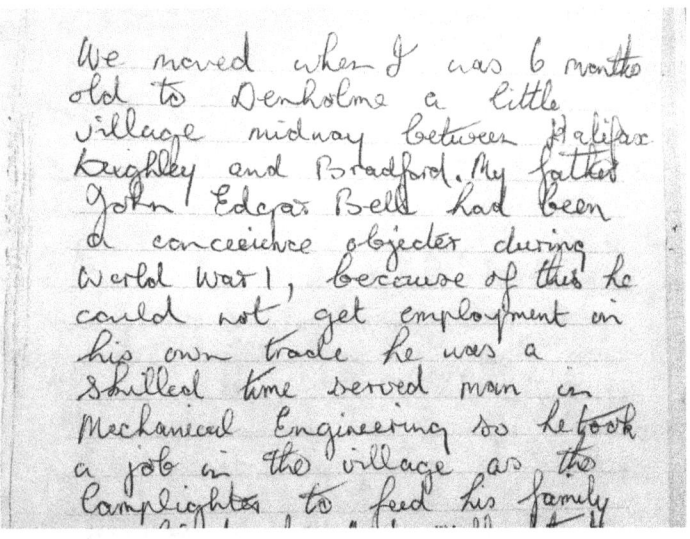

Figure 14.1 Extract from the diary of Myrtle Andrew (formerly Myrtle Bell), 2004

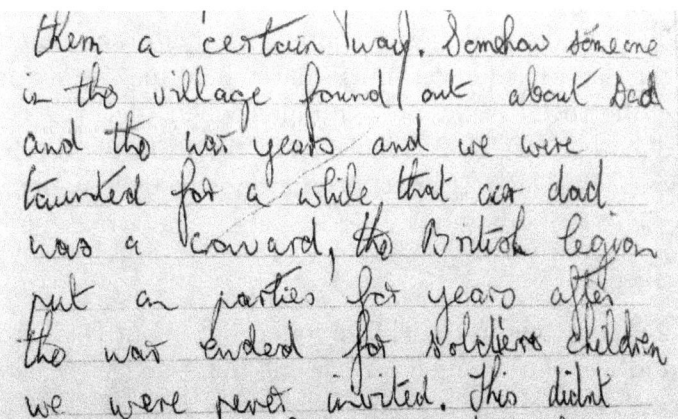

Figure 14.2 Extract from the diary of Myrtle Andrew (formerly Myrtle Bell), 2004

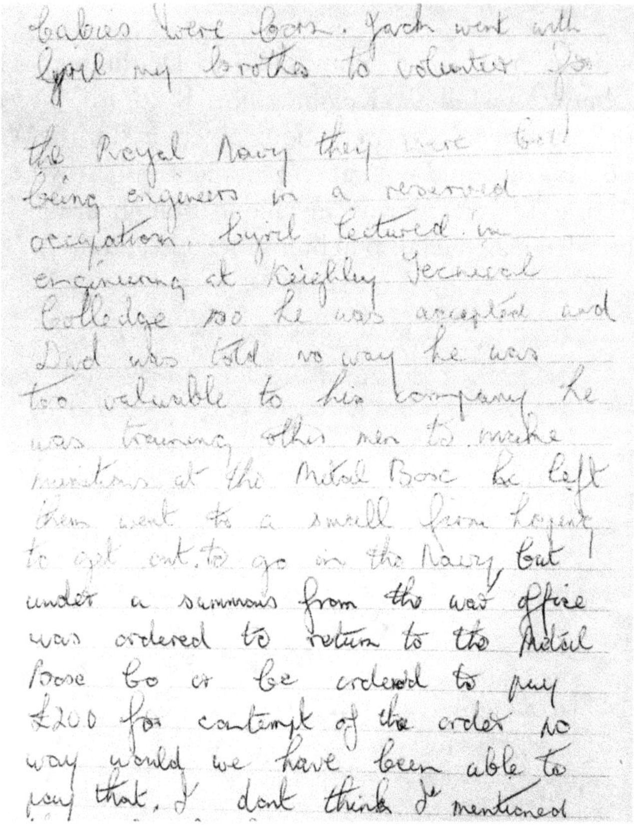

> babies were born. Jack went with Cyril my brother to volunteer for the Royal Navy they were but being engineers in a reserved occupation. Cyril lectured in engineering at Keighley Technical College so he was accepted and Dad was told no way he was too valuable to his company he was training other men to make munitions at the Metal Box he left them went to a small firm hoping to opt out to go in the Navy but under a summons from the war office was ordered to return to the Metal Box to or be ordered to pay £200 for contempt of the order no way would we have been able to pay that. I dont think I mentioned

Figure 14.3 Extract from the diary of Myrtle Andrew (formerly Myrtle Bell), 2004

As a child Myrtle would accompany her father on his nightly rounds to light the lamps. She recounts that when the family moved to Denholme the social exclusion continued when the local community discovered he had not fought. Graffiti in the form of 'X' crosses and derogatory words were scrawled on the door of their home, and they also experienced more direct verbal abuse. She writes in her diary (Figure 14.2):

> Somehow someone in the village found out about Dad and the war years and we were taunted for a while that our Dad was a coward, the British Legion put on parties for years after the war ended for soldiers' children, we were never invited.

The social exclusion gradually abated, only to resurface many years later in the Second World War when Myrtle had married. Her husband Jack was in a reserved occupation as an engineer in the manufacture of ammunitions, so he could not fight for his country, although Myrtle's diary shows (Figure 14.3) that he wanted to enlist in the navy:

> Jack went with Cyril my brother to volunteer for the Royal Navy; they were both being engineers in a reserved occupation. Cyril lectured in engineering at Keighley Technical College so he was accepted and Dad [Myrtle refers to her husband Jack as Dad as they had a child by that time] was told no way, he was too valuable to his company, he was training other men to make munitions at the Metal Box. He left them, went to a small firm hoping to get out to go in the Navy, but under a summons from the War Office was ordered to return to the Metal Box Co or be ordered to pay £200 for contempt of the order, no way would we have been able to pay that.

Although Jack's exemption from military service was not due to conscientious objection, the associations with the past remained attached to the family for many years, as subsequent generations in their community learnt of John Edgar Bell's pacifist beliefs and imprisonment as a 'conchie'.

Richmond Castle cells

Richmond Castle is one of the few locations where the prison cells of World War I conscientious objectors are preserved. To gain a better understanding of the conditions faced by the objectors during their incarceration, English Heritage was contacted to arrange access to the cells. The visit revealed the cramped, dimly lit, unheated conditions the conscientious objectors' experienced (Figure 14.4), and why this may have led some absolutists to agree to non-combatant service. The lime plaster on the cell walls was covered with a small number of portraits of loved ones and decorative drawings (Figure 14.5), but motivational and religious writing, and Christian symbols, were predominant underneath the writing 'Henderson, York, John Smith, Leicester, NCF, June 24, 1916' is written "It matters not how straight the gate, how charged with punishment the scroll, I am the master of my fate, I am the captain of my soul" with the signature Mr C. Henley. NCF was an acronym for the 'No Conscription Fellowship' who required its members to "refuse from conscientious motives to bear arms, because they consider human life to be sacred and cannot, therefore, assume the responsibility of inflicting death."[21]

Figure 14.4 Images from the cell block at Richmond Castle, and Richmond Castle ruins, North Yorkshire. Photography: S. Andrew. Photography by kind permission of English Heritage

Further research on the drawings and texts provided more specific information on the experiences of individual prisoners, with drawings such as 'N.Gaudies mothe' cross-referenced to Norman Gaudie, writer of the 1922 publication 'The Courage That Brings Peace'.[22]

What remains of the crumbling lime render on the cell walls at Richmond Castle is testimony to the faith of the imprisoned conscientious objectors of World War I. Drawings by the guards are also visible on the corridor walls outside the cells, and later writing inside the cells shows that World War Two objectors were also kept there.

---

[21] ppu.org.uk.
[22] co.project.org.uk.

An inscription above the name 'H. Conlin, Green Howards, 1939' states:

> The only war which is worth fighting is the class war. The working class of this country have no quarrel with the working class of Germany or any other country. Socialism stands for Internationalism. If the workers of all countries united and refused to fight there would be no war.

Figure 14.5 Drawings on the cell walls in the prison block at Richmond Castle, North Yorkshire. Photography: S. Andrew. Photography by kind permission of English Heritage

Visual representation of John Edgar Bell's story

The photographs from Richmond castle provided a record of the writing and drawings from the cell walls, but also captured the quality of light and the physical spaces. They contributed to a collection of World War I images that enabled translation of John Edgar Bell's conscientious objection story into visual form via a series of textile panels as installations in public spaces. These works functioned as an act of individual remembrance and commemoration, and an exploration of how narrative textiles may function as mnemonic products. This allowed not only a visualisation of John Edgar Bell's story, but also

Figure 14.6 Panel one from the triptych 'The Ties That Bind (I)'. Photography: S. Andrew

examination of the relationship between authorial intention and viewer interpretation of the visual narrative. It revealed how the history of a past life, shown through an image based narrative, can engage audiences in reflection on aspects of war, society, family and faith, their responses revealing the impact of shared cultural understanding and the projection of personal memory on their construction of meaning from the artwork.

Narrative content

The textile panels needed to communicate the values and social exclusion of the objector's family, the imprisonment of the objector, and the post war stigma the family endured. With these three objectives, a triptych format was developed. The left panel was designed as the start of the family narrative, with John Edgar Bell's imprisonment as the central panel, and an image of his daughter Myrtle in the final panel to continue the family signification into the post war era. Kress and van Leeuwen[23] (2001) note that this left to right construction of visual narrative is common in Western cultures, but less prevalent in others, and enables a sequential transformation to take place, often through the actions of the centre image, to transfer viewer perception from one paradigm of meaning to another. A photographic portrait of John Edgar Bell therefore became the focus of the centre panel. The aim of this was to establish the objector as the main character in the visual narrative, surrounded by images to connote imprisonment, war, family and faith across the panels. Family photographs were a vital element in the construction of the compositions, but there were only a limited number of images to form any visual history of John Edgar Bell. By consolidating John's story in a visual form based on the fragments of oral history, diary extracts, and photographs, an enhanced 'archive of memory' was created via the textile panels.

Two textile triptychs were developed, and each tested in a range of public spaces. In both triptychs the communication function of the first panel was to convey the family's pacifist stance, the burden of conscientious objection on the family, and being singled out for their belief. The visual content also needed to indicate the period and begin the narrative chronology of the panels. The central panel intended to convey the imprisonment of John Edgar Bell, so signifiers associated with this were trialed. The final panel in both triptychs was the most difficult to compose on both communication and aesthetic levels. Conveying the post war stigma the family endured proved challenging, as this part of the narrative spanned many years.

The colours applied across the triptychs fulfilled both conative and emotive communication functions. The sepia and grey tones of old

---

[23] Kress, G. and Van Leeuwen, T. (2001) *Reading Images: The grammar of visual design*. London: Routledge, pages 181-229.

photographs, and the blue, taupe and khaki shades of military uniforms were incorporated into the triptychs.

Figure 14.7 Stamp detail from the triptych 'The Ties That Bind (I)'. Photography: S. Andrew

These colours were intended to connote war as entropic signifiers and allude to the past, but also fulfill the emotive function of communicating a sombre mood. Van Leeuwen (2005) notes that people are not always aware of the connotations of colours and may, for example:

> wear military colours without intending to convey any form of identification with the military... Yet the military connotation is objectively there. The military is objectively one of the places - perhaps one of the most important ones - 'where this colour has come from'.[24]

---

[24] Van Leeuwen, T. (2005) *Introducing Social Semiotics*. London: Routledge, page 62.

Figure 14.8 Centre panel detail from the triptych 'The Ties That Bind (I)'. Photography: S. Andrew

The images incorporated into the compositions for each triptych were chosen to communicate specific meanings to viewers. For example, a white feather to signify cowardice and a portrait of mother and child to connote the maternal and familial. The images chosen ranged, in semiotic terms, from the redundant and easily understood, to the entropic that required more specialised knowledge to decipher.[25] Images to represent Christian faith, therefore, ranged from white crosses to

---

[25] See, Barthes, R. (1974) *S/Z*. New York: Hill and Wang (originally published in French by Editions du Seuil, Paris, 1970); Fiske J. (2010) *Introduction to Communication Studies*. London: Routledge.

crossed keys (symbol of Saint Peter and gates to heaven), and fleur de Lys (symbol of the Virgin Mary). Shadows cast by the bars of cell windows, keys, a lock, barbed wire and lines 'marking time' were selected to connote imprisonment. To represent war, images such as bombs, warships, and a crane loading munitions at a quayside, were considered.

In the first triptych crossed out medals of a hybrid design were included to communicate rejection of war and 'not heroic', as signifiers of the cultural perception of the conscientious objector's actions and the ongoing social exclusion the family faced from World War I to World War II. Circling marks were added around the mother and child image to signify 'marking out' by others, to try and communicate a family being 'singled out' in their community, and stamp images (Figure 14.7)from 1910 - 1915 were incorporated to indicate the period and provide an icon of the ruling monarch. The stamps also represented the dominant cultural code of 'serving king and country' in wartime.

In the central composition of the first triptych the eyes of the objector were covered to connote loss of identity. The absence of the mouth had a dual connotation of 'a voice unheard' and losing freedom of speech, but when combined with the shadows of prison bars, also signifying imprisonment for speaking out. A World War I uniform pattern was also included as entropic signifier to represent the pressure of conscription, with the placement of the uniform over the objector's torso to reinforce the idea of the military uniform being imposed on him (Figure 14.8). In the final panel, a postcard image of a boy wearing an army uniform and a girl waving a British flag was added to denote the end of the war, whilst a photograph of Myrtle Andrew with her husband Jack aimed to represent the family in the later post-war years (Figure 14.9). Juxtaposition of the couple with a warship and white feather particularly intended to create a 'micro-visual syntagm' to communicate the ongoing stigma they faced during World War II.

Responses to the Visual Narrative of John Edgar Bell

The textile triptychs were exhibited without a title or content description at a range of venues in England. Each panel was numbered to direct the viewer from panel to panel in the correct order.

In 2007 triptych one was exhibited at Walford Mill Crafts Gallery in Dorset, Lloyds TSB regional banking headquarters in Birmingham, the textile gallery of Manchester Museum of Science and Industry and Saltaire United Reformed Church (part of Saltaire world heritage site in West Yorkshire). Viewer feedback on the triptych informed the design of three new textile panels. Unsuccessful images were removed from the design process and the second triptych developed.

Visual signifiers with a greater degree of redundancy were incorporated into the textiles to try to obtain a more accurate reading of John Edgar Bell's story from viewers. Juxtaposed with the family photographs were images of a World War I bomb and gun, barbed wire, tally marks, lock and key, and crossed out British flags. Photographic images

Figure 14.9 Family photograph of Myrtle and Jack Andrew

Figure 14.10 The second triptych 'The Ties That Bind (II)' displayed at the Bankfield Museum, Halifax, West Yorkshire. Photography: S. Andrew

of hands praying, bound and bandaged and larger decorative white crosses were also included. The second triptych (Figures 14.10, 14.11 and 14.12) was exhibited in 2008 at the Bankfield Museum and Art Gallery in Halifax, West Yorkshire, and the textile gallery of Manchester Museum of Science and Industry.

Figure 14.11 'The Ties That Bind (II)' panel one detail

Figure 14.12 'The Ties That Bind (II)' centre panel detail of Harriet Bell, John Edgar Bell's wife

Viewers' interpretations of the triptychs were gathered via on site questionnaires and 1:1 interviews during the exhibition periods with responses from over 450 people collected. Viewers responded about the meaning conveyed by the triptychs and gave details about specific elements in the textile panels that informed their perceptions of the visual narrative. Both triptychs predominantly signified war, loss, and families in wartime. The image of John Edgar Bell in the centre panel of the first triptych, with eyes covered and mouth omitted, elicited a range of responses. At Manchester Museum of Science and Industry one viewer suggested that "eyes are covered" signified "someone who wants to say something but can't be seen saying it", whilst two respondents at the Saltaire site read the strip over the eyes literally, as blindness, rather than reading the image as a visual metaphor. At the LloydsTSB site a viewer noted "The gentleman in the middle one where his face is missing, or where his eyes are missing I should say, covered with the bar, made me think of the faceless soldier." Several viewers across the sites commented on the image of John Edgar Bell being the unknown soldier in their responses to the first triptych, and omission of the mouth from the image also generated several responses focusing on this aspect. At Manchester Museum of Science and Industry one viewer felt that the "man with no voice" signified "Anti-war." In the interviews at Lloyds TSB a viewer noted "The chap in the middle I think that's to do with someone betraying someone else - his mouth isn't there." A further viewer at the Lloyds TSB site stated:

> Although I don't know why the gentleman's, the figure in the middle one's mouth is covered up, I don't know. Maybe, oh, now you start to see a theme, maybe he was a soldier, maybe that's why the cross through the medal, who was dishonoured during the war. Maybe deserted under fire and then later on found, as we're now finding, that they were treated rather harshly.

Other viewers used combinations of signifiers to generate a series of linked meanings to decipher the central panel. For example:

> And in the middle one its just one man by himself and the medal is crossed out, and his eyes are also blacked out and I think that signifies that he, that all the soldiers, were just almost anonymous, and didn't really have their own identity, and all sort of merged into one as cannon fodder for the army.

Although the majority of viewer interpretations of both triptychs related to war and family in general terms, the second triptych generated a greater number of responses that reflected on pacifism, conscientious objection and faith that correlated with the intention of the visual narrative. Responses included:

> A man separated from his family because he is a conscientious objector - imprisoned - then released, but bearing the scars of the whole ordeal.

> The struggles of those conscientious objectors and their courage and dire consequences for them and their families.
>
> The overall impression is of an ancestor of yours who was misunderstood when he became a conscientious objector in WW1. He was shown the white feather and was 'obliged' to become an active participant. He was subsequently taken prisoner of war and interned for a long time. He always was an enigma to his family who misunderstood his motivations and his change of personality when he returned home from his ordeal.
>
> Wartime devastation, family separation, conscientious objector? Imprisonment, incarceration, counting the days, loss, bereavement. War is dreadfully sad.
>
> It's a family saga and that only impinges on me more strongly as I look and see the same people in different pieces. Its about war and imprisonment, the way the women back home are trapped behind their windows, in domestic staticness, in a way similar to the man trapped behind the barbed wire of his POW camp. I wonder if he was imprisoned for being a conscientious objector - as there is a crucifix and a crossed out projectile? And his hand suggests attesting - e.g. to a belief.

Imprisonment due to religious belief, belief in peace, and the communication of an anti-war message featured in other responses, such as "Pacifists dying for a faith", "Consequences of faith/objection/resistance runs throughout" and "White feather, symbol of conscientious objection, standing up for beliefs.

Conclusion

Whilst the triptychs were successful in functioning as an archive of personal memory for John Edgar Bell's descendants, interpretations of the work from the general public were, as expected, quite broad. Whilst the second triptych generated a greater number of readings related to conscientious objection, the range of responses still expressed what Barthes (1974) termed as 'a galaxy of signifiers',[26] the textile panels often functioning as mnemonics that triggered reflection on oral histories from a viewer's own family, or a friend's family. Some interpretations were close to the encoded intentions of the work, but many others diverged from it, one viewer even described the image of John Edgar Bell as Hitler. Depth of knowledge of British history informed the accuracy of audiences' understanding of triptychs, with readings reflecting on World War II emerging, in addition to those about World War I. Knowledge of local history also impacted on how viewers interpreted the textile panels. This created some variance in responses based on the regional location in which the textile panels were shown. In the West Midlands several respondents thought that the panels related to the local lock and key making industry that used to be prevalent in that area, whilst in Saltaire, the history of tailoring in Leeds, and ancestors who had worked in Salts mill, featured in the responses.

In the ten years following the studies both triptychs were selected for a range of national and international exhibitions. In 2014 the work was also archived via an online exhibition on the Arts and Humanities Research Council Image Gallery, and in their World War I Centenary commemorative publication 'Beyond the Trenches, Researching the First World War'.[27] Accompanied by a written content description, these exhibitions shared the hidden narrative of John Edgar Bell's conscientious objection with new audiences across the world, providing an alternative voice from World War I through his story.

---

[26] *Op.cit.* Barthes (1974), page 5.
[27] See, ahrc.ac.uk and for further details on the construction and interpretation of the triptychs can be found in the following publications: Andrew. S. (2013) The Medium Carries the Message? Perspectives on Making and Viewing Textiles. In *The Journal of Visual Arts Practice*. Vol. 12: 2 (August 2013), pages 195 - 221. *This paper focuses on responses to the textile medium and processes in the first and second triptychs.* Andrew. S. (2014) Image and Interpretation: Encoding and Decoding a Narrative Textile Installation. In *The Journal of Textile Design Research and Practice*. Vol.2: 2 (November 2014), pages 153-186. This paper focuses on the development and interpretation of the second triptych only. Triptychs images in colour, with accompanying text can be retrieved from:
ahrc.ac.uk/research/readwatchlisten/imagegallery/2014galleries/atextilenarrativeofjohnedgarbellconscientiousobjector/.

www.ingramcontent.com/pod-product-compliance
Lightning Source LLC
Chambersburg PA
CBHW050327230426
43663CB00010B/1762